THE UNION MUST STAND

THE
UNION
MUST
STAND

THE CIVIL WAR DIARY OF
JOHN QUINCY ADAMS CAMPBELL,
FIFTH IOWA VOLUNTEER INFANTRY

Edited by
MARK GRIMSLEY
and
TODD D. MILLER

Voices of the Civil War
Frank L. Byrne
Series Editor

The University of Tennessee Press / Knoxville

The Voices of the Civil War series makes available a variety of primary source materials that illuminate issues on the battlefield, the homefront, and the western front, as well as other aspects of this historic era. The series contextualizes the personal accounts within the framework of the latest scholarship and expands established knowledge by offering new perspectives, new materials, and new voices.

Frontispiece. John Quincy Adams Campbell, c. 1900. From *History of the First Presbyterian Church of Bellefontaine, Ohio* (Bellefontaine: Press of the Index Printing & Publishing Co., 1900), 64.

Library of Congress Cataloging-in-Publication Data

Campbell, John Quincy Adams.
The Union must stand : the Civil War diary of John Quincy Adams Campbell, Fifth Iowa Volunteer Infantry / edited by Mark Grimsley and Todd D. Miller. — 1st ed.
p. cm. — (Voices of the Civil War)
Includes bibliographical references (p.) and index.
ISBN 1-57233-069-4 (cl.: alk. paper)
1. Campbell, John Quincy Adams Diaries. 2. United States. Army. Iowa Infantry Regiment, 5th (1861–1864) 3. Iowa—History—Civil War, 1861–1865. 4. United States—History—Civil War, 1861–1865 Personal narratives. 5. Soldiers—Iowa Diaries. I. Grimsley, Mark. II. Miller, Todd D. III. Title. IV. Series: Voices of the Civil War series.
E507.5 5th.C36 2000
973.7'81'092—dc21
[B]
99-6744

CONTENTS

Illustrations

Figures

Maps

Foreword

Like several other volumes in the Voices of the Civil War series, the diary of John Quincy Adams Campbell speaks for those often overlooked in the traditional emphasis on the Civil War in the East. Its writer was a northwesterner, originally from Ohio, who had migrated farther west to Iowa, where he joined that state's distinguished Fifth Infantry Regiment. He began his military career as a sergeant and in less than a year rose to the rank of lieutenant. Besides keeping a personal record, this literate journalist also wrote letters for newspaper publication which are here reproduced. When many of his unit failed to reenlist in 1864, Campbell finished his service in the Fifth Iowa Cavalry, whose history is also partly related in this volume.

Campbell recounts such often-ignored battles as New Madrid, Iuka, and Corinth, and he vigorously describes attacks at Champion's Hill, Vicksburg, and Missionary Ridge. The editors have effectively placed Campbell's account of army life in the context of the historical controversy over the extent of ideological commitment among Civil War soldiers. In Campbell's diary readers meet an ardent churchgoing reformer—a man well acquainted with conductors of the Underground Railroad in Ripley, Ohio, who readily supported converting the Civil War into a struggle for freedom.

Those familiar with editor Mark Grimsley's *Hard Hand of War* (1995) will not be surprised that Campbell's advocacy of war against slavery led to a desire to remake Southern society. Campbell met Jeremiah Clemens, a prominent reunionist of Huntsville, Alabama (and a relative of Samuel Clemens), and tells of a meeting there of those supporting restoration of the Union. Campbell also took a dim view of any resistance by civilians, such as guerrilla activity in northern Georgia. Significantly, he looked with an appraising eye at the economic potential of Tennessee and other parts of the South and in so doing anticipated the coming of the Northern settlers who would be branded as carpetbaggers.

With a thoughtfulness and detail rare in the diaries of Civil War soldiers, Campbell depicts life in the Union army and life behind the lines in both the North and South.

Frank L. Byrne
Kent State University

Acknowledgments

Many people helped us in the preparation of this book, and it is a pleasure to have the opportunity to thank them. The Western Reserve Historical Society, which owns the John Quincy Campbell manuscript diaries (Ms. 3560), graciously extended permission to publish them, while the society's staff gave us plenty of courteous, professional assistance during our many visits. Jennifer Siler of the University of Tennessee Press never lost enthusiasm for the project—or patience with its editors. Frank Byrne Sr. and Daniel E. Sutherland, the readers for the press, gave us excellent feedback and advice. Ron McLean of the Ohio State University prepared the maps that accompanied the text and, as always, was a joy to work with.

Roger Davis of Keokuk, Iowa, permitted us to use a number of photographs from his extensive collection on the Fifth Iowa. Kevin Hymel of Leesburg, Virginia, Larry Steiner of Ashland, Ohio, and Larry Strayer of Dayton, Ohio, supplied photographic assistance and advice. Dan Ehl of Newton, Iowa, photographed a mural, on display in the county courthouse, that depicts the Fifth Iowa going off to war. Chris Daley of Middletown, Maryland, James Miller of Manassas, Virginia, and Dana Shoaf of Burkittsville, Maryland, gave us the benefit of their extensive knowledge of Civil War drill manuals and terminology. Rick Baumgartner of Blue Acorn Press, Huntington, West Virginia, provided us with illustrations and research advice. Robert Hodge of Alexandria, Virginia, assisted us with research at the National Archives in Washington, D.C.

Hans Brosig, museum director of the Jasper County Historical Society in Newton, Iowa, generously opened the society's doors to Todd Miller on a day when they ordinarily would have been closed. We would also like to thank the staffs of the Ashland County Historical Society, Ashland, Ohio; Brown County Historical Society, Georgetown, Ohio; State Historical Society of Iowa, Des Moines; Old Courthouse Museum, Vicksburg, Mississippi; and Ohio Historical Society, Columbus. These organizations greatly assisted us in our research and permitted us to use photographs and other illustrations from their collections.

A portion of this diary dealing with the Vicksburg campaign has been previously published. It appeared in Edwin C. Bearss, ed., "The Civil War Diary of Lt. John Q. A. Campbell, Company B, 5th Iowa Infantry," *Annals of Iowa* 39, no. 7 (1969): 519–41.

Mark Grimsley
Todd Miller
March 1999

INTRODUCTION

I

Combat affects men in many ways. No one can say in advance the response it will claw from them. For some Civil War soldiers the experience was completely unnerving, for others—a few—invigorating and sublime. Most men stood at their posts white with fear but also taut with determination. Their reactions could vary not just from day to day, according to morale or physical condition, but even from moment to moment. The acerbic writer Ambrose Bierce, who fought in the western theater, recalled one regimental battle line as "irregularly serrated, the strongest and bravest in advance, the others following in fan-like formations, variable and inconsistent, ever defining themselves anew."[1]

Though he had been a soldier for well over a year, until September 19, 1862, Sgt. John Quincy Adams Campbell had no idea how battle would affect him. Nor did any but a handful of men in his regiment, the Fifth Iowa Infantry, one of the first regiments organized in response to the firing on Fort Sumter. Although often at the fringe of combat, the unit had escaped all but the most minor of skirmishes. At the Battle of Iuka, however, that abruptly changed. Thrown into the fiercest sector of the action, the regiment suffered 217 casualties, the worst single loss of its entire three-year career. Despite the horrendous losses, most of the men were able to master their fear of wounds and death. "Nobly the boys stood up to the work," Campbell wrote of his comrades, "loading and firing amid a storm of lead, as if they were drilling—only showing much more enthusiasm and earnestness." Of his own reaction, he wrote with a kind of stunned amazement, "I was utterly unconscious of danger, and although the dead and dying were dropping at my feet, I felt no emotion nor sorrow—there was a strange, unaccountable lack of *feeling* with me that followed me through the entire action. Out of a battle and in a battle, I find myself two different beings."[2]

We know of Campbell's response to his first combat experience because of a diary that he meticulously kept throughout the war. Although many Civil War soldiers kept such diaries, they are often so cursory as to make them of limited historical value. Some are little more than itineraries giving the number of miles marched on a given day and the state of the weather. Campbell's is one of relatively few to offer a clear and extended picture of what it was like to be a Civil War soldier, and more than that, what motivated him to endure the harrowing dangers and make the sacrifices required by service in a war that killed 2 percent of the population of the United States—North and South—and 8 percent of its men of military age.

Born on September 28, 1838, John Quincy Adams Campbell—his family called him Quincy—was the third of six children. His parents, Charles Fenlon and Harriet Essington Kephart Campbell, lived in Ripley, Ohio, a bustling market town on the Ohio River about sixty miles southeast of Cincinnati. His father was trained in law, active in the Whig and, later, Republican Parties, and publisher of the local newspaper, the *Ripley Bee*. His mother, by all accounts, was strongly religious and a devout Presbyterian. The family lived comfortably but not extravagantly: the 1860 census credits Charles Fenlon Campbell with two thousand dollars in real estate and six hundred dollars in personal property.[3]

The Campbells resided in a modest house on Third Street, a short walk from the river. On the high bluff above the town they could see the residence of John T. Rankin, an outspoken abolitionist whose home was a stop on the underground railroad. Rankin was a significant influence on Quincy Campbell— in later life he would write an admiring article about him—and early on Quincy became an earnest antislavery man. He was also a teetotaler and an enthusiastic churchgoer: it was not unusual for him to attend Sunday services at several different churches. Indeed, so steeped was he in high moral ideals that, in his diary, he comes off as more than a little priggish.

In 1860 Quincy was twenty-two years old and working at his father's newspaper. But in December of that year, he left Ripley for Jasper County, Iowa, where he joined his brothers Angus and Frank, copublishers of the *Newton Free Press*. The three were living in Newton when the Confederates fired on Fort Sumter in April 1861.[4] The two elder Campbells stayed on to manage the newspaper (though Frank eventually would join the Fortieth Iowa). Quincy, however, promptly enlisted in a local infantry company dubbed the "Jasper Grays." The company rosters were filled within three weeks, but deluged by the organizational headaches of the sudden mobilization, it required more than two months for Governor Samuel J. Kirkwood to recognize and accept the company into service. Mustered into one of six regiments initially organized by the state, the Jasper Grays officially became Company B, Fifth Regiment, Iowa Volunteer Infantry.[5]

Quincy's wartime diary commences on July 9, 1861, six days before the members of the Fifth were formally sworn into service at Burlington. By that time he had already been appointed first sergeant, a promotion due less to Quincy's martial prowess—he had no previous military experience—than to his conscientious deportment and facility with a pen. The regiment spent its first seven months of service in Missouri, where it helped secure that border state to the Union, inconclusively pursued a few secessionist bands, but otherwise saw little action. In the spring of 1862, the Fifth Iowa participated in two major operations, the siege of Island No. Ten on the Mississippi River in March–April and the advance against the strategic railroad junction of Corinth, Mississippi, in May. But both campaigns were nearly bloodless, and the summer that followed was spent rather quietly. For Campbell, the principal development was his field promotion to lieutenant, a rank he held for the balance of his service.

Campbell's baptism of fire took place at the Battle of Iuka at the end of summer 1862. More fighting came three weeks later in the savage Battle of Corinth. Then ensued Maj. Gen. Ulysses S. Grant's long campaign for Vicksburg, in many respects the high point of Campbell's military career. He was present for all of it: the initial overland advance into Mississippi from western Tennessee, aborted by a timely Confederate cavalry raid against Grant's principal supply depot; the efforts in the winter of 1863 to find a viable waterborne route to approach or bypass the rebel fortress; and eventually Grant's classic campaign of maneuver by which he placed his army south of the fortress and in three weeks managed to wall up an entire Confederate army within the Vicksburg entrenchments. The Fifth Iowa then took part in the May 22 attempt to take the Confederate fortifications by storm—an episode that Grant would recall as one of two attacks made during the war he regretted having ordered.[6] Campbell depicts its missed chances and bloody failure in unsparing terms.

After the city's surrender following a forty-seven-day siege, Campbell and his regiment lingered in central Mississippi until events in far-off East Tennessee led to their urgent transfer to that region. Defeated at the Battle of Chickamauga on September 19–20, 1863, the Union Army of the Cumberland had gotten itself cornered in the railroad town of Chattanooga. Reinforcements rushed to assist the beleaguered force, including twenty thousand men from Grant's Army of the Tennessee. On November 25, 1863, the combined Union troops shattered the Confederate army on Missionary Ridge just east of Chattanooga and sent it in headlong retreat into northern Georgia. It was a great day for Union arms— unless one happened to be a Federal soldier fighting on the northern end of Missionary Ridge, as Campbell was. There the attacking forces experienced nothing but bloody failure in one valiant charge after another. "We were whipped," Campbell acknowledged bitterly, "but it was the fault of our generals, not of the men. Our charge is highly spoken of by lookers on." For Maj. Gen. William T. Sherman, the Union commander in that sector, he had hard words: "Gen. Sherman has certainly not improved his reputation by operations today. He has not gained a single position and his army has lost heavily. I am not now (nor ever was) an admirer of Gen. Sherman for he has only succeeded at failing. In every expedition and undertaking he has tried during the war and has sacrificed more lives than any other general in the Western Army."[7]

Feeling as he did, it was perhaps just as well that Campbell and the Fifth

Iowa were not called upon to participate in Sherman's Atlanta campaign during the spring and summer of 1864. Instead their duty was to defend the sprawling rear area against incursions by Confederate cavalry and guerrillas—a grueling, savage little war in which a man could march as hard and get killed as dead as in any major battle. During this period, Campbell left the Fifth to become an adjutant at brigade headquarters; the Fifth itself went out of existence in the summer of 1864, when the men's enlistments expired. Those who reenlisted were ordered to report to the Fifth Iowa Cavalry. Campbell also joined the unit, but served in it only a few months before word came that his father had died. His mother needed him at home and so, in November 1864, Campbell resigned his commission and went home, having served precisely three years, five months, and one day.

In January 1865 Campbell moved to Bellefontaine, Ohio, purchased the *Bellefontaine Republican,* and spent the rest of his life as its editor and publisher. He used the newspaper unstintingly as a vehicle for his prohibitionist views, and it was said that he did more to make Bellefontaine "dry" than any other single individual. He also became a ruling elder of the First Presbyterian Church, which ordained him in 1872 and was known with considerable justice as a pillar of the community. Though he never held political office (save as a presidential elector for James Garfield in 1880), Campbell served as Bellefontaine's postmaster and a trustee of the local water works, and he spearheaded campaigns for such projects as a new courthouse and improved county roads. He was twice married—first to Isabella Darwin in 1866, who died barely a year later, then in 1872 to Estelle Hoge. He had a son by the first marriage and two daughters by the second. He died in his sleep on March 2, 1922, at the age of eighty-three.[8]

II

In a sensitive study published in 1987, historian Gerald F. Linderman maintained that *courage* was the core value at the heart of the volunteer soldiers of 1861–62, by which he meant not merely fearlessness but a whole constellation of related values: manliness, religious faith, honor, and chivalry. Linderman argued that many Civil War soldiers believed in a link between the qualities that made a good man and those that made a good soldier. He described how the realities of Civil War combat placed a breaking strain on this ethos of courage. By the latter years of the war, Linderman suggested, the volunteers of 1861–62 had become disillusioned with courage, coarsened by the death and degradation around them, and more willing to visit terror on enemy civilians.[9]

The Campbell diary supports Linderman's thesis—up to a point. From Campbell's entries it is overwhelmingly evident that he saw a strong connection between being a good soldier and being a good man. It particularly dis-

turbed him, for example, when comrades drank or committed sexual indis-
cretions. For him, the link between courage and moral rectitude could never
be severed. One might suppose otherwise: Campbell, after all, participated
in two needless and costly failed assaults. And he indeed became disillusioned—but with military life, not the values with which he began the war.
These survived intact.

An ethos of courage was not the only thing that sustained Campbell. His
diary also portrays a soldier keenly aware of the political issues at stake in the
conflict and strongly motivated to help secure the benefits he expected from
a Northern victory: the preservation of the Union and republican government,
for a start, but also the death of slavery and the elimination of the antidemocratic, slaveholding aristocracy he perceived as the core of the rebellion. Not
many years ago, it was commonly assumed that Civil War soldiers were essen-
tially as apolitical and nonideological as their American counterparts in World
War II are said to have been. Two classic works by Bell Irvin Wiley, *The Life
of Billy Yank* and *The Life of Johnny Reb,* concluded as much, and a 1970
article by Pete Maslowski confirmed the portrayal.[10] James M. McPherson,
however, powerfully challenged this thesis in his 1994 study, *What They Fought
For, 1861–1865,* and pointed to a mountain of diaries and letters by Civil War
soldiers that testified eloquently to their political and ideological convictions.
Persuaded by McPherson's work, Charles P. Roland, a former Wiley protégé
and now a distinguished historian in his own right, wondered how his men-
tor, "a man of particularly keen sensitivity to the convictions and emotions of
persons whose lives he examined"—could have missed their significance in the
mindsets of Civil War soldiers.[11]

A perusal of Campbell's diary might have saved Wiley from the oversight.
In the very first entry he wrote: "I have left the peaceful walks of life and 'buckled on the harness of war' not from any feeling of enthusiasm, nor incited by
any hopes of honor [or] glory, but because I believe that duty to my country
and my *God* bid me assist in crushing this wicked rebellion against our government, which rebellion men have instigated to secure their own promotion
to place honor(s) and to secure the extension of that blighting curse—*slavery*—
o'er our fair land."[12] Campbell's conviction that slavery lay at the heart of the
rebellion was profound and unswerving, even at a time when it was the official policy of his government to harm the institution as little as possible. He
and his comrades enthusiastically did what they could to assist runaway slaves
in the war's first year, and even Lincoln's preliminary Emancipation Proclamation did not fully satisfy him. "Better late than never," was his initial response. After a day or two to mull it over, he became more enthusiastic: "The
President has placed the Union pry under the corner stone of the Confederacy
and the structure *will* fall." Yet even while recording his elation at the surrender of Vicksburg in July 1863, Campbell could not resist the thought that "the
chastisements of the Almighty are not yet ended. . . . My firm conviction is

that the Almighty has taken up the cause of the oppressed and that he will deny us peace until we 'break every yoke' and sweep every vestige of the cursed institution from our land."[13]

Campbell did not merely inform his diary of these convictions. In a stream of letters to newspapers in Iowa, Missouri, and Ohio—fifteen of which survive and are reproduced in this book's appendix—he pressed his views upon the folks back home. In this respect he illustrates a powerful dynamic during the Civil War that historians have only recently begun to explore: the continued bonds between soldiers and their home communities, and the mutual influence of one upon the other.[14] From an army camp outside Memphis, Tennessee, in January 1863, Campbell told the readers of his hometown newspaper about the slaves' unmistakable desire for liberation. Responding to those who suggested that most slaves were content with their lot, and that the recent Emancipation Proclamation needlessly roiled the waters, he wrote:

> I do not intend to deny that the slaves are well fed and well clothed— that they are happy—that they love slavery—nor will I deny that they love their masters. Perhaps they do. Perhaps they don't. But do they desire to be free? I answer emphatically, they do. Nothing, but the innate love of liberty in man, could have caused the wide spread desire for freedom that is manifested among the slaves wherever our army goes. In regions where an Abolitionist was never heard of, the Yankees are hailed by the darkies as their deliverers. And their masters as far as they are able (though they talk loudly about the happiness and contentment of their slaves) keep shoving them farther south as our army advances. The darkey is not to be trusted (contented or discontented) where Freedom is in question.[15]

But although Campbell probably had more humanitarian sympathy for African Americans than most Union soldiers, his enlightenment had limits. As the reference to "darkies" indicates, his diary contains a number of the racist stereotypes and demeaning characterizations common to his day and age, while the news that some of his comrades had slept with Negro prostitutes filled him with a moral contempt strongly laced with revulsion: "Men(?) whom I had *before* considered men of principle and mind, have given way to their passions and sunk the *man* into a mere *animal*, disgracing themselves, their company, their regiment, their friends, and *their race*."[16]

Like most antislavery Northerners, Campbell disliked the "peculiar institution" as much for its effects on whites as on African Americans. It was a common (though distorted) belief of the period that Southern whites were sharply divided into two classes: the planter "aristocracy," which monopolized social status and political authority thanks to its slavery-based wealth, and the nonslaveholding "poor whites," who lived primitive, degraded lives in the shadow of the great plantations. Conditioned by this belief, much that Campbell saw when he entered the South seemed to confirm it. From a troop transport plying the Tennessee River in April 1862, he wrote, "As we passed up the river, we had frequent evidences of the existence of slavery, in the miserable looking dwellings and farms(?) of the poor whites, on both banks."[17] The parenthetical question mark was Campbell's way of saying that the farms really did not merit the term. A subsequent use of the same device underscored more sharply Campbell's convictions about what slavery had done to the nonslaveholding white: "Came across a genuine Mississippi *Union* man(?) today. He was one of the *poor whites.*"[18] Sharing his encounters with the readers of the *Ripley Bee,* he wrote, "Every one of these men recognized slavery as the cause of the war, and heaped their imprecations upon slavery and slaveholders for bringing them and their families to misery. The Abolitionists don't all live outside of Mississippi." With emancipation, however, the poor whites would be liberated as much as the slaves: "Slavery has bred ignorance and treason. Freedom will breed light and loyalty."[19]

Of only slightly less importance than opposition to slavery in Campbell's moral pantheon was his opposition to drunkenness—indeed, his distaste for alcoholic beverages of any kind. "The officer's mess . . . celebrated Washington's birth-day by drinking and feasting," he snorted in February 1863. "Satan was more honored than Washington by it."[20] His diary churns with indignation at the peccadilloes of thirstier comrades, affording a reminder that the America of this period had just passed through one substantial temperance crusade and would see another, even more extensive one in the future (a crusade that Campbell would wholeheartedly support). In addition to his proclivity for moral declarations—so pronounced in the diary that Todd and I briefly considered calling the volume "Bluenose Bluecoat"—Campbell was also a staunch Republican and a keen though not especially penetrating political observer. Northern elections rarely passed without his notice, and Campbell was not reluctant to press his views even upon officers of higher rank. Concerning a discussion of the 1863 gubernatorial election in Iowa, he noted, "This evening I had a talk with Col. B., which did me some good, but agitated *him* considerably—'facts are stubborn things.'"[21]

Indeed, Campbell evidently "agitated" a good many of his fellow soldiers during his three and a half years of service. Reading between the lines, it is not hard to discern that his strong opinions and judgmental temperament made him a trial to his comrades. Campbell himself seldom grasped this, and his reaction when he did—that their disapproval only showed their own debauched nature—was not calculated to improve matters. Things got worse for Campbell in January 1863, when he filed charges against two men in his company for being away without leave to visit the fleshpots of Memphis. They culminated in June of that year when, near the conclusion of the siege of Vicksburg, his company held an election to choose a new captain. As the third-ranking officer in the unit, Campbell was an obvious choice, but instead the men reached past both him and another lieutenant to choose the second sergeant, William Pennywitt. Deeply hurt, Campbell confided the bitter news to his diary: "The vote of the company has unmistakably indicated a lack of confidence in me as an officer and I shall embrace the first opportunity (after termination of our present Vicksburg campaign) to remove 'my obnoxious presence' from the company."[22]

But Campbell did not leave the company. Instead, the regimental commander overruled the election results, vowing that "officers who have been on the battlefields that you have, and not found wanting, should not be overridden." The senior lieutenant in the company was thus appointed captain and Campbell became first lieutenant. Ironically, just weeks later Campbell was placed in temporary command of the company, a post he held for the next four months. "Not a desirable position," was his laconic reaction.[23] It was the worst of both worlds: all the responsibility of a captaincy with neither the rank nor the recognition (though he did receive a temporary bump in pay). His tenure as company commander saw further insult to his sense of dignity and fairness. In early November, as the Fifth Iowa marched to the relief of Chattanooga, a private in Campbell's company discharged his musket without authorization and was arrested by the colonel. Then Campbell was also placed under arrest for having failed to arrest the offending private, despite the fact that at the time of the incident, Campbell was off duty and another officer had charge of the company. "I may have deserved censure," Campbell fumed helplessly, "but . . . it looks much too much like *spite* work."[24]

Campbell's final year of service brought additional disappointments. The enlistments of the Fifth Iowa soldiers were due to expire in July 1864, but government policy decreed that if three-quarters of them chose to reenlist, the unit could remain in existence. It did not happen—the regiment failed to reach the cutoff by just twenty-one men. Then Lieutenant Pennywitt, the same Pennywitt whom the men had chosen over Campbell the previous June, was appointed company commander. Finally, in mid-September 1864, Campbell's father died. Shaken by the loss, within a few weeks Campbell began to ponder resigning his commission: "Since Father's death, Mother has been solicitous that I should come home and I have hardly spent a day nor a night during the past six weeks that I have not earnestly considered the propriety of yielding to her solicitations."[25] He left the army a short time later.

Aside from the self-portrayal of an ideologically motivated Civil War soldier, Campbell's diary, like most Civil War journals or letter collections, offers a useful corrective to our tendency to think of the struggle as a series of uninterrupted campaigns. The service of Civil War soldiers, like that of soldiers in other wars, was characterized by a certain ebb and flow: periods of camp life and little activity, expeditions that went nowhere, unexpected small epiphanies about one's comrades, one's enemies, and oneself. And only then, at long last, the tidal pull of a major military campaign: the purposeful road marches, the rising anticipation, the climactic but comparatively brief moment when the world exploded in urgency and blood and barely contained chaos, and the aftermath, in which a soldier would discover which of his comrades were absent because of wounds and which would be absent forever. Then always a moment of summing up—in rage or pride or disappointment or all of these—what the combat had meant and what it had cost.

Campbell's diary also affords a sense of the steady wastage of men's lives from causes having nothing to do with battle. The many illnesses that stalked the encampments killed more soldiers in the Fifth Iowa than did combat. Simple mishaps also took a toll: during his three years' service, for instance, no fewer than two men in his regiment died from gunshot wounds inflicted accidentally.[26] Death could come at virtually any time. "Some of the boys who came from Camp Clear Creek today brought news of the death of *Jacob Stern* of our company," Campbell wrote on July 3, 1862. "He died yesterday while out gathering blackberries." As if to reassure himself that such a death was not meaningless, Campbell added staunchly: "He died for his country."

III

I first encountered the diary of Lt. John Quincy Adams Campbell in the autumn of 1990, while researching my doctoral dissertation.[27] Archival research is frequently a crapshoot, and never more so than when one is pursuing a general historical problem—in my case, the nature and extent of the Union army's attacks on Southern property—rather than the experiences of a few people or a specific individual. Serendipity takes a large hand. A soldier who marched with Sherman to the sea turns out to have filled his letters home not with news of the march but rather with plaintive pleas for mail. Another participant who routinely commented on precisely the matters most of interest to my research turns out to have been taken prisoner just before some crucial episode—a misfortune for me as well as the captive. Many other letter and diary collections are simply uninformative, their comments too general or simplistic to be of much use.

Only rarely does a Civil War diary display both detailed observations and intelligent understanding of what a soldier was experiencing. J. Q. A. Campbell's is such a diary. As I read it, I discovered much that was helpful to my own research—and much, I quickly realized, that would be valuable to other historians as well. It was, indeed, considerably better than most published diaries and letter collections I had examined, for all too many owe their publication more to a descendant's zeal than a dispassionate assessment of their historical value.

What made Campbell's diary so striking? First, his entries were regular, fleshed out when events warranted, and extremely lucid. Second, he noticed a great deal—the antics of his fellow soldiers, the attitudes and behavior of Southern civilians (both white and black), the rhythms of camp life, the strange, almost out-of-body sensations of battle. But perhaps most important, Campbell had well-articulated opinions about what all of it *meant*. We know a great deal about what Civil War soldiers did. Campbell's diary tells us much about why they did it.

I was sufficiently impressed with the diary to have it microfilmed and sent to several other Civil War historians for their evaluation. They confirmed my opinion. I also showed it to my good friend Todd D. Miller, a junior high school teacher and a close student of the Civil War who has read hundreds of diaries and letter collections from the period. He was as impressed with it as I was, and we soon agreed that we should prepare the diary for publication. Todd carefully transcribed the entries into a word processor and did practically all the research into Campbell's background and that of his unit and comrades, a task that took him as far afield as Iowa and Washington, D.C. Without his efforts, *The Union Must Stand* would not have become a reality.

Campbell's manuscript diaries now repose in the Western Reserve Historical Society in Cleveland, under accession number Ms. 3560. From the condition of the notebooks and the internal evidence of the text, they are probably not the originals but were transcribed some years after the war, apparently with little or no embellishment. The spelling, capitalization, and style are those of a person closely acquainted with the written word, and in general we have left Campbell's sentences exactly as he wrote them. Exceptions were made in only two cases. First, Campbell tended to fill his sentences with unnecessary commas. These have been silently edited; more rarely, a missing comma was inserted where needed. Second, Campbell habitually spelled "today," "tomorrow," and "tonight" as "to=day," "to=morrow," and "to=night." These have been changed to their modern forms. We do not think that either of these small editorial intrusions have detracted from Campbell's style or from the historical integrity of his diary. Campbell also occasionally inserted parenthetical question marks for ironic effect. These should not be confused with editorial notations, which are in brackets.

Mark Grimsley
Columbus, Ohio

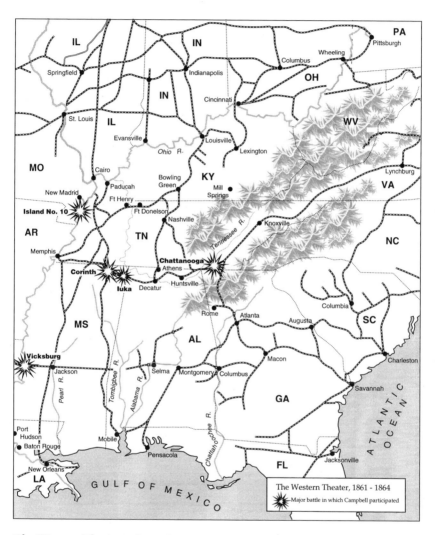

The Western Theater, 1861–1864.

1

———◦◦◦◦———

BUCKLING ON THE HARNESS OF WAR
Sojourn in Missouri, July 9, 1861–January 30, 1862

The Civil War was not yet three months old when John Q. A. Campbell mustered into the Fifth Iowa Volunteer Infantry Regiment, and few yet knew what sort of war it would be. Most believed it would be a relatively brief conflict fought in much the same way as the war with Mexico fourteen years earlier. Some even thought it might end without any serious fighting. Scarcely anyone foresaw that it would take four years and the lives of 620,000 Americans before it was over.

Even at the outset, however, it was evident that the Lincoln administration had a formidable task ahead of it. Eleven states—a geographic expanse the size of western Europe—had not only left the Union but also organized a government and fielded an army nearly as effective, if not so well established, as the force at the disposal of the North. True, the North possessed a much larger population and economy, but these advantages were somewhat latent: it would take months if not years for them to significantly influence the struggle. In the short run, the political complexities of civil war far outstripped any material edge the North might possess.

To begin with, the Northern population was not united in its understanding of the nature or purpose of the war. Some thought it a tragedy that might have been avoided but for blundering politicians and troublemakers like the "fire-eating" secessionists of the South and the rabid abolitionists of the North. Many held that, though war might be necessary, it should be prosecuted in a careful, conciliatory manner calculated to keep bloodshed to a minimum and avoid as much as possible the bitterness that might endanger a true reunion of the warring sections. Others—like Campbell—saw the war as the product of an entrenched "slaveholding aristocracy" that was despotic, antidemocratic, and dedicated to the preservation of chattel slavery at all costs. Such people did not necessarily view all white Southerners as enemies, but they believed that secessionists must be punished and, as a rule, that slavery must be destroyed. The Lincoln administration had to prosecute the war without alienating either of these groups.

The administration also had to avoid driving the border states—Missouri, Kentucky, and Maryland—into the Confederate camp. All three states were southern in culture and all three held a sizable contingent of slaves. A harsh program of retribution against the South would deeply offend them, as would any attempt to convert the war for union into a war against slavery. The danger was less extreme in Maryland, which rapidly came under firm Union military control, than it was in Kentucky, where the Union's grip was far more tenuous. It was worst of all in Missouri, where the secessionists had a strong military presence of their own.

The struggle for Missouri lasted from May 1861, when the first confrontations between Unionist and secessionist forces occurred, to March 1862, when the Union victory at Pea Ridge, Arkansas, ended any real hopes that the Confederacy might gain control of the state.[1] Campbell and the Fifth Iowa were very much part of this struggle. Between August and October the regiment shuttled from one threatened district to another, never quite getting into action but bolstering Federal authority in the region. Autumn was quieter. Campbell came down with a serious fever and spent several weeks in a military hospital, followed by more dead time before he could rejoin his regiment at Syracuse in central Missouri. There they saw the old year out and waited to see what the new year, 1862, might bring.

Tuesday, July 9, 1861. I left Newton, Jasper County, Iowa this day in Captain Samuel H. Chapman's Company (B), of the Fifth Regiment of Iowa Volunteers. The officers of our company are: *Captain, Sam'l H. Chapman; First Lieut.—Alex. L. Mateer; Second Lieut.—John H. Tait.* Our company, which had been "in quarters" in Newton for upwards of a week, was drawn up in line in the Court-House yard and relatives of the volunteers bid them "farewell." It was the most affecting scene I ever witnessed. After the parting, two pictures of the company were taken by Mr. Webster, the artist of the place. About noon, the company jumped into the wagons and started for Burlington, the place of rendezvous for the regiment. Many of the citizens followed out of town and the *"Newton Band"* accompanied us to Burlington. I have volunteered to fight in this war for the Union and *a government*. I have left the peaceful walks of life and "buckled on the harness of war" not from any feeling of enthusiasm, nor incited by any hopes of honor [or] glory, but because I believe that duty to my country and my *God,* bid me assist in crushing this wicked rebellion against our government, which rebellion men have instigated to secure their own promotion, to place honor(s), and to secure the extension of that

"Off to War," a mural painted in the Jasper County Courthouse in Newton, Iowa, c. 1910. Photograph by Dan Ehl.

blighting curse—*slavery*—o'er our fair land. We reached *Monroe,* a small town, some 12 miles from Newton, about sundown and remained there over night. I stayed overnight at *Col. Shelledy's.* The name of our co[mpany] is "The Jasper Greys."

Wednesday, July, 10. This morning, those of the company who lived in Monroe had an affecting parting from their friends. Our company started on their journey about 7 o'clock A.M. We reached Pella, about noon, where we dined. We were escorted into and out of the town by the Home Guards. We started for Oscaloosa [*sic*] as soon as we had dined and reached there before sundown. We were met at the outskirts of the town by the Home Guards and the *Oscaloosa band,* who escorted us through the town, to the residence of *Mr. Loughridge,* where we were presented in behalf of the ladies of Oscaloosa with 101 havelocks.[2] Who would be a bachelor, while there are single ladies in Oscaloosa? The presentation speech, by *Mr. Loughridge,* was brief and appropriate. I took "tea" with S. H. M. Byers, at his Father's, where I also spent the night, retiring very early as I was tired and sore.[3]

Thursday, July 11. We started for Oscaloosa this morning at 6 o'clock A.M. We passed through *Eddyville,* on our way to *Ottumwa,* about noon. Eight miles from Ottumwa our wagons train passed the R.R. station just as the cars (bound for Ottumwa) came along. Together with some 25 of the boys, I jumped aboard the train, determined to exchange the jolting of the wagons and the heat of the Sun for a ride on the cars. I paid 40 c[ents] for my ride of eight miles— just *five cents a mile*. Some of the boys plead[ed] "dead-broke" and had to hand over their old combs, knives, &c. We took dinner in Ottumwa and then boarded the cars for Burlington, where we arrived after sundown. We were immediately marched out to the campgrounds (Fair Grounds), arriving there after dark. We were furnished with some bread and beef and then "*shown to our beds.*" We slept in long board tents, open at both ends. There was hay in the tents, and with my blanket for a covering, I slept very comfortably, although the night was quite cold. Some of the boys, who brought no blankets with them, suffered from the cold, and got to sleep little.

Friday, July 12. Today I was appointed *First Sergeant* of the company by the Captain. The *non-commissioned* officers of the company are as follows: *First Sergeant—J.Q.A. Campbell, Second Sergeant—John E. Shelledy; Third Sergeant—James Vanatta; Fourth Sergeant—Thomas R. Keislar. Corporals— S[amuel].M.H. Byers, Miles Humphrey, Wm. H. Dungan, Isaac G. Jones, Duncan W. Teter, J[ames].W. McCroskey, Willard C. Winslow, and James P. Banks.* I spent the day with some eight or ten of the boys in fixing up "quarters" for our company.

Saturday, July 13. I had nothing to do today but stay in camp. Nothing to do, and plenty of help.

Sunday, July 14. In the forenoon, our company was engaged building tents for companies which were expected to arrive. As there were prospects of rain, it was thought proper to have dry quarters for the boys, should they arrive (which they did). In the afternoon I attended divine service on the camp ground—sermon by the Rev. Mr. Jocelyn, of Burlington. In the evening, the boys thinking the *grub* set out for them was insufficient and *tainted,* kicked over the table and raised quite a breeze. Considerable apprehension of trouble was felt but all passed off quietly. No arrests were made but *grub got better.*

Monday, July 15. Our company was sworn into U.S. service today by Lieut. [Alexander] Chambers [an officer in the regular U.S. Army]. No one of the company was rejected—one (McCroskey's brother) refused to be sworn in.

Tuesday, July 16. Doing nothing, today.

Wednesday, July 17. Lying in my *bunk,* sick, with an attack of diarrhea— a prevailing disease in camp.[4]

Thursday, July 18. I have been able to drill today.

Friday, July 19. Drill and eat and sleep.

Saturday, July 20. Ditto! Ditto!! Ditto!!!

Sunday, July 21. With the Captain and a good portion of the company, I attended divine service at the Congregational Church in Burlington today. The sermon of the pastor, Rev. Mr. Salter, was an excellent course. After sermon, by invitation I took dinner with the pastor, with whom I had formed a slight acquaintance while he was at Newton, during the installation of Rev. Jones.

Mr. Salter's good woman proved that in preparing things for "creature comfort" she was as expert as her husband in preparing that better "bread." I was able, without any effort, to eat what was before me, asking no questions.

Monday, July 22. I did nothing and saw nothing today that would astound or astonish!

Tuesday, July 23. Ditto! I believe.

Wednesday, July 24. Ditto, and Also.

Thursday, July 25. Company drilled in evolutions.

Friday, July 26. Company drilled same as yesterday.

Saturday, July 27. I went to Burlington early this morning to take the stage to Uncle William's, but found the stage had started some three or four hours before its time.[5] So I was fooled out of my expected visit, much to my disappointment.

Sunday, July 28. A good portion of the company attended divine service at the M[ethodist].E[piscopalian]. Church in Burlington—Rev. Mr. Jocelyn. We heard a good sermon. Our company commenced cooking by "messes" today.[6]

Monday, July 29. Uncle William came in with his buggy today to take me out but I could not go, as the company (and regiment) had orders to be ready to march to Keokuk in the morning.

Tuesday, July 30. We failed to start to Keokuk this morning but are to start tomorrow morning. [James] Dun. Peregrine came into camp and joined our company. Good!

Wednesday, July 31. We failed to start to Keokuk this morning but are to stand "ready."

Thursday, August 1. Company engaged in drilling.

Friday, August 2. Our regiment left Camp Warren today at 8 1/2 o'clock P.M. for Burlington. Camp Warren for a week or so past has been extremely disagreeable owing to a lack of water and a superabundance of dust. We, therefore, left it without any reluctance. We marched down to Burlington through a cloud of dust and took up a position on the wharf [on the Mississippi River]. At 11 1/2 o'clock P.M. we started for Keokuk on the steamer Pomeroy—a very small boat. Our company was stationed on the hurricane deck. Some of the companies were placed in the barges alongside. I slept with Lieut Mateer in the hawser box on the hawser.[7] We slept soundly.

Saturday, August 3. We arrived at Fort Madison at daylight. We here took the cars for Keokuk. Owing to the locomotive being too light for his load, we were delayed and did not reach Keokuk until 9 1/2 o'clock A.M. We were there assigned quarters in the 2nd story of a big brick building, doing our cooking "out doors."

Sunday, August 4. I attended Sabbath School at the N[ew].S[chool]. Presbyterian Church today, but was prevented from attending preaching by "official duties."[8]

Monday, August 5. About noon, we received "arms" and were sent out on the Keokuk and Ft. Desmoine R.R. to *whip* the saucy rebels under Martin Green who had attacked Athens, Mo. this morning.[9] We got off the cars about four miles below Athens and marched into the interior to a point about five miles in the rear of Athens, hoping to get Mr. Green and his band "in a fix." The march, owing to the extreme heat, was very oppressive and we found it difficult to procure water for drinking. We camped about dark on the prairie without either coats or blankets.

Tuesday, August 6. We slept well last night. During the night we had a "false alarm" caused by a sentinel (Dave Cowman) shooting at a cow while on post. About daylight we learned from an escaped prisoner that Green's forces (all mounted) were some twenty miles in the interior, having been whipped at Athens yesterday morning by the Home Guards under Col. Moore, and having retreated on "double quick."[10] Not thinking we were prepared to pursue mounted men, we started back for Athens, after a breakfast on hard crackers and ham.[11] On the road to Athens, our Surgeon extracted a ball from the neck of a wounded secessionist—who lay in a farm house, near the road. On arriving at Athens, we camped on the battle-ground of the previous day. Evidences of the conflict were to be seen on all sides—among which was a big hole through the house of a secessionist, caused by a ball fired from a cannon, in the hands of Green's forces. Said hole was all the damage done by the *cannonading.* Quite a number of the wounded of both sides were lying in the hospital in town. After fording the [Des Moines] river, we got aboard the cars (at 11 1/2 o'clock A.M.) and returned to Keokuk.

Wednesday, August 7. "Busy as a bee"—expecting our regiment to be moved to Missouri.[12]

Thursday, August 8. Our company, with four others, again went to Athens. News came to Keokuk that Green's forces had again made an attack on Athens. Five companies of our regiment under the command of the Major [William Robertson] accordingly started for Athens this morning on the cars. On arriving at Athens, we found all quiet—no signs of an enemy. While waiting for the "down train" to come, the Major heard thunder, and mistaking it for the reports of cannon, dispatched a locomotive for the Colonel [William Worthington].[13] All sorts of rumors were spread through Keokuk upon the arrival of the locomotive and soon the city was alive with excitement. A train full of soldiers and citizens, armed as best they could be soon started to our relief, but they were met on the road by another locomotive (which the Major dispatched, when he found his mistake), and their fears dismissed by a report of "all's well" and they returned to the city. We returned on the afternoon train.

Friday, August 9. We are preparing to leave tomorrow. I had my likeness taken today and sent it home. We gave up our muskets—will get more in St. Louis.

Saturday, August 10. The boat did not arrive last night and we were busy all day *watching for her.*

Wartime photograph of Col. William H. Worthington. Courtesy of the State Historical Society of Iowa.

Sunday, August 11. We started for St. Louis at 6 o'clock this morning on steamboat "Die Vernon." We had a short allowance of crackers, ham, cheese, and molasses to eat, and our appetites grow keen. I was disappointed in the scenery on the banks of the river—it did not come up to my expectations.

Monday, August 12. We arrived at St. Louis at noon today—had nothing but crackers and raw ham to eat. After an hour's rest on the wharf, we started for "Jefferson barracks" on the "*Jeannie Deans*."[14] We remained on the boat all night, at the barracks landing.

Tuesday, August 13. We marched off the boat and spent the day doing nothing in particular but waiting "orders to march." We spent a good part of the night cooking "rations for three days." We expect to start somewhere tomorrow.

Wednesday, August 14. We marched aboard the "War Eagle" early this morning, and started for St. Louis. We stopped at the Arsenal, where we took aboard arms, ammunition and blankets for the regiment—Companies A & B received Springfield rifles for their arms. We moved on up to St. Louis where five companies (including B) were transferred to the "Satan." The two boats then started with the "Iowa Fifth" for Lexington, Mo.

Thursday, August 15. Plowing our way up the Missouri—passed St. Charles at sunrise. As we passed different places today, [we] were loudly cheered by the populace. We stopped overnight at Hermann.

Friday, August 16. We passed several bridges today which [Confederate captain William Hicks] Jackson attempted to burn in his flight—all guarded by soldiers who "presented arms" as we passed.[15] We arrived at Jefferson City about 3 o'clock P.M. and remained there over night.

Saturday, August 17. I bought a "Jeffersonian Examiner"—a secesh paper—this morning. The meanest, lowest article in it,—was from the "*Debuque* (Iowa) *Times.*" We left Jefferson City, and traveled to within 20 miles of Boonville where we tied up at an island overnight. We have met the 5th Missouri Regiment—3 month volunteers—on board two stern wheelers bound for St. Louis, to be discharged. They have been stationed at Lexington. They reported that they have been fired into everyday since they left Lexington. Today they had one man killed and several wounded by rebels firing from the shore.[16]

Sunday, August 18. A consultation of officers was held last night and as the Col. of the Missouri regiment reported that it would be imprudent for us to proceed farther without artillery, we this morning turned back to Jefferson City to get cannon and more ammunition. We arrived at the City at 10 o'clock A.M. Our chaplain [A. B. Medeira] preached his *first* sermon this afternoon!!!

Monday, August 19. We spent the day lying around on the boat. At midnight three companies of our regiment went on the R.R. to Osage to guard the bridge as danger is apprehended there. The remaining companies were marched up to the ground in front of the Penitentiary. We then lay down in the road (newly McAdamized) "on our arms" and *slept soundly until morning.*[17] The intention was for us to retire into the Penitentiary and fight from behind its walls if attacked by a *very* superior force as it was expected we would be.

Tuesday, August 20. There was no attack last night (just as many of us believed). We received our tents and went into camp today. Part of the regiment camped in "contraband" houses and the rest of us, in tents, pitched in the streets about the Seminary in the lower end of the city.

Wednesday, August 21. Company drilled in the "manual of arms."

Thursday, August 22. There was a hard rain last night and the water rushed into some of the tents (not properly "ditched") and chased the boys out. "Mess No. One" kept dry. This morning the weather "cleared up" and the company drilled.

Friday, August 23. Company drilled in the "manual of arms."

Saturday, August 24. Nothing worth noting.

Sunday, August 25. Today our Captain was placed under arrest for refusing to make the company swear or "pledge their word of honor" that they knew or did not [know] anything about certain threats said to have been uttered by someone of our company against the life of Howe, a *secessionist*, who was searching for men in camp who had taken fruit out of his orchard. The Captain has endeared himself by his conduct to all his men—*the Colonel* [William Worthington] *hasn't*.

Monday, August 26. The Captain is still under arrest—he takes it cheerfully. So many men taken from the company "for duty" this morning that we have no drill. I went up into town and sent home 17 (old) stamped envelopes.

Tuesday, August 27. We received our caps, pants, shirts (all blue), and canteens today.

Wednesday, August 28. "Our Captain" was released today and five companies (including B) were sent to the mouth of the Osage to guard the R.R. bridge.

Thursday, August 29. The boys went out into the country today and procured an abundance of peaches.

Friday, August 30. More peaches—company shot at a target. *Milt Campbell* made the best shot.

Saturday, August 31. I went out with a scouting party after night, about 3 miles down the Railroad where firing had been heard. We found that a German had been shooting off his revolver! While we were gone, one of [the] sentinels at the camp was shot in the hand by some would be assassin who unfortunately escaped in the dark. After being shot, the sentinel fired at the fellow but missed his mark.

Sunday, September 1. I spent this day in the woods near camp reading, singing and sleeping. There was more of the quietness of *Sabbath* in camp today than any Sabbath since we left home.

Monday, September 2. We left camp at Osage at 8 o'clock this morning on the cars for Jefferson City where we remained during the day. Leaving "Camp Worthington" near Jefferson about 8 o'clock P.M. on a secret expedition. The night was as dark as the absence of light could make it. We marched down to the steamboats and got aboard just as a heavy rain began falling.

Tuesday, September 3. Our regiment and a company of Home Guard Cavalry, which came aboard the boats during the rain last night, started up the river on the War Eagle and Satan. The boats would have run last night but the night was too dark to navigate. We captured a horse and two skiffs on the way up the river. Five companies (including B) got off the boats about dark at

Rocheport and started for Columbia, 12 miles into the interior. Co. B led the van and kept up a brisk pace—so brisk that Co. K requested the Lieut. Col [Charles Matthies] (who was in command) to let them march in front.[18] They seemed to be tired of our quick step. Soon after they got ahead, their complaints of being tired caused the Lt. Col. to halt till daylight. We were then 6 miles from Columbia. The road we traveled over was the worst I ever traveled on. *It was awful.*

Wednesday, September 4. This morning, just after we resumed our march, we were informed that a company of 60 secessionists were camping about half a mile from us. Company B and the cavalry company were detailed to capture them. We found the distance to be not less than three miles and the number of the enemy not more than *six*. When we had marched about a mile and a half, the Col. thinking he was close on to the prey, ordered us to "double quick" while he led the cavalry ahead on a "charge."[19] We followed on the *run*. The cavalry chased several *"seceshers"* out of some bushes where they had been sleeping and fired on them but hit no one.[20] We arrived about three minutes behind the cavalry and the col. said *we would have passed them* if we had had another half mile to go. We ran the mile and a half with our cartridge boxes on, and our knapsacks on our backs. After chase the Col. *pressed* a wagon and we were relieved of our knapsacks.[21] We started for Columbia, where we arrived at 10 A.M., and found the regiment camped on the State University grounds.[22] Five companies (under Col. Worthington) reached the place by a different road from ours. In the evening we had a fine "dress parade" in town, many of the citizens being present. Columbia is strongly secesh.

Thursday, September 5. We started from Columbia at sunrise and marched 12 miles on the road to Jefferson City, camping at night in a "woods-pasture." The day was very hot and the march tedious. [William] Fouts, John Rhinehart, [Miles] Humphrey, and others threw their knapsacks into the wagon during the march. I learn that we are on the look-out for Maj. Harris' forces.[23] No signs of them yet.

Friday, September 6. The regiment moved forward towards Jefferson City today, arriving at the river about four miles above the city. We waited at this point for the Satan which carried us to Jefferson, arriving there after dark.

Saturday, September 7. Our company got their blouses. I sent a letter to the "Free Press" and got a good letter from a good Mother—Father is getting better. "Blessed be God" who, heretofore, hath blessed us as a family and called us to mourn the loss of none of its members and who still extends his merciful hand toward us.

Sunday September 8. This morning the orderlies were furnished with swords. In the evening an inspection of arms took place. Oh! for a Sabbath properly observed. Verily the food of war is broken commandments.

Monday, September 9. I spent the day in camp, drilling, washing, &c. Wrote two long letters—one to Bill and one to Archie.[24] We had a battalion drill in the afternoon.

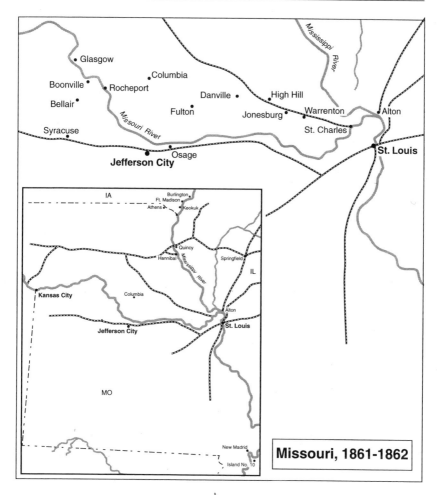

Missouri, 1861–1862.

Tuesday, September 10. Our company is on picket guard today. I spent most of the day in camp making out "muster rolls," &c.

Wednesday September 11. In camp—no men on duty. Company, squad, and battalion drill. Our regimental "drill master" made his first appearance today. Our company "on picket" were treated to a heavy rain and a big *ducking* last night.[25]

Thursday, September 12. In camp, dribbling.

Friday, September 13. In camp.

Saturday, September 14. The regiment left camp at 6 o'clock this morning and marched down to the *Satan* and War Eagle in a rain. We started for Boonville at 10 A.M., having with us some artillerists and a section of a battery. Our purpose is to reenforce the Home Guards at Boonville who were attacked yesterday morning by 600 Secessionists. The Home Guards (160 in number) were stationed inside earthworks, 100 yards long by 25 yards wide. They repulsed the secessionists, killing and wounding upwards of sixty. They lost two men, and had one wounded. Among the killed on the secession side, was Col. Brown, a brave man and a prominent leader among the secessionists.[26] All honor to the brave Germans of Boonville for their devotion to our flag!

Sunday, September 15. We arrived at Boonville at two o'clock this morning and found the Home Guard anxiously awaiting us. Company B was stationed inside the entrenchment (built by General Lyon) inside which the Home Guards were stationed during the fight.[27] The home Guards marched over to town and took up their quarters there on our arrival.

Monday, September 16. In camp at Boonville. Our company has been busy "policing" inside our intrenchment. We soon made a decided improvement in the looks of things. The 18th and 22d Indiana regiments arrived this afternoon.

Tuesday, September 17. In camp. Nothing to note.

Wednesday, September 18. The 26th and the remainder of the 22d Indiana regiments arrived this morning from Jefferson and the three Indiana regiments started up the river on the War Eagle, Satan, White Cloud, and Desmoine.

Thursday, September 19. What is represented (in my "diary") as occurring yesterday occurred today. I made a mistake of one day. Nothing of note Wednesday.

Friday, September 20. Our regiment commenced throwing up a new intrenchment today. Our company was busy repairing the old one. Five of six companies went out at noon on *some* expedition. The 18th and 22d Indiana regiments came back today. They had a battle among themselves last night through mistake. They put out their pickets when the boats tied up for the night a few miles below Glasgow. Several companies were also sent ashore to scout. As the boats were some distance apart, the pickets mistook each other for enemies and the scouting companies fired on each other, killing several and wounding quite a number (including Major Larner, of the 22d, among the latter) before they found their mistake. The sad affair was caused by criminal dereliction of duty among the head officers in not acting in concert. There seemed to be no *head* officer.

Saturday, September 21. Work was continued on the intrenchments today. The 26th Ind reg. came back from up the river today. The companies of our regiment which went out yesterday came back today. I am as ignorant of their deeds as I was of their designs.

Sunday, September 22. Today was *Sabbath* as well as Sunday. We were excused from duty and permitted to attend church in Boonville.

Monday, September 23. News came today that Price has captured Lexington.[28] "Whom the Lord loveth, he chasteneth." A battery of flying artillery came up from Jefferson today *enroute* to Georgetown.[29]

Tuesday, September 24. Two of the Indiana regiments started for Georgetown today. (Our regiment is busy drilling and *catching mules.*)

Wednesday, September 25. Our regiment left Boonville and started for Glasgow this morning on the War Eagle. We had to march down to the boat while the rain was coming *straight down.*

Thursday, September 26. I slept last night doubled into a knot on a pile of tents on deck. The boat stopped over night about four miles below Glasgow. We reached Glasgow about 9 o'clock A.M. and camped on a grassy ridge in back of town. As we marched through town, the ladies welcomed us by the waving of handkerchiefs, showing that there were Union-loving citizens in Glasgow who were not afraid to manifest their love for the country of Washington and Jefferson.

Friday, September 27. In camp at Glasgow. There are rumors afloat today of "danger ahead" but danger seems to be a fast craft and keeps ahead.

Saturday, September 28. Our company was out on picket guard last night. I had one squad on the Boonville road. We had no trouble or alarms. Today I have been busy running around town and washing. Glasgow is full of beautiful houses and pretty girls. Our company today received 16 pairs of pants as their share of a present from Iowa. My birthday.

Sunday, September 29. I attended divine service in town and at camp— Rev. Mr. Vincent preaching on both occasions. Had a talk with Uncle John's brother-in-law (a Union man) who lives near camp. He says Uncle John is a "hot secessionist." Poor fellow!

Monday, September 30. Sent a letter to Mother and one to the "Free Press." I have not received a letter since we left Jefferson on the 14th.

Tuesday, October 1st. A "false alarm" last night caused by the sentinels firing on a crazy man, who escaped from the guard house and ran by the sentinels. The regiment formed in good order *in a very short time.* Company B was the first company "on the ground." The crazy man (who, luckily, was not hit by either of the sentinels) was found next morning 1 1/2 miles from camp.

Wednesday, October 2. We "pulled up stakes" and started for Boonville this morning on the "War Eagle" and "New Gaty." Before the boats left our Colonel was presented with a beautiful bouquet by the ladies of Glasgow. The "stars and stripes" were waved from different dwellings by loyal ones of the fair sex; and many a *hat* was raised to cheer the soldiers of the Union by the *"lords of creation."* We arrived at Boonville at dark.

Tuesday, October 3. We marched off the boats and camped on "the old camp ground." No mail for the regiment—yet!!! Where lies the blame? Echo answers "Where?" But we are "only *soldiers*"—there's the rub.

Friday, October 4. In camp.

Saturday, October 5. Our company started out to "press" wagons about noon through a rain. We travelled till night (having three covered wagons with us to carry our provisions, &c.) making about ten miles and camping at the "Widow Magruder's." I ate supper with [the] Lieutenant at her table by invitation. We (the Lieut. and I) slept in one of the wagons with some of the boys, while others slept in the hay in the barn loft. We slept with our wet boots on as we did not know how near an enemy might be to us and we desired to be ready.

Sunday, October 6. We returned to Boonville by another road arriving at camp about four o'clock with fifteen wagons. We had great difficulty in getting wagons as the farmers generally had hid them and we had to hunt them out of the bushes in several cases. No mail yet!

Monday, October 7. In camp—sick with bad cold. Received news that New Orleans was taken by our forces.[30] I won't vouch for the truth of the report. No mail yet!

Tuesday, October 8. Sick in my tent—unable to do duty—eating nothing.

Wednesday, October 9. Still sick with no appetite. No mail yet!

Thursday, October 10. I went on the "sick list" this morning—got two "blue mass" pills.[31] I received two letters today! the first I have received since we left Jefferson on the 14th of last month. One of the letters, of a late date was from Sister and one dated September 12 was from Angus and Frank.

Friday, October 11. The Dr. said this morning that I have the "intermittent fever" and placed me on the *"quinine list."* I took six quinine pills today.

Saturday, October 12. I got no medicine today by reason of a mistake on the part of the Dr. In the evening I was sent to the hospital in Boonville as the regiment is expected to march next morning. When I arrived at the hospital, I found a good straw mattress to sleep on and a covering for the bed. Slept in a room by myself and would have suffered for water had not a soldier who was attending a sick man in next room, attended to my wants.

Sunday, October 13. This morning I received a month and a half's pay ($30.66) from July 15 to August 31. My fever is worse today and I am kept busy *dosing* with medicine. [William] *Rice* came over to attend on me.

Monday, October 14. My fever is worse, and I am pretty sick. The regiment started for Springfield this morning. Dr. Halliwell has been prescribing for me since I came here. He says that I have "intermittent-bilious" fever.

Tuesday, October 15. Fever is still high and I am correspondingly low. Lieut. Mateer is sick in the same room with me. Since we have been in the hospital, the Union ladies of Boonville have treated us very kindly. *Mrs. P. A. Whitehurst* has furnished us all that we have to eat and says that she will continue to do so while were are ill and that she doesn't want us to eat anything but that which she sends.

Wednesday, October 16. My fever is somewhat abated. In the room (15 x 20) with us is a sergeant from Company A. (Mr. Wm. Elliott) who has been sick for some time but is now able to walk about. Lieut. Mateer is getting better.

Thursday, October 17. I am still getting better—ditto the Lieutenant. We have a small stove in our room and as the evenings are cool, we find fires quite agreeable.

Friday, October 18. Still getting better—am about rid of the fever. *Mrs. Whitehurst* furnishes us with food both wholesome and *palateable* [sic].

Saturday, October 19. I am clear of the fever and taking no medicine. The Lieut. is well enough to walk into town.

Sunday, October 20. Better!—taking no medicine. Mr. Elliott and the Lieut. went to church.

Monday, October 21. Dr. Halliwell was dismissed today on charge of fraud. I am still getting better—was able to sit up some today.

Tuesday, October 22. I am still "on the mend." My principal business now is to "gather strength" which I think I am doing "as fast as the law allows." I sat up some today.

Wednesday, October 23. Still getting better and stouter. Sat up some again.

Thursday, October 24. All who were able left here today with a train of 100 government wagons to join their regiments. I wasn't quite stout enough to make the trip, although [I] sat up all day and wrote part of a letter to Sister.

Friday, October 25. I felt strong enough today to walk down town. I bought a *twenty-five cent pocket knife.* I stood the walk better than I thought I would.

Saturday, October 26. Sent my letter to Sister. Went down town—had my hair cut and was shaved—purchased some letter paper and envelopes.

Sunday, October 27. Took a walk in the forenoon and one in the afternoon. Wrote a letter to the "Free Press" and Angus. A difficulty occurred this evening between the Home Guard and a squad of the Illinois 37th under Capt. Powell in which three of the latter were wounded.

Monday, October 28. I walked down town twice today. Wrote a letter to Uncle William and also one to Frank.

Tuesday, October 29. I was down town twice today—weather pleasant but rather windy and dusty.

Wednesday, October 30. I received a letter from the regiment from George Work this morning. It was "thrice welcome." It reported the regiment (on 27th) 10 miles south of the Osage.

Thursday, October 31. I spent the day lying about my room eating a great deal and reading a little—more material to work on in the eating than the reading line. I am still getting better. I took a walk down town and made a short stay.

Friday, November 1. The Lieut. and I made arrangements for boarding with *Mr. Burgher* at $2.50 per week as the warden informed us that we would have to give up our room to sicker men.

Saturday, November 2. I took a walk into the country 1 1/2 miles and got some apples and sweet cider. Finding out that we would not be removed from our room, we *un*made arrangements for boarding with Mr. Burgher. I walked out to the Fair Grounds this morning.

Sunday, November 3. I attended service at the Catholic church this morning. Lieut. Mateer left this evening on steamer "Rowena" to join the regiment via St. Louis. The Rowena was searched while here for secessionists said to be aboard but none were found.

Monday, November 4. I wrote a letter to the *Free Press*, which was quite lengthy and occupied most of my time, in the morning, in writing. I commenced eating in the "kitchen." "Woods" was brought into our room.

Tuesday, November 5. I wrote a letter to Sister Bell—took a walk into the country—bought a St. Louis Democrat—heard a report of a battle between Price's and our forces in which our forces were said to have gained a great victory.[32] I believe there has been no battle yet.[33]

Wednesday, November 6. Nothing worth noting today.

Thursday, November 7. I took dinner at the City Hotel where I got a New York Tribune.

Friday, November 8. I got some medicine this morning for diarrhea—stayed in my room and lay on my cot most of the day on account of a "pain under the apron." News came today of the removal of Freemont [*sic*] causing general regret among the Unionists of this place and the soldiers.[34] The Secesh have no tears to shed.

Saturday, November 9. No news of a battle yet. The Secessionists profess to be confident of Price's success in the event of a battle. Don't believe they will be so confident in a few days. *Mr. Elliott* left for home on a furlough this evening.

Sunday, November 10. I attended service at the Baptist Church this morning. In the afternoon I went to the graveyard with the corpse of a soldier (belonging to our regiment) who died last night.[35]

Monday, November 11. News came today of the battle of Belmont.[36]

Tuesday, November 12. Nothing to note.

Wednesday, November 13. This morning all of those who had recovered sufficiently to do duty were sent from the hospital to camp on the Fair Grounds. I was placed in command of the squad. We marched out to the camp and were placed in a frame house (of two rooms). The company (27 in number) was divided by the Captain into two messes—one mess to each room. The boys from the Iowa Fifth and the 37th Illinois constituted "Mess No. One." The boys from the 9th Missouri constituted "Mess No. Two." I have to act the part of Captain, Lieutenant, and Orderly for the company. News came today of the victory of our fleet at Port Royal [South Carolina].[37] The blow, I hope, will have a salutary effect upon the infatuated citizens of *Palmettodom.*

Thursday, November 14. Today, Company "X" received their arms which looked much the worse for rust and dust. We also received the balance of our "ten days rations." Two very large racks of hay were burned in camp this morning—caught fire by accident. I think a dutchman's "pipe" did it.

Friday, November 15. The boys are busy cleaning their guns. We are getting along very well. News came of the battle of Piketon (Ky).[38]

Saturday, November 16. I went over to town today—received a letter from Lieut. Mateer from Tipton. The boys have been busy washing.

Sunday, November 17. Company "X" appeared on "Dress Parade."

Monday, November 18. I received word this morning to get ready to join my regiment. I was placed in command of the (2) teams and the squad of men (48 in number) from the hospital who were being sent to join their regiments at Syracuse. After trading our rations for food that needed no cooking, we started for Syracuse at one o'clock P.M. We traveled about 13 miles stopping over night at Mr. Leonard's. Mr. Leonard is much of a gentleman and (of course) a good Union man. He furnished us everything we desired. I partook of supper at his table on invitation. A number of the weaker members of our squad accepted his invitation to sleep in his house over night.

Tuesday, November 19. We started at 7 1/2 A.M. on our journey and reached Syracuse (12 miles) distant before noon. I walked two thirds of the way. A heavy rain came on just before we reached Syracuse. After the rain ceased, I walked out to camp (2 miles) and joined my company. I found the boys looking hale and hearty. I received quite a number of letters that had been awaiting my arrival.

Wednesday, November 20. I visited the camp of the Brown County Cavalry (near Syracuse) this morning and saw several old acquaintances.[39] In the afternoon I wrote a letter to Father and drew my overcoat, jacket, and cap.

Thursday, November 21. I resumed my duties in the company—received two letters.

Friday, November 22. Our camp was moved off the prairie to a sheltered nook near the timber where the wind don't blow icicles through us.

Saturday, November 23. Weather very cold. I drilled with the company in the forenoon and afternoon. Recieved [*sic*] a paper today containing Halleck's Fugitive Slave "Order No. 3."[40] Oh! when will the blunders of this war cease?

Sunday, November 24. The old woman has commenced picking her geese— snow this morning. I went on the sick list on account of sore-throat, hoarseness, and a bad cold generally. Dave McCord came into camp to see us.

Monday, November 25. Still on the sick list, but my cold getting better. Jim McCord came into camp today. The First Iowa Cavalry is camped near Syracuse. A rumor prevails through camp that we will have to march soon.

Tuesday, November 26. Captain Chapman resigned his position as commander of our company this morning on account of ill-health—i.e. "piles." Non-commissioned officers drilled this morning.

Wednesday, November 27. Nothing startling!

Thursday, November 28. Today is Thanksgiving Day at home. We have spent the day eating hard crackers instead of turkies. The regiment started about 8 o'clock A.M. on a march for Otterville. After marching seven miles a messenger overtook us bearing orders for us to return. We then countermarched to the old camp, arriving there about 3 P.M.

Friday, November 29. I went to town and bought a box of Ayer's Pills, two sticks of cough candy, and a daily paper. While in town, I saw Cal. Rankin and others of the Brown County Cavalry.[41]

Saturday, November 30. Battalion drill in the morning—afternoon devoted to washing. I received four papers today, (including a Free Press) from John Lamb.

Sunday, December 1. No drill today. Dress Parade in the evening. Wrote a letter to Mother.

Monday, December 2. Snow to the depth of four inches covered the ground this morning. The snow in camp was scraped up by "fatigue" parties and hauled off.

Tuesday, December 3. Battalion drill in the morning (through the snow). Brigade Review (by acting Brig. Gen. Worthington) and drill in the afternoon. During our few leisure moments we (King, Byers, and I) put up a chimney with sods at the end of our tent. The embers glowing in the fire-place are not only pleasant to the sight but their heat diffuses comfort through our canvas habitation.

The glowing coal makes a happy soul.

Wednesday, December 4. I wrote a letter to the *Free Press* and received a *Bee.* Brigade Drill in afternoon.

Thursday, December 5. Captain Chapman's resignation having been accepted, he started for home this morning.

Friday, December 6. Battalion Drill. Wrote to Cousin Esther.

Saturday, December 7. A *very* heavy rain last night—caused an overflow of most of the tents. Our tent was slightly inundated. My boots opened their mouths and took a big drink much to the discomfort of my feet in the morning.

Sunday, December 8. Our company was paid off for September and October. After being payed off, we were sent to Syracuse on "detached service."

Monday, December 9. I have been busy doing nothing today—have been busy employed by running about town, and eating *pies.* The country-people bring in apples, chickens, cakes, pies, &c., every day, and sell to the soldiers at paying rates.

Tuesday, December 10. Agreeably to orders from Pope's headquarters, our company detailed 27 men for guards today. We have to furnish sentinels for guarding army stores in town and also for guarding some secession prisoners who are confined in a house near our camp. I took "tea" out in town—price $.25—"washing not included."

Wednesday, December 11. "Mother Earth" received quite a treat today. An Irishman came into camp today for the purpose ostensibly of selling pies— but Madam Rumor whispered into Lieut. Mateer's ear that "Pat" was selling *pies* on. A search was ordered and (73) seventy three bottles of *whiskey* were found secreted in the bottom of the Irishman's wagon. The wagon was soon unloaded and a corporal broke the bottles and spilled the Irishman's "spirits" upon the earth.

Thursday, December 12. A difficulty occurred in camp today of an unpleasant nature. Wm. Hill and Jarred Metsker, coming into camp intoxicated, were ordered to be taken to the guard-house by Lieut. Mateer (commander of the company). They resisted, when a scene occurred disgraceful to them, and through them to the company. They were placed in the guard house, however, and quiet restored in the company.

Friday, December 13. Seven companies of the regiment, under command of Lt. Col. Matthies, marched to Boonville today as there are apprehensions of trouble there. Companies A and I came to town and camped with our company. The Col., Major, Adjutant, Quartermaster, and Chaplain remain with us.

Saturday, December 14. Nothing to note. No guards around camp.

Sunday, December 15. I attended divine service in a church in Syracuse—sermon by our Chaplain. The discourse was a very fair effort—some of the points were new and good. This is, I believe, the *second* sermon our Chaplain has preached to us!

Monday, December 16. Intelligence by a late foreign arrival, intimates that England will demand delivery of Mason and Slidell.[42] Let her demand! Five prisoners taken at Cole Camp were brought in today.

Tuesday, December 17. Intelligence came today of the great fire in Charleston. The weather during the present month has been extremely mild and pleasant for this time of the year.

Wednesday, December 18. A beautiful day—company drill. Milder news from England—not quite as bellicose as it was.

Thursday, December 19. Weather cooler.

Friday, December 20. Weather cool but pleasant. No drill.

Saturday, December 21. News came today of the victory of Pope's forces at Rose Hill—1300 prisoners captured.[43] The commission of Lieut. John H. Tait as Captain of the company came last night—also the commission of *R[obert]. A. McKee* (private) as 2nd Lieutenant. The commissions were both procured through the influence of Colonel Worthington. The appointment of Tait was a good one. The appointment of McKee was unexpected by the whole company. Not a single member of the company suspicioned that he (McKee) had any aspirations *or qualifications* for the office. The appointment caused much ill-feeling in the company. The company desired to choose their own officers but were satisfied with the appointment of their captain.

Sunday, December 22. A heavy snow for this region (4 inches) fell last night. Our chaplain having resigned started home today. The prisoners captured by Pope, at Rose Hill, passed here last night.

Monday, December 23. Wrote a letter to Archie, enclosing $10. "Mess No. One" divided, temporarily today.

Tuesday, December 24. Wrote a letter to the Free Press—had a good time snow balling. Milt Campbell was appointed regimental postmaster today.

Wednesday, December 25. I partook of a Christmas Turkey Dinner out in town—also a dish of oysters in the evening. An Indiana soldier (belonging in a hospital here) was shot today at the edge of town—supposedly by some secessionist. The company was disgraced today by a number of the boys getting drunk.

Thursday, December 26. An election of Corporals today resulted in the choice of David Heron and James Taylor. Squirrel for dinner.

Friday, December 27. John L. Payton, one of our best men, died today in the hospital.

Saturday, December 28. Payton was buried today with military honors. "May the clods of the valley be sweet to him."

Sunday, December 29. I attended divine service—sermon by Matthew Sparks. Dress parade with part of the 39th Ohio regiment. Wrote a long letter to Mother. Rabbit for dinner.

Monday, December 30. News came tonight of the surrender of Mason and Slidell—to the British government. After a careful reading of Secretary Seward's State paper, I am convinced that the course of our government was correct—and judicious. Busy today making out muster rolls.

Tuesday, December 31. I made out the "Monthly Return" and finished the Muster Rolls today. Oysters in the evening. Farewell 1861!

Wednesday, January 1 [1862]. Took dinner out in town at Sergeant Pennywitt's expense. Only *one* man was drunk today in the company. Today our company began making details to patrol the Pacific Railroad between Syracuse and Larmine bridge—one man is sent out from each company, (A, B & I) every hour and a half, during the day and night.

Thursday, January 2. I received a letter from Father per Walker Ellis of Georgetown, Brown co., Ohio.[44] Mr. Ellis took observations of our tents and improvements to make a report on his return to Ohio. He found this situated: Our tent is a small *wedge tent*—8 ft. X 6 ft. At one end of the tent is a sod chimney with a fireplace which serves to cook in and keep us comfortable. A pork barrel on top of the chimney increases its draught and prevents the chimney from smoking. In one corner of our tent is our bed—a small pile of straw (scarcely enough for a hen's nest)—on which we spread our blankets and overcoats at night. In another corner of the tent is our cupboard—a small box, containing 3 tin cups, 3 tin plates, 3 spoons, one knife, one fork, and a mess pan. Along side the cupboard is a box containing our library, which is not very large. Along one side of the tent is a pole, on which we hang our blankets during the day. Overhead hangs my sword—in a corner stand the guns. In the center of the tent are three candle boxes which serve as seats for "King, Byers, and me." Over the fire-place is the mantlepiece, above which is posted a "birds-eye view" of Washington and vicinity—on the margin of which is written (for the benefit of loafers) *"Read Proverbs, XXVc and 17 verse."*[45] This ends the description of our *home.*

Friday, January 3. I spent the day in sewing, writing, &c. Wrote a letter to the *"Free Press."*

Saturday, January 4. I spent the day in my tent, cooking, eating, playing chess, &c. Patrols still continue to be sent out to the railroad.

Sunday, January 5. We have prairie chicken for breakfast and dinner. No chaplain—no preaching.

Monday, January 6. Nothing of *importance*.

Tuesday, January 7. Squirrel for breakfast—rabbit for dinner.

Wednesday, January 8. Nothing unusual—the same old routine of business—roll calls, school, &c. &c.

Thursday, January 9. Spent my leisure time writing letters.

Friday, January 10. We had an interesting game of foot-ball today.[46]

Saturday, January 11. I played foot-ball and "town's ball" in the forenoon and did some mending in the afternoon.[47] I played well but sewed indifferent.

Sunday, January 12. A very cold day. Wrote a letter to Archie.

Monday, January 13. Weather still very cold making me keep near the fire. A cloth habitation in cold weather is not very warm but we manage to live very comfortably. Fatigue parties go to the woods everyday and cut a wagonload of fuel for the company. Every tent has a fire-place.

Tuesday, January 14. We had Dress Parade this evening during a big snow storm—mittens and gloves were in demand.

Wednesday, January 15. Today we had Battalion Drill through the snow. I wrote a letter to Captain Chapman. News came of Cameron's removal and Stanton's appointment as Secretary of War.[48] Alas! he is a *conservative!*

Thursday, January 16. Mr. McFadden of Brown co., Ohio called to see me. He came to Syracuse to procure a furlough for his son (a member of the Brown County Cavalry) who is here sick.

Friday, January 17. Wrote a letter to the *Missouri Democrat*, in favor of Jim Lane's policy.[49] Dress Parade in the evening—good music by band of 39th Ohio.

Saturday, January 18. Recited—snow-balled—played chess—made details—ate apples and sewed my unmentionables.

Monday, January 20. The *"Missouri Democrat"* with my letter in came today. We receive the daily papers by the cars every evening.

Tuesday, January 21. I receive a pair of nice buckskin gloves by mail today—a New Year's gift from Archie. Thanks to the "judge" for his present. News came today of the victory at Mill Springs, Ky., and the death of Zollicoffer.[50] Thank *God* for the victory.

Wednesday, January 22. Having received new gloves, I disposed of another pair which I had just purchased.

Thursday, January 23. I received a letter with wafers in for my throat. *Haller* [William Haller, Thirty-ninth Ohio Volunteer Infantry] called to see me.

Friday, January 24. The camp was thoroughly policed today.

Saturday, January 25. Six regiments passed here today *enroute* to St. Louis from Larmine cantonment—they were marching. I saw Lt. [Stephen] Porter of Brown co. Cavalry.

Sunday, January 26. We had dried peaches, rice, milk, beef-steak, liver and crackers for dinner.

Monday, January 27. New canteens and haversacks were drawn today. A thunderstorm payed us a visit in the afternoon. Sergeant Kiesler telegraphed to St. Louis today to inquire if any transfer could be made from our regiment to the gunboat service—the government having called for gunboat recruits from the infantry regiments.

Tuesday, January 28. A thunderstorm this morning caused a deluge in camp and a heavy detail was made to ditch the camp in the midst of the storm. Toward evening the rain turned to sleet.

Wednesday, January 29. Snow fell today.

Thursday, January 30. The regiment was payed off today to December 31, 1861. The company signed State Pay Rolls. We have orders to cook two day's rations, preparatory to marching—to Leavenworth, probably to join Jim Lane.

2

————⊸●⊶————

"Our Turn to Send Compliments"
The Island No. 10 Campaign, January 31–April 16, 1862

For Campbell and his comrades, the business of war recommenced only at the end of January 1862, when the Fifth Iowa was ordered to join the Union army's first great offensive in the western theater. As they dismantled their Syracuse winter camp and began the long trek south, the overall military situation looked as follows. In far-off northern Virginia, the massive Army of the Potomac—led by Maj. Gen. George B. McClellan, who doubled as general-in-chief of all Union armies—contemplated an advance against the Confederate capital at Richmond. In Missouri, Union forces had largely secured the state and were about to advance against a Confederate army in northwest Arkansas. Elsewhere, a Union naval blockade of the South was underway, and Federal forces had secured a few modest enclaves along the Southern coast.

West of the Appalachian Mountains, Rebel general Albert Sidney Johnston commanded a lengthy defensive line that ran from East Tennessee to the Mississippi River. Its eastern anchor had been broken at Mill Springs, Kentucky, just days earlier, but a sizable body of Confederates defended Bowling Green in the south-central part of the state, while additional Confederates manned river fortifications at Fort Donelson on the Cumberland, Fort Henry on the Tennessee, and Columbus, Kentucky, on the Mississippi. Twenty-five miles southwest of Columbus, still another complex of Confederate fortifications commanded the Mississippi at New Madrid, Missouri, and Island No. 10.

The Fifth Iowa was still en route to the theater of war when word came that Union forces under Brig. Gen. Ulysses S. Grant had captured Forts Henry and Donelson. Campbell celebrated the news, but aware that he had not yet been in battle, innocently hoped it was "only the beginning of the end." Realizing that the loss of the two forts rendered Columbus exposed and untenable, the Confederates abandoned that post in mid-February. Nashville, Tennessee, fell to Union troops without a struggle by month's end. Unopposed, Federal gunboats steamed triumphantly up the Tennessee River as far as Muscle Shoals, Alabama. For all practical purposes, the Confederacy had lost the entire western half of Tennessee.

Along the central Mississippi River valley, only the rebel forts at New Madrid and Island No. 10 continued to defy the Union juggernaut. Campbell and the Fifth Iowa now joined eighteen thousand Federals under Brig. Gen. John Pope in a month-long campaign to reduce these Confederate strongpoints. The initial clash occurred at New Madrid, where from March 3 to 14 Pope's force besieged the town. During this period, Campbell witnessed his first combat, a noisy but bloodless skirmish on March 6. After the fall of New Madrid, Pope spent an additional three weeks attempting to capture the surviving enemy fort at Island No. 10. The trick was for the Union gunboats north of Island No. 10 to run past the enemy's guns, link up with Pope's force at New Madrid, and cover Pope's river crossing as he shifted to the Tennessee bank of the Mississippi. Not until April 4 did the first gunboat, USS *Carondelet*, make the trip, followed by several others. That completed, Pope moved rapidly to cross the river and cut off the Island No. 10 garrison while gunboats and a flotilla of mortar boats shelled the fort. The trap shut on April 7; nearly seven thousand Confederates went into the bag. Although slightly disappointed that his unit was not in on the kill—"we would have been pleased to 'have a hand in the pie'"—Campbell and his comrades "cheered right lustily." Visiting with Confederate prisoners a day later, Campbell found the "majority of them sick of rebellion and not at all sorry they were taken."[1]

Even as Island No. 10 collapsed, McClellan's army began its ponderous but massive offensive against Richmond. And on April 6–7, Grant's army repulsed a major counteroffensive by Albert Sidney Johnston at Shiloh. The way was now open for a further Union advance against the strategic railroad junction at Corinth, Mississippi, just twenty miles from Shiloh. Richmond and Corinth: with the fall of these points, it was widely believed, the rebellion was finished.

Friday, January 31. We had reveille at 4 1/2 o'clock this morning in order to prepare for marching. After getting breakfast we "struck tents" and loaded our wagons. After taking down the tents, the following *ode* was found in one of the chimneys. The writer(s) was doubtless deeply affected.

An Ode to our Chimney

Old Chimney, I love thee, for what thou hast done.
To cheer us and warm us, and keep us in fun—
Without thee, I fear that we'd frozen our toes,
Or, perhaps, brought our days to an untimely close.

Like man, thou wert has made of the dust of the earth—
But thy nature detracts, not one whit from thy worth.
Like woman, our helper thou always hast been—
How can we forsake thee, and yet have no sin?
I love thee, old chimney, for well thou hast *drew*—
Without thee, old chimney, what, what shall we do?
Without thee, I fear, lest the pitiless storm
Shall beat on our poor pates and do us much harm.

Fare*well*, then, old chimney! Adieu! we must part,
But thy mem'ry shall linger fore'er in my heart.
See! the blest little water-drops steal from my eyes—
Curs'd, Curs'd, be the hand, that thus severs dear ties,
Adieu.

We bid good-bye to our winter home and started for Boonville at 10 o'clock, A.M., travelled 13 miles, camping at night in a barn near Bellair. The officers stopped at Mr. Leonard's.

Saturday, February 1. We started for Boonville at 7 A.M. (company B being in the lead) and reached there at noon. We were escorted into town by the *remainder* of our regiment, who came out to meet us. On our arrival in town we were quartered in a brick building. I took dinner at Mr. Burghers.

Sunday, February 2. Last night—I made my bed on a box and slept very well. I ate a good dinner at Mr. Burgher's where the Captain and Lieutenants board.

Monday, February 3. I called to see my friend Mrs. Whitehurst this morning and received a hearty welcome. I wrote to the *Free Press, Bee,* and Archie and received a letter from Father dated September 21.[2] A battalion of the 39th Ohio Regiment came into town today. A fight occurred in quarters today between [William] Hill & [Jarrod] Metsker and [Thomas] Preston & [Hiram] Hall. *Whiskey did it.*

Tuesday, February 4. General Inspection today. The 47th Illinois arrived today. Also the 11th Ohio Battery.

Wednesday February 5. The Illinois regiment and the Ohio battery crossed the river today. We have orders to march in the morning. A heavy rain fell today—we have a promise of plenty of mud tomorrow.

Thursday, February 6. We had reveille at 4 1/2 A.M. and after getting breakfast we prepared to march. We crossed the river about 10 o'clock and camped near Franklin 2 miles from the river in our tents. The ground was frozen so hard (the weather having changed during the night) that we had to chop holes with axes to drive our tent stakes into the ground.

Friday, February 7. Having no bed-fellow and but two blankets, I was "frozen out" last night—a few minutes before midnight and spent the rest of the night sitting by a fire. Today we had skirmish drill. In the afternoon, we had a good game of "shinny" on the ice.

Saturday, February 8. We had reveille at 5 1/2, and started on a march for Columbia at 8 o'clock. We marched 12 miles over the *iceyist* road I ever saw. We camped at night on an ice-field, digging holes again, to drive our tent-stakes.

Sunday, February 9. Before starting this morning, we had a *show* that exacted considerable merriment. Some of the battery boys had stolen a pig during the night and were caught dressing it. Col. Worthington (commander of the force) had them stand guard over it all night, and this morning, he compelled them to carry it along the whole line of troops, after we were drawn up. Two soldiers with reversed arms marched before them and two behind them, to increase the effect of the scene. The boys showed themselves good *pork packers* notwithstanding the jeers and laughter of the soldiers.

Monday, February 10. I was waked up about midnight last night by a bad attack of cholic [*sic*] and kept awake till morning. We marched 15 miles today, passing through Columbia and camping six miles beyond. We passed through Columbia *in style*. Since we left Boonville, several contrabands have joined us.[3] One was captured today by his owners and taken back a few rods when he was rescued by the boys of the Ohio battery.

Tuesday, February 11. Marched 12 miles and camped in timber.

Wednesday, February 12. Today we had a hard march, owing to the bad state of the roads—the mudding—being deep and sticky—boot jacks were rendered useless. During the day we passed through Fulton where we were met by the 3rd Iowa Cavalry and escorted into town. We camped 4 miles South-east of Fulton. After marching a whole day through Missouri mud, I am decidedly in favor of Macadamized roads—an institution I have failed to find in Missouri.

Thursday, February 13. We marched 14 miles today, through a snow storm camping 2 miles east of Williamsburgh. Several of the boys had their *windward* ear frozen during the march. The weather being warm in the morning, I put my overcoat in the company clothing box but would have been glad to get it before night. After starting in the morning, Col. Worthington announced to us our destination—i.e. Tennessee. *Elisha*, a contraband, joined [our] company today.

Friday, February 14. *David*, another contraband, came into camp last night. We marched 18 miles today (passing through Danville) and camped near High Hill on the railroad. Water was very scarce during the march today. During our march from Boonville, we have been able to get chickens, butter, &c. from the inhabitants at reasonable prices. The 81st Ohio regiment was quartered at Danville.

Saturday, February 15. We marched 18 miles parallel to the railroad, passing through High Hill, Jonesburgh, and Warrenton. We were met and escorted into Warrenton by a company of cavalry. A Missouri regiment is stationed at

Warrenton. Another contraband accompanied us today. Let them come. "I repeat it, let them come." I was troubled with colic all day.

Sunday, February 16. Being still unwell this morning, I received permission to march "out of ranks." Our course having been along the railroad, I concluded to walk in the track as being a smoother and shorter road. In company with Sergeant [Thomas] Kiesler and private [William] Hurling, I accordingly started "by rail." We had not walked many miles when we found that the road our regiment was traveling diverged from the railroad and that we were consequently getting farther away from one another. Nothing daunted, however, we pressed on preferring the straight and narrow way. We walked 7 miles when we were overtaken by a government R.R. train at a station. We jumped aboard the cars and rode 7 miles farther. As soon as we got off the cars, we took a cross road to make our way onto the road on which the regiment was marching. Before reaching the state road, we stopped at the house of Mr. Wilson, a rich secessionist, to get our dinner. Mr. Wilson was not at home, but his son-in-law, a son of Hon. Edward Bates invited us in, and we spent an hour or more in conversation with him.[4] He took the side of the South, but professed to be a *neutral!* We gave him some plain words and left him in no doubt as to what our opinion of a *neutral* was. Before leaving, dinner was set out *by request*—but as nothing but *cold grub* was offered, I refused to partake, having plenty of that style in my haversack. The boys offered to pay for their meal, but their pay was not accepted. Mr. Bates is a St. Louis merchant—he is the only son of one worthy attorney General who is not loyal to his country. Woman's influence makes him disloyal. After leaving Mr. Wilson's, we soon came onto the state road (distant 4 miles from the railroad) and were not long in discovering that our regiment had not passed. We accordingly took the back track and had 8 miles to travel before we came to the regiment. Luckily we had a opportunity to ride most of the way in a huckster's wagon.[5] The regiment marched only 10 miles, while we traveled at least 25! Quite a joke on a sick man.

Monday, February 17. The regiment started before daylight this morning and as I was suffering from a violent attack of colic, I remained behind until the troops and most of the teams had left. I then started on walking as best I was able. I had walked about a mile when Sergt. Byars [Byers] came along on the Sutler's horse and finding that I was unwell, he got off and helped me on the horse.[6] As the road was crowded with the teams, I rode along a path next to the fence. I had ridden some distance when the horse suddenly scared and rearing up, fell backward into a deep ditch *with me under him.* It was quite a jolt—and I was deprived of sensibility for a short time. The first thing I remembered after the horse fell back, was Dr. [William] Daro [Darrow] and one of the boys leading me to a wagon and helping me in it. I then gradually "came to," and learned what happened *in my absence.* When the horse fell on me, those who were near thought I was killed *but they were mistaken.* It was with some difficulty that I was extricated from under the horse and placed on a *proper footing.* My injuries amounted to a bruised thigh and shoulder. The narrowness of the ditch at the bottom saved me from being crushed. The jolting of the wagon pained my thigh somewhat and John Rhinehart helped me on his horse, an easy riding, tractable animal.[7] On horseback, once more, I got along very well until Phillips, Brigade Wagon Master, made me get off the horse to let John attend to his business as Regimental Wagon Master. Phillips having *ordered* me to get off the horse and having spoken to me in a very ungentlemanly manner, I refused to get in one of his wagons and ride. I accordingly limped along about two miles when I stopped at a Farmer's on the road and hired a horse to ride across to O'Fallon's station on the railroad. The house where I stopped was only half a mile from and in sight of Cousin Samuel McClure's. I thought of calling to see him but I did not wish to stay behind the regiment without leave and as I was *lame*, I did not know but they might consider me as asking for *charity* On arriving at O'Fallon's station, I quartered myself in the depot—and doctored my bruises while waiting for the cars. Before the cars arrived, Cousin Robert McClure called to see me having heard of my whereabouts. He wished me to go home with him but the same reasons prevented me that prevented me going to Samuel's. The cars came along at 11 o'clock and at midnight I arrived at St. Charles and took up my quarters in the depot. At the depot I learned of the capture of Fort Donnelson [*sic*].[8] May this only be the beginning of the end. The regiment arrived at St. Charles about 2 o'clock P.M. having marched 28 miles.

Tuesday, February 18. I procured breakfast at the American Hotel and then went out into town and had my picture taken and sent it home. I then went out to camp and had been there but a few moments, when the bugle sounded and we started for town, enroute to St. Louis. We left here our contrabands after giving them instructions for getting into Illinois. We left them because Halleck's orders compelled it.[9] We crossed the river at St. Charles and took the cars (hog cars) for St. Louis. On our arrival at the city, we were marched aboard the steamer Ed. Walsh on board which boat were also stowed an artillery company and part of the 2nd Iowa and part of the 2nd Michigan Cavalry. The crowd aboard the boat was so great that there was no convenience or comfort. The men were highly indignant at this treatment and for awhile confusion and cursing reigned supreme. A leader was all that was wanting to make a mutiny. The noise and confusion were kept up until several barrels of bread and meat were brought aboard when the men addressed themselves to a new undertaking and a calm ensued. The officers occupied the cabin of the boat and were crowded as well as the men. At St. Charles we parted from the 39th Ohio, 47th Illinois, and the Ohio Battery, our companions on the march.

Wednesday, February 19. We started for Cairo [Illinois] this morning on the Walsh. On our way down the river, we passed several boats loaded with *secesh birds* (captured at Ft. Donnelson) on their way North. Before leaving St. Louis I bought a Bacon's Cartridge Revolver, paying $25 for it and 200 cartridges.

Thursday, February 20. We passed several boats today going to St. Louis with assorted cargoes of secesh on. We arrived at Cairo in the afternoon, where we found more Ft. Donnelson butternuts.[10] We remained aboard the boat over night where we were visited by several Newton boys of the 10th [Iowa] Regiment.

Friday, February 21. We were marched ashore and quartered in the barracks at Camp Defiance this morning. We are without anything to cook with or to eat. A small amount of bread and a few spoonfulls of Molasses were furnished but this only served to aggravate our appetites which we had to satisfy at our own expense at the eating houses in town. I had a conversation with some of the secesh prisoners and found them blinded and deluded beings— some were penitent, others were spunky and saucy. This is my first visit to Cairo—may it be my last. Oh! what a mud hole! I wrote to the Free Press.

Saturday, February 22. Washington's Birth Day. I celebrated the anniversary by visiting the Newton boys of the 10th Iowa Regiment at Bird's Point [Missouri]. I took dinner with Corporal [James] Banks and supper with Capt. [John] Garrett. Failing to make the connection with the ferry boat, I remained at Bird's Point over night—sleeping with Mr. Harris, with whom I took breakfast—eating my share of buckwheat cakes, and other *goodies*. Today we received the news of the taking of Nashville by our forces.[11]

Sunday, February 23. After breakfast with Mr. Harris, I returned to Camp Defiance. A reconnoitering expedition went down to Columbus today—returning in the evening. In the evening, I attended divine services at the Episcopal Church with the Captain and several others of the company.[12]

Monday, February 24. I bought my breakfast and dinner in town, owing to the scarcity of grub at the barracks. In the afternoon, we were marched aboard the steamer E. H. Fairchild and started *up* the Mississippi to Commerce, Mo. We are considerably puzzled to understand this move, as we were informed that we were going to Tennessee.

Tuesday, February 25. We arrived at Commerce last night and this morning we left the boat and marched out 2 miles on the road to Benton and camped. Our regiment here drew new clothing and new tents. A pretty large force gathered here portends some expedition of importance. Among the regiments, I found the 27th Ohio and got to see Cousin Hi[ram]. Reynolds.

Wednesday, February 26. Today we marched 10 miles, camping 2 miles Southeast of Benton. From this camp, the boys sent back half their blankets (by order) to Commerce in order to lighten their loads on the march. All extra baggage, tents, &c. were also sent back.

Thursday, February 27. General Inspection today. Eight days rations were issued to the companies.

Friday, February 28. The regiment was mustered today.

Saturday, March 1. We marched 12 miles southward from Benton today through a swampy country. After marching 4 or 5 miles, we began to see signs of an enemy ahead—such as trees felled across the road, through the swamp and bridges burned. This was the work of Jeff Thompson's men but they failed to delay us any as our *pioneers* had removed all obstructions before we came along.[13] At night, our company was detailed for picket duty but was excused. *Good!* During the day we came across a butternut who gave us some knowledge of Jeff Thompson's movements. Said butternut was considerably frightened by the boys who chastised him pretty closely while they were *resting.*

Sunday, March 2. We marched 14 miles on the road to New Madrid whither we are evidently ending our way. During our march we passed through Sikeston where we left our knapsacks in order to make our loads still lighter. During the forenoon, we marched through the deepest of mud and during a *very* heavy thunderstorm. We got a good soaking. After passing through Sikeston the road became pretty good and as the rain had ceased, we marched along at a brisk pace.

Monday, March 3. We marched 12 miles and arrived at New Madrid. Our advance went near enough the town to draw the fire of the enemy's gunboats which threw several large shells among them, killing two or three of our men. Our batteries replied with the design of drawing the enemy's fire and learning their strength and position. After reconnoitering, Gen. Pope (Commander of our forces) withdrew his command out of reach of the enemy's guns.[14] We expect a fight tomorrow. Our regiment is camped in timber.

Tuesday, March 4. We changed our position today, camping nearer the enemy and in line of battle. Our camp is in the center of a large level cornfield. We soon made use of the cornstalks for beds. They are not very soft, but they serve to keep our blankets out of the mud. Our regiment, together with the 59th Indiana, 10th Iowa, and 26th Missouri, and Constable's Ohio battery, form a Division commanded by Gen. [Charles] Schuyler Hamilton. Our regiment occupies the center of the line of our forces. Gen. [David] Stanley commands the Division on our right, and Gen. [Eleazer] Payne [Paine], the one on our left. A feigned attack was made on the enemy after dusk this evening. One man in company A of our regiment was killed.[15] Our regiment [company] was not in the affray—only half of our regiment being sent out.

Wednesday, March 5. Our teams having to go beyond our pickets after forage, our company was detailed as their escort. We went within sight of the enemy's pickets, who kept a close watch on our movements.

Thursday, March 6. This afternoon, our company and Company A, with 3 rifle companies of the Indiana regiment, were detailed to make a reconnaissance. We were placed under Col. [Gordon] Granger's command—Major Robinson [sic] having immediate command of us. On arriving at our line of pickets, we deployed as skirmishers—Company A being of the right of our company and the Indiana company on our left. A reserve of 500 men remained at our picket line to support us but they did not advance a foot from their position and might as well have stayed in camp. We advanced as skirmishers through corn-fields keeping a lookout for the enemy. We had advanced some three-quarters of a mile, when the enemy sent as their compliments in the shape of a volley from their grand guard.[16] Their heaviest fire was in front of our right and the left of company A. The balls whizzed past and over us in a rather *un*musical manner. We dropped on our knees and the balls cut the corn stalks about us in a manner that showed they wished to cultivate a close acquaintance. The Major gave the word "fire" and it then became our turn to send compliments. We fired at random, not being able to see the enemy but the marks of the balls on the fence showed that "we intended well." After firing, we loaded and advanced on reaching the fence at the edge of the field, we found that the enemy had fallen back some 500 yards and were drawn up in line. On the right of our line, we jumped the fence into a lane and took our position behind the fence next [to] the enemy. We were within good range of the rebels but were ordered not to fire till we got *orders*. The enemy soon perceived the error of remaining drawn up in a body and they deployed. We lay behind the fence some ten or fifteen minutes, with our men picked out but we finally had to retire without firing. While we lay behind the fence, our Major kept riding up and down our lines to see if all was right and each time as he passed along some of the rebel marksmen attempted to pick him off but, most fortunately, failed. They however made some close shots. Notwithstanding this aggravation, we were not permitted to pull trigger. When the order to retire came, the left of our line (through misunderstanding of the order) fired on the enemy before entering; with what effect is not known. We retired about a quarter of a mile, where we lay flat on the ground to await the enemy in hopes that they would follow us. But they were too wary. The enemy's gunboats in the meantime had commenced throwing big shells at us and they fell close around us, much to our *terror*—luckily no one was hurt by them. One of them fell so close as to throw dirt on some of the boys. Their *music* as they whistled through the air was anything but melodious, and we were not grieved when after half an hour's practice, they stopped throwing their cast-iron pumpkins at us. It is not much *fun* to have an enemy doing his best to put an end to your existence when you can do nothing in return. When the gun-boats ceased firing, we fell back to our reserve and returned to camp. Our casualties were one man killed in an Indiana company and three of Company A slightly wounded. Providentially our loss was small. No one of our company was hurt in the least. The loss of the rebels is of course unknown to us.

Friday, March 7. This morning, our company and Company A were detailed *to take one of the enemy's gunboats.* The boat was said to be tied to the bank and her gunners and pilot were said to be exposed. The plan was for an attack to be made on the left of the enemy's line and draw their infantry force that way—we were then to rush in to the river bank on the right and pick off the crew and gunners of the boat with our rifles and take possession of her in the name of Uncle Sam. The plan was a very foolish one but was fortunately for us disarranged and we were not led to the slaughter. Few, if any of us, would have been left to tell the tale if we had attempted to carry out the plan. The gunboats kept steam up all the time and their gunners were not exposed. A rebel fort (whose existence seems to have been unknown to our commanders) commanded every approach to the river and we would have made a sorry show getting to the bank. The 27th Ohio drove in the enemy's pickets and our field batteries fired a few shells, waked up the rebel gun-boats, which moved up and down the stream firing shells at us. No damage done. Maj. Robinson and command were complimented by Gen. Hamilton for their conduct during the skirmish yesterday.

Saturday, March 8. The rebels were busy, all last night burning houses, chopping, &c. What they are doing, time will tell. We have no good water near our camp and "fatigue details" are at work digging a well. From Benton to New Madrid we did not cross a single stream of water. Skirmish drill today.

Sunday, March 9. Forty men of our company on grand guard today. I paid a visit to cousin Hiram today and heard a sermon by the Chaplain of the 27th.

Monday, March 10. More troops arrived today. Pope's force is now about 25,000—infantry, artillery, and cavalry.

Tuesday, March 11. Company and Battalion Drill. Our camp has been cleared of corn-stalks and levelled off and now presents a very neat appearance. It is swept every morning and kept in good order. Part of Pope's force has been sent to Point Pleasant a few miles below New Madrid, where they have thrown up works and planted a battery that virtually blockades the river and cuts off the rebel communications with Memphis except by their gunboats which have to run the gauntlet.

Wednesday, March 12. I went on the sick list this morning on account of a bad cold and sore-throat. Two large siege guns and a 64-pound howitzer arrived this evening from Cairo *via* Sikeston. They are to be placed in position tonight. We have orders to be "ready to fall in by daylight."

Thursday, March 13. At day-break, our big guns (which had been planted within 800 yards of Fort Thompson) opened fire and were soon throwing shells into the enemies' works. The enemy was not slow in replying from his forts and gunboats. The contest became interesting and the howl of the shells as the went whirr-r-r-r-ing through the air spoke of *business.* We were soon in line and marched down to support our batteries. Two Ohio regiments (39th and 27th) and two Illinois regiments were stationed in trenches and rifle pits around the batteries, while we (the rest of Pope's forces) remained out of reach of the enemy's fire as a reserve. Our batteries were planted last night and the trenches dug and occupied (by the Illinois and Ohio regiments above named) without the enemy suspicioning that anything was going on. The first they heard of us was the morning salute of our howitzer. We stacked our arms in a pasture and lay down to wait for something to turn up. There being no danger where we were, the firing became uninteresting to us and we betook ourselves to reading, sleeping, &c., as best suited us. At sundown, we returned to camp. The result of the days fight may be summed up as follows: one of our big guns placed *hors du combat* and four or five men killed and as many or more wounded. The enemy's loss, of course cannot be known. Several of their guns, however, were silenced.

Friday, March 14. At 3 o'clock this morning, our regiment was called up to go down and take the place of the regiments occupying the trenches. A heavy thunder storm had occurred during the night and the fields and roads were flooded so that we waded rather than marched down to the batteries. We got into the trenches (full of mud and water) just at day-break. The clouds looked threatening and we were promising ourselves a 24 hour treat of mud and rain in the trenches. We had been but a short time in the trenches when "a man came riding by" who announced to our eager ears that *the enemy had evacuated!* Confirmation of the report soon came and we got out of the trenches and gave three rousing cheers that were echoed and re-echoed by our forces till they reached the camp to there die away in the feeble echoes of the sick and *drones* left behind us. Companies A and B were soon ordered on a scout to scour the woods below the fort, which we did with much fatigue and little profit. On our return from the scout, our company was detailed to assist Bissell's Engineer Company in mounting the cannon in Fort Thompson and putting it in proper repair. I thus had an opportunity of viewing the fort and the effect our guns had had on it the day before. Fort Thompson is a *very* strong earthwork—mounting 13 large pieces, mostly 32-pounders. Outside, the fort is protected by a deep ditch and a *rampart* of brush, which encircles the fort about 15 feet outside the ditch. None but cowards would have been driven out of such a fort by four guns. Besides this fort, the rebels had another at the upper end of town mounting 8 or 10 guns. This fort was probably constructed after our appearance before the place. Besides those two forts, the enemy had three or four gunboats with heavy armaments to assist in their defense. Notwithstanding all this strength, they took advantage of the storm and deserted their works during the night and *fled* on their gunboats. Their *evacuation* was so precipitate that they left some of the pickets on duty and one or two of their dead unburied—several of their number were left asleep and knew nothing of the flight of their friends until the yankees informed them of it. The guns in the forts were spiked but it was done so hastily that it required but little labor to unspike them.[17] Knapsacks, haversacks, buckets, cooking utensils, provisions, spades, wheelbarrow, &c, &c., &c., were left lying around in confusion showing that the flight of the rebels had been very precipitate. Five hundred horses and mules were left in the stables. Nearly a million dollars worth of property fell into our hands. A large amount of ammunition fell into our hands. In the afternoon, I returned to camp as it was raining and I did not wish to expose myself needlessly while my throat was sore. The company remained at the fort at work.

Saturday, March 15. The company remained at the Fort today.

Sunday, March 16. The company returned to camp. I wrote to the *Free Press.*

Monday, March 17. This afternoon, the different regiments of our Division were marched through New Madrid and the fort by order of Gen. Pope by way of compliment to us. Our company remained in town over night. Heavy firing was heard in the evening in the direction of Island No. 10.

Tuesday, March 18. Our company returned to camp. Heavy firing was heard all day at Island No. 10.

Wednesday, March 19. Firing at Island 10 continued. Battalion drill.

Thursday, March 20. No firing at No. 10 today. Our company commenced drilling in the bayonet exercise.

Friday, March 21. No firing at No. 10. Drill, Drill, Drill! Received a "*Press.*"

Saturday, March 22. No firing at No. 10. Drill.

Sunday, March 23. No firing at No. 10. Inspection of arms.

Monday, March 24. Battalion Drill. Camp put in "apple pie order."

Tuesday, March 25. Firing commenced, again, at No 10.

Wednesday, March 26. Division Drill under Gen. Hamilton.

Thursday, March 27. General Inspection and Review by Gen. Pope. The weather during the past week has been delightful.

Friday, March 28. Division Drill. Weather beautiful.

Saturday, March 29. Wash day. Our spare time we spent playing ball.

Sunday, March 30. No firing heard at No 10. Inspection.

Monday, March 31. A beautiful Day. Firing again at Island No. 10. How long will we have to wait for "*the gunboat fleet?*"

Tuesday, April 1. Weather hot and very windy. Firing at No. 10 continues. I called on Hiram, Haller, &c. We have drill every day.

Wednesday, April 2. A heavy wind and rain storm last night caused quite a stir in camp. Tents were blown down and boxes and pans sent whirling through camp at a lively rate. The tent I was sleeping in was blown down and I had to skedaddle through the rain and hunt other quarters. Weather clear today.

Thursday, April 3. Drill, Drill, Drill.

Friday, April 4. Ditto, Ditto, Ditto.

Saturday, April 5. I got through our picket lines and went to town this morning where I saw one of our gunboats (the Carondelet) which ran the blockade at Island No. 10 during a storm last night. She passed the rebel batteries without injury although they did their utmost. I returned to camp and found that our regiment had orders to cook three days ration[s]. This means *action.*

Sunday, April 6. I attended divine services at the 43d Ohio regiment this morning. The *Carondelet* has been fighting a rebel battery located on the

Kentucky shore a short distance below Ft. Thompson. The firing was heavy. Our tents, blankets, & c., which we left at Benton, came up today. A large fatigue party was sent to town this evening—for what purposes I am ignorant.

Monday, April 7. Another gunboat ran the blockade at Island No. 10 last night during another storm—no injury done to her. Four transport steamers arrived at the upper fort last night having come through by the *overland route*— i.e. through a channel cut by Bissell's Engineer regiment through the woods beginning at a point above No 10 and ending at the upper fort where the boats again came into the river. They were nearly three weeks making the trip—distance 12 or 14 miles. At day-break, the two gun-boats (Carondelet and Cincinnati) attacked the rebel batteries on the opposite shore and soon silenced them. In the meantime Pope's force was moving to the river to cross on the transports and attack the rebels at Island No 10 in the rear. Our regiment started to the river at 10 o'clock. Payne's Division crossed first—Stanley's second, and ours (Hamilton's) last. We landed at the enemy's battery which mounted (before it was dismounted) one 84-pounder siege gun and the 64-pounder howitzers. The gunboats had placed all these pieces *hors du combat* and the enemy fled leaving a great number of intrenching tools in our hands. Each division started "No. Tenward" as soon as it crossed the river. We got across the river about sundown and started after the other divisions. We marched until 8 o'clock P.M. over a very muddy road, when we halted in a piece of timber and rested for night. We had no blankets but slept with tolerable comfort.

Tuesday, April 8. A deserted secesh camp was found near our bivouack this morning and a secesh flag picked up in it. We started ahead on the march at 8 o'clock. Soon after starting we received news of the evacuation of Island No. 10 by the rebels and their flight towards Tiptonville. Our course was accordingly changed to Tiptonville to intercept the rebels in their retreat. We soon overtook Stanley's Division and we pressed on towards Tiptonville. Before reaching the place, news came that Payne's Division had surrounded and captured the whole secesh force numbering 5,000. Although we would have been pleased to "have a hand in the pie," we were nevertheless rejoiced at the news and cheered right lustily. We reached Tiptonville about noon, where we found Payne's forces guarding their captives. Part of Payne's force, however, were out hunting up the stragglers who were being brought in, in squads every half hour. The prisoners were a motley set—"blue devils and white, black devils and grey." They were from Tennessee, Alabama, Mississippi, Louisiana, and Arkansas—a few being from Florida. The Alabamians were the best uniformed and best looking of the lot. I circulated among them and conversed freely with different ones. I found the majority of them sick of rebellion and not at all sorry they were taken. Many of them denounced their leaders bitterly. A great many said they were *forced* into the service. A few were spunky and sullen. Among the Alabamians I found two lieutenants who were acquainted with Uncle Samuel D. Campbell. They spoke of him as a Union man and a *Yankee*. Hamilton's Division remained at Tiptonville to assist Paine's Division in guarding the prisoners. Stanley's Division marched across to Island No. 10, scouring the country as they went. Payne surrounded and captured the rebels without a fight, they being frightened too badly to fight.

Wednesday, April 9. Last night a cold drizzling rain drenched our forces and the prisoners who had no tents or other protection from the elements. I was fortunate enough to get sleeping room in a deserted home. Our prisoners were sent to New Madrid today on transports. These prisoners were part of [Gen. Braxton] Bragg's force at Pensacola. They were sent to New Madrid and No. 10 on the evacuation of Pensacola. The secesh who evacuated New Madrid went to No 10, *via* Tiptonville.

Thursday, April 10. Last night I slept in the woods near Tiptonville under a *"fly."* We returned to Mew Madrid on steamer in the forenoon. The prisoners were sent *north* today. News came of the battle at Shiloh.

Friday, April 11. We have orders to get ready to march. *I put on a clean shirt.*

Saturday, April 12. Companies drew 10 days rations. At 8 o'clock we "struck tents" and marched to the river where we got aboard the steamer *"Chonteau."*

Sunday, April 13. Early this morning we started down the river *for Fort Pillow.*[18] Hamilton's Division were all aboard the *Chonteau, Emma,* and *City of Alton.* Payne's Division and Stanley Davis' Divisions started before day. The gunboat and mortar fleet preceded them. We arrived at Plum Point, Tennessee (nearly opposite Osceola, Arkansas) where we joined the remainder of our fleet about 3 o'clock P.M. I slept last night on a coal pile. I have slept worse on feather beds.

Monday, April 14. This morning the fleet moved across the river and the whole force was landed at a point below Osceola, 9 miles above Ft. Pillow by water and 4 by land. Two or three of our mortar boats were towed to a position about 3 miles from Ft. Pillow by land and the mortars commenced firing about 2 o'clock P.M. The enemy soon replied. No harm done. The firing was done *across* Craighead point. The whole land force was put ashore to stay during the day. At night, we returned to the boats. The plantation we spent the day on belongs to a secessionist who fled on our approach, taking his slaves with him. The plantation is protected by a levee. We have a very pleasant abiding place.

Tuesday, April 15. All the troops marched ashore again. We are "pestered" a great deal by the mosquitoes, which are thick and blood-thirsty. I went down to the levee this morning to within 300 yards of the mortar boats and witnessed the firing between them and the fort. The sight of the shells as they leaped from the monster mortars and flew [through] the air was grand, while the roar of the mortars was terrific. The enemy made some close shots in reply to our mortars but happily missed their mark. Cane brakes are numerous about us in low places. We returned to the boats at night.

Wednesday, April 16. Troops went ashore again. After going aboard the boats again in the evening, Gen. Hamilton came aboard our boat and held a consultation with our officers. Our company was detailed on "fatigue" soon after and were put to work carrying and chopping up rails and taking them aboard the "Chonteau" for fuel. It was evident from this haste in procuring fuel that some move was intended soon. We could get no clue to it, however, and were left to our own conjectures, which were not very satisfying.

3

———◦◦◦———

"UPHOLDING UNCLE SAM'S AUTHORITY"
The Siege of Corinth and After, April 17–September 17, 1862

After the victory at Island No. 10, most of Pope's force went to join the over-whelming concentration of Union troops at Pittsburg Landing, Tennessee—scene of the recent Battle of Shiloh. Not only was Grant's army already there, but it had been joined during the battle by a second army under Brig. Gen. Don Carlos Buell. With the arrival of Pope's troops, which included Campbell and the Fifth Iowa, the Union host numbered well over one hundred thousand. Commanding the combined force was Maj. Gen. Henry W. Halleck, the highest-ranking Union general in the western theater.

Halleck's objective point was Corinth, Mississippi, where the Confederacy's main east-west railroad intersected a major north-south railroad. Mindful that many of his troops lacked experience and that the fight at Shiloh had come per-ilously close to disaster, Halleck saw little reason for a hasty advance. Although he handily outnumbered the fifty thousand troops possessed by his opponent, Gen. P. G. T. Beauregard, Halleck moved his army slowly, carefully, at a rate averaging scarcely a mile each day. But at the end of May the Confederates evacu-ated Corinth and the town fell without a fight. It was another triumph for Union arms to add to a gleaming stream of victories: Fort Henry, Fort Donelson, Shiloh, and Island No. 10, as well as the defeat of a Rebel army at Pea Ridge, Arkansas (in March) and the capture of New Orleans (in April).

All eyes turned to Richmond, where McClellan had advanced to within six miles of the city. At the end of June rumors began to fly of a great struggle outside the Rebel capital. They continued for over a week. "We have been kept in a painful suspense of mind today by conflicting rumors of events at Rich-mond," Campbell wrote on July 5. "We have a report one hour that McClellan has taken Richmond and the next, that he has been whipped." The latter news proved correct. McClellan fell back from Richmond in defeat, and a war that had seemed nearly over now seemed anything but.

Even before word of McClellan's repulse, the momentum had drained from the big Union offensive in the West. After Corinth's capture, Halleck dispersed his large army to garrison the vast territory that had been won. Before the month of June was over, Pope was off to Washington, D.C., to take command of a new Union army; Halleck followed him less than a month later to become the new general-in-chief. Now under Brig. Gen. William S. Rosecrans, Campbell and his regiment spent the summer of 1862 in relative quiet. But around them the nature of the war was changing. In July the U.S. Congress passed a law authorizing the confiscation of Rebel property; soon afterward, President Abraham Lincoln issued a call for three hundred thousand additional three-year volunteers to join Campbell and the other "boys of '61." In the field, Union soldiers no longer regarded white Southerners as wayward brothers who might be wooed by mild treatment. It now became accepted practice to seize supplies directly from enemy farms. Campbell approved. "We are going to fight the enemy henceforth with every available weapon." he wrote.

Northern newspapers called the new mood "making war in earnest," but the Southerners were also in earnest. In August, having bested McClellan, Gen. Robert E. Lee's Army of Northern Virginia thrashed Pope on the Manassas plains southwest of Washington. Two more Confederate armies embarked on an invasion of Kentucky. And yet another two—these under Maj. Gen. Sterling Price and Maj. Gen. Earl Van Dorn—came marching toward Corinth in a bid to retake the town. Campbell and the Fifth Iowa were at last about to stare into the face of battle.

Thursday, April 17. This morning early, Pope's fleet pushed out from their moorings below Osceola and started *up* the Mississippi. The gunboat and mortar fleet with an Indiana brigade remained behind to attend to Fort Pillow. The scene on the river as the large fleet steamed along was lively and animating. We are still ignorant of our destination, but Madame Rumor says it is Pittsburg Landing on the Tennessee river. As we passed up the river, we had frequent evidences of the existence of slavery, in the miserable looking dwellings and farms(?) of the poor whites on both banks. Some of the inhabitants seemed anxious to hear from the *world* once more and came out in skiffs to get newspapers which were thrown out to them.

Friday, April 18. Our boat tied up at Riddle's Point last night and remained there until she "wooded." About 10 o'clock she started on up the river, but her boilers began to leak, and she made poor headway. At New Madrid, we found the City of Alton awaiting us. She was lashed to the Chonteau and we proceeded on our journey at a better speed. We passed [Island] "*No 10*" at sundown, and had a good view of the rebel stronghold. Rain, today and yesterday.

Saturday, April 19. We reached Cairo last night. I saw Drs. Parker in a grocery in Cairo. We, here, left the *Chonteau* and got aboard the *Nebraska,* a better and faster boat. I sent $45.00 home in a letter. We started up the Ohio in the evening.

Sunday, April 20. The boat stopped at *Metropolis, Ill.* last night, where we remained until 2 o'clock P.M. today when we started up the river. Between 3 and 4 o'clock we entered the Tennessee river and went ploughing up that now historic stream. We passed Paducah at 4 o'clock, and continued on our course. Paducah is one of the most beautiful places I ever saw. Rain, again. Our cooking accommodations(?) while on transports are always miserable. This trip is no exception. Our treatment in this matter is mean and criminal.

Monday, April 21. Our boat stopped last night at Fort Henry but I was asleep while we remained there and missed the sight.[1] As we passed up the river today, I remained on deck (in spite of the rain) to view the magnificent scenery that graced the banks. Nothing that I ever beheld in Nature was so grand and beautiful. And yet it is a wilderness, almost, on account of slavery's baneful influence. As we passed up the river we were greeted at different points by hearty manifestations of welcome.

Tuesday, April 22. When we awoke this morning, we found our boat lying at Pittsburg Landing. About 8 o'clock we moved up the stream three miles to Hamburgh. We then disembarked from the boat and camped half a mile from the river on a beautiful grassy ridge.

Wednesday, April 23. Today we had "General Inspection." Gen. Hamilton's Division has been enlarged by the addition of four more regiments. Gen. Buford of Illinois is commander of our brigade.[2]

Thursday, April 24. Regiment drew clothing today. Company drill.

Friday, April 25. We are under marching orders—have two days rations in our haversacks. Rain.

Saturday, April 26. A beautiful day. "Wash day" for me.

Sunday, April 27. There is apprehension of an attack today. We are all ready. Our *new chaplain* [J. C. Sherron] preached today. He seems to be a good man. I hope he will be a useful sort. We want a working chaplain.

Monday, April 28. We had no fight yesterday. Today we advanced our camp four miles on [the] Corinth road. Our cavalry had a skirmish with the enemy. After getting in to our new camp, I took a stroll into an old cotton field and did my first *"cotton-picking."*

Tuesday, April 29. I was employed today making out pay rolls. One year ago today, I volunteered to serve my country as a soldier.

Wednesday, April 30. Our regiment was detailed on "fatigue" today. We were detailed to work the road on which we were to advance. A regiment or two accompanied us as an escort. Bissell's Engineer regiment does the bridge building for us. Before we returned, we repaired the road beyond the Mississippi line and I for the first time placed my foot in that treasonable commonwealth. I dined with an old couple who appeared to still love the old Union.

The old lady was a cousin of Mr. Lincoln. Rations of *whiskey* were issued to the company on our return. I poured mine out, much to the indignation of some who would rather have wet their throats with it.

Thursday, May 1. A beautiful day. Our company was mustered.

Friday, May 2. We advanced our camp 5 miles towards Corinth, camping on the Mississippi line. I am unwell today—symptoms of biliousness.

Saturday, May 3. I am still unwell—have a violent headache every forenoon. There was brisk cannonading in front this evening.

Sunday, May 4. I went on the "sick list" this morning.

Monday, May 5. My head still persists in aching during the forenoon. I am taking quinine and blue mass. A heavy rain fell last night.

Tuesday, May 6. I used a mustard plaster on my forehead yesterday morning and in consequence *am* much better this morning. Today we moved camp half a mile towards Corinth. The intention was to go 5 miles but a bridge was found washed away and our progress was stopped *pro tem.*

Wednesday, May 7. I have deserted the sick list and reported for duty. I sold my revolver this morning to Lt. McKee for $25.00. We advanced four

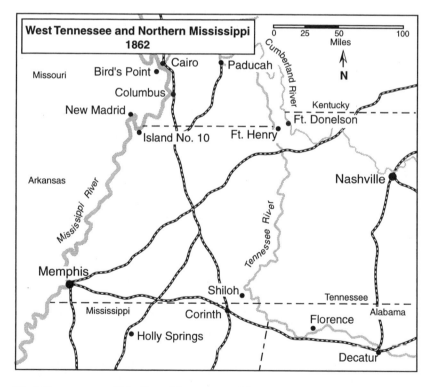

West Tennessee and Northern Mississippi, 1862.

miles, Corinthward, passing through an upland country timbered with oak and pine. We have a good camp, distant *six* miles from Corinth.

Thursday, May 8. Preparations for battle, or to guard against surprise and prepared for an emergency, were made today. One hundred rounds of cartridges were dealt out to each man. *Later,* We (Pope's force) advanced to Farmington, 3 miles from Corinth, on an armed reconnaissance and our advance drove in the enemy's pickets. At night, we returned to camp.

Friday, May 9. Quite a severe skirmish occurred on our advance, today. The rebels came out and attacked a few regiments of infantry and cavalry which were posted at Farmington by Gen. Pope. The rebels were in considerable force and our troops had to fall back for supports. The 2nd Iowa Cavalry made a brilliant charge on a rebel battery but were not properly supported and retired with loss. Pope's whole force was drawn up in line—the artillery posted—and every preparation made to give the rebels a hearty welcome if they should venture to cross the *swamp.* Our regiment marched out a mile from camp and took a position to support a battery. As we marched out, we met our wounded coming in from the field. Those of them who spoke to us urged us to "give it to them." But with the wounded we also met a gang of cowards, straggling back from their regiments, who, with doleful countenances, warned us that we "would catch it," "see enough of them," &c., &c. Some of the specimens of cowardice which I saw were shameful and disgraceful. They were not in our regiment, however. "The Fifth" showed no signs of cowardice. The enemy being satisfied with driving in our outposts, retired and we returned to camp.

Saturday, May 10. Today the signal gun "announced" an alarm and we turned out in double-quick style. Our regiment was the first in line. The alarm was false and we returned to our quarters. Pope has a telegraph line connecting his headquarters and his outposts, and the first appearance of the enemy is signalled over the wire, and announced to us by the discharge of a six-pounder at headquarters. We had another false alarm after dark.

Sunday, May 11. Gen. Halleck passed our camp today. I was gratified with a sight of "our general" but more gratified to see Cal. Rankin and Lieut. [Stephen] Porter of his escort. Preaching by our Chaplain. Prayer-meeting after Dress Parade. Our Chaplain proposes to have a prayer meeting every night after Dress Parade. May he succeed. The exercises are reading a chapter of scripture, and prayer, by the Chaplain. Our company attended *en masse,* this evening.

Monday, May 12. Nothing doing today.

Tuesday, May 13. Company drilled in bayonet exercise.

Wednesday, May 14. Regiment drew new pants, blouses, and hats. Company drilled in bayonet exercise and skirmish drill.

Thursday, May 15. The regiment was called up at 3 o'clock this morning and preparations made for fighting. Two days rations were put in our haversacks and everything put in readiness to march at a moment's notice. But our preparations were all to no purpose, as we remained in camp all day.

Friday, May 16. I was unwell this afternoon.

Saturday, May 17. This morning we were again ordered to get ready for marching at an early hour. At 3 o'clock P.M. we advanced 3 miles and camped at Farmington. The roads were dusty and the weather hot and the march of course, fatiguing. I have been suffering from an attack of diarrhea all day. We left all our tents at the old camp, which we left this morning.

Sunday, May 18. Last night heavy details were constantly at work, throwing up breastworks, digging trenches, rifle-pits, &c., &c. We slept in the woods. Firing between the pickets was kept up all night and continued today. This morning a long line of earthworks (extending as far as we could see) greeted our eyes on coming out of our leafy beds. Our boys have done a good night's work. Today the work goes bravely on. Masked batteries are planted at different points along the line. I saw cousin Hiram today. We have cleared a new camping ground and our tents have come up.

Monday, May 19. We are now camped on the *safe* side of a ridge in supporting distance of our batteries. Several large Parrot[t] guns have been planted on the line of earthworks in front of our camp.[3] Considerable cannonading was heard this evening in front of Buell's position. I am still unwell.

Tuesday, May 20. A heavy rain fell last night. There was heavy firing on the picket line today. I am still unwell.

Wednesday, May 21. Cannonading in front of Buell's Division again. Not well yet—taking medicine and dieting.

Thursday, May 22. Col. Worthington was shot last night by one of our pickets belonging to an Illinois regiment. The Colonel was on guard duty and was going the "grand rounds" about 3 o'clock in the morning, when by a mistake of the picket, he was shot and died in a few moments. His body was sent home for burial. The regiment was drawn up in line to pay its last tribute of respect to the remains of the deceased as they were taken from camp.[4]

Friday, May 23. Rain. I feel well enough for "duty."

Saturday, May 24. The company is on guard. I wrote to the *Bee.*[5]

Sunday, May 25. Our regiment and two companies of the 4th Minnesota were employed on a reconnaissance today east of Corinth. Companies A, B, and D and the Minnesota companies were deployed as skirmishers—the rest of the battalion followed as our reserve. A section of a battery and a few cavalrymen accompanied us. We advanced and scoured the woods, as far south as the Memphis and Charleston Railroad, coming to it at a point about two miles east of Corinth. Just as we reached the railroad we came upon the enemy's pickets, who fled after firing one shot at our cavalrymen. Having accomplished all that was desired by the reconnaissance we returned to camp. Preaching at prayer meeting in the afternoon. Drs. Ault and Hunter who have been with us some time, awaiting "the coming battle" started home today. Dr. Hunter takes the remains of Major [Thomas] Miller of the 13th [Iowa] home with him. Major Miller was a gentleman and a soldier. We mourn his loss.

Monday, May 26. The 10th Iowa was in a skirmish today. William Hunter and James Rodgers of the 13th [Iowa] paid us a visit.

Tuesday, May 27. A warm day. Among the notable things about this region is a "look-out" of General Pope's. It consists of a long beam, with cross-pieces on, fasted upright in the top of a tree. By ascending this look-out, he can, with a glass, get a view of Corinth. "May we get a nearer view of Corinth," is my wish.

Wednesday, May 28. This morning we started out of camp with two day's rations in our haversacks, supposing that we were probably going on some reconnaissance. On getting out of the woods, however, we saw troops advancing all along our line and we soon became convinced that *our army was advancing on Corinth.* After advancing a mile and a half, Hamilton's Division halted and the force was disposed so [as] to protect our batteries, which were soon planted. Our company and company A were thrown out as skirmishers with a battalion of Yate[s]'s sharp-shooters. We entered a piece of timber on the left of our batteries to keep a lookout for any demonstration the rebels might attempt on the flank of our batteries. We lay in the woods all day. Soon after entering the woods, our batteries opened on the rebels and they instantly replied from a battery about half a mile in front of us. The firing at times was terrific. We had the advantage in the number of guns but the rebels had the heaviest metal. As we were not in range, we could listen to the roar of the guns and the shriek of the shells without trepidation. The firing was kept up between the batteries at intervals during the entire day. At one time, the rattle of musketry was mingled with the roar of cannon and it was evident a contest was going on near our batteries with small arms and stout hearts. Soon the musketry firing ceased and loud cheering was heard, which we judged (correctly as we afterward learned) was occasioned by the repulse of the rebels who had attempted to take one of our batteries. At sundown we were notified that we would have to remain in our place until morning acting as pickets. We accordingly made our arrangements to spend a night on duty in the woods. During the entire night, we could hear the movements in our own and the enemy's camp. In the latter we heard rattling of wheels as if moving gun-carriages and beating of drums as if troops were marching. A locomotive was also heard moving about whistling and making itself noisy, generally. About 3 o'clock in the morning we heard a heavy train move off on the Mobile road.

Thursday, May 29. This morning we were relieved and returned to our regiment. We here found that our army had thrown up a new line of breast-works. We also learned that Gen. Buford had reported during night that he had no doubt that Maj. Robinson and companies A and B were all taken prisoners! It was news to us. We remained in the woods near our intrenchments all day ready for action.

Friday, May 30. The firing between our batteries and the enemy's was kept up at intervals yesterday but not so briskly as the day before. This morning we were called up by our cannon making its *morning report,* for us to "up and not be caught napping."[6] It has been customary, lately for us, to have reveille before day and be in readiness, should the enemy attempt to surprise us. A cannon is fired every morning to awake the boys. This morning it sounded its *reveille* and we arose and got our breakfasts. At daybreak a cloud of smoke was seen rising over Corinth. We at first supposed it to be the smoke of a locomotive. But as the cloud grew larger and blacker, it became evident that there was something unusual burning. We were not left long in doubt, for soon an explosion was heard and *felt* that announced the destruction of Beauregard's magazines *and the evacuation of Corinth.* The first explosion was followed by others equally heavy and our generals were not long in finding out their meaning. Troops were ordered forward and Corinth was soon occupied by Uncle Sam's troops, and the Stars and Stripes raised over the late rebel stronghold. Just after the explosions were heard, a beautiful rainbow—red, white and blue of heaven—was visible over Corinth. As soon as it was known that Corinth was really evacuated, our cavalry was started in pursuit and the infantry and artillery were ordered to follow. Our Division did not get started, however, until sundown. We marched until 11 o'clock at night when we stopped and lay down in the dust by the roadside to sleep, being then five miles south of Corinth.[7]

Saturday, May 31. On awakening this morning, I found that we were near the Mobile railroad at a point where the enemy had thrown up intrenchments to command the approach to Corinth from the South. As our regiment did not move on this morning, I had an opportunity to visit a deserted secesh camp near this earthwork and on the railroad I found that the rebels had left here quite a quantity of mess beef, sugar, and molasses, and a lot of small arms, and other property, and had burned a number of tents, wagons, &c., &c. A considerable quantity of molasses was also spilled on the ground. Our regiment remained at this point all day. Most of Pope's force is lying near us. We are waiting for the construction of bridges which the rebels have burned in their flight.

Sunday, June 1. Our regiment exchanged our old rifles and muskets for new *Whitney rifles,* with sword bayonet today. The number of my gun is 5,784. The new gun is a neat piece, and is highly recommended.[8]

Monday, June 2. Starting at half-past five this morning, we marched 12 miles on the road to Mobile, passing through the towns of Danville and Rienzi. We halted at noon (as a rain came up) near Rienzi. Near Tuscumbia river, we passed a secesh earthwork which they had built to cover their retreat. The country through which we passed, presented the same half-civilized appearance that the South generally does—poor houses and waste fields. The stores, groceries, &c., in the villages were all *evacuated.* Several graves along the road have been *opened* and found full of *rifles!*

Tuesday, June 3 We remained in camp near Rienzi until 3 o'clock today, when we started on and marched 6 miles camping within a mile-and-a-half of Booneville [*sic*]. The clouds treated us to a good ducking during the march. At mi [*Entry ends abruptly.*]

Wednesday, June 4. At midnight, last night, we were called up and our regiment moved to another position in line of battle with the remainder of our forces as there were apprehensions of an attack by the enemy. This morning quite a "slaughter of innocents" took place to get fresh meat. I gathered a cup of huckleberries and had a good stew for dinner.

Thursday, June 5. Drill. Papers of May 30th, in camp today. Our mail accommodations since we went to New Madrid have been very good. We have a general Post office at Pope's headquarters and post offices (subordinate) at division and regimental headquarters.

Friday, June 6. Whiskey-rations were drawn again today but not by me. The guzzlers growled not a little because I objected to engaging in the "liquor business." Let them growl. In the afternoon, we moved camp one mile southwest.

Saturday, June 7. Our new camp was *policed* today and fitted up as if there was an intention to stay here. I wrote a letter to the "Free Press."

Sunday, June 8. Weather pleasant. Inspection. We have orders to cook three day's rations.

Monday, June 9. We received our tents, knapsacks, &c., &c. today. Gen. [William] Nelson's Division passed our camp, *enroute* to Jacinto. I saw Gen. Ammon [Ammen] and had a friendly chat with him.[9] He is the same "Old Jakey."

Tuesday, June 10. We have orders to prepare for marching tomorrow.

Wednesday, June 11. We started this morning on the road to Corinth the whole army taking the back track. We marched 11 miles, camping on the Tuscumbia river. The roads were *very* dusty and the weather hot. Our regiment was "rear-guard" and we had a tough time of it. It was the hardest march our regiment ever had. "General Stanley's brother" furnished us a little entertainment on the way. Thanks to the "brother to the General."

Thursday, June 12. We marched 4 miles today and camped at our camp ground. Our company was detailed for Grand Guard.

Friday, June 13. I have been busied today making out muster rolls. Three Captains claimed to be commanders of Company K today. The blame lies between our departed Colonel and Gov. [Samuel] Kirkwood.

Saturday, June 14. We moved camp one mile eastward this evening. Our new camp is a beautiful place. Our whole Division is camped on a series of high ridges covered with oaks and pines. At the foot of the ridges, gushing springs are found which supply us with the clearest, coolest water.

Sunday, June 15. We received news of the great gunboat fight at Memphis today.[10] Good for our Western Navy. Bravely done.

Monday, June 16. Our camps are being "fixed up" for a permanent stay. We will probably remain here during the summer. A spring is being put in order near Gen. Hamilton's headquarters, which is estimated to run 70 gallons per minute of the purest, coolest water.

Tuesday, June 17. I received my "Warrant" of office today, as did also, the other non-commissioned officers—"better late than never."[11]

Wednesday, June 18. We are still improving our camp. I wrote to *Mag* and *Hat.* today. *Soldiering* is making me *desperate!*

Thursday, June 19. Generals Pope and Hamilton have both left us. Pope has gone east.[12] Hamilton has gone home on sick furlough.

Friday, June 20. Wash-day, for me. In the afternoon our brigade took a *jaunt* to the Memphis and Charleston Railroad.

Saturday, June 21. I have assisted in building a schoolhouse for "non-commissioned officers school" today. One year ago today, we were ordered into quarters at Newton.

Sunday, June 22. Signed Pay-rolls today. Preaching in the afternoon by our chaplain. Prayer meeting in the evening.

Monday, June 23. School commenced today. Our school house was chopped down at noon by some *poor simpleton.*

Tuesday, June 24. I took a stroll after blackberries today and got a good mess. Berries are plenty but soldiers are too.

Wednesday, June 25. Received several letters from home today.

Thursday, June 26. Company is on Grand Guard.

Friday, June 27. We had reveille at 3 1/2 o'clock this morning and started on a march for Holly Springs at daylight. We marched 14 miles and camped 2 miles west of Rienzi on State road leading to Ripley, Holly Springs, &c. The day has been hot and we suffered more from marching than we ever did on any other march. At noon we halted and lay in the woods until late in the afternoon, when we marched ahead. When we halted at noon not half of the men (of our and all the other regiments) were in the ranks. More than half were unable to keep up and had dropped out of ranks. One man in the 4th Minnesota regiment was sunstruck but recovered. I kept my place in ranks but I was agreeable to stopping when we did. All of Gen. Hamilton's Division is along. Jeff Davis' Division will also accompany us.

Saturday, June 28. We marched 11 miles westward, camping on head-waters of the Hatchie river. We stopped at noon—and the *army* started for the fields and picked their fill of blackberries which were very plenty all along the route we have passed. I took a swim in the creek.

Sunday, June 29. We marched 12 miles through Pine country and camped within two miles of Ripley. We passed some respectable (for this country) looking houses today and some good farms.

Monday, June 30. We marched 4 miles today, camping 2 miles west of Ripley. We passed through Ripley with flags flying and drums beating but we could draw very few secesh out to us. Most all the houses were closed and but few *white* people showed themselves. The Ripleyites evidently did not fancy our visit. Ripley is a pleasant looking town of some 1200 inhabitants and has some very neat dwellings in its limits. In peace times, it is probably a business place. It is undoubtedly *a strong secesh hole.*

Tuesday, July 1. For some reason (unknown to me) we turned back this morning and marched (16) sixteen miles towards Rienzi camping again on Hatchie river. We found Ripley about the same as yesterday. The male population is doubtless "off to the wars." A rain today and a cloudy sky, made our march pleasant.

Wednesday, July 2. We marched 15 miles today passing through Rienzi and camping one mile east of it on the road to Jacinto.

Thursday, July 3. I have been employed making out pay-rolls today. Some of the boys who came from Camp Clear Creek today brought news of the death of *Jacob Stern* of our company. He died yesterday while out gathering blackberries. He died for his country.

Friday, July 4. This, our National Anniversary, we celebrate by upholding Uncle Sam's authority in a rebel state. There is not much *show* but considerable of the *substantial* in our mode of celebrating. The only fuss we have had was the firing of national salutes by our different batteries. Their rapid and continued firing would have been *wonderful* a year ago but today it is common. This afternoon, we marched a mile further east and camped. After camping, I gathered quite a luscious mess of blackberries. Among the boys who came up from camp yesterday, was *Ike Loudenback.* He has been home on a furlough. He was returning *via* Memphis when about 17 miles east of Memphis the train he was on was thrown from the track, and most of the passengers (principally unarmed soldiers) were captured by a party of secession guerrillas. Ike made his escape by good running. Bully for Ike!

Saturday, July 5. We have been kept in a painful suspense of mind today by conflicting rumors of events at Richmond. We have a report one hour that McClellan has taken Richmond and the next, that he has been whipped, all his siege guns taken, and his army compelled to retreat 17 miles. During the whole day, we have had these reports each confirmed and contradicted, as often as a rumor could travel from headquarters to camp.[13]

Sunday, July 6. I have spent the day in camp. Thanks to friends at home for the entertainment which reading some *N.Y. Independents* has furnished me. Rumors "from headquarters" about events at Richmond still continue.

Monday, July 7. This morning some *"Mess Beef"* was issued to the regiment in lieu of good meat. Considerable disturbance in camp was the consequence. *Loud and deep bellowing* was soon heard through camp and one [not] acquainted with the facts, would have judged that the ghosts of *the departed* had begun to cry aloud. But, not so. It was only another way the boys had of expressing their indignation at such treatment from the Quartermaster (which was *this time* not to blame). Our Colonel [Matthies] became very indignant and called the regiment into line and gave the boys a lecture. He said *"every ox will have* to carry a knapsack!" In the afternoon, we moved back to the camp, nearer Rienzi as there is news of the approach of the enemy in force by way of Booneville. We will be ready for them if they come. Rations have been poor and scant for several days past.

Wartime photograph of Col. Charles Matthies. Courtesy of Roger Davis.

Tuesday, July 8. No enemy yet. We were paid off today for March, April, May, and June. I received $80. Company on Grand Guard.

Wednesday, July 9. No enemy yet. We have orders to arrange our camp, for a permanent stay. The tents, knapsacks (which latter were sent back, yesterday), and baggage are to be brought up tomorrow.[14]

Thursday, July 10. This morning at day-break, we received orders to return to our old camp on Clear Creek, much to our satisfaction. At 7 o'clock, we started and reached camp about 3 o'clock and our regiment was "rear guard" again and we suffered this inconvenience and troubles attending this position. A heavy rain layed the dust and cooled our heated blood during the march.

Friday, July 11. Sent $5.00 to Mr. [John] Rankin today. Regimental Inspection this morning.

Saturday, July 12. "Inspection" again. We received news today of the President's call for 300,000 more men.[15] Let them come, I repeat it, "Let them come." "The more the merrier."

Sunday, July 13. "Inspection" again! Twenty of the company are on grand guard today. The "Independent" has again furnished me Sunday reading.

Monday, July 14. This day ends my first year in Uncle Sam's Service. I hope that I have been of some service to my venerable Uncle. Major Robertson has resigned and started for home today. He carries with him the respect and best wishes of the 5th. May his place be as well filled by his successor. I received a letter from Hat. from Ripley, today.

Tuesday, July 15. More Inspection! Ugh!

Wednesday, July 16. A "shower bath" has been put up for our regiment near the spring which if properly used, will be a blessing to us all. More water and less quinine is needed.

Thursday, July 17. Capt. Tait started for Iowa this morning on the recruiting service. I sent $85.00 home by him. A very heavy rain fell last night—as much as three or four inches.

Friday, July 18. A short drill in the morning and one in the afternoon is now our daily *task.*

Saturday, July 19. I paid a visit to the 7th and 13th Iowa regiments today to see some of my Newton friends. I also visited the famous city of Corinth and found it a very common looking village. I also got a glimpse of Beauregard's extensive earthworks which he threw up and *evacuated.*

Sunday, July 20. News came today of the President designs vetoing "Confiscating Bill" just passed by Congress. I hope, for his sake, and the sake of the country, that he will do no such thing.[16]

Monday, July 21. Rebel guerilla bands are doing considerable mischief in Tennessee and Kentucky. "Up and at 'em."

Tuesday, July 22. The rebel guerrillas, emboldened by the success in Kentucky, have crossed the Ohio, and made a dash into Newberg, Indiana![17] The audacious scamps! Lincoln's veto turns out to be only some very sensible objections to the portions of it which he thinks are unconstitutional. The bill has been amended according to the suggestions and is now a law. Good!

Wednesday, July 23. Had my likeness taken in "soldier gear" and sent them to Alma. Weather pleasant.

Thursday, July 24. Inspection! I today, handed over the "Orderly" books to Sergeant Vanatta and began acting the part of Lieutenant, *pro tempore* by

order of the Colonel. Easier times for "your humble servant" will be the result. How long *pro tempore* will last, I can't tell.

Friday, July 25. I received a letter from Sister today, giving an amusing
account of *the great scare* at home (Ripley, Ohio) caused by reports of the
approach of Morgan's guerrillas to Maysville, Ky. "The Judge" is said to have
shouldered his gun and gone to war *on a tow boat!*[18]

Saturday, July 26. Battalion Drill. I am slightly unwell.

Sunday, July 27. Today I have served my first turn of guard duty. I am
"officer of the guard." I am still unwell.

Monday, July 28. I am still "indisposed." A dose of *blue mass* was pre-
scribed and taken last night. Company is on guard today.

Tuesday, July 29. I wrote a letter to the *Bee* today. The weather is pleasant and the health of the regiment is good.

Wednesday, July 30. General Inspection by Brig. Gen. [Morgan L.] Smith.
Rain this afternoon. Weather warm.

Thursday, July 31. Battalion drill this morning. *"Old Dutchy"* is on a mad
and he has "put us through" today.[19]

Friday, August 1. Division Drill in skirmishing. I had charge of Company
B. Weather pleasant.

Saturday, August 2. I paid a visit to cousin Hiram in the 27th Ohio Regiment today. I borrowed "Chambers Miscellany" to read at my leisure hours.[20]
I also visited the 39th Ohio and saw *Haller.*

Sunday, August 3. I have spent most of the day reading "Chamber's Miscellany." I have had charge of the company today. Lieut. Mateer being "on
duty" and Lieut. McKee on the "sick list."

Monday, August 4. Company Drill this morning. This afternoon, I paid
another visit to the 27th Ohio to return the borrowed book. We have orders
for marching tomorrow.

Tuesday, August 5. We had reveille at 4 o'clock this morning and started for
Jacinto at sunrise. The day has been very warm and the marching, consequently,
wearisome. Three horses died on the road in the Ohio Battery from the effects
of the heat. I stood the march very well. We lay by during the hottest of the day.
We arrived at Jacinto a few minutes before sundown and camped about 3/4ths
of a mile south of town. Our force (Buford's brigade) consists of the 11th Ohio
Battery, and the 4th Minnesota, 59th and 48th Indiana, 26th Missouri, and 5th
Iowa regiments. Jeff C. Davis' brigade is camped near us.

Wednesday, August 6. We have been employed in arranging our new camp
today. The camp is called *"Camp Cold Spring,"* from a Spring of very cold
water which we have found for our use.

Thursday, August 7. We are still fixing up our new camp. We have very
nearly as good a camp as we had at Clear Creek. A large corn-field in front of
our camp has been dedicated to our use by the General. We have "Hot Corn,

hot corn, smoking hot corn," for our meals. Other vegetables and fruits are also brought to our table from secesh farms. The Kansas Jayhawkers will have to look out for their laurels.[21] We are going to fight the enemy henceforth with every available weapon.

Friday, August 8. In camp living on green corn, sweet potatoes, chickens, peaches, &c. We are living off the enemy.

Saturday, August 9. I am serving as "officer of the guard" again today. We received news today of the President's call for a draft of 300,000 more troops.[22] That looks like something was to be done.

Sunday, August 10. Our company is on Grand Guard today. Weather very warm.

Monday, August 11. Some of the boys on grand guard yesterday had their blankets and clothing *fly-blowed! Jiggers* and *flies* are the plagues of Tishomingo County. I wrote a letter to the *Bee* today.

Tuesday, August 12. Skirmish Drill in the woods this morning by the battalion.

Wednesday, August 13. I have been busy today "squaring up" the company clothing book. I received a new silk handkerchief by mail from Mother for which I am much indebted. "Thanks" till better paid.

Thursday, August 14. On duty today as "officer of the guard." Four companies of the regiment were sent up town yesterday to act as provost guard, hence I [was] glad to go on duty sooner.

Friday, August 15. Today *drafting* begins in the North.[23] The remainder of our (Gen. Hamilton's) Division came up today from Clear Creek. I wrote a letter to the *Free Press.*

Saturday, August 16. I have been employed to day "posting books." The boys have found another spring near camp.

Sunday, August 17. I have spent my leisure time today reading. Four companies of our regiment are on grand guard, leaving only two companies in camp.

Monday, August 18. In camp "posting books." The companies which have been acting as provost guards came to camp today.

Tuesday, August 19. We left our old camp this morning and marched to a point 2 miles southwest of Jacinto where we camped on a ridge formerly occupied as a camping ground by the 22d Indiana. We had a dirty place to camp on but we soon changed the appearance of things.

Wednesday, August 20. I am on *grand guard* today for the first time since I have been in the service. Weather pleasant.

Thursday, August 21. Our company was relieved from grand guard this morning and returned to camp. Weather warm.

Friday, August 22. "Posting Books." Our mails are becoming irregular much to our inconvenience. The Secessionist who was shot by Sergeant [William] McElrea of Company A on Wednesday night (while on grand guard) was buried today in Jacinto. Well done, McElrea.

Saturday, August 23. I (and the regiment generally) were *sold* today on "target shooting." "For particulars, see small bills." We witnessed, however, the target practice of the Ohio battery with interest. The Quartermaster made an excursion into the neighborhood today and procured a supply of apples, peaches, &c., for the regiment. Weather pleasant.

Sunday, August 24. I spent my time today mostly in reading. On Dress Parade our company commander was *non compos mentis.*[24]

Monday, August 25. Weather pleasant, for the season.

Tuesday, August 26. Company on Grand Guard.

Wednesday, August 27. Company came off Grand Guard. I spent most of the day reading "Tales of my Landlord"—"The Surgeon's Daughter."[25]

Thursday, August 28. Lt. Col. Matthies received his commission as colonel last night and an election was called to fill the vacant places of Lt. Colonel and Major. Adjutant [Robert] Patterson was chosen Lt. Colonel and Capt [Jabez] Banbury (of Co. D) Major. Good selections. Today, the regiment has been practicing at "target shooting." Co. D did the best shooting. Company B did good shooting.

Friday, August 29. Our company and the others, (with four companies from each regiment of the brigade) accompanied our teams as an escort on a *foraging* expedition today. We went nine miles from camp eastward and procured a supply of corn from the farm of a rebel Colonel. We had a hot, dusty and tiresome march. We reached camp (on our return) at sunset.

Saturday, August 30. I have occupied my time today reading the *"Tales of my Landlord—Castle Dangerous."*[26] Weather warm. *Mahoney* the editor of the*Dubuque* (Iowa) *Times* has been arrested and sent to Fort Lafayette for discouraging enlistments. This is tardy justice. See diary, August 17, 1861.

Sunday, August 31. A heavy rain today has rendered our camp more pleasant and camp life more comfortable. I received a letter from my brother Frank. He has volunteered in one of the Iowa regts [40th Volunteer Infantry].

Monday, September 1. Summer is gone and Fall has stepped upon the threshold of time. We have spent a summer in the "sunny South" and have fared well. In spite of the rebel declarations, hopes and prayers, we have *not* been decimated by diseases but have enjoyed good health. Our company is on grand guard again today. *Capt.* [Ezekiel] *Sampson* of Company F received a commission as Lieut. Colonel of our regiment today from Governor Kirkwood. This was wholly unexpected by the regiment and is another evidence of Kirkwood's knavery (trickery, perhaps, is the more appropriate word).

Tuesday, September 2. The company came off grand guard this morning. We had no alarms yesterday and our cavalry had a fight with the rebel cavalry at Booneville. The rebels were too strong for our force and the latter fell back, bringing several prisoners with them.

Wednesday, Sept 3. In company with Corporal Banks, I today visited the 10th Iowa to see my Newton friends in Company I. Before starting for the 10th, our regiment spent an hour at target practice. Weather pleasant.

Thursday, Sept 4. Weather pleasant. News of the battle between Pope and

Jackson, near Washington, reached us, today.[27] We are anxiously awaiting news of the final result.

Friday, Sept 5. Further details of the battle near Washington reached us today. We are still left in painful anxiety. Weather pleasant.

Saturday, Sept 6. Four companies of our regiment went to town today to serve as Provost Guards.

Sunday, Sept. 7. The 59th Indiana and the 48th Ind. regiments left last night for Rienzi. About dusk we were ordered to put "two day's" rations in our haversacks, strike tents, and prepare to march immediately. We had soon complied with orders and our wagons stood ready for *skedaddling.* Such property as could not be loaded on the wagons was piled up ready to burn. The cause of all this commotion was the report that Price's force (40,000 strong) was marching northward, being only a few miles south of Booneville. We were making preparations to fall back to Corinth and leave him a deserted camp on his approach. After loading the wagons we stacked arms on the color line and lay down to sleep until Price's arrival—the design being (I suppose) to give a fair race.[28]

Monday, September 8. This morning we found ourselves safe and sound and a *little hungry.* Our company was sent out on grand guard.

Tuesday, September 9. Private James Shelledy accidently shot himself (in the foot) while on guard last night. Weather pleasant. News from Washington still *unsatisfactory.*

Wednesday, Sept. 10. Target practice this morning.

Thursday, Sept. 11. On police guard as officer of the guard. This evening two or three companies were sent out to fell trees across the road leading to Booneville at which place Price is reported to be with a strong rebel force. Mess No. One has dissolved—no cook.

Friday, Sept. 12. Last night about 9 o'clock, we were aroused from our slumbers and ordered to cook two day's rations. At two o'clock we struck tents and loaded our wagons. We then stacked arms on the color line and awaited the approach of the enemy(?) if there was any near. We were ready to fight or retreat, according to the strength of the enemy. At daylight, forty rebel cavalry made a dash on our pickets capturing one of Company E and securing a number of blankets. A rain came up this afternoon and we "pitched our tents in the old camp ground."

Saturday, Sept 13. This morning at 3 o'clock, we were again aroused, and struck tents and stacked arms on the color line. At daylight we had battalion drill. This morning our officers announced that our hitherto inexplicable moves are but measures of caution to guard against surprise—they are in consonance with order eight of Gen. Buford—*"this Division must not be surprised."* At noon we again pitched tents.

Sunday, Sept 14. Our company is on grand guard today. We arose at 3 o'clock and loaded wagons this morning as usual. This afternoon, some of the boys saw some suspicious characters at a house about half a mile from our guard lines. They reported to me and I sent a corporal with a squad to investigate the matter. On their arrival at the house they found *"the birds had flown"* but there was conclusive evidence of their having been there. The supposition is that they were rebel scouts, who stopped to get their dinners and gather information of our force and its position and doings. I reported proceedings to the officer of the day who approved my course and coincided with my opinion.

Monday, September 15. After dusk last evening, the *"officer of the day"* sent another company out to support us. Part of the force was sent to watch the suspicioned house during the night. This morning they reported that during the night they heard enough to convince them that all was not right and this morning early they made a scout through the adjoining woods and fields and found where a small cavalry party had stayed during the night. We came off grand guard this morning.

Tuesday, Sept. 16. Our baggage, tents, &c. were sent to Corinth today, preparatory to marching soon.

Wednesday, September 17. We did not march today but were soon treated to a hard rain, which lasted throughout the day. We had anything but a "dry time." At dusk, we received orders to cook three days' rations and prepare to march by 3 o'clock in the morning.

4

"Nobly the Boys Stood Up to the Work"
Fighting in Mississippi, September 18, 1862–March 1, 1863

Although relatively forgotten today, the Civil War saw few battles more fierce than those at Iuka and Corinth. The Confederate commanders, Maj. Gen. Earl Van Dorn and Maj. Gen. Sterling Price, intended to recapture Corinth and prevent Grant from going to the aid of Buell, who was then trying to contain a major invasion of Kentucky led by troops under Gen. Braxton Bragg. Fortunately for Grant, Van Dorn and Price functioned as a coequal partnership, with neither able to command the other. Although cordial enough—"I shall always be happy to be associated with you in this noble struggle," Van Dorn assured Price—the arrangement was awkward. Each general worked independently with only informal cooperation. Grant hoped not only to turn back this offensive but, if possible, to wreck the Confederate forces that were making it. Finding his own army between Van Dorn and Price, he took advantage of his central position to strike Price alone. Led by Brig. Gen. William S. Rosecrans, one wing of the Union army collided with Price outside Iuka on September 19.

In Missouri back in 1861, Campbell had written, "There are rumors afloat today of 'danger ahead' but danger seems to be a fast craft and keeps ahead." The same had been true for the Fifth Iowa during much of 1862. But at Iuka, danger stopped and glared. The Confederates took the tactical offensive and lunged directly for the Fifth; in the ensuing fire fight, 217 of Campbell's comrades became casualties. The Federals held their own. Two weeks later the Fifth was in action again, this time at Corinth, where Rosecrans's force beat back a determined assault by the combined forces of Van Dorn and Price. After this second defeat, the Confederates abandoned their offensive and withdrew farther south.[1]

After Corinth, Grant spent another month preparing his army for its own long-deferred offensive. Rosecrans, meanwhile, left to assume command of a force at Nashville soon to be dubbed the Army of the Cumberland. "Thus we are served—we no sooner make a General than they take him from us," Campbell noted. His new commander, Grant, was not yet the legend of later years; indeed, he remained rather under a cloud after the surprise of his army at Shiloh. Nor was the new offensive auspicious.

With the fall of Island No. 10, New Orleans, and Memphis, the sole portion of the Mississippi River still in Confederate hands was a 130-mile stretch between Port Hudson, Louisiana, and Vicksburg, Mississippi. Both places were fortified, but Vicksburg was the key, and it became Grant's objective point. Grant intended to take his army overland to attack Vicksburg, more than 250 miles south-southwest of Corinth, while a secondary force under Maj. Gen. William T. Sherman steamed down the Mississippi and launched a diversion against the Vicksburg defenses. Campbell was part of the overland campaign, which began in early November. By mid-December Grant's army was deep in Mississippi but still far from its objective. Then, on December 20, Rebel cavalry under Van Dorn seized and destroyed Grant's forward supply base at Holly Springs, while raiders under Brig. Gen. Nathan Bedford Forrest knifed into western Tennessee. Suddenly cut off from regular supply, Grant's army began to withdraw. Rumors circulated that Gen. Braxton Bragg's Army of Tennessee—the principal Confederate army in the West—was about to fall upon them, but Campbell did not credit them. In any case: "We are not alarmed—but are ready for Bragg, or whoever may cross our path." Meanwhile, Sherman's force unsuccessfully assaulted the Vicksburg defenses on December 29.

By New Year's Eve Campbell was in Memphis, where his regiment spent the next three months. Grant soon took the bulk of his army down the Mississippi to Milliken's Bend, a low expanse of dry land some twelve miles northwest of Vicksburg. Although geographically close to the Confederate fortress, he was no nearer to seizing it.

Thursday, September 18. At *one* o'clock this morning we were called up, and at half-past three we started on the march, through rain, mud, and darkness. We passed through Jacinto and marched to the eastward on the road to Iuka. We halted in the road at 10 o'clock and remained where we halted until night. Our cavalry went ahead to *feel* the enemy. During the day we marched about 8 miles. Near where we halted, we found a lot of broken muskets which some secesh had left in the road.

Friday, September 19. At sunrise, this morning we took up our line of march towards Iuka, where *Price* was said to be with his army, having captured the place a few days before. About 10 o'clock our cavalry came upon the enemy's pickets and drove them in. We kept steadily advancing and at noon came upon the enemy's infantry pickets. Our cavalry then retired, and companies, E, G, and D, of our regiment were thrown forward as skirmishers. The remainder of our regi-

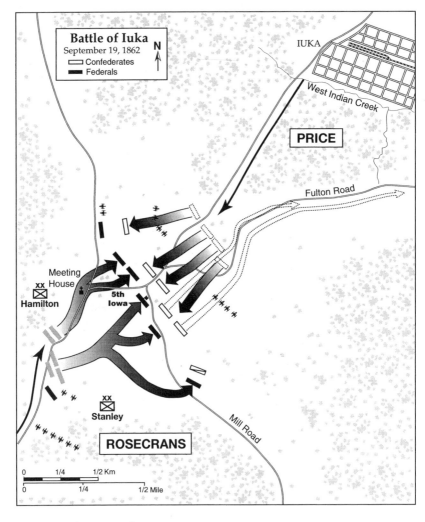

Battle of Iuka, September 19, 1862.

ment moved by the flank along the road, close behind our skirmishers, to support them. The 11th Ohio Battery followed close to us, and behind it the remainder of Hamilton's Division. Gen. Stanley's Division followed. Our skirmishers steadily drove back the enemy's pickets, for better than four miles, with occasional losses on both sides. About sundown, our skirmishers (the companies from the 26th Missouri regiment—who had relieved our skirmishers a few moments before) got *into a hornet's nest!* They came upon the enemy in force and were compelled to fall back. At the same time, the rebels opened on us with artillery and attempted to flank us on the left. We were then on the point of a wooded ridge along which the road led. Our Colonel immediately got our regiment into line and prepared to meet the enemy. The battery got into position on the point, and we waited (but only for a few moments) for the enemy. Gen. [William S.] Rosecrans (who was in command) had just left us to go and examine another road leading into town. The battery was in a bad position, but it was the best that could be had. Soon the enemy appeared and opened a fire on us. The Fifth replied with a will and an effect that was admirable. Nobly the boys stood up to the work— loading and firing amid a storm of lead, as if they were drilling—only showing much more enthusiasm and earnestness once we made a charge and the rebels gave way before us. But the nature of the ground and the darkness prevented us following farther than the brow of the ridge. We then fell back to our original line and resumed our fire. The enemy was strong and bold and their leaden hail swept our ranks with a besom of destruction. The boys flinched not, but stood over their dead & dying comrades and beat back thrice and quadruple their numbers for more than an hour, and until darkness had enveloped the field. Again and again the rebels charged upon us, but again and again they reeled and broke before the steady fire of Iowa's sons. At times they came so close to us that in a few instances the bayonet was used. We had to stand before the steady fire of the rebels besides the heavy *volleys* which *reliefs* of the rebels poured into us at intervals from another ridge. While we were thus engaged, the 4th Minnesota, 48th Indiana, 17th Iowa, and part of the 26th Missouri (respectively) were engaged with the enemy on the left of the battery. But the rebels brought their principal strength on us, and on the *Fifth* fell the brunt of the battle. The battery did good execution until the men and horses were most all placed *hors du combat* by the destructive fire of the rebels. The rebels then gained our flank and we were subjected to a terrible cross fire. At length, after fighting an hour and a quarter, when our ranks were almost *annihilated*, when most of the men had fired all their cartridges away, the *remnant* of the Fifth fell back before the superior force of the rebels. As we retired, the 11th Missouri received the rebels and gave them a fitting entertainment. The Fifth withdrew from the field and formed in the rear of the 11th. After a half hour's further fighting, the rebels were repelled from the field and our forces occupied our original ground. Part of the battery was captured by the rebels. Our loss is great but our *honor* is safe. I cannot particularize instances of daring, or bravery, for all did well.[2]

Saturday, September 20. This morning our forces moved on Price but found him *non* est—he having skedaddled during the night. Rosecrans followed as far as Iuka, where he met Grant, and the latter followed Price while Rosecrans started his army back to Jacinto. Iuka is full of wounded rebels left behind by Price in his flight. Our regiment was halted on the battlefield as we marched out this morning and details were made to bury the dead. Most of the wounded were brought off the field last night, but a few were found there this morning. The loss on both sides was great in the battle yesterday, but only from the official report can we gain exact returns. Our company lost six killed on the field and two mortally wounded who died at the hospital. Twenty-one others were wounded. The killed were John Bodley, Elias Babcock, Moses Cottrell, Oscar Piper (the last two died in the hospital) George Lowe, [James] Henry Smail, Leroy Shelley, and Samuel Pitman. They died as the brave die—at the post of duty. The wounded were Sergeants Vanatta and Dungan, slightly, Corporals McCroskey & Banks, slightly, and Corporals Work (seriously) and Heron (perhaps mortally). Privates Borden, [Luther] Carey, [Barnett] Dewitt, [Joseph] Delong, [John] Hall, [David] Loudenback, [Charles] Norris, Peregrine, Rice, [Asbury] Romans, [William] Sparks, Wm. Scott, [William] Warrell and Winslow were wounded—Borden, Delong, Rice and Scott seriously. Peregrine was wounded in the foot and is missing—perhaps taken prisoner. Lieut. Mateer was shot in the breast and can hardly survive.[3] The conduct of our officers (regimental and company) was highly praiseworthy. They showed themselves fit officers for their regiment of *braves*. Our regiment fought (during the engagement) the 11th and 37th Alabama, the 5th Missouri, 3d Louisiana, and 38th Mississippi regiments. No wonder our loss was heavy, when we fought such odds. The battle field, however, showed that while we suffered, our foe suffered equally with us. At times the contest was a hand to hand one. Rice, of our company, received three bayonet wounds. Col. Matthies recieves the highest praise for his bearing during the battle. Our regiment is the object of praise from all our generals. It is styled "the plucky Fifth." This morning, the two pieces belonging to the Ohio Battery (which were captured by the rebels) were found near the battle-field. During the battle, I was acting as Lieutenant. My duty was to cheer and encourage the men, and aid the company commander in managing the company. For a time I turned *exhorter* and plead[ed] and cheered with an earnestness (I perhaps might say enthusiasm) that seriously affected my diseased throat. I was utterly unconscious of danger, and although the dead and dying were dropping at my feet, I felt no emotion nor sorrow—there was a strange, unaccountable lack of *feeling* with me that followed me through the entire action. Out of a battle and in a battle, I find myself two different beings. During a part of the fight, I assisted the boys in loading by taking out their cartridges and tearing them, ready for loading. Corporal Banks was wounded while recieving a cartridge from my hand. Private Shelley was shot dead and dropped at my feet. Private Smail fell dead at my feet on my left, grasping hold of me as he fell. But enough of this. After the engagement, I lay down on a couple of rails to sleep. I had slept but a few moments, however, when I got up and went to the hospital. From thence I assisted in carrying Lieutenant Mateer to a hospital a mile and a half from the battlefield. By the time I returned our regiment was called up and we moved back half a mile and prepared our breakfasts. About noon we marched back on the road to Jacinto. After marching five miles, we camped with the remainder of our brigade. The whole of Rosecrans' army camped near us.

Sunday, September 21. We started at noon today and marched back to

Camp Cold Spring near Jacinto, arriving there after night. Our wounded were left at Iuka.

Monday, September 22. We changed our position this morning to our old camp south-west of town. I wrote a letter to Mother and one to the Free Press. Distance from Iuka to Jacinto 20 miles.

Tuesday, September 23. In camp, resting. Weather cloudy. Our wounded have been removed from Iuka to Corinth.

Wednesday, September 24. In camp. Corporal Heron has died of his wounds. Another good, brave boy has been taken from us.[4]

Thursday, September 25. I received a very interesting letter today from a friend whose patriotism is strong and hatred of rebels intense. The telegraph announces that the President has issued a proclamation respecting the emancipation of all slaves in states that may be in rebellion, on the first of next January.[5] The President will be sustained in this by the loyal North. His proclamation would have been in better time, however, if it had been made a year ago. But better late than never.

Friday, September 26. Our baggage is still at Corinth and the Sutler is coining money—practicing extortion—taking advantage of the wants of the boys. Weather pleasant.

Saturday, September 27. In company with Sergeant Pennywitt, I visited my friends in the 39th Ohio regiment today. I received a letter from Frank— he is in the 40th Iowa regiment. Papers came last evening containing President Lincoln's Emancipation Proclamation. The 1st of January 1863 is to be the day of our nation's second birth. God bless and help Abraham Lincoln— help him to "break every yoke and let the oppressed go free." The President has placed the Union pry under the corner stone of the Confederacy and the structure *will* fall.

Sunday, September 28. Twenty-four years old today and *no whiskers, no duck!!* Weather damp.

Monday, Sept. 29. On grand guard in command of the company. Lieut. McKee has gone to Corinth to see Lieut. Mateer.

Tuesday, September 30. In camp.

Wednesday, October 1. Marched to camp near Corinth.

Thursday, October 2. Moved camp nearer to Corinth.

Friday, October 3. We were aroused this morning at 2 o'clock and at sunrise we marched into Corinth. As we marched into Corinth, we could hear the reports of our cannon—our forces eng[ag]ing Price's army, which was advancing upon Corinth from the west. Price having been joined by General Van Dorn and [Maj. Gen. Mansfield] Lovell, with their commands, has marched upon this place expecting to capture it. He will meet a foe worthy of his steel. After our division marched into town, our regiment was sent to the North of town, to guard the road leading in from Pittsburgh [Pittsburg Landing]. The

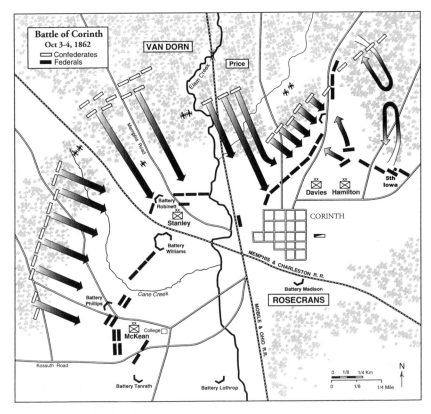

Battle of Corinth, October 3–4, 1862.

position was assigned us by Gen. Rosecrans who said he wanted a regiment there that would hold the position. It was a post of honor for us. We e[n]sconced ourselves behind the old earthworks of the enemy, where we remained without molestation, during the day. About noon, the enemy approached the vicinity of town on the West (having driven our advance forces in), and during the afternoon a severe engagement was fought, resulting [in] the repulse of the enemy. During the engagement the 2d Iowa thrice repulsed charges of the rebels.

Saturday, October 4. During all of last night, there was noise of busy preparation in Corinth. At 2 o'clock this morning we joined our brigade in Corinth. Our brigade was placed in position as a reserve. Shortly before daybreak, the big guns in our forts commenced shelling the enemy. The noise made by our 64-pound howitzers was terrible, and must have made many a poor rebel quake like an aspen. The rebels replied from a battery and shelled all our wounded out of our hospital. This battery was taken by a charge of our forces at day-break. We expected and were ready for a fierce attack from the rebels at dawn, but nothing (excepting the artillery firing) was done till nine o'clock, save fighting by the pickets. We began to think Price had given us the slip during the night, but our delusion was soon apparent. Price had received 15,000 reinforcements during the night and had no notion of skedaddling. At nine o'clock the battle began on our left and the conflict there was terrific. After nearly an hour's fighting there the rebels seemed to give way or slacken their fire. We then had a short cessation—the lull before the storm. At *ten* o'clock the rebels came sweeping down upon our right and center with the design of sweeping us before them by a grand charge. They came charging upon our lines—into the very mouths of our cannon—with a bravery and desperation that threatened calamity to our army. Our first line was compelled to fall back, and the enemy gained our breastworks and captured one [of] our big forts. Success seemed lighting upon their banners. Bravery and might seemed giving away before daring and desperation. But the enemy is taken in his toils. His desperation is to prove his destruction. Now Gen. Rosecrans generalship becomes manifest. He has permitted the enemy to come within the "death circle" and now the work of destruction commences. Our second line offers a terrible fire of musketry and our field-batteries which had been silent, scatter death and destruction through the rebel ranks, with their fire of grape, shell and canister. Now the 5th Iowa, 4th Minnesota, and 26th Missouri, with the 11th Ohio battery, start forth upon the double-quick and flank the rebels on their left. They give way. Their line wavers. Our counter charges upon them with the bayonet and they break—they fly. It becomes a rout, and the *victory* is ours. Thanks be to God. But the work of destruction still continues. Our batteries continue their terrible fire, and hundreds of rebels fall before their death-hail. Our big guns are double-shotted with grape and the rebels fall by fifties at each discharge. The work is continued until distance intervenes between the foe and danger, when our forces return to their original position. The part played by our regiment was important, but we suffered no loss. Our double-quicking was very fatiguing. After the battle, the wounded were cared for and the dead buried (or rather preparations made to bury them). At sundown, Gen. [James] McPherson arrived with reinforcements, (5,000) having made a forced march to join us in time for the fight, but without avail. We have achieved a great victory, at which the Nation may rejoice.[6]

Sunday, October 5. This morning, after putting three day's rations in our haversacks, we started after Price. Our Division was in the rear. We marched about 12 miles west of Corinth and camped for the night. Parties of straggling rebels were picked up all along the road. We found the bodies of the rebels who had been killed Friday, along the road, still unburied. Our advance has been engaged with the enemy, but we are without particulars of the result. Reports, however, are encouraging. We passed three companies of rebels who had been left by Price to bury his dead.

Monday, October 6. Today, we marched west, south, and east, about 12 miles. On the road we saw wagons, ammunition, guns, &c., &c., which the rebels had left and thrown away in their flight. We camped in a burr-patch at night. We are now marching for Rienzi.

Tuesday, October 7. We marched 25 miles today, arriving at Rienzi after night. Most of the boys have sore feet and marching is hard on them. They bear it well. After arriving in camp, we got fresh meat.

Wednesday, October 8. This afternoon we marched 13 miles towards Ripley, camping on our old camp ground on the Hatchie. My feet are very sore. Price is said to have made a stand at Ripley. We are marching to join Rosecrans who is there in line of battle.

Thursday, October 9. Price evacuated Ripley yesterday, and we have remained in our camp on [the] Hatchie, all day. *Foraging* is good. We received a mail today.

Friday, October 10. We marched back to Rienzi this morning. This afternoon a cold rain came up, and the weather is quite *winterish.* Fires are in demand.

Saturday, October 11. We marched from Rienzi to camp near Corinth today. We marched the whole distance (14 miles) without resting once. Weather cool.

Sunday, October 12. In camp near Corinth.

Monday, October 13. Our Division changed its position today. We are now camped in line of battle, north-east of Corinth just inside the old rebel breastworks. Weather pleasant.

Tuesday, October 14. Lieut. Mateer died today at 10 o'clock A.M. of the wound he received in the battle of Iuka. How long will we survive him?—but a brief period at best.

Wednesday, October 15. Lieut. Mateer is buried today with military honors. Corporal [Ethelbert] Edmonds has died in the St. Louis hospital of chronic Diarrhea—so the St. Louis Democrat of the 13th reports.[7] Corporal Heron (who was reported dead) is living and doing well. Weather pleasant—nights frosty.

Thursday, October 16. The vote of our regiment Tuesday, for State Officers, was a stunner for the Mahoney clique. The total vote was 269. It stood as follows: Republican candidates 259. Democratic candidates 10 (*ten*).[8] Bully for the *"Fifth."* I commenced boarding with the Lieutenant today.

Friday, October 17. In company with Capt. Skiff, of the 13th Iowa, I visited the 10th Iowa regiment. The company has been busy today *policeing* our camp. Dress Parade in the evening.

Saturday, October 18. "Indian Summer" weather. Brigade Drill in the forenoon.

Sunday, October 19. Company on grand guard. Weather pleasant.

Monday, October 20. In camp. Nights too cool for pleasant sleeping—days warm. Mrs. Hawk and *daughter* were in camp today.

Tuesday, October 21. Lieut. Mateer's brother arrived last night. Brigade Drill this morning.

Wednesday, October 22. In camp—nothing doing.

Thursday, October 23. In camp. Weather cool, but pleasant.

Friday, October 24. I sent my diary home, today, by Mr. David Mateer, of Monroe, Iowa.

Saturday, October 25. Mr. Merrill, our new Chaplain, arrived this morning. In company with him, I visited the 13th Iowa Regt. this morning, and took a stroll over the battle-ground. This afternoon, snow fell to the depth of an inch.

Sunday, October 26. Weather cool. Mr. Merrill preached for us this afternoon. I hope we may have the opportunity of hearing him frequently.

Monday, October 27. Our regiment was on *fatigue* today—throwing up *breastworks.* Corinth is being strongly fortified and a great deal of *dirt* has to be thrown up. Gen. Rosecrans left this morning, to take command of Buell's army.[9] Thus, we are served—we no sooner *make* a General than they take him from us. May success attend him.

Tuesday, October 28. Weather cool but pleasant. Speaking of the weather being pleasant, reminds me that the weather has been favorable for any movements our army could wish to make, but the opportunity has not been improved. This fact is discouraging. The result of the elections in the North is discouraging.[10] Much, very much, there is to discourage the soldier, but I still trust that God will enable us to overthrow the armies of the Confederacy and re-establish the Supremacy of our law, over every foot of Southern Soil. I trust (now, that we are fighting for *Liberty* and Union and not Union and *Slavery*) that the God of battles will be with us. I feel confident that I am fighting for a righteous case, from true motives and whether successful or not, I will fight on and leave the result to God—in acting well *my* part, is where all honor lies. We had a chimney built in our tent, today.

Wednesday, October 29. Company on Grand Guard.

Thursday, October 30. Gen. Hamilton is in command of the Army of the Mississippi, *vice* Rosecrans transferred. Gen. [Ferdinand] Quinby is in command of our (3rd) Division.

Friday, October 31. Our Regiment has been working on Fort Madison, today. The fort is nearly completed. The fortification[s] about town are being steadily pushed to completion. Regiment mustered.

Saturday, November 1. Weather warm.

Sunday, November 2. Quimby's, Stanley's, [Brig. Gen. John] McArthur's and [Col. John K.] Mizner's Divisions left Corinth this morning for Grand Junction. We marched 18 miles and camped near the Tuscumbia river.

Monday, November 3. We marched 21 miles this day, and camped on a branch of the Hatchie. During the march, we crossed the Tuscumbia and Hatchie Rivers, and one or two tributaries of the latter. We also passed over the battle-field of Hatchie where we was abundant evidences of the conflict.[11]

Tuesday, Nov. 4. We marched 18 miles today, camping 3 miles South of Grand Junction, on Scott creek, a tributary of Wolf river. The march from Corinth to this point has been very fatiguing owing to the dust. All along the

line of our march, fences and houses have been ruthlessly burned by straggling soldiers. Such deeds are disgraceful to our army, and the offenders merit
the severest punishment. McPherson's Division arrived at Grand Junction,
from Bolivar, simultaneously with us.

Wednesday, Nov. 5. In camp on Scott creek. A reconnoitering expedition
left our army, today. A house (belonging to Rev. Mr. Milliken, a rebel Chaplain)
near our camp, was plundered and burned by some of our vandals today.

Thursday, Nov. 6. In camp, on Scott creek. Stringent orders (from Generals Hamilton and Grant) were read today. They speak in terms of strongest con-
demnation of the acts of vandalism committed by our troops, and prohibit all foraging by the troops. All house-burners will be severely punished if found out.

Friday, Nov. 7. Regiment on grand guard—pleasant times.

Saturday, Nov. 8. We came off grand guard at Noon. In the afternoon, we
marched five miles on the road to Holly Springs, camping at night at Davis Mills.

Sunday, Nov. 9. We marched six miles today, towards Holly Springs, on a
reconnaissance. A force from McPherson's army preceded our Division. Our
advance captured 142 rebels. In the afternoon we returned to Davis' Mills. The
country we passed through today was the finest I have seen in the South. Large
plantations, covered with cotton and corn, bordered both sides of the road.

Monday, Nov. 10. Moved camp 3/4ths of a mile, forward.

Tuesday, Nov. 11. Regiment on grand guard—headquarters at a planter's
deserted home. Most of the plantations near here are deserted. The whites
gave gone South—the darkies "Norf."

Wednesday, Nov. 12. We had a rain, today, "laying the dust," much to our
satisfaction. We received orders to cook three days' rations this evening.

Thursday, Nov. 13. Some of the Recruits for our Regiment arrived today—our company received seven. Battalion drill this afternoon.

Friday, Nov. 14. Col. Matthies returned to the Regiment today. Adjutant
Patterson has been appointed Lieut. Col. of the 39th Iowa Regiment. Colonel
Matthies was warmly greeted by the Regiment. On dress parade this evening, a
letter was read from Gen. Schuyler Hamilton, complimenting our Regiment for
its action in the battle of Iuka. Praise from such a source is not *flattery.*

Saturday, Nov. 15. Drilled the recruits today. On dress-parade this
evening, the finding and sentence of a general court-martial in the cases of
two house-burners (from the 4th Minnesota) were read. They are to be imprisoned in the Alton Penitentiary during the war and forfeit all their pay. Our
Chaplain preached a good sermon to a full house this evening at the church
near our camp.

Sunday, Nov. 16. Gen. Grant reviewed our Division this morning. In the
afternoon the chaplain preached at *our* church.

Monday, Nov. 17. At 8 o'clock this morning, we received "marching orders,"
and at 9 o'clock, started for Lagrange, Tenn. We arrived at Lagrange about noon
and halted there for a few moments. We then started westward for Moscow, Tenn.

Soon after leaving Lagrange, it commenced raining and marching became very disagreeable. We plodded along thro[ugh] the mud and rain, until after night when we halted and bivouacked in a piece of timber. After halting, we built fires, put up a few tents, got our suppers, and then threw ourselves into the arms of Morpheus to take a comfortable *snooze*. Just before we entered Lagrange, we crossed Wolf River. Lagrange is a barren-looking, uninviting place in itself, but is surrounded by magnificent scenery.

Tuesday, Nov. 18. We were called up this morning at half past three and at daylight, started for Moscow. We reached that place in about two hours, where we found the 2nd brigade of our Division, they having reached there the evening before. Moscow is ten miles west of Lagrange on the Railroad and is a miserable Southern village. I hope our visit to Moscow may not terminate as fatally as Napoleon's did. I understand that we are to remain here, until the Railroad and bridge (which have both been destroyed) near this place, are repaired.

Wednesday, Nov. 19. Our Regiment went out this morning with the Division for forage. We went some five miles South-west of town and returned by three o'clock having procured a full supply of corn.

Thursday, Nov. 20. Company Drill.

Friday, Nov. 21. The forage train of our Division was attacked this afternoon by a band of guerrillas about a mile beyond our pickets. Eleven six-mule teams and their drivers were captured. The guerrillas did not have time to destroy the wagons, but made their *exit* on *double-quick.* The teams that were taken had started to camp, ahead of their escort, and consequently fell an easy prey to their captors. Two regiments of cavalry started after the guerrillas as soon as the alarm reached camp, but it is doubtful whether they will accomplish anything. When the alarm came to camp, the nature of the attack was not known, and in apprehension of a general attack, our whole force was called out. Our regiment was first in line.

Saturday, Nov. 22. Our cavalry were unable to overtake the guerrillas and our loss of mules will have to be made up from the surrounding country.

Sunday, Nov. 23. Our chaplain preached a very good sermon this morning, in a church in town. In the afternoon, the chaplain of the 17th Iowa preached a forcible sermon on "profane swearing" at the camp of the 17th. This evening an interesting "conversation meeting" was held in town. The church was crowded to overflowing. Preaching is well attended and I hope good results may flow from the faithful labors of our chaplain.

Monday, Nov. 24. Company drill this forenoon—Battalion Drill in the afternoon—the latter a good drill. I went to town to attend a meeting this evening, but the church was so crowded I could not gain admittance. Two new Illinois Regiments (the 109th and 72d) came here a day or two since.

Tuesday, Nov. 25. Battalion Drill. I attended church this evening.

Wednesday, Nov. 26. Company Drill.

Thursday, Nov. 27. I have been on duty today as officer of the guard.

Friday, Nov. 28. Our Division has been divided into three brigades. Our regiment has been put in the third brigade, which consists of the 5th and 10th Iowa, and 26th Missouri, and 109th Illinois. Col. [George] Boomer of the 26th, commands our brigade. This morning, our Division started on a march for Holly Springs. We marched south over a broken country and camped at 11 o'clock P.M. on the hills south of Coldwater creek, 19 miles from Moscow. We were in rear of the 1st and 2nd brigades and our march was slow and tedious.

Saturday, Nov. 29. We joined Grant's army at Coldwater last night and this morning the army moved South for—Price. We passed through Holly Springs about 11 o'clock A.M. and found most of the inhabitants *non est.* Holly Springs is a town of about 4,000 inhabitants and has evidently has been *a business place.* There are many fine residences in and about the town. From Holly Springs we marched South through a broken and poor country some 7 or 8 miles and camped on the hills south of Lumpkin's Mill. During our march today our advance (cavalry) skirmished with the enemy, killing several of them and losing one or two men. We marched 12 miles today.

Sunday, Nov. 30. A slight earth-quake was felt this morning in camp. Our reconnoitering forces are feeling the enemy today. We have heard the booming of cannon ahead all day. We have remained in camp near the Mill.

Monday, December 1. A heavy wind and thunderstorm visited us last night, blowing over some tents and washing into others. "Our tent" was "built upon the sand" but it was well *ditched* and *staked* and *we* suffered no inconveniences. We remained today in camp near the Mill. A report has been circulated through camp to the effect that Burnside's army has suffered a serious defeat. The report (though probably untrue) has caused great depression in our spirits. I hope that it is merely a "camp rumor."[12]

Tuesday, Dec. 2. We started this morning at day-break on our "forward march." Soon after starting, the rain commenced falling and continued during the entire day. We marched about 3 1/2 miles, when we halted and lay by the road-side until 3 or 4 o'clock P.M. Soon after halting the boys kindled fires, and the fences on each side of the road furnished excellent fuel to keep the fires burning brightly. In the afternoon we marched ahead a half mile farther and camped in a open field. Luckily for us, there was a large straw stack nearby and we had what we had not dared hope for—dry beds. It was an amusing sight to see the straw-stack walking into camp by "piece-meal." It reminded me of a lot of ants, busy carrying stores to the[ir] subterranean homes.

Wednesday, Dec. 3. This has been a clear, pleasant day. Our Division marched forward one mile this afternoon, and camped near the Tallahatchie river. The enemy left here Sunday evening *for a more congenial clime.* We will probably remain in our present camp for three or four days. The report of Burnside's defeat has been contradicted. Good! General [Frederick] Steele is said to have possession of Grenada, Miss., hence the departure & the flight—the skedaddling of the butternuts from this point.

Thursday, December 4. This morning, I took a stroll over the river bottom and viewed the works the rebels threw up here, and left as monuments of their folly. On this (North) side of the river, they have two heavy forts (having each six embrasures) and a long line of breastworks. These works command the river bottom, but are so situated that they in turn are commanded by positions which we undoubtedly would have occupied. On the other side of the river were their main works, and they were indeed formidable. They were so placed as to command the wagon road and the railroad. They consisted of a series of forts and breastworks and were strongly built. One strong fort with six embrasures is built immediately on the R.R. track. Both bridges were destroyed and the tressle-work of the R.R. injured to a considerable extent. The river-bottom is heavily timbered and to give their guns full range, the rebs have made quite a "clearing." The clouds are again treating us to a rain.[13]

Friday, Dec. 5. A 4 o'clock, this morning, we were "called up," and at daylight, "struck tents." At 8 o'clock we started for Oxford through mud and *snow*. During the entire night, rain had fallen and the roads had become very muddy. This morning the rain changed to snow; but soon after started, it ceased to snow, and during the day, "the weather cleared up." The left-wing of our regiment was let behind for rear-guard. As we had crossed the river, we got on to the R.R. track, where we found less mud to march through. Our regiment and the 26th Missouri, continued to travel "by rail," until we reached Oxford, where we arrived at Sundown and camped on the hills east of town. We made good time and passed by the first and second brigades of our Division and overtook Logan's Division. We halted two hours, when we had arrived within four miles of the town. We passed the *dwarf-village* of Abbeville on the march. The rebels had burned the depot and a lot of commissary stores at Abbeville. From the Tallahatchie to Oxford, we found the Railroad *very* little injured. The rebels were in too much of a hurry to destroy the road. They had been repairing the road, and new timbers, ties, and rails lie scattered along the road in numbers more than sufficient to do all repairing that is needed. The distance from the River to Oxford is 16 miles— the road lies through a very broken country. Oxford is situated on "the hills."

Saturday, Dec. 6. This morning I went over to town and found John Woodward and through him, the Brown County cavalry and saw quite a number of old acquaintances. Oxford is a pretty place—much like Holly Springs. The citizens deserted the place almost *en masse,* when our cavalry approached here. This is the first time the town was ever visited by the yankees. The "State University" is situated here. We have about 800 prisoners quartered in the Court House and other buildings in town, "and still they come." The first and second brigades of our Division came in this morning. Our wagons arrived late this afternoon. Sherman's, McPherson's, and Hamilton's forces are camped near town. Last night was a very cold night and the boys "felt it" keenly.

Sunday, Dec. 7. In camp east of Oxford. Our company went on grand guard this afternoon. Weather quite cool.

Monday, Dec. 8. On grand guard. Several citizens passed through our lines today into town to be "cussed" into the United States again. Among others was one old man from Indiana, who has always been true to the old flag, though his sons have been pressed into the rebel army. His secesh neighbors bear testimony to his *treason* (loyalty). After "taking the oath," the butternuts returned to their homes with light hearts and easy consciences. This afternoon our company was relieved from grand guard.

Tuesday, Dec. 9. Our regiment was inspected by Gen. Grant this morning. This afternoon, we had a short company drill.

Wednesday, Dec. 10. Our regiment accompanied the Division train on a "foraging" expedition, as escort, today. We went eight miles southeast of town and foraged on the plantation of a Mr. Porter, who has run off to Alabama with his slaves. One or two old darkies are left on the place "to see to things."

> "De massa run, ha! ha!
> De darkey stay, ho! ho!"[14]

About sixty bales of cotton were taken on Mr. Porter's plantation yesterday by "our folks." We reached camp, on our return at 4 o'clock, P.M., tired and hungry.

Thursday, Dec. 11. Several of our teams were sent out today for cotton that was found yesterday by our foraging party. The cotton was concealed in the woods.

Friday, Dec. 12. Today our Division marched six miles S.E. to the Yacona (pronounced "*Yockny*") river where we camped. The design in coming here seems to have been to get where *forage* was plentier.

Saturday, Dec. 13. I came across a genuine Mississippi *Union* man(?) today. He was one of the *poor whites*, but was a man of good sense and some information. He had been conscripted into the rebel army, but deserted three times. He wouldn't take Secesh *scrip!* He says there are a number of Union men living near here—*poor whites*.

Sunday, Dec. 14. I was detailed as Lieutenant of a fatigue party (for repairing the road across the river bottom) this morning. We finished our work and returned to camp by noon. While at work, I met a *poor white* who lives just across the river. He is bitter against slavery and slaveholders—says they have caused all the trouble and have always oppressed the poor white man. He is for the *Union* and has been throughout. He says many of the poor whites are going to move North from this neighborhood. He remarked that the road which we were repairing, was getting better *worked* than it had been for many a year.

Monday, Dec. 15. A heavy, cold rain has kept me in my tent all day, but I have improved my time by reading Victor Hugo's "Les Miserables"—"Fautime."[15]

Tuesday, Dec. 16. A clear day, which I have spent in reading "Fautime," &c. We received news today of Burnside taking Fredericksburg.

Wednesday, Dec. 17. I have spent the day in reading "*Cosette*" (part 2nd of "Les Miserables") drilling the company, and studying my lesson in tactics. Our chaplain has organized an *army church*, of which I am a member. We held prayer meeting at the hospital this evening.

Thursday, Dec. 18. A clear pleasant day, as Wednesday also was. I have been busy reading "Cosette," drilling, &c.

Friday, Dec. 19. A beautiful day. I have occupied my time in discharging company duties, writing and reading.

Saturday, Dec. 20. Reading "Marius."[16] Our Division is still suffering from the "*Yells!*" This disease, which has become so deeply seated, is new and novel in its nature. The subjects are generally afflicted with the disease about "tatoo." It is no doubt a *noxious* epidemic. When it begins to work, the screams of the sufferers can be heard, here and there, through camp, and soon it spreads from regiment to regiment, from brigade to brigade, until the whole division camp becomes an uproar, and one, uninvited, would think Pandemonium was let loose. The stronger the symptoms, the louder and longer the *yelling*. It is a lung disease, probably produced by hilarity. It is novel at least. Adam is said to have had the disease when a boy.

Sunday, Dec. 21. Our Division marched back to Oxford today from Yacona and camped on the old camp ground. As we came into town, McArthur's Division came in *from the South* on another road.

Monday, Dec. 22. The rebel cavalry having captured Holly Springs a day or two ago, we are cut off from communication with the North.[17] There are rumors of Bragg being between us and Grand Junction. They are not credited, however. We are not alarmed—but are ready for Bragg, or whoever may cross our path— not *anxious*, but *ready* for a fight. After *retiring* last night, we were called up at ten o'clock "to fall in on the color line, immediately, without any noise." We were soon on the color line and formed, found that a cavalry raid was threatened by our *lively* enemies. Our brigade was posted with a battery, on the hill above camp, on the road leading into town from the east. Other forces guarded other roads. We remained "in line," on the watch until next morning, but our *guests* failed to come. Either the alarm was false, or they heard of our good(?) intentions and held off. A bright light could be seen during the night several miles east of camp, which was probably made by camp fires, or burning cotton. At sunrise we returned to camp, satisfied that we had not been surprised. In the language of Gen. Buford, "this Division *must* not be surprised." At nine o'clock this morning, our Regiment was sent out on grand guard. Our company was sent out west of town to guard the Panola road. In the evening we were relieved by some of [Maj. Gen. John] Logan's Division, which had come into town from Water-valley during the day.

Tuesday, Dec. 23. Our Division marched (from Oxford) today northward and camped two miles north of the Tallahatchie. Our *army* is evidently falling back, taking its own time, burning nothing but bridges and mills. How far we will continue to *retrograde,* is more than we can guess. Evidently, "something is up,"—what that "something" is, I can[']t tell better, if I live another month. [Brig. Gen. James] Denver's Division, of Sherman's force, is camped between us and the Tallahatchie, having coming in, just ahead of us. During the march today, I had the great pleasure of meeting Will McClanahan, an old school-mate, now 2nd Lt. in 17th Ills. Regiment. He heard that our Reg. was passing and he called to see me.

Wednesday, Dec. 24. This morning I visited the camp of the 70th Ohio and saw Col. [DeWitt] Loudon, Qr. Master [Israel] DeBruin, Capt. [Benjamin] Wiles and other old acquaintances, who gave me a hearty greeting. Our Division marched today to Lumpkin's Mill where we camped. "On the march." Who, that never marched, knows the meaning of that phrase? What an interesting thing a regiment, a company is, when "on the march." Watch a company, see its charac- ters, hear them talking, laughing and joking—and catch their spirit. There they go, merrily, jogging along—some laughing and joking at each other, at everybody and everything they pass—others spouting politics, talking of the elections, of the probabilities of war and the possibilities of peace—others singing—others look- ing about, eyes wide open, "viewing the landscape o'er." Here you have a man laughing, "fit to split his sides," at the humor of his "file leader." At his side, some mischief is relating his adventures while pursuing butternut hogs and digging for rebel potatoes. There you see a man, plodding along, with his head down, brood- ing over the reverses of our army, and muttering "good for my three *years*," while by his side his more hopeful comrade is singing "Hail Columbia" or "There's a good time coming." Just behind him a pensive lad is humming the air of "Home, Sweet Home," while *his* "right hand man" is munching a hard cracker, and greas- ing his throat with a piece of rusty bacon. There you see a man, whose "ideal" is a good Iowa farm, laughing at the farms and farming of the Southern nabobs, occasionally joining an ex-Supervisor in the imprecations on southern roads and southern mud-holes. So they go. "A company on the march." Look on them and you see, in reflection, the human race on the journey of life.

Thursday, Dec. 25. Christmas! *minus* the turkeys—*minus* the dough- nuts—*minus* the firecrackers—and (I may add, with pleasure) *minus* the *whiskey.* After marching, shaving, brushing my clothes and blacking my boots, I took a short stroll and then returned to write and read my Christmas away. I did not hang my socks up last night, for fear old "Kriskringle" might put them on and wear them, and I get up minus *goodies* and *socks.* I had tomatoes and strawberries for dinner.

Friday, Dec. 26. Our Division started for Memphis this morning as es- cort for a provision train of 500 wagons. Soon after we started, rain commenced falling and we had to travel all day through mud and rain. We camped at night, near Tallaloosa, Miss., thirteen miles from our starting point.

Saturday, Dec. 27. Owing to the mud, our wagons did not get up to camp last evening, & we spent the night in the woods without tents and blankets. We slept (as well as the rain would permit) by fires and this morning, we found our selves pretty well "used up." The *toughest* night I have spent in the service was last night. Our wagons came up about noon today and the rain having ceased, we started again on the march at 2 o'clock P.M. We camped at night about a mile east of Myhalia, Miss., having marched twelve miles. I discovered (to my disappointment) when our wagons came up today, that my knapsack, with my "possessions," was missing.

Sunday, Dec. 28. We marched 22 miles today and camped with[in] 6 1/2 miles of Memphis. During the day's march, we passed through the town of Myhalia, and through a section of country that excels anything our eyes have seen, for months, in beauty of situation, fertility of soil, and general adaptation for farming. The road we have traveled is a superb road for marching on. Today, several of our regiment (and a number from other regiments) were taken by guerrillas and paroled. Those who were thus taken, had straggled from their commands for the purpose of *"foraging."* According to Gen. Grant's order, each one of the persons so taken and paroled will forfeit all his back pay and bounty, and be dishonorably discharged from the service. Among those taken was Capt. Foley, Adjt. Gen. of the First Brigade.

Monday, Dec. 29. We marched into Memphis and camped just outside the fortifications, south of town. After camping, our Company was put on Division Guard. The weather this evening is cold and windy.

Tuesday, Dec. 30. We were relieved from grand guard this morning and most of the boys and Lt. McKee went into town. I remained in camp, in command of the company—i.e. what was left of it.

Wednesday, Dec. 31. We were mustered this morning at eight o'clock. Our train started back with provisions for Grant's army, about nine o'clock—the first brigade marching in advance, the 2nd brigade in the center of the train, and the 3rd brigade in the rear. While the train was getting started, I took a stroll through Memphis. I found it a very nice city, containing many elegant residences. The public buildings are nothing extra. The wharves are very common. The business houses are good structures. The inhabitants are very reserved and grim—as might be expected. Memphis, in my opinion, is noted (or should be) for its beautiful residences and pretty women. Our train took the "State-Line" Road leading to Grand Junction and we marched 15 miles, camping at Germantown, Tenn. The country through which we passed today, like that on the Holly Springs road, is rich and rolling—such as Adam would not have "sneezed at" just after coming out of paradise, However, on neither road, except after [the] city, [was] the cultivation and improvement that would be expected in farms, on the main thoroughfares leading to a city.

Adieu!

1862

January 1 [1863] *(Thursday)* Our train (which had been to Memphis), for rations for Grant's army, and was returning by the State Line Road travelled 16 miles today, halting at Lafayette, where we found McArthur's Division *and the locomotive.* The road we have marched over from Memphis to this point is the straightest and best dirt-road I ever saw. It is smoother than a pike. After camping this evening, *Will McClanahan,* (an old school-mate) called to see me and we had quite a lengthy and interesting chat, about Union School boys and girls, and other matters of days gone by.[18] Just as we came into camp, I also met John Matthews, of the 13th Iowa. Quartermaster DeBruin also added his phiz to the group of old acquaintances, met on New Year's Day.

Friday, January 2. Gen. Grant having determined to open the Memphis & Charleston railroad from Lagrange to Memphis, our Division has been detailed to guard that section of it lying between Collierville and Memphis. We accordingly marched to our station, today. Our brigade is to guard the road for seven miles—2 miles east and 5 miles west of Germantown. We marched to Germantown, where we are now encamped.

Saturday, January 3. It has rained during the entire day, and we have remained in the camp resting. This afternoon I was sent out in command of an escort for a forage train. We procured forage within a mile of camp, and returned without any adventure. The locomotive passed here this morning for Memphis.

Sunday, January 4. The first train from Memphis passed this morning. We received a small mail this evening. *"Nothing for me."*

Monday, January 5. In camp. Trains are running regularly to and from Memphis. Weather pleasant.

Tuesday, January 6. Our company was detailed for grand guard this morning and Lt. McKee being unwell, I have command of the company. We are stationed on the Hernando road south of town. *Forage plenty.* We received a mail, today from Memphis—the first mail *through* since the rebel raid on Holly Springs. I received, among other things, a nice Christmas Gift from Sister in the shape of a Portfolio. I also received my commission, as 2nd Lieutenant, of Company B. My commission dates from December 9, 1862. But for the *carelessness* of someone, it would have dated from October 15, 1862.

Wednesday, January 7. Half of our company being required to "stand to arms," during the night, and the weather being quite cold, I got but little sleep, last night. On coming into camp this morning I found that a cavalry dash was apprehended—Van Dorn having camped last night at Tallaloosa, with 3,000 cavalry. Let him come. Stockades are being built near our camp.

Thursday, January 8. Our company acted as escort for our forage train today. We procured abundance of forage about 3 miles from camp.

Friday, January 9. I am on duty, patrolling the railroad today. Our headquarters are in town. One commissioned officer and 12 privates are sent two miles down the road every two hours. Dun. Peregrine arrived tonight on the cars.[19]

Saturday, January 10. Our force was called up at an early hour this morning to be in readiness for a cavalry attack which was threatened by Van Dorn. Morning came, but Van Dorn *didn't.*

Sunday, January 11. I attended church in town, and heard an interesting sermon by Rev. Warren, Chaplain of the 26th Missouri regiment.

Monday, January 12. We signed the payrolls today, preparatory for payment for July and August!

Tuesday, January 13. A very warm day. In the evening, I attended divine service in town—sermon by our Chaplain.

Wednesday, January 14. I am on duty today as officer of headquarters guard. It has rained all day and bids fair to continue all night. News came today of the capture of "Arkansas Post."[20]

Thursday, January 15. The rain turned to sleet and snow during the night and this morning the ground was covered with snow, to the depth of five inches. The snow continued to fall during the day, and by night, the ground was covered the depth of from 9 to 12 inches. A pretty deep snow for the "*Sunny South.*" I received a very nice Christmas Gift by mail today from Lizzie H.

Friday, January 16. A very cold day for *Dixie*—doing nothing in particular.

Saturday, January 17. On railroad patrol duty, "again." Weather cold. Our regiment was payed today for July and August.

Sunday, January 18. A train was thrown off the track near town last night and five soldiers killed and 40 or 50 wounded by the accident. The cause of the accident was the rottenness of some of the ties and the heavy loading of the cars. John Woodward and John King stopped to see me today. They were on their way to Memphis.

Monday, January 19. In camp. Rain.[21]

Tuesday, January 20. Our company acted as escort for brigade forage train today. We procured forage on a farm 5 miles south of town. The 11th Wisconsin regiment arrived here today. I have preferred charges against two of the boys for leaving the company. I expect no thanks and much ill will from my action, but discipline has become so lax that *something must be done.* I am conscious that I have done nothing but my duty on the matter and I am willing to abide the results.

Wednesday, January 21. In camp. Weather wet.

Thursday, January 22. Weather clear. Our camp was thoroughly policed today.

Friday, January 23. Weather wet. Our regiment drilled in the woods this forenoon. We made two or three *famous* bayonet charges in the course of the drill.

Saturday, January 24. Weather wet. I have spent my leisure time today reading "Japhet in search of his Father."[22]

Sunday, January 25. Weather wet. I received several interesting letters tonight. Guards were placed around camp today by order of our brigade commander.

Monday, January 26. Weather wet. Lieut. McKee preferred charges against some three or four of the boys for going to Memphis without leave.

Company B now has four representatives in the guard house. William Hill, of our company, who was in the guard house for going to Memphis without leave, escaped from the guard house a night or two since and has *deserted*. My diary mourns for the honor of the company, not for the deserter. One of our "prisoners" has his trial today. As I expected, I have drawn upon myself the ill-will and the maledictions of the individuals I preferred charges against. I have also incurred the censure of the *accomplices*—or those who like a "loose rein." "No rogue e'er felt the halter draw, with good opinion of the law." It is desirable to have the good will of all with whom we may be called to associate, but it is more desirable to be *right*. As an officer, I have duties which must be performed "come weal or woe." An evidence of the laxity of discipline in our brigade and the necessity for its correction, may be found in the number of cases before the court-martial in session in town.

Tuesday, January 27. Weather clear and cool. On duty as officer of camp guard.

Wednesday, January 28. Weather clear and cold. We had battalion drill today.

Thursday, January 29. Weather clear and cold. We have orders for marching tomorrow. We will have no tears to shed on leaving Germantown, and I suppose the citizens of the *burgh* will shed none for us. A brigade of [Brig. Gen. Leonard] Ross' Division takes our place here.

Friday, January 30. We left Germantown at 9 o'clock this morning and marched 12 miles on the road to Memphis, camping about 4 o'clock P.M. in a piece of timber 2 1/2 miles from Memphis. The road today was very muddy and marching difficult—weather clear.

Saturday, January 31. I have been busied today in making out a bunk and otherwise improving my new home. Weather wet.

Sunday, February 1. Weather cloudy. This forenoon our Chaplain preached a sermon from the text, "Let your light so shine," &c. This afternoon the chaplain of the 26th Missouri regiment preached a sermon on the subject of "true riches."

Monday, February 2. A clear day. McKee being absent, sick, I have not had an opportunity to get to Memphis yet. From a combination of causes, I am not in the best of spirits just now, but hope looks forward to a better day. With Cowper I can exclaim:

> "Never despair; the darkest day,
> Leave till tomorrow, will have passed away."

Tuesday, February 3. Weather clear.

Wednesday, February 4. Today, I visited Memphis and made purchases to the amount of $112.00. I also had myself *photographed*. While in town, I met Capt. Thompson ("Pretty Bill") of the 120th Illinois, formerly of Ripley.

Of course, we had a long talk over "old times." This afternoon, snow fell to the depth of two inches.

Thursday, February 5. With 13 of our company, I was detailed on picket guard today. We are stationed on the "Hernando road" about a mile from camp. We have had a busy time passing citizens "in" and "out," and searching for "contraband goods." The snow continued to fall this morning, but by noon the clouds began to break and this evening the sky is clear.

Friday, February 6. Last night was a *biting* cold night for standing picket but by keeping up a big fire at "headquarters," we managed to keep from freezing. I slept but little during the night. Today is clear and cold.

Saturday, February 7. I went to Memphis this afternoon and purchased some *grub* for "the family." Butter 35c. a lb., peaches 40c a gallon, eggs 30c a doz., &c., &c., &c.

Sunday, February 8. Preaching this forenoon by our Chaplain on the parable of "the rich man and Lazarus." Weather cloudy.

Monday, February 9. I went to town today in one of the ambulances and made some purchases for myself individually, and our mess collectively. On returning to camp, I found a bundle had been left for me by Mr. Johnson of Ohio. I soon made the strings and paper fly, and found the bundle to contain some socks and *etcetera* from home. "Do they miss me at home?" They *think* of me *at least.* Several of our company returned to camp from Memphis this evening, *drunk.* This is an everyday occurrence, not confined to our company, or our regiment, however. Our proximity to Memphis is taken advantage of by many to indulge in the grossest and lowest dissipation. Men(?) whom I had *before* considered men of principle and mind, have given way to their passions and sunk the *man* into a mere *animal,* disgracing themselves, their company, their regiment, their friends, and *their race.* The presence of temptation is no excuse. He is no *man,* that is one only when he has no opportunity to be otherwise. The *man* shines the brightest through trials and temptations—the *creature* bows to every adverse wind. He is only the true sailor, who braves the storm, and rides upon the ocean's roughest billows. "A diamond sparkles brightest in the mine." The being who is a man merely because those around him are men is but a parrot mimicking his suspicions. Such creatures demand our pity. The true man challenges our admiration. He alone who puts his trust in God, is certain that he will be able to avoid the vices of this world and live, *a man.*

Tuesday, February 10. Weather wet. While in town yesterday, I heard a rumor to the effect that we would leave here for Vicksburgh [*sic*] next Thursday. This passes for what it is worth, but it suggest[s] to me the fact that Vicksburgh is not yet *ours.* When I think of what *might* have been done and what has been done since last February, it causes a gloomy feeling to creep o'er my mind. And when I see the discontent that exists in our army, and the *treason* that is showing itself in the North, that gloom grows darker and heavier.

When I hear of traitors boldly proclaiming their hostility to our government in the legislative halls of the North—and when I hear *so many* privates in our army express a desire to have the war closed *on any terms,* my faith in the American people is much shaken, and I have at times my *misgivings* as to the final result of our struggle for nationality. But the contest must be continued and directed by the *true patriots* of the land. The *sheet lightning patriotism* of our country has spent itself, but those who will not fight as *patriots* must fight as *subjects.* The Union must stand, undivided, entire, triumphant. Many sacrifices will have to be made, many trials endured, and perhaps many temporary reverses met. But what is success, unless obtained over difficulties? The end, *I believe,* will be the complete triumph of our cause. And such an end is worth the sacrifices and sufferings of a generation.

Wednesday, February 11. A very warm day, which I have spent in camp doing nothing in particular. The prevailing opinion in camp now is that we will leave for Vicksburgh in a few days.

Thursday, February 12. Weather wet. The 1st and 2nd brigades of our Division having joined us again, our guard duty is not as *heavy* as it has been for two weeks past. Mess of officers was formed today.

Friday, February 13. Part of our brigade went out on a "foraging expedition" this morning. Weather cloudy.

Saturday, February 14. Our cavalry that accompanied the foraging expedition yesterday had a skirmish with some guerrillas, killing a few and capturing several. Weather wet.

Sunday, February 15. I am on duty today as Lieutenant of Camp Guard. This afternoon, Lt. Porter of Fosters Cavalry and Mr. Cyrus Howard of Ripley, called to see me. Weather clear and pleasant.

Monday, February 16. I was taken ill last night, and this morning. I found that I was "no better fast." I have been unable to sit up today. I bought a watch to day from Lt. [John] Cosad for $20. I received a very nice "smoking cap" today by mail—a present from Miss Frank Rankin. Our regiment went out to Nonconna river this afternoon, to have a fight with Blithes [*sic*] guerrillas but the guerrillas couldn't be found and the regiment returned to camp at dark.[23] Weather wet.

Tuesday, February 17. I feel considerably better this morning. "Blue mass and quinine" have done a good work for me. This afternoon I was very agreeably surprised by Frank [Campbell], stepping into my tent. He came to Memphis on duty, and of course had other duties than those military to perform and he "dropped in on me."

Wednesday, February 18. In company with Frank, I went to Memphis today where I met Missrs. Howard Wiles, Martin Dragoo, and other old acquaintances. Frank took passage for Columbus on the *Diadem* and I returned to camp. I am sad at the parting and can hardly say whether the pleasure of meeting counterbalanced the sadness of parting. Will we ever meet again—if not on earth—may we *"meet ne'er to sever—Where love will wreath her chain 'round us forever."*

Thursday, February 19. The weather "cleared up" this morning and today has strongly indicated the approach of Spring. The wind blew a large tree down in camp today, crushing two tents and injuring four men, in Companies K and I—one severely.

Friday, February 20. A warm clear day. Spring is dawning. Logan's Division embarked for Vicksburgh today. I have been reading the *"Iliad."*

Saturday, February 21. This morning on waking, I found the prodigal clouds again pouring forth their contents. Mother Earth is filled to satiety and cries "hold—enough!" But the clouds in giving know not where to hold.

Sunday, February 22. A sad accident happened in my tent this morning, resulting in the death of Frank Johnson. He was placing a loaded revolver away when it accidently went off and the ball entered his head at the corner of the right eye. He lived about two hours after the accident. I was seated behind him when the unfortunate occurrence took place. Nothing, not even the horrors of the battlefield—ever gave me such a shock as this. Our Chaplain preached this afternoon, the weather being favorable. The officer's mess, of the right wing, celebrated Washington's birth-day by drinking and feasting. Satan was more honored than Washington by it.

Monday, February 23. Frank Johnson was buried today by the company in Elmwood Cemetery. Our Chaplain offered up a very fervent prayer over the grave. Weather "beautiful."

Tuesday, February 24. A beautiful day. Our Chaplain preached this evening.

Wednesday, February 25. Weather wet. It has rained all day. I have spent the day in reading, writing, playing chess, and talking politics.

Thursday, February 26. It rained hard all last night, but this morning there are appearances of a "clear up." I have been engaged in making out muster-rolls today.

Friday, February 27. A beautiful day. I have been engaged on the muster-rolls again. Uncle W. G. Kephart arrived this afternoon. He has been appointed Chaplain of the 10th Iowa.

Saturday, February 28. This morning we were mustered, and this afternoon I went to town to make some purchases.

Sunday, March 1. A beautiful Spring day. Our Division has been marching to Memphis and embarking on transports for Lake Providence, today. The first and second brigades marched in early this morning. Our brigade expected to march in today, but we were detained. I have been on picket today.

5

***

"GLORIOUS VICTORY"
The Vicksburg Campaign, March 2–July 12, 1863

Grant's new base at Milliken's Bend was not a good position from which to conduct military operations. Vicksburg was protected not only by high bluffs, heavy guns, and an entire Confederate army under Lt. Gen. John C. Pemberton but also by terrain. East of the Mississippi the Yazoo River Delta—a forbidding network of bayous, streams, and lowlands two hundred miles long and forty miles wide—sprawled from Memphis to Vicksburg, barring the way to any maneuvering army. A similar network dominated the Louisiana side of the river. The Walnut Hills immediately north of Vicksburg ruled out a direct assault on the city, as Sherman had discovered at considerable cost in December 1862. All in all, simply getting into a position from which one might operate against Vicksburg seemed a nearly impossible task.

Conceivably Grant might have withdrawn his army from Milliken's Bend and renewed the advance from northern Mississippi, but political considerations ruled that out. In the forlorn winter of 1863, hard on the heels of defeat at Fredericksburg, Virginia, and bloody stalemate at Murfreesboro, Tennessee, such a move would have looked too much like another ignominious failure. Instead, Grant tried to make the waterborne approach work. He put labor parties to work digging a canal to divert the Mississippi River so that it would bypass Vicksburg. He tried cutting water channels to connect the bayous and streams on the Louisiana shore into a navigable route for warships and transports. And he made two attempts to do the same in the Yazoo River Delta, hoping that navy gunboats could carry troops through the delta to the high ground beyond. Campbell and the Fifth Iowa spent two hapless weeks on one such expedition before the project was given up.

During the same period, Grant's army had to deal with the Lincoln administration's new emancipation policy. So many African Americans flocked to Union lines that Grant briefly issued an order barring any further refugees. The Lincoln administration, however, instructed him to rescind the order. It also dispatched Adjutant General Lorenzo Thomas to supervise recruitment of black soldiers and explain the new policy to Grant's army. Although some white troops objected to the enlistment of blacks, Campbell and his comrades applauded. Hearing an address by Thomas on the subject, Campbell wrote, "The plan meets with favor and will (at least) be earnestly carried out."

Thwarted in his early attempts to attack Vicksburg, in April 1863 Grant launched one of the most daring campaigns of the entire war. The naval flotilla under Adm. David Dixon Porter ran past the fortress guns under cover of night and linked up with Grant's army as it moved along the Louisiana shore to a point well south of the city. Then, after crossing the Mississippi River at Bruinsburg, Grant lunged eastward toward the state capital at Jackson, cut Vicksburg off from reinforcement, and forced Pemberton's army to fall back into the city's fortifications.

Although these fortifications were well-sited and forbiddingly strong, Grant believed that the Rebels were demoralized by their recent defeats and that an immediate assault would cause their complete collapse. He launched one attack on May 19 and suffered a thousand casualties for his pains. Campbell's unit, on this occasion, was not involved. Grant organized an even larger attack on May 22. This time the Fifth Iowa was involved, and with a vengeance. Summoned from their encampment in a deep ravine just behind the Union line, the Fifth Iowa was sent into action against a monstrous Confederate earthwork called the Railroad Redoubt. By the time they entered the battle the attack was already well underway and looked like a failure, but in the Railroad Redoubt sector the local corps commander, Maj. Gen. John C. McClernand, sent word to Grant that with additional support he might break through. Grant, who distrusted McClernand, also distrusted the report, but he had little choice but to accede. The result, for the Fifth Iowa, was a harrowing ordeal that cost them heavily and gained them nothing. Grant later called the May 22 attack one of only two during the war he regretted having ordered.

It did not matter except to the families of the men thus lost. Full-scale siege operations now began. They continued for forty-seven days. But at the end, Vicksburg capitulated on July 4, 1863. For Campbell as for the other members of Grant's army, it was a moment of triumph.[1]

Monday, March 2. We had reveille at an early hour this morning and at 8 o'clock A.M. I was relieved from picket. At 10 o'clock, we struck tents, and at 1 o'clock P.M. we started for the river. On arriving at the river, we were marched aboard the *Henry Von Phul*.

Tuesday, March 3. On board the *Von Phul*, lying at the Memphis levee, John Dixon and Hayden Reynolds (of our company) were shot by the guards in town today, as they were attempting to avoid being arrested. They were both shot through the fleshy part of the thigh. Our boat pushed out and started down the river at 9 o'clock P.M. Four of our company deserted before the boat left. Their names are Ewing McReynolds, Alfred Dodge, William Warrell, and Wesley Matison. Their motives for desertion (as near as I can judge) were about as follows: McReynolds deserted because the rest did—Dodge because he thought he could make more money peddling raisins—Warrell because he though it was too worthy a cause for him to be engaged in—and Matison because *he was a coward from the crown of his head, to the sole of his foot.* Moreover, I am convinced that neither of them wanted to go to Vicksburgh. The first three, however, behaved bravely in the battles we have been in. It was *moral* not *physical* courage they lacked. Their desertion has raised a query in my mind. "Has their *desertion* disgraced the company more than their *presence* did?"

Wednesday, March 4. On arising, this morning, I found that we were some distance below Helena [Arkansas] and the boat [was] moving on at a good speed. The scenery on the banks of the river today has been barren and uninteresting. The river is at a high stage and the country is flooded *from "Dan to Beersheba."*[2] The dark forests of cypress that live by both banks may be very inviting to beasts and reptiles, but they have very little attraction for the human eye, at this season. The clusters of white negro-huts on the plantations along both banks afford rest here and there to the wearied eye. The villages are too few and insignificant to attract attention. The cane-brakes to a Northerner are a novelty—but one that he soon tires of. The river, itself, in its immensity and *crookedness,* is an object of interest.

Thursday, March 5. Our boats stopped at a landing in Chicot county, Arkansas last night, and this morning our Division marched off and camped on a large plantation *that has, evidently, been inhabited some time or other.* We are about three miles from the Louisiana line. The plantation we are on is almost surrounded by water. Our camp reminds me very forcibly of that of New Madrid where we were just one year ago. The peach trees are in bloom here.

Friday, March 6. One year ago today our company first "smellt powder"— in the skirmish at New Madrid. The boats that brought us down are still here, and there are rumors that we will leave here for Lake Providence tomorrow. This afternoon, I took a ride on an *extempore* raft in a bayou. The current and the wind set against me on my return, and it was with extreme difficulty that I reached land again.

Saturday, March 7. We embarked on our transports today and started *up* the river. Our destination is said to be Yazoo City, *via Yazoo Pass, Coldwater* and Yazoo River. This is a beautiful day.

Sunday, March 8. On arriving this morning, I found our boat was just passing the mouth of White river. At 6 o'clock P.M. our boat tied up, about 3 miles below Helena, nearly opposite the entrance to Coldwater ("Yazoo Pass"). Our Chaplain preached twice for us today.

Monday, March 9. Our fleet has remained tied up, where we stopped yesterday. I took a trip across the river today on the Anglo-Saxon, John Patterson Commander—Henry Hopkins, Clerk. Weather cool.

Tuesday, March 10. It has rained almost the entire day, and I have remained aboard the boat. Our fleet still remains at its mooring below Helena. Our company received three recruits today from Davenport.

Wednesday, March 11. Our Division marched off the boats today and the boats will leave tomorrow to bring another division from Lake Providence. Our regiment is camped in the timber on the river bank about four miles below Helena. This is a beautiful day.

Thursday, March 12. This is another beautiful Spring day. I visited Chaplain Meyer's company of the 28th Iowa near Helena today. Helena is "lowest deep." I thought when I was in Cairo that I had seen the *ultima Thule of muddom,* but Cairo is a jewel in comparison with Helena.[3]

Friday, March 13. Another beautiful day! Will Work and Capt. Meyer are here on a visit to us today. My throat has been unusually *sore* for a few days.

Saturday, March 14. Still another beautiful day. The first brigade of the Division has gone into "the pass" [the Yazoo River Pass]. We are waiting the arrival of small boats. Capt. Tait arrived today. He bought a great many kind remembrances for the boys from their friends at home. My throat is not better today.

This wartime sketch of Lake Providence, Louisiana, shows the sort of bayous with which Union soldiers had to contend during the Vicksburg campaign. Courtesy of the Ohio Historical Society, Columbus.

Sunday, March 15. Our Chaplain preached two good sermons today. I also heard an excellent discourse by the Chaplain of the 10th Iowa. This has been a pleasant day, but somewhat cloudy. Part of [Maj. Gen. John] Smith's Division reached here from Memphis today. They had a difficulty (which threatened to become very serious) with the Provost Guard at Helena. My throat is "no better fast."

Monday, March 16. A beautiful Spring day. We received a large mail today.

Tuesday, March 17. Weather pleasant but very warm for this season.

Wednesday, March 18. Weather pleasant—throat better. The *"boys"* are making traps to catch fish in the bayous. They have already caught some fine fish. The river is still rising.

Thursday, March 19. The weather still continues pleasant—and we continue to *fritter* away our time on this sand bank. Why this delay?

Friday, March 20. My throat is still getting better. Weather continues pleasant.

Saturday, March 21. Weather pleasant. We have received "marching orders." We will have to leave here soon or climb trees. The river still continues to rise and our camp is being submerged. Levees have already been thrown up to stay the waters but we are surrounded and must succumb or leave.

Sunday, March 22. Our brigade embarked on steamer this afternoon. Our regiment is on the steamer "Amanda."

Monday, March 23. The rain, which began to fall last night, has continued to day and renders it very uncomfortable for the boys on the hurricane deck. Our company was detailed on "fatigue" this morning to load a section of the 6th Wisconsin battery on the boat. This afternoon our brigade started into Yazoo Pass and entered Moon Lake, where we tied up for the night, near the exit from the Lake. The pass is extremely narrow and the current very swift. Moon Lake is a beautiful crescent-shaped sheet of water, about 1/3 of a mile wide and four miles long. Its shores are lined with forest trees which are just putting on their livery and render the scenery of the lake very attractive.

Tuesday, March 24. At sunrise this morning, our boat started into the Pass. Our progress today has been very slow and tedious. Our boat is the largest that has ever gone through the pass, and we have to move very cautiously. Most of our progress today has been made by *"kedging."*[4] The pass is very narrow and also very crooked—there is hardly a *"stretch"* in the whole pass two hundred yards in length. Often the distance between bends is not more than a length of a boat. The limbs of the trees almost continually brush both sides of the boat. The country on both sides of the pass is flooded as far as the eye can reach. For the first five hours after we entered the pass, there was not a foot of land to be seen on either side. We have seen but two or three plantations today, and they were "well watered." We passed the wrecks of two small boats (the *Jenny Lind* and the *Luella*) that had been sunk in the pass, and pulled out to one side. At sundown, we tied up in the woods somewhere. The distance from Moon Lake to Coldwater is *twelve* miles. How much of that distance we have made today is more that I can *guess at*. The weather "cleared up" this afternoon.

Wednesday, March 25. A clear, pleasant day. Owing to accidents happening to boats in front of us today, we have made but poor progress—travelling only two miles. We passed two or three good plantations.

Thursday, March 26. The "pass" today has been but a repetition of the pass of yesterday, and we have progressed slowly. We are now (8 oclock P.M.) tied up "in the woods" about 2 miles from Coldwater.

Friday, March 27. Weather cloudy with appearances of rain. We started at sunrise, this morning, but owing to accidents happening to boats ahead of us, we did not reach Coldwater till after one oclock P.M. Coldwater is but little wider than Yazoo Pass (as far as we have descended it today), but it is much less crooked and is, of course, better for navigation. Our boat tied up at sundown at a large plantation and (for once in four days) we had the delightful privilege of treading *terra firma.* We traveled only about two miles on Coldwater this afternoon. The plantation where our boat is tied up is deserted and *sacked.*

Saturday, March 28. A heavy thunder storm passed "our way" last night, and the boys on the hurricane deck were wet to the skin. We have met several boats today coming up from Greenwood, bound for Helena, to procure rations. Our progress today has been considerably of an improvement on our previous travelling.

Sunday, March 29. A cold wind blowing this morning rendered it very uncomfortable on deck and also rendered navigation difficult, and our boats landed at 10 o'clock and the soldiers and *stock* were taken off the boat and the boat cleaned. This afternoon we had quite a sprinkle of *snow!* Our Chaplain preached on the boat this morning.

Monday, March 30. A cold, windy day with more *snow!* We reached the Tallahatchie at 10 o'clock A.M. We have made very respectable progress since we reached that stream. Our boat is tied up tonight at "Charleston Landing."

Tuesday, March 31. A warm, pleasant day. We have remained at Charleston Landing today waiting for the balance of our fleet to "catch up."

Wednesday, April 1. Our fleet started this morning at 8 o'clock. Owning to rumors of "guerrillas ahead," the troops on all the boats were ordered to prepare for action. Half of each regiment has stood to arms all day. We have made very good progress. The country we have passed through today is more thickly populated than any we have seen since we left Helena. We passed quite a number of plantations on which we saw some fields of excellent looking wheat, apparently within two weeks of "*heading.*" The "improvements" on most of these plantations might more appropriately be called some other name. On one or two plantations, however, we saw improvements that were very creditable. The *negro-cabins* are the same all over the south;—a small one story frame (or log) [building] with a chimney at one end and a door in the middle— no window and but one little room.

Thursday, April 2. A very pleasant day. Our boat arrived at our destination at 11 o'clock this morning. In the afternoon, we cleared off our camping ground. We are about three miles above the rebel fort at Greenwood.[5]

Friday, April 3. We marched off the boat at an early hour this morning and pitched our tents. Our camp is on the banks of the Tallahatchie, in "timber." The rest of our fleet arrived this morning. They were delayed by wind. The 10th Iowa were fired into by guerrillas yesterday on their way down. We are in the peninsula formed by the junction of the Yalabusa and Tallahatchie rivers. We can hear (every hour in the day) firing at the rebel fort. The *palm* plant grows "very thick" in the woods where we are camped. In the manner of its growth, the shape and size of the leaves, and length and shape of the leaf stems they are similar to the rhubarb, or "pie plant." Weather pleasant.

Saturday, April 4. A beautiful day. This morning I spent in writing. At noon, orders came for us to "strike tents" and load our i[m]*movables* on the boat. By the time half the things were loaded, orders came to "stop loading." Many were in conjectures as to the cause of the orders and countermanding orders. The rumor that gains no credence is that we are bound [to the] Red River, *via* Lake Providence. Part of [Brig. Gen. Leonard] Ross' Division started *up* the Tallahatchie this afternoon. The battery was sent out this evening to shell rebels—a *blind* to cover our retreat.

Sunday, April 5. The remainder of our property was brought on the boat last night and at an early hour, our boat started *up* the Tallahatchie for the Mississippi. Our retrograde movement is made in accordance with orders from high authority. We are needed elsewhere. We had Divine services this forenoon and afternoon in the cabin. Our boat tied up after dusk about an hours' run below Charleston landing. We met two boats today, one of them reported being fired into by guerrillas about two miles above. The boys were instantly on the alert but we saw no guerrillas. We, however, passed the ruins of a house that had been burned by those on the boat that had been fired into. The family were sitting around in the yard, looking very disconsolate, as well they might. This is severe retribution, but guerrilla warfare *must* be stopped.

Monday, April 6. Weather pleasant. Our boat tied up this evening at a plantation six miles below the mouth of Coldwater.

Tuesday, April 7. Weather pleasant. Our boat tied up this evening at a plantation on Coldwater (2 1/2 miles below the mouth of the Pass) where we stopped on our downward trip.

Wednesday, April 8. Our boat started at an early hour this morning and has made extraordinary time through the pass. At six o'clock P.M. we entered Moon Lake when the flag was run up and three hearty cheers given, and the boat was *"let out"* before a quick run through the lake. At dusk, we tied up at "the old sand bank" below Helena, where we landed on coming up the river from Grand Lake.

Thursday, April 9. Our boat has been lying at the sand bank today. The

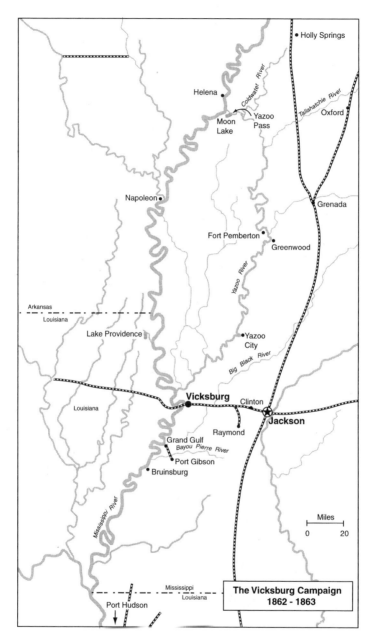

Holly Springs

Helena

Coldwater River

Tallahatchie River

Oxford

Yazoo Pass

Moon Lake

Napoleon

Grenada

Fort Pemberton

Greenwood

Yazoo River

Arkansas
Louisiana

Lake Providence

Yazoo City

Big Black River

Vicksburg

Clinton

Louisiana

Jackson

Raymond

Grand Gulf

Bayou Pierre River

Port Gibson

Bruinsburg

Mississippi River

Miles

0   20

Mississippi
Louisiana

**The Vicksburg Campaign
1862 - 1863**

Port Hudson

The Vicksburg Campaign, 1862–1863.

remaining boats of our brigade and the boats of the 2nd brigade arrived today. We received a very large mail this afternoon. Weather pleasant.

Friday, April 10. The 1st brigade and the gunboats got out of the pass this morning. This afternoon, our boat came up to Helena to *coal.* Our company is detailed to assist in the *coaling.*

Saturday, April 11. Our company was up till 11 1/2 o'clock last night loading coal. This morning we took some hay and then started down to the sand bank. This afternoon every thing has been loaded on the boat, preparatory to leaving for Vicksburgh. A heavy rain this evening.

Sunday, April 12. Our fleet has remained at the *sand bank* today. [Brig. Gen. Charles] Hovey's Division left for Vicksburg this morning. We had divine services this afternoon and evening.

Monday, April 13. Our fleet started for Vicksburgh this afternoon. Weather cool—with rain.

Tuesday, April 14. A very windy, rainy, disagreeable day. We arrived at Lake Providence a 8 o'clock P.M., where we tied up for the night.

Wednesday, April 15. This morning I sallied out into town, and found Will McClanahan and other friends of the Brown [County] Cavalry. The country about Lake Providence is very fertile and extremely pleasant to look upon. The town of New Providence has *been* a very pretty burgh. The water from the Mississippi is running through the *"Lake Providence Canal"* at a fearful rate and deluging the country in the interior. We started from Lake Providence for Milliken's bend at noon, and arrived there about 3 o'clock P.M. *Thursday, April 16.* This morning our Division went into camp at Milliken's bend—20 miles above Vicksburg by land, and 12 by water. The plantations we are camped on, are large, fertile, and well improved. The *negro-huts* are *wanting.* They have either been destroyed by the soldiers or are stuck away in some corner of the plantation "out of sight."

Friday, April 17. Last night about 12 o'clock, a fleet of five gunboats and two transports ran the blockade at Vicksburgh. One transport was burned by the carelessness of our men (her crew). The casualties on the blockade runners were trivial. We could hear very distinctly the reports of the enemy's heavy guns as they thundered away at the yankee boats. The rebels had large bonfires burning while the fleet was passing to light up the river and render their firing effective. This morning, our Division was reviewed by Adjutant General [Lorenzo] Thomas.[6] After review, Gen. Thomas and others made speeches proclaiming and advocating the policy the Administration has adopted with regard to arming the contrabands. The plan meets with favor and will (at least) be *earnestly* carried out. This afternoon our regiment was mustered—preparations to being filled up with conscripts. I am on guard today.

Saturday, April 18. I have been busy most of the day trying to get into Uncle Sam's service. Having been discharged as an enlisted man, and not having yet been mustered in as a Lieutenant, *I am not in Uncle Sam's service.*

I took dinner with Capt. Foster today, and to and fro from Gen. McPherson's headquarters, but have failed to get mustered into the service. Our regiment was paid today up to February.

Sunday, April 19. We had a very heavy storm last night, and this morning every thing is filled with life. I succeeded in being mustered today.

Monday, April 20. A very warm day. Company Drill in forenoon and Battalion Drill in afternoon. After a few day's stay in Louisiana, I am convinced that the inhabitants of this part of the State *"lived at home."* The green fields, the hedges, the mocking birds, and the many other adornments and songsters that Nature has lavishly bestowed on their land make it almost an Eden.

Tuesday, April 21. A warm day with rain in afternoon. Late papers from the North bring intelligence of the repulse of our ironclad fleet at Charleston.[7] The news is discouraging as we had been led to expect better things.

Wednesday, April 22. A very warm day. Battalion drill in afternoon.

Thursday, April 23. Six of our transports, loaded with commissaries, attempted to run by Vicksburgh last night. Five of them got through safely, in spite of the heavy fire from the rebel batteries. One boat was sunk, as far as the cotton on her would permit, but was floated by the batteries and secured by our forces below. Weather very warm today. Our Colonel has been ordered to report for duty as Brigadier General and the company officers will meet tonight to elect a new Colonel.

Friday, April 24. The election, last night, resulted in the choice of Major [Jabez] Banbury for Colonel, and Adjutant [William] Marshall for Major. I paid a visit to the 13th Iowa today and took dinner with the officers of Company B. Weather warm.

Saturday, April 25. We had "reveille" at 3 1/2 o'clock this morning and at 6 o'clock we took up our line of march for Richmond, leaving our tents behind. The country we have marched through today is flat and low (as I suppose most of the State is). The land, which is very fertile, is mostly cleared and under cultivation—or *was* before the war. The day has been hot and oppressive, and the boys had a hard march. More straggling was done than I ever saw, with the exception of one time. The straggling was occasioned to a great extent by the commander of the brigade marching the boys too long between *rests.* We reached Richmond at 2 o'clock P.M., having marched 15 miles. Richmond is a small village, 20 miles west of Vicksburg on Roundaway bayou, a channel through which the water flows from the Mississippi into the Tensas, in high water and *vice versa* in low water.

Sunday, April 26. We had reveille at 3 1/2 o'clock this morning and at daylight started for Carthage. At 10 o'clock A.M. halted at Holmes' Plantation, nine miles from Richmond. This plantation (which is but a *sample* of all) contains about 600 or 1,000 acres of improved land, which was mostly planted in corn last year, but will raise nothing but weeds this season. On the plantation is a large mill, which consists of a large two-story frame and a one-story brick

Wartime photograph of Col. Jabez Banbury. Courtesy of the State Historical Society of Iowa.

building. A thirty-horsepower steam engine runs the machines for a grist mill, a saw mill, and four cotton gins. Besides the mill there are several other large buildings (warehouses, barns, &c.) which with the rows of negro cabins, give the plantation the appearance of a village. The groves of trees and hedges of roses on some of the plantations make them very beautiful at this season. At 4 o'clock P.M. we started on our journey again and after marching seven miles stopped at dusk at another plantation just as a heavy rain commenced falling. We stowed ourselves away in the plantation buildings and soon resigned ourselves to the arms of Morpheus. On Holmes' plantation, we saw the "first alligator."

Monday, April 27. This morning at sunrise we started on the march but had scarcely got out of camp when we were ordered back and remained on "*Sussett's*" plantation all day. Logan's Division passed, during the day—they had [a] "hard (muddy) road to travel."[8] During the day I have conversed with some of the "superannuated" niggers that were left on the plantation and learned much about plantation life that was new *to* me. One old man (of 88 years) gave me an account of the cruel conduct of the overseer on this plantation towards the slave, and an amusing account of his (the overseer's) actions when the "*yankees*" came.

Tuesday, April 28. We left *Sussett's* Plantation at an early hour this morning and marched some 7 or 8 miles and camped. The roads were very muddy—weather very warm. Or destination appears now, to be some point on the Mississippi below Carthage.

Wednesday, April 29. At daylight this morning, we started again on the "tramp." During the day we crossed two pontoon bridges built by our forces across bayous. Our company was detailed to follow the regimental wagons and we did not get into camp until dark, owing to the delay caused by crossing the bridges. The regiment got into camp at noon. Distance travelled about 10 miles. We are now *bivouacked* half a mile from the Mississippi, a few miles above Grand Gulf. Gen. [Brig. Gen. Marcellus] Crocker now has command of our Division.

Thursday, April 30. A very warm day. We have marched 15 miles down the river, mostly along the shore of Lake St. Joseph. On this land there are some of the finest plantations in Louisiana. On one of these (Dr. Bowie's) there is a splendid dwelling home or mansion, that far surpasses anything I have seen in the South. All these plantations were deserted on the approach of the yankees—the planters fleeing with their families and "chattel" to Mississippi and Red river, leaving only the "*worthless niggers*" behind. The fine furniture left in these houses had been mostly destroyed by the *vandals* of our army before we came. After looking upon these plantations and seeing the despotic sway that these few planters wielded over this whole section, I am not surprised that they should be aristocrats, nor do I wonder that the cling to their "pet institution." "Where their treasures are, there will their heart be also." "Give me neither poverty nor riches."

Friday, May 1. At 7 o'clock this morning we "started on," and marched about a mile and a half down the river when we marched aboard our gunboats and transports (that ran the blockade at Vicksburg) and crossed the river landing at a plantation four miles below, whence a good road leads to Port Gibson. The troops ahead of us have evidently been fighting today, as there has been brisk cannonading ahead. At noon we started on the Port Gibson road and marched eight miles through a very hilly country. Weather hot.

Saturday, May 2. Our forces completely routed the rebels in the fight yesterday, taking some 500 or 800 prisoners. The rebels lost some 2,000 in killed, wounded and prisoners—our loss was about 450.[9] The rebels evidently were "caught napping." Several new Iowa regiments won laurels in the fight. On feeling for the rebels this morning, they were found *non est,* and our whole force pushed on into Port Gibson, where we remained until the bridge over bayou Pierre, at the north side of town (which the rebels had burned), was replaced by a pontoon bridge of *"our manufacture."* At 12 o'clock the bridge being completed, we started after the rebels on the Vicksburgh road—our Division being the advance of our forces. After a march of eight miles, we halted and camped for the night, at Big Bayou Pierre where the rebels had partially burned another bridge. During the march this afternoon, we found a lot of bacon the fleeing rebels had left in the woods. Port Gibson is a pleasant business-looking place of about 2,000 inhabitants. The inhabitants deserted the town on our approach—only a few families remaining. Weather hot. Roads good but very *up and downy.*

Sunday, May 3. After repairing the bridge, our forces crossed the bayou and started in pursuit of the rebels this morning—Logan's Division being in the advance. They caught up with the rebels after a few miles march and slowly drove them before them—the rebels keeping up a running artillery fight. About three o'clock our Division was ordered to the front, while Logan's made a circuitous movement to get in rear of the rebels and catch them. Our Division was thrown into line of battle and advanced on the rebel battery, which was planted on the crest of a high hill. Our movements were made slowly in order to give Logan time, but the rebels "smelt a rat," and skedaddled and Logan was only able to gobble up about fifty men of their rear guard. We followed the rebels to Big Black river, where we camped—the rebels stopping on the North side of the stream. They succeeded in partially destroying the pontoon bridge across the river. Weather warm.

Monday, May 4. Our pickets had some skirmishing with the rebel pickets last night. We had reveille at 3 o'clock A.M. About 8 o'clock our pickets and the rebel pickets had a "set-to" and the artillery on both sides, for a short time, lent a helping hand. Before noon, the rebels left for another standpoint. They have displayed good generalship in their retreat since the battle of Friday. Their rear guard has kept back our whole army, by taking positions in commanding places and shelling our advance as it came up—thus compelling us to form lines of battle and advance slowly and with caution, lest we might come on the rebels before we were ready for them. I have spent my time, today in washing, repairing, writing, &c. Grand Gulf was evacuated by the rebels Saturday night, and is now our base of operations.[10]

Tuesday, May 5. Rain last night. This afternoon our regiment, the 10th Iowa, and a battalion of cavalry made a reconnaissance across Black River, going three miles out. We found the enemy's pickets, drew their fire, and then returned to camp. Heavy firing was heard at Vicksburg this evening.

Wednesday, May 6. Preparations are being made for a forced march. All our baggage was sent back to Grand Gulf today. Weather cool and pleasant. We received a [shipment of] mail today.

Thursday, May 7. I have been sick today with fever and sore throat. Weather very cool for this season.

Friday, May 8. I have been *doctoring* and feel better today. Weather still cool.

Saturday, May 9. We left our camp on Black River this evening and marched eastwardly on the Raymond road, ten miles through a hilly country, and camped at night at Utica Cross roads. The weather during the day has been pleasant. My health has improved.

Sunday, May 10. Marched 10 miles on road to Raymond, passing through and camping about four miles east of Utica. The country as we approach Raymond is getting less hilly and more fertile. After going into camp, our company was sent out on picket. As we approached our picket post, sharp skirmishing began a short distance ahead of us and we loaded our pieces and pushed ahead to take part in the action. Just as we got up the firing ceased, and we learned from Company D of our regiment that they had just repulsed an attack made on them by a squad of rebel cavalry. About half an hour afterward, a flag of truce came in, and we learned that the cavalry were the 6th Missouri instead of butternuts. Fortunately no one was hurt. The mistake was on the part of the cavalry in the beginning. My health is better.

Monday, May 11. Marched only one mile and a half. Roads dusty— weather warm.

Tuesday, May 12. We marched 12 miles today arriving at Raymond just as Logan's Division was driving the rebels out of town—(or rather driving them off their battle ground and through town). For six miles we could hear the roar of the conflict and expected to take part in the engagement on arrival at the battlefield, but our services were not needed. The rebels under [Brig. Gen. John] Gregg—although they gained a decided advantage in the beginning of the fight—were badly whipped.[11] During the march today, and for several days past, our Quartermasters have scoured the country along our line of march for *bacon,* and have succeeded in obtaining a reasonable supply. The ration to each man is now about two crackers each day and such meat and sugar as our Quartermaster can *"press."* Coffee is issued in about half rations. The weather today has been very warm, & I have been somewhat unwell.

Wednesday, May 13. At 7 o'clock this morning we started for Clinton, but by mistake got on the road to Jackson, *via* Mississippi Springs. After marching about a mile (our regiment being placed in advance) we turned back and got onto the Clinton road. Our skirmishers were kept deployed ahead of us from the start. At 11 o'clock they came upon some rebel scouts (supposed to be pickets) and our regiment was thrown into line of battle and preparations made for a fight. As soon as the skirmishers found there was no force of the enemy ahead, we recommenced our march and arrived at Clinton at 3 o'clock P.M. The topography of the country at Clinton is very favorable for defensive operations and we here expected to meet stubborn resistance, especially as the town lay on the railroad (from Jackson to Vicksburgh). But our skirmishers slowly ascended the hill and marched through the town, followed by our regiment, without seeing sight of an armed rebel and before we could realize it, we found ourselves in peaceable possession of Clinton. The rebels were completely surprised at our arrival among them—they having supposed that our army was going to Jackson on the Mississippi Spring road—they not supposing we had force enough to march on both roads and meet their forces. A train of cars passed through Clinton for Vicksburg about one hour and a half before our arrival. We were prevented from capturing a train that was expected, by the telegraph operator giving the rebels at Jackson timely notice of our arrival. As we passed through town, the inhabitants—men, women, and children—turned out to see the first yankee troops that had ever visited their quiet *burgh*. We marched through town without halting and camped about a mile east. In the town, we found several rebel hospitals with sick and wounded in [them], whom we paroled. The heat during the march today was excessive. Soon after getting into camp, a heavy rain came up and cooling the atmosphere and settling the dust—much to our satisfaction. For our regiment, I claimed the honor of being the first yankee to reach and cut off the rebel line of communications between Vicksburg and Jackson. Logan's Division marched in rear of ours today. We are camped in line of battle tonight as usual on the march.

Thursday, May 14. At 7 o'clock this morning we started for Jackson—the 2nd brigade of our Divison [*sic*] being in advance. A heavy thunder storm came up soon after we started and continued during our march. About four miles from Jackson, our advance came up with the enemy skirmishers and found the enemy in force in position about 3 miles from the capital—this at eleven o'clock A.M. Dispositions for battle were made as rapidly as the condition of the roads would permit. The enemy occupied the rest of a hill with a cleared slope, about three quarters of a mile long, in their front. Their batteries were planted in the road, and to the right of the road, at the crest of the hill. The infantry was in timber. When our brigade arrived in sight of the battlefield, the 1st Missouri and 6th Wisconsin batteries were in position near a cotton gin about half way up the slope. The first brigade was in line on the right of the batteries and the 2nd on the left. Our brigade was halted for about 20 minutes just as we came in sight of the battlefield and we had a good view of an interesting artillery duel that soon commenced between our and the rebel batteries. Our brigade was then ordered into line and took position on the left of the second brigade forming the left wing of our line of battle. As soon as we got into position, our whole line advanced and soon came on to the enemy. On the right and left wings we met nothing but a heavy line of skirmishers, the whole rebel force being placed in support of their batteries, and in front of the 2nd brigade. This brigade made a gallant charge and routed the enemy and sent them flying into Jackson. The rebels were principally South Carolina troops who had just come from Charleston. The loss of the Second brigade was heavy—the largest proportion falling on the 17th Iowa. To the Second brigade belongs the laurels of the fight. Our regiment lost only four (4) wounded. After the rebels fell back, our line advanced cautiously, expecting to find the rebels in their earthworks ready to give us another trial. Our company was thrown out as skirmishers in order to extend our skirmish line. We advanced close up to the rebel works, when the skirmishers discovered that they were evacuated and no rebels were to be seen. Our company was first to make the discovery and Lt. McKee with an artillery major first entered the rebel fort, where we found four cannon still warm from firing. Word was sent back of the *status* of affairs and the skirmishers assembled in the fort and started into town through the mud. We were thus the first troops to enter Jackson. In the streets we found citizens, straggling soldiers and darkies, [and] quite a few small pieces of cannon. Our regiment followed soon after us and we camped on the outskirts of the west side of the town. Sherman's force fought the enemy on the Mississippi Springs road at the same time we were engaging them, but they did not get into town until our flag was on the State House. The rebels skedaddled out of town, on the Canton road. They were commanded by Gen. Joe Johnston.[12] After getting into camp our first care was to wash the mud off our clothes and build fires to dry by. My shoes were bursted at the sides and they had taken in mud and water to their satisfaction. By washing my shoes, socks, & pants, and drying myself by a big fire, I managed to get my clothing in a *tolerable* condition by bedtime. We had a hard day's march through the mud (the rain falling during the whole march and most of the fight) and we were greatly wearied and thankful for an opportunity to rest.

Friday, May 15. We started from Jackson *for Vicksburg* at 7 o'clock this morning. We passed through Clinton about the middle of the afternoon and camped at dark six miles west of that place. The weather has been pleasant today and the roads good. Sherman's corps remained at Jackson to destroy public property and works, railroads, and bridges.

Saturday, May 16. This has been another eventful day in our military life. At 7 o'clock our Divison started on the march again—our brigade being in front. After marching a few miles we passed the teams of Logan's and Hovey's Division *corralled* by the side of the road—a certain indication that there was an enemy ahead. Soon after passing the teams the occasional boom of the cannon could be heard engaging the enemy. About 11 o'clock A.M. our brigade reached the battlefield and formed in line at the double quick. The position of the enemy was well chosen. They had formed their line on a wooded ridge along which the Vicksburg and Jackson road ran. From this main ridge small ridges projected from each side (like ribs from a backbone) forming natural breastworks for the enemy to fight behind. The main Jackson road, as it ascends the ridge leads from an open field in a Southern direction—again

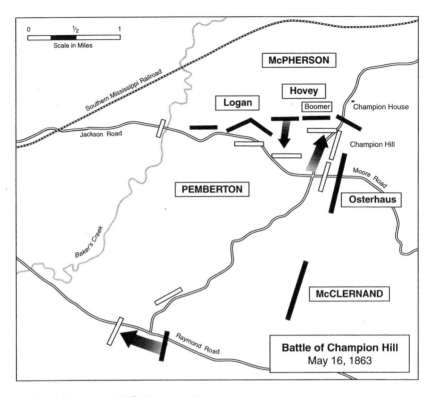

Battle of Champion Hill, May 16, 1863.

taking its westerly course on reaching the top of the ridge. Hovey's Division occupied the center of our line (stretching across the road), Logan's Division was on the right of Hovey's and [Brig. Gen. Peter] Osterhaus' on the left. Our brigade, on coming up, was formed in rear of Hovey to support him, he being at that time warmly engaged with the enemy on the ridge. We moved forward in line, and started up the ridge, but had gone but a short distance when we were marched by the right flank out into the open field on the right of the ridge where we were ordered to be held as a reserve. The Division of Hovey's was driving the enemy so rapidly before it, that it was deemed unnecessary for us to follow it for support. This (as the sequel proved) was a great blunder. We took our position in the open field and the First Brigade of our Divison moved around to the right to support Logan. We had not been long in our new position when it became evident from the firing that Hovey's Division was falling back. After capturing two batteries and driving the enemy for a half a mile, Hovey's troops were compelled to fall back—the enemy being heavily reinforced in their front. Hovey sent for reinforcements again and again but owing to "red tape" circumlocution he could get no help till he was driven back over most of the ground he had gained. Half of our brigade was finally ordered to his support. The 93d Illinois and the 5th Iowa started up the hill—marching by the left flank. Before reaching the top of the ridge, "double quick" was ordered and we went up the hill on nearly a run. On arriving at the top of the ridge, where the road turns to the right, we found there was no opportunity to form a line, as Hovey's troops were breaking back through our ranks and the rebel bullets were whizzing by us in rather a careless manner. We accordingly moved "by the right flank" (gaining the top of the ridge) without halting or dropping the "double quick" step. On moving forward "in line" the same causes prevented our preserving an alignment that forbid our forming a line on reaching the top of the ridge. As we moved forward, the order was given to "fix bayonets" but there was so much noise that but few heard the command and not one in ten fixed his bayonets. We charged with a yell (but without bayonets) and chased the rebels from their position on one of the side ridges, where they were standing and pouring a murderous fire into a few brave Indianans, who were fighting them from the ravine below. This ridge was one hundred yards or more from the place we ascended the hill. Taking position at the brow of the ridge (after driving the rebels off it) our boys opened a terrific fire which they maintained for upwards of half an hour. By some unaccountable blunder, the order was given for the 93d to fall back. They accordingly started back, and had reached the ravine when the blunder was discovered and they were rallied again to the brow of the ridge. The rebels, taking advantage of it, commenced a flank movement on our left and soon had the 93d completely flanked and opened a raking fire down their lines. After standing for a short time under this fire, the 93d gave way and fell back in confusion. Our regiment was thus left alone (with one company of the 93d Illinois), with an enemy in our front and on our flank. The fire in our front, it is true, had been nearly silenced, but the enemy was there. Company A of the 93d did not fall back with their regiment but remained with ours. We held our ground for a short time after the 93d fell back, when the order was given for us to retreat, the Colonel seeing that our only choice was to run or be "*gobbled.*" On the left of the regiment, we did not hear the command, and our company & Company I (and Company A of the 93d) did not start back until our colors had crossed the ravine and were going up the other ridge. Being behind in starting, we made the better time after getting under way. Individually, I made 2:40 time going over the ridge back of us, where the whizzing of the balls plainly told me I was going none to fast for safety. On clearing the brow of the ridge, I struck "common time," which I continued till I was out of sight of the rebs. Our right wing moved off into the open field by a left oblique movement and continued this fight from a new position they there gained. The left wing fell back towards the point they advanced from and became more scattered. It was rallied by Captain Tait and formed in rear of one of the batteries for "a support." About the time our demi-brigade was forced back, the balance of the brigade was ordered into the fight. They, like us, went up the hill on double quick, under fire. The enemy came onto them just as they reached the top of the hill, and the strife for a time was terrific. Unable to drive the 10th Iowa and 26th Missouri back by a *front* attack, the rebels flanked them as they had done us and compelled them to fall back to a new position. By this time Second Brigade had arrived on the field, and they entered the fight, and charging the rebels, soon had them skedaddling to the *Black River!* About the same time Logan routed the rebels on our right and the whole rebel army were put to flight. Thus ended the battle of *"Champion Hill"* or *"Baker's Creek."* The general result of the fight was gratifying—being a glorious victory for our army. About 3,000 prisoners were taken and 23 pieces of artillery captured. To our Brigade—to myself individually—the result was not altogether satisfactory. The boys fought with a determination and valor never surpassed, and it is to be regretted that they were compelled (for the first time) to give way to a line of rebel troops. It is to be regretted that owing to *somebody's* blunder, we were not sent into action in proper time and the whole brigade together. The loss on our Brigade was about one third of our whole force—as follows: *5th Iowa*—killed 19, wounded 75; *10th Iowa*—killed 37, wounded 130; *26th Missouri*—killed 18, wounded 71. *93d Illinois*—killed 50, wounded 99. Our company lost four wounded (none killed)—as follows: Wm. McCully, severely in the head; Wm Spurling, severely in the arm; Thos. Poor, slightly in the hand; Simeon Kennedy, slightly in the thumb. Our company had good protection when fighting over the brow of the ridge, hence our small loss. McCully and Spurling were wounded by needlessly exposing themselves. After the fight we lay for a short time on the battlefield and then marched ahead about a mile and camped for the night about 25 miles from Vicksburg and three or four from Edward's station. To *Him* who hath preserved me through so many dangers, I return thanks that I have again passed safely through the perils of the bloody field.[13]

Sunday, May 17. About 8 o'clock this morning we started on the march and passed Edward's Station about 11 o'clock. At one oclock, we halted at Cook's plantation, 3 1/2 miles from Big Black bridge. During the whole morning we had heard heavy firing in front and when we halted our General announced to us that McClernand had whipped the enemy badly at Big Black bridge, capturing 2,000 prisoners and 17 pieces of artillery.[14] The 11th Wisconsin, 21st, 22nd, and 23d Iowa particularly distinguished themselves. We are now *bivouacking* in Cook's "dooryard."

Monday, May 18. At 9 o'clock this morning, our Divison crossed Black River (on a bridge built during the night) at Cook's plantation. Sherman crossed the river above us, and McClernand below, at the Big Black bridge. We halted about half an hour after crossing the bridge and then moved on by a bye-road to the main Jackson road on which Sherman was moving. After halting a number of times to let other troops get out of our way, we finally got into the main road and marched 3 miles and camped for the night—being about 6 miles from

Black River. Black River is a very insignificant looking stream to be designated by the appellation of "*Big.*" Gen. Quinby has returned and resumed command of our Division. Gen. Crocker has highly complimented our brigade for their conduct in the action at Champion Hill. He says we "saved the day."

Tuesday, May 19. Starting about 7 oclock we marched 8 miles on the Vicksburg road, when we arrived in view of the enemy's works. Our company was "rear guard." This morning when we arrived at our hospital location, we were detailed for hospital guards and to police the hospital grounds. After getting things in order, an order came for us to join our regiment. By this time, our forces had taken their positions around the fated city and while we were on the way to our regiment (2 oclock P.M.) a furious cannonade was opened up along our line. The rebels replied spiritedly and during the rest of the day there was a constant roar of artillery.[15] The country about Vicksburg is very broken—being simply a mass of hills jumbled together in every conceivable shape. The topography of the country is thus very favorable to us in approaching the rebel works. Our batteries are placed along the brow of the hills, while the infantry support finds a safe position back of the hills. During the afternoon our company was thrown out as skirmishers to watch the flank of Degolya's battery, which was advanced about 200 yards in front of the other batteries. Our batteries are in position about half mile from the rebel works. Our sharpshooters are several hundred yards in front of the batteries. Our forces invest the rebel stronghold from the Mississippi above to the Mississippi below Vicksburg. Our line is in the shape of a "horseshoe"—Vicksburg lying within the shoe. Sherman's Corps occupies the right of our line—McPherson's the center—and McClernand the left. Our Division is the left of McPherson's Corps.

Wednesday, May 20. Earthworks were thrown up at different points along a line last night. This morning the whole line advanced several hundred yards. Our regiment advanced to the crest of a timbered ridge, about 700 yards from the rebel works. We are in full view of the rebel works—or rather we would be if we did not keep ourselves concealed. Our brigade is supporting an Illinois battery which has been advanced to a position just on our right. The rebels have fired but little with their artillery today. A few of their shells passed our way, but did no damage. Our sharpshooters have kept us an incessant firing today, much to the annoyance of the rebel gunners.

Thursday, May 21. We have remained today in the position we advanced to yesterday. Our 13-inch mortars have been throwing their huge missiles of destruction into the rebel stronghold from a point on the river above town. Our skirmishers have abated none of their vigilance and today as yesterday, they have kept up a constant fire. Our artillery has been at work all day—the different batteries firing by turns. The rebels have fired very little today. This evening our pickets had a friendly chat with the rebs.

Friday, May 22. This morning at 7 o'clock, our brigade was moved forward

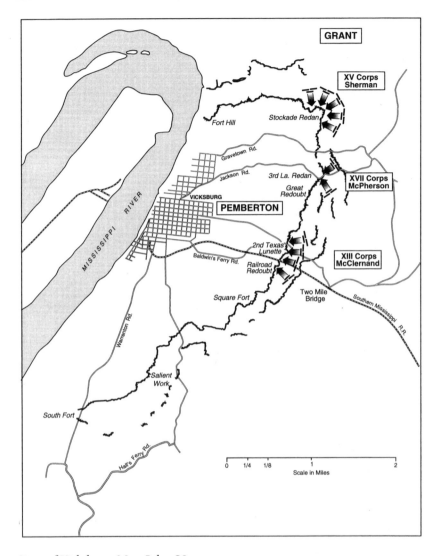

Siege of Vicksburg, May–July 1863.

over a ridge, in our advance to a ravine within 400 yards of the rebels works. We were there drawn up in line and ordered to *"rest."* Thus far we know nothing of the *meaning* of our move but the riddle was soon solved by [Brig. Gen. John] Stevenson's brigade of Logan's division coming up and passing us with twenty or thirty *ladders*. There was no mistaking this sign—the rebel works were to be *stormed*. We soon moved to a position at the brow of the ridge in our front. Along this our brigade was posted in two lines. Stevenson's brigade was assigned the task of charging the rebel works. They advanced steadily up the slope with "bayonets fixed" and orders not to fire guns. The 7th Missouri was in the advance. No rebels were to be seen until our force had approached close up to the rebel works, when their breastworks and forts swarmed with butternuts who poured volley after volley into our advancing columns. Our brigade and our batteries opened fire on the rebels as soon as they showed themselves and with considerable effect. Most of our brigade, however, was unable to fire from the position we were in. Our company was exposed to the fire of the enemy but was unable to return the fire without endangering the lives of our own men. We were compelled to lie flat on the ground for protection and the heat was so great that our suffering became almost intolerable. Several men were sunstruck and carried off. I never suffered more from heat at any time and I think, never as much. By some blunder, the 10th Iowa was moved over the brow of the hill, and by the time it could be brought back to the proper position their loss was quite heavy. Stevenson's brigade moved steadily on till they reached the rebel works when they found their ladders were too short and after standing awhile under a withering fire, they were ordered back. Their loss was very heavy. In our company, Isaac Courtwright and Charles Norris were wounded—the former severely. I have learned since the charge that our brigade was ordered to follow Gen. Stevenson's but (fortunately for us) Col. [George B.] Boomer [Campbell's brigade commander] did not so understand the orders he received. After remaining in our position for several hours after the charge, we were ordered down off the hill and marched to the rear. We supposed we were going back to camp, but we were only "getting out of the frying pan into the fire." Our Division was ordered to reinforce [Brig. Gen. Eugene] Carr's Division which had been partially successful in a charge on our left—the 22nd Iowa having succeeded in driving the rebels out of one fort and planted their flag on it, although they could not occupy the fort as the rebels could command it from the rear. But the brave fellows of the 22nd, occupying the rifle pits and ditches of the enemy, held their position and kept the enemy at bay. To complete their success, reinforcements were ordered to their relief, but unfortunately much too late. Reinforcements that might have made the success certain at noon, were powerless for good at 5 o'clock in the evening. Each of our brigades was sent to a different point and operated separately. Our brigade marched around to the left and took position to the right of the railroad within 500 yds of the enemy's works. We could then see the flag of the 22nd Iowa proudly waving on the rebel fort, and the boys of the 22nd (and other regiments of the brigade) stubbornly holding their position. Our position was formed under cover, preparatory to a charge, in two lines—the 5th Iowa and 93d Illinois in the front line and the 26th Missouri and 10th Iowa in the 2nd line. Col. Boomer took his position between the two lines. In front of us were two ravines and over this ridge we were ordered to charge in order to reach the rebel works. About half past seven o'clock (as soon after our arrival as our dispositions could be made), Col. Boomer commanded "right shoulder shift arms," "forward—common time—march," and our brigade moved forward in perfect line. As soon as we reached the top of the rise in our front, we came in plain view of the rebels and they instantly opened fire on us with musketry and artillery from our front and flanks. We moved steadily down the slope in our front at common time, presenting a perfect line until we were half way down, when the line was broken by the nature of the ground and we "double quicked" the remainder of the distance into the ravine. We were not under fire for more than a minute, but the balls flew about us like hail and our loss was considerable. *George L. Jones,* of our company, one of the "bravest of the brave," was shot through the heart. Wm. Adamson was knocked down and slightly wounded in the head. Sergeant Heron was struck by three spent balls and knocked down. Just as we reached the ravine, the rebels (who had been re-inforced from some other point in their line) drove our men from their positions around the fort and captured the flag of the 22nd Iowa. By the use of "hand grenades" they drove our men from the rifle pits without exposing themselves, and thus regained their fort. Although the purpose for which our brigade was ordered to charge was thus already thwarted, Col. Boomer immediately reformed the brigade to continue our charge. We advanced to the brow of the hill that lay between us and the rebel works, when the brigade was formed in mass—our regiment and the 26th Missouri forming in rear of the 10th Iowa and 93d Illinois. While Col. Boomer was forming our brigade in this manner, he was mortally wounded by a ball from the rebel fort on our left flank. He lived but a few moments, and his last words were: *"Tell Col.* [Holden] *Putnam* (of the 93d [Illinois]—our next senior Colonel) *not to go over that hill."* It was then dusk and Col. Boomer well knew that a further advance would incur a fearful sacrifice of life without the possibility of accomplishing ought. Col. Putnam then sent an orderly back to Gen. Carr to report these facts. Gen Carr immediately sent an order back for the brigade to hold their position until it was fairly dark and then retire to the position where our brigade first formed. After falling back, we gathered in our wounded and dead.[16] We then threw ourselves on the ground, wearied and exhausted, for a night's rest—not knowing what the morrow might bring forth. The results of today's fighting are heavy losses and small gains on our side.[17]

Saturday, May 23. At an early hour this morning, we buried Geo. Jones in the peach orchard where we were lying and placed a very respectable board at the head of his grave, on which his name, company, and regiment, and date of death, were well engraved by Sergt. Pennywitt. About ten o'clock I found *Henry Crozier* in a battery [17th Ohio Independent Battery] which was stationed just on the right of our regiment. At three o'clock P.M., our brigade was relieved and we marched back to our Army Corps, where we were placed in the reserve line for a *"rest."*

Sunday, May 24. There has been but little firing today. I attended preaching this morning—sermon by the Chaplain of the 10th Iowa. This evening our company was sent to the rear on picket.

Monday, May 25. Our company came off picket at an early hour this morning. There was but little firing this forenoon. This afternoon the rebels sent in a flag of truce. The proceedings on both sides during the cessation of hostilities was extraordinary and enigmatical. From the proceedings of both parties, I thought a surrender was *on* tapis, and was surprised to hear that the *"lull* in the storm" was to permit the burying of the dead, who had fallen near the enemy's works on the 22nd inst. When I learned that a flag of truce had been sent in, I went to the top of the hill where I could get a view of the rebel works and I was astonished to see "bluecoats" and "butternuts" mingling in numbers about their works. Strange as it may seem, our men were permitted to go up to and examine their works and they came down and passed their remarks on our tunnels and trenches. It was emphatically a *"dutch mix."* Some rebels took advantage of the opportunity and came out "to stay." In the evening, I paid a visit to Will McClanahan.

Tuesday, May 26. We remained in camp on the hillside in the reserve line during the day. At 10 o'clock P.M., we moved to our old position on the brow of the hill in the advance line.

Wednesday, May 27. Firing is more brisk today than for two or three days past. The 6th Wisconsin Battery has been placed in position on the hill in our front, within 500 yards of the rebel works. Our sharpshooters are within 150 and 200 yards of the rebel works and woe to the *horse, mule,* or rebel who risks his body in their sight.

Thursday, May 28. Nothing outside the regular *routine* today.

Friday, May 29. For half an hour this forenoon, and the same length of time this afternoon, our batteries all along the line kept up a constant fire on the rebel forts. The roar of the artillery was grand, beyond anything of the war. The *rebels* certainly *appreciated* it. Rain today.

Saturday, May 30. Weather pleasant. Nothing unusual transpiring. Hundreds of dead mules and horses have floated by Warrenton which were killed inside the rebel fortifications by our shot and shell and were thrown into the river by the rebels.

Sunday, May 31. There was very heavy firing by our batteries before day[light] this morning. Weather warm today. Preaching in forenoon. Our regiment entered the rifle pits this evening at 8 o'clock and relieved the 26th Missouri.

Monday, June 1. Our company occupied the rifle pits last night and is on the reserve today. Weather very warm. This afternoon our reserve was compelled to change its position by reason of some 20-pound shells from Sherman's guns coming entirely over the rebel works and light[ing] in our midst. One of Company E was slightly wounded. Col. Banbury, who has been at home on sick leave, returned to the regiment today. Lt. Col. Sampson who has been in command of the regiment for two months past has won the esteem and respect of both officers and men by his gentlemanly conduct in camp and his gallantry and bravery on the field of action.

Wartime photograph of Col. Ezekiel Sampson. Courtesy of Roger Davis.

Tuesday, June 2. There was a large fire in Vicksburg last night caused by shells from our 13-inch mortars. Our baggage came up today from Grand Gulf. Weather very warm. At 8 o'clock P.M. our company and four others of our regiment entered the trenches alongside the Wisconsin batteries.

Wednesday, June 3. Our company has been in the trenches today. Weather cloudy. About 4 o'clock P.M. the rebels opened a battery from the fort in our immediate front and for about fifteen minutes, they threw shot, shell, and canister over our heads in a very *unhealthy* manner. Our batteries, however, answered the rebels from several points and their career was cut short before their accolade could do much damage. One man in the 6th Wisconsin Battery had his eye shot out by a piece of shell. We have become so used to firing, since the commencement of the siege, that the report of a 6-pounder sounds no louder to our ears than the report of a musket formerly did, while the crack of a rifle resembles the report of a firecracker. Gen. Matthies has been placed in command of our brigade, and Gen. [John E.] Smith in command of our Division. Reports are flying about camp, that Joe Johnston is marching with a large force to raise the siege of Vicksburg. Gen. Grant has been making preparations for his reception, and we are no ways alarmed at his coming. It will be better to fight him on our own ground, and in our own works, than to have to hunt him up and fight him in *his* works at some future day. We can certainly get reinforcements as fast as Johnston can, and our line of communications is much better than his can be.

Thursday, June 4. We were called up and into line at 2 o'clock this morning, as it was thought the rebels were going to make a sally on Sherman's line. The rebels didn't come but daylight did. Weather warm. Our regiment entered the rifle pits at 8 o'clock this evening.

Friday, June 5. Our company has been in the rifle pits today and we have done considerable sharpshooting. Early in the morning, the rebels showed themselves about their forts and rifle pits pretty freely but we put the minies in so thick about them that they soon learned better and it was very rarely we could get sights of one during the remainder of the day.[18] Their sharpshooters fired several times during the day, but never more than two three shots from one place. I fired about 100 rounds of cartridges during the day.

Saturday, June 6. We were relieved last night by a regiment from the 1st Brigade and today, we are in camp *resting.* There has been the usual firing today. Weather very warm.

Sunday, June 7. There has been but little firing today. Preaching this forenoon by the Chaplain of the 10th Iowa and this evening by our Chaplain. Weather very warm.

Monday, June 8. Weather very warm and roads dusty. Water is getting scarce but the boys are digging wells. We received news today of the fight at Milliken's Bend yesterday morning. Sergeant [Thomas] Keisler of our company was in the fight, and he speaks of the conduct of the colored troops in terms of highest praise.[19] "Logan's Car" was burned by fire balls thrown from the rebel fort this evening.[20]

Tuesday, June 9. Weather more pleasant. Rumors still circulate of the presence of Johnston in the neighborhood of Black River with a large force. Grant has gone to the rear. Our army has received heavy reinforcements from the North.[21] Today I built myself a bunk with cane, and wrote a letter to the Des Moines Register.

Wednesday, June 10. We have had a heavy rain today. There has been but little firing. Rumors are flying about camp today of a battle of Black river, resulting in the defeat of Johnston.[22] Among the reinforcements we have received are [Brig. Gen. Jacob] Lauman's and [Brig. Gen. Leonard F.] Ross' Divisions, from Memphis and Helena, and [Brig. Gen. Francis] Heron's Army Corps from Missouri. Burnside's Army Corps is expected to arrive in a few days.

Thursday, June 11. Weather pleasant. I have been suffering today from a slight attack of numb ague. A large "nine-inch gun" has been planted on the hill near Logan's headquarters and is thundering away at the rebel fort today with considerable effect. The "good shots" are numerous as the frequent cheering of the gunners attest[s].

Friday, June 12. Weather pleasant. Having taken some "quinine and blue mass" I feel better today. Our company has been in the trenches today. The rebels commenced firing from a big howitzer from the fort in our front this afternoon. The howitzer is so planted as to throw shells like a mortar. It throws nine-inch shells. It is so concealed that our guns can not be brought to bear on it. It has thrown shells only in the direction of our big guns. No damage has been done by it.

Saturday, June 13. Weather pleasant. The rebels have fired a few nine-inch shells today, but have done no damage. I am not as well today as I was yesterday. I heard from Frank today. He is at Haine's Bluff.

Sunday, June 14. A pleasant day. I attending preaching in forenoon and afternoon—sermons by Chaplain of the 10th Iowa. The sermon in the afternoon was very good. There was but little firing this morning, but the rebels began throwing their nine-inch shells pretty briskly just after dinner, and there has been pretty lively firing this afternoon.

Monday, June 15. At an early hour this morning, the rebels opened fire from a battery on our right, which was in a position to rake our brigade (from right to left) its entire length. They threw quite a number of 30-pound shells which struck on the high ground on our right and bounded entirely over our regiment and fell on the left of the brigade and beyond. Fortunately but few of the shells exploded. The first shell did no harm, the second killed one of the 17th Iowa, and the third mortally wounded one of the 56th Illinois. None of the others did any harm, although quite a number struck in our regiment and in the brigade. This flank firing has given quite an impetus to "excavating."

Tuesday, June 16. Our company was working on the new fort, which is being thrown up in our front during all last night—coming into camp at daylight this morning. The rebels opened fire from their flank battery again this morning but fired only a few shots. Weather pleasant. Logan has been digging a ditch towards the rebel fort on the high ground at night. The ditch is so directed and the dirt thrown in such a manner as to protect the workers as they advance. This ditch is now within 20 feet of the rebel fort.

Wednesday, June 17. Weather pleasant. The rebel howitzer in the fort in our front has been throwing its big shells quite briskly today—about 4 an hour. No harm done by these big shells yet.

Thursday, June 18. Our company was at work on the fort again last night—

working till dawn this morning. I did not go out. I took a stroll this afternoon into Smith's Division on our left and saw Dr. Hamer Wiles and Adjutant Bill Thompson. Weather warm.

Friday, June 19. A warm day. Dr. Hunter and his brother, from Newton, visited us today. Firing about as usual today.

Saturday, June 20. At 4 o'clock this morning, our batteries opened along our entire line and kept up a constant cannonade until 10 o'clock. While our batteries were firing, the rebels fired scarcely a shot. Our whole force was kept "under arms" during the cannonade to be ready for emergencies. At 10 o'clock I started for "Sherman's Landing" on the Yazoo, to procure provisions for "our mess." At 2 o'clock we reached the landing and after various delays procured a supply of *grub*. The teamster stated that it was then too late to return this evening and we had to make preparations to sojourn overnight at "the landing." Weather pleasant.

Sunday, June 21. At 7 o'clock, this morning, we started for our regiment where we arrived at 11 o'clock A.M. There has been but little firing today. "Logan's Ditch" is still progressing—being now dug *around* the rebel fort.[23] Yesterday evening some of Logan's men got out of their ditch, crossed over to the rebel fort, and dug a hole half way through its bank, when for some reason they were ordered back into their ditch. One poor fellow was killed *on* the rebel fort. He had crawled to its top and *was reaching over with a boarding pike to haul a butternut out,* when he was shot through the head. A light work was thrown up and two guns planted on our skirmish line in our front last Friday night. It is within 300 yards of the rebel forts.

Monday, June 22. Weather pleasant. I visited Capt[.] Foster's company this morning. At 7 o'clock this evening we left our *bivouack* on the hillside and marched to the rear with the remainder of our brigade. After marching six miles in a north-easterly direction, we halted and made our beds by the roadside and threw ourselves into the arms of *Morpheus.* Just after leaving our Vicksburg bivouack, Frank met us, as he was on his way to see JQA, and turning back, he accompanied us on our march and slept with me over night.

Tuesday, June 23. Frank started back to *Vicksburg* this morning to see the "*sights*" and some of the boys who were left there in camp. About 7 o'clock we started again on the march. After marching 10 miles over a dusty road, we camped at a church. In the evening a rain came up and cooled the atmosphere and laid the dust, much to our satisfaction.

Wednesday, June 24. I slept in an old log schoolhouse last night but had no dreams of "school boy days," as I reasonably expected to! Before starting this morning, our company held an election to fill the office of Captain made vacant by the resignation of *Capt. Tait.* The election resulted in the choice of W.C. Pennywitt, 2nd Sergeant, as Captain of the company. This result was brought about by various influences. I did not expect nor desire the election to the office, nor did I expect a candidate from the ranks to be elected over

Dugouts used by Union soldiers during the siege of Vicksburg. Courtesy of the Old Courthouse Museum, Vicksburg.

my head. However, I abide by the decision of the company. Sergeant Pennywitt will make a very good officer. *"May his shadow never grow less."* The vote of the company has unmistakably indicated a lack of confidence in me as an officer and I shall embrace the first opportunity (after termination of our present Vicksburg campaign) to remove "my obnoxious presence" from the company. At 8 o'clock our bugle sounded the *"assembly"* and we again started on the march. After going four miles, we halted at Bear Creek. There has been very heavy firing at Vicksburg today. Weather very warm. In the evening our regiment was sent out on picket. This afternoon, Colonel Sampson gave in his decision, with regards to the election of Captain in our company—the result of the election having been made known to him by a committee from the company. He stated that Lieutenants McKee and Campbell were officers who had been tried on the field of battle and never found wanting and that the promotion of a Sergeant to the office of Captain over them would be an act of gross injustice and he would, therefore, recommend Lieut. McKee for Captain, and Lieut. Campbell for 1st Lieutenant and Sergeant Pennywitt for 2nd Lieutenant of the company. Although this expression of confidence on the part of the Colonel is especially gratifying, I shall nevertheless abide by my original resolution to put *distance* between myself and the company. Lieut. McKee will accept the position of Captain. We look through different glasses.

Thursday, June 25. We had very little sleep last night, being compelled to "stand to arms" more than half the night. The weather is very warm today. Blackberries are ripe and very plenty near our camp. We were relieved from picket this evening. After returning to camp I took a good wash in Bear Creek.

Friday, June 26. We had reveille at 4 o'clock this morning. About sunrise our pickets exchanged a few shots with some rebel cavalry. This forenoon I visited a beaver dam on the creek a short distance above camp and saw some of the ingenious workmanship of those animals. This afternoon we were relieved by a force of cavalry and at 5 o'clock P.M. we took up our line of march to the rear. About dusk we halted at Hill's place, 5 miles from Bear Creek.

Saturday, June 27. I was busy this forenoon making a bunk. This afternoon I went back to the *corral* to see Uncle William who is there, sick in the hospital. Weather warm. My throat is somewhat inflamed.

Sunday, June 28. Preaching this forenoon and prayer meeting this afternoon. Our company was detailed for picket this evening. Weather pleasant.

Monday, June 29. On picket on the "Benton Road" north of camp. I was cheated out of my sleep by the mosquitoes last night, getting only a fifteen minute snooze during the whole night. Weather very pleasant today. A brigade of Eastern troops belonging to the 9th (Burnside's Army Corps) camped near us this afternoon.[24] We were relieved from picket this evening.

Tuesday, June 30. We "pulled up stakes" and left *Hills' place* at 7 o'clock this morning. We marched about 3 miles South and camped by the roadside. After building our *shanties* we lay in the shade and rested the remainder of the day. At 6 o'clock P.M. we were mustered. Bob Courtney called up to see me this evening and we had quite a lengthy and friendly chat.

Wednesday, July 1. Weather warm. Heavy details have been made from our brigade today to throw up fortifications and clear out the roads between our camp and Vicksburg. I paid a visit to the 100th Pennsylvania this evening.

Thursday, July 2. Weather very warm—thermometer standing at 95 in the shade. The work on the forts near our camp is still progressing. Among the *good things* we are now living on are apples, peaches, green corn, and blackberries. The following is the reply of Colonel Sampson to the company in regard to the election of Captain[:]

Head Quarters, 5th Iowa Infantry,
     In the field, June 24, 1864.
     Co. B. In view of the facts—that but little over half of the company could take part in the election—that the person chosen had but a small majority—and also, considering that officers, who have been on the battlefields that you have, and not found wanting, should not be overridden, except for the gravest of reasons—my judgement dictates to me that in justice to you all, I should recommend Lieutenant McKee for

Captain, Lieut. Campbell for 1st Lieutenant, and seeing your decided expression of confidence in the abilities of Sergeant Pennywitt, that I should recommend him for 2nd Lieutenant. My course will, therefore, be as above indicated.

> Yours respectfully,
> E. S. Sampson, Lt. Col.
> Comd'g 5th Iowa Inftry.

Friday, July 3. Weather warm. Most of the company is on picket and fatigue today. At 5 o'clock this afternoon we received news of the surrender of Vicksburg. The report is pretty reliable but needs confirmation.

Saturday, July 4. "The glorious Fourth" made doubly *"glorious"* by the confirmation of the news of the capture of Vicksburg. At 10 oclock this morning the surrender was completed and at 10 1/4 the rebel army marched out and stacked arms and then marched back as prisoners of war. The number surrendered is not yet known.[25] The news was received in camp very coolly, but little excitement being manifested. Some looked upon the report as a *canard,* but I determined from the first to believe it and *feel good over it* as it was *the 4th* and I wanted to enjoy it. I celebrated *"the 4th"* by *putting on a clean paper collar.* This afternoon we received the official announcement of the capture of Vicksburg from Gen. Sherman. The great stronghold has fallen! To Him who hath crowned our arms with victory is an important one and the questions naturally arises to our minds "what will be its effects?" Can we see the end of war any nearer than when the rebel stronghold defiantly denied our navigation of the Mississippi? The victory is too important to not be followed by important results but I can not recognize the fall of Vicksburg as the fall of the Confederacy. Many hard battles are yet to be fought, and months, perhaps years, of fighting stand between us and peace. To me it appears that the chastisements of the Almighty are not yet ended—that the nation has not yet been brought down into the dust of humility and will not *let the oppressors go free.* My firm conviction is that the Almighty has taken up the cause of the oppressed and that he will deny us peace until we "break every yoke" and sweep every vestige of the cursed institution from our land.

Sunday, July 5. A very warm day. Preaching in forenoon and evening. Sherman's Corps has been marching by today, *en route* for *Joe Johnston!* Other corps have been marching for the same destination on other roads.

Monday, July 6. Weather very warm. [Maj. Gen. Francis] Blair's Division of Sherman's Corps passed this morning *en route* for *Joe Johnston!*

Tuesday, July 7. Weather very warm—thermometer 97 in the shade. (On the 1st of July 97—on the 2nd of July 98) This afternoon we marched to Black River Bridge—5 miles distant. A heavy rain fell in the first part of the night. I lay down and spread my gum blanket over myself and slept very well, getting but little wetted by the rain.

Wednesday, July 8. At an early hour this morning our regiment moved to a new camping ground. We are now camped on a beautiful grassy ridge, well shaded and clear of trash and underbrush. We have a beautiful camping place—about 1/4 of a mile from the railroad. I have been busy today, building a booth. We were paid this afternoon for March & April by Major Haggerty.

Thursday, July 9. Two years ago today our company left Newton for the rendezvous at Burlington, Iowa. We little thought, at that time, that we would have to spend two years in Uncle Sam's service. But so it has been. Lieut McKee went to Vicksburg this morning and I have been busy today attending to "company duties," including the signing of our pay rolls for May & June. The *iron horse* came out from Vicksburg this afternoon. We have had various rumors today of successes at Port Hudson, Jackson, Helena, Tullahoma, and in Virginia.[26] The reports need confirmation. Weather moderately warm.

Friday, July 10. Rain last night. Weather pleasant for this season. This evening I took a swim in Black River near the bridge.

Saturday, July 11. Weather warm. The rebel army (captured at Vicksburg) has been passing our camp, today *en route* for their camp of instruction.[27] They straggle along, each to suit his own convenience. I conversed with a number of them and found a great many who were anxious to go home. They are a motley crew.

Sunday, July 12. The rebel army is still moving by today. We received news this morning of the capture of Port Hudson with 8,000 prisoners and our official dispatch from Gen. Halleck to Gen. Grant announcing a great victory in the east—Gen. Mead[e] having whipped Lee after a three days' fight.[28]

6

"The Hand of God Is in This"
Vicksburg to Chattanooga, July 13–December 2, 1863

After Vicksburg several months of relative quiet ensued for Grant's army. The fall of the Confederate bastion doomed the second Rebel fortress at Port Hudson, Louisiana, some 130 miles to the south, which surrendered on July 9. With these two capitulations the strategic purpose of a thrust down the Mississippi River reached its logical culmination. Temporarily at least, there was nowhere else to go.

Hundreds of miles to the north, the Union Army of the Cumberland stirred from its encampments near the end of the Vicksburg siege and began its long-deferred offensive against the Confederate rail center of Chattanooga, Tennessee. The Federal commander was one of Campbell's favorite generals: Maj. Gen. William S. Rosecrans, the victor at the Battles of Iuka and Corinth as well as a subsequent hard-fought clash at Stone's River in December 1862. Disenchanted with head-on collisions that at best simply shoved the enemy back a few miles, Rosecrans contrived to maneuver the opposing Confederate army out of Middle Tennessee with a minimum of bloodshed.

In one of the war's most remarkable campaigns, he succeeded in doing exactly that. By early September Rosecrans had captured Chattanooga almost without a fight. The Confederate army under Gen. Braxton Bragg withdrew sullenly into northern Georgia. Believing the Rebels demoralized, Rosecrans pursued vigorously, unaware that thousands of reinforcements were en route to Bragg and that Bragg was planning a major counteroffensive. On September 19–20, 1863, the Confederates suddenly hurled themselves against Rosecrans in the Battle of Chickamauga. A tactical mistake on the battle's second day turned a critical situation into an outright disaster for the Federals. Rosecrans withdrew his army to Chattanooga and holed up in the city. Bragg promptly planted troops on the heights that overlooked the town and inaugu-rated a quasi-siege.

Although able to receive a trickle of supplies via a single wagon road that wound through the mountains, the Army of the Cumberland's predicament was dire. Worse, Rosecrans seemed psychologically crushed by the reversal—"like a duck hit on the head," in President Lincoln's expressive phrase.[1] The War Department sent Grant in person to review the situation and placed him in command of all Union forces between the Appalachians and the Mississippi. Grant relieved Rosecrans from command, replaced him with Maj. Gen. George H. Thomas, and oversaw the transfer of thirty-seven thousand rein-forcements to break the siege of Chattanooga. Among those reinforcements was Lt. J. Q. A. Campbell and the Fifth Iowa.

Campbell spent the bulk of this period as acting commander of Company B, a position he found more onerous than desirable. But by the time his regi-ment neared Chattanooga, after a lengthy journey by steamer, railroad, and on foot, he had resumed his normal duties, and it was as a simple lieutenant that he fought in the Battle of Missionary Ridge on November 25. Although the engage-ment as a whole resulted in a dramatic triumph for Union arms, for Campbell it was tarnished by a bloody reversal in his own sector of the fighting.[2]

Monday, July 13. I "sat up" with Uncle William Kephart last night, he having been taken much worse yesterday, and being dangerously ill. At 3 o'clock this morn-ing our brigade had reveille. I remained with Uncle until our regiment com-menced moving out of camp, when I had to bid him a sad adieu and follow my company. Soon after we started, it commenced raining and rained lightly during most of the day. We crossed Black River and took up our line of march East. In the afternoon we camped on the battle-field of Champion Hill. During the day, we marched along side the rebels who are still thronging the road coming out of Vicksburg, and going to a *"paroled camp,"* agreeable to terms of surrender.[3] It was a queer sight to see the rebels and Federals marching along side each other on (comparatively) *good terms.* The *rebs* made a great many remarks about the appearance and marching of our brigade as we passed them. "Very fine looking troops," "the *purtyest* sight I ever saw," "*you-all* must be expecting a fight, you march so fast," "*You-uns* are never sick any way, are you?" &c., &c. After getting into camp, I took a stroll over the battle-field and examined the ground over which we fought on the 16th of May. Weather pleasant.

Tuesday, July 14. We left camp at 5 o'clock this morning and reached Clinton (13 miles distant) at noon, where we camped "for the remainder of the day" and the night. In the afternoon I took a stroll through Clinton. This is the last day of our second year in Uncle Sam's service. Few regiments have done more or better service in this time than ours. Of our original company, *Sixty-four* (present and absent) still remain. Firing can be heard at Jackson.

Wednesday, July 15. At 8 o'clock this morning we left Clinton and marched

7 miles on the road to Jackson. We camped at noon on the battle ground of the 14th of May. A regular camp was laid out in the afternoon, and we had begun to police and build bunks when we received an order to be "ready to march." At dusk, we left our *embryo* camp and started on the march for Clinton(!) where we arrived about 11 o'clock P.M. and bivouacked east of town.

Thursday, July 16. At daylight we were "called up." We had barely got our eyes open when word was brought to General Matthies that the rebels were approaching town on the north side. Our brigade was instantly started through town to meet them. On arriving on the north side of town, we found the rebels were skirmishing on the hill (about half a mile from town) with the skirmishers of the 78th Ohio regiment. This regiment (from Logan's Division) had been stationed in the town since noon of the 14th. Our brigade was formed for battle, but the sight of us was enough for the rebs and they withdrew. Many of the rebs were captured and from them we learned that their force was Jackson's cavalry (numbering 1500) with a section of artillery.[4] Their intention, no doubt, was to capture the 78th Ohio and stop our supply train, which was expected up from Black River, but our appearance frustrated their plans. At 11 o'clock A.M. word came to the General that the rebels had burned our train between Clinton and Champion Hill. Logan's Brigade having arrived with the 10th Ohio Battery (from Jackson), about this time, our brigade and the battery started towards Champion Hill. Three miles west of Clinton we met our train. It was escorted by the Iowa brigade of [Brig. Gen. John] McArthur's Division and had not been troubled. Nine wagons, however, which were ahead of the train, were burned by the rebel cavalry. We halted alongside the road until the train passed us, when we marched on to the crossing of the Raymond railroad where we camped for the night.

Friday, July 17. At 6 o'clock this morning we started on the march for Champion Hill where we arrived about 10 o'clock and camped. In the afternoon we policed our camp. A rumor has been in circulation in camp this afternoon that the rebels have evacuated Jackson. (I have neglected to state in the proper place that our army, which went in pursuit of Johnston, has had his force—numbering some 30,000 to 40,000—penned up in Jackson for the last ten days, and there have been strong hopes of their capture.)[5] The movements of our brigade have been in cooperation with our besieging force at Jackson. Since we left Black River we have received full confirmation of the capture of Port Hudson and the defeat of the rebels at Helena and Gettysburg.[6] (Thrice Hail to the Army of the Potomac!) Weather moderately warm. Water very scarce.

Saturday, July 18. This morning we have a confirmation of the report of the evacuation of Jackson, but no particulars.[7] Our brigade (since we left Vicksburg), together with a brigade of Logan's Divison and the "Iowa brigade" of McArthur's Division, had been under the command of Gen'l McArthur. We will now probably return to our Division. Two regiments of our brigade—the 10th Iowa and 93d Ill.—left today for Edward's Station. Weather pleasant.

Sunday, July 19. Five companies of our regiment (including B) are on picket duty. Our company is stationed on a road leading South from our camp. Weather very warm. It is reported today that our forces captured 1,000 prisoners and 20 pieces of artillery at Jackson, and that they are in pursuit of the rebs.[8]

Monday, July 20. Company came off picket at 9 o'clock A.M. Weather warm, Mercury 93. Sherman pursued Johnston as far as Brandon where he captured the rear-guard of Johnston's army. Our whole army is now returning to the neighborhood of Vicksburg. The railroads about Jackson have been destroyed for a distance of 50 miles.

Tuesday, July 21. At 6 o'clock this morning we moved camp to a pleasant location a mile west of our former position. Soon after we had completed the erection of our bunks and booths, "orders for marching" came. We are to move at 8 A.M. tomorrow to Black River. The greater part of our army is returning *via* Raymond. Weather warm.

Wednesday, July 22. McArthur's and Logan's brigades passed our camp this morning *enroute* for Black River. They had 500 prisoners in their charge. The time for moving our brigade was postponed till 3 1/2 o'clock P.M. At 4 o'clock we started out of camp. The roads were then very dusty and the weather very hot. By the time we had got fairly started the sky was clouded over and a strong breeze [was] blowing. Just as we reached Edward's Station, rain commenced falling and for about two hours it "came down the near way." This was what we had been hoping for and we jogged along in the best of humor. Our gum-blankets kept us pretty dry and we much preferred *mud* to *dust.* Where we reached Black River bottom, we found the road *flooded.* For three miles we had everything but a *dry* march. Every 400 or 500 yards, we had to wade through water up to our knees—this, too, after dark. We reached our old camp ground, near Black River, at 9 o'clock P.M. As there was a prospect of more rain during the night, I made a bed off the ground (by placing three railroad ties side by side) and then lay down for rest and sleep.

Thursday, July 23. At sunrise this morning, I waked, after a sound sleep and found myself *dry.* We received Northern papers of the 16th today giving particulars of Morgan's raid through Indiana and Ohio and the attack on Charleston by our fleet and land forces.[9] Weather warm, with showers. Troops been moving by constantly today.

Friday, July 24. In camp on Black River. Weather *showery.*

Saturday, July 25. Our brigade started for Vicksburg at 5 o'clock this morning. We marched on the R.R. track and reached the "two-mile bridge" at 9 o'clock. After resting at that point a few moments, we started ahead but instead of going straight in we made a circuit for about four miles (passing near our old camp and through Fort Hill) and came back to the R.R. at a point just inside the rebel works. We there halted and stacked arms on the ridge and lay there until dark—our officers being on the hunt of a camp in the meantime. The circuit of four miles which was uselessly made in the heat of the day, caused much straggling in the brigade so that not one third of the men were in ranks when we stacked arms. So much for *somebody's* blunder or stupidity. By dark our General succeeded in finding camping ground for our regiment. We will move in the morning.

Sunday, July 26. At 7 o'clock this morning our regiment moved to its camping ground on a hill about three-fourths of a mile in rear of Vicksburg. We have a rather pleasant camping place. About noon our *old tents* came up and were torn to pieces by the boys and put up in *scraps.* In the afternoon I went down to the steamer Nashville to see Uncle Kephart whom I found somewhat better, and recovering. I took a "running peep" at Vicksburg as I passed through. I have not seen enough of the city, however, to form an opinion if it. We had a *glorious* rain this afternoon.

Monday, July 27. We were visited by another heavy rain last night. This afternoon I took a ride into town and visited the Brown co. Cavalry. I also called on Friend Will McClanahan, whom I found just starting for Ripley! having resigned. I confess it made me *homesick* to bid him good bye, thinking where he was going. Long life and happiness to him.

Tuesday, July 28. This morning our company was paid for months of May & June. Lt. McKee has been detailed as Asst. Ad[jutant] General of our Brigade, and I am now in command of Company B—not a desirable position. I have been busy this afternoon arranging the company papers.

Wednesday, July 29. This forenoon I spent in writing. In the afternoon I went down town and visited the *Nashville.* I found that Uncle William was about to start North on a hospital boat. May the change in climate soon restore him to health. I have been through the greater part of Vicksburg and find it a very irregularly built, but not uninteresting place. It is well termed the *"Hill City."* There is scarcely a house that does not bear evidence of the siege. The caves in the different hill-sides in town, will long remain objects of interest. McPherson commands the Department of Vicksburg and his Army Corps (with the exception of one brigade) is all within the line of fortifications. [Maj. Gen. E. O. C.] Ord's Corps is at present camped on the river bank below town, but is not expected to remain there long. [Brig. Gen. Thomas] Ransom's brigade of McArthur's Division is at Natchez. Burnside's Army Corps is at or near Snider's Bluffs.[10] [Brig. Gen. Nathan] Kimball's Divison of [Maj. Gen. Stephen] Hurlbut's Corps has gone up the river to Helena & Columbus. Sherman's Corps and our cavalry are camped on Black River. [Maj. Gen. Francis] Heron's Corps is said to have gone somewhere down the river. Such is the situation of the Army of the Mississippi at present. Many of our generals and other officers have gone home on leave of absence. Weather is warm. We have got no tents yet.

Thursday, July 30. Two men ([Thomas] Poore and [William] Fouts) of our company received furloughs for 30 days and started for home today. Weather warm.

Friday, July 31. I went downtown this morning on business, and called on John Woodward. This afternoon I was slightly indisposed. Weather *very* warm. "Late New Orleans Papers" were selling in camp this morning. Late in the afternoon I took a stroll around part of the line of fortifications, and examined the rebel works in front of our position in the besieging line.

Saturday, August 1. Weather very warm—Therm. 94 Fahr. Sickness is on the increase in our regiment but there is as good as state of health as usual at this season. A good rain and a strong breeze made the weather more pleasant this afternoon. A great many officers in our army are going home on leaves of absence. I have not yet made up my mind to go.

Sunday, August 2. A warm day but not as warm as yesterday. Inspection at 8 1/2 o'clock. The guns and clothing were in excellent condition. Preaching at 9 o'clock. I have spent a good portion of my leisure time, today reading the "History of the Waldenses."[11] Dress Parade this evening.

Monday, August 3. Boats arriving from New Orleans bring watermelons and peaches here, which are sold at marvelous prices. I took a bath in the Mississippi this afternoon. Weather warm.

Tuesday, August 4. I have had the company organized into one mess today and a kitchen shade built. A bake oven was built yesterday.

Wednesday, August 5. I spent the forenoon in writing and reading. The afternoon I spent *variously.* Weather warm.

Thursday, August 6. By order of President Lincoln, this day is set apart for National Thanksgiving.[12] At 11 o'clock A.M. I attended religious services at the Presbyterian church in town, and heard a very good sermon by an army Chaplain. The congregation was composed of soldiers. *One lady* represented *the fair sex* at the meeting. Through the kindness of a soldier from Chicago, we had good music from the organ. Company B has been in town today on Provost Duty. I took dinner with Lieut. Porter. This afternoon, a good shower has rendered the atmosphere very pleasant.

Friday, August 7. I have been "on duty" in command of a fatigue party today working at the City Hospital. Weather warm in the forenoon—pleasant in the afternoon.

Saturday, August 8. I have spent the forenoon in posting books, reading late papers, and writing letters. The afternoon I have spent in writing and posting books. Weather warm.

Sunday, August 9. After inspection this morning I went to town and attended preaching at the Presbyterian Church. The church was well filled with soldiers and a very good sermon preached by an army Chaplain. In the evening, Rev. Mr. Russell of Jacksonville, Ills., preached an excellent sermon in camp. Weather warm.

Monday, August 10. The forenoon I spent in writing. In the afternoon I went to town [and] attended prayer meeting at the Presbyterian Church. Weather warm.

Tuesday, August 11. A very warm day. I have spent the entire day in posting company books. Dress Parade in the evening. There were only about 100 men on parade—the balance of the regiment being on duty. For a week past, our regiment has had a great deal of duty to do in town.

Wednesday, August 12. I have spent the day in posting company books, writing letters, reading Irvings *"Conquest of Granada."*[13] In the afternoon we had a pleasant shower. Weather warm during the day. The mercury during the first part of the month, has ranged from 85 to 95—getting above 95 but seldom and below 85 quite as seldom during the heat of the day. This evening I was detailed as Lieut. of the Guard at the *"rebel arsenal"* near our camp.

Thursday, August 13. My slumbers were very much disturbed last night by rebel mosquitoes. The weather during the day has been very warm. A very heavy rain fell this evening just after I was relieved from guard.

Friday, August 14. This forenoon I spent in town. The afternoon I employed in attending to company duties. A pleasant shower in the afternoon. We had a company desk made out of an old mess chest today and I now have a respectable and convenient repository for the company books and papers. Weather warm. To this "weather" remark I guess, I had better write "ditto" for the next two months.

Saturday, August 15. A very warm day, which I have spent in camp, reading and writing. In the evening I visited the city cemetery about a mile from camp. I found it a very pretty and interesting place, but the weather was so extremely warm, that I suffered in the flesh more than I have at any time, this summer, from the heat.

Sunday, August 16. I attended Church in town this morning. This afternoon, I spent in reading the History of the Waldenses. A heavy rain this evening.

Monday, August 17. A pleasant day, which I spent in my tent—reading and writing. Ten rebel cavalry were captured today between Vicksburg and Black River by a company of Negro cavalry. The rebels had captured a few forage wagons of ours a few hours before.

Tuesday, August 18. Weather moderately warm. I have spent the day at "home," writing, reading, and posting books.

Wednesday, August 19. A very pleasant day which I have spent in my tent. Dress Parade in the evening. About 11 o'clock in the forenoon, while sitting in my tent, I heard a terrific explosion in the direction of town. Running out of my tent I beheld a large column of steam or smoke rising apparently from some point at the land. We soon after heard of the sad accident, which was the blowing up of the steamer *City of Madison,* which was being loaded with ammunition at the wharf. A fatigue party was engaged in loading the boat when by some sad accident the powder took fire and blew the boat into fragments. The number of killed and wounded has not yet been ascertained, and perhaps, never will. About 100 persons were on and near the boat, all of whom were either killed or wounded. The boat is a complete wreck. The bodies that were found today were horribly disfigured. Several ladies were on the boat at the time of the accident, and were all killed. The Ed. Walsh was lying near the City of Madison and was badly damaged by the explosion. For two or three squares back in the city, the glass was shattered from the windows by the shock of the explosion. The source of the explosion is not known, and in all probability never will be, as all who may have known were blown into eternity.[14]

Thursday, August 20. It rained gently almost the entire day and I have remained in my tent attending to company duties and reading.

Friday, August 21. I spent the forenoon in town among my Brown county friends. I spent the afternoon in my tent reading "*Mabel Vaughan*"[15] Weather very pleasant.

Saturday, August 22. "Mabel Vaughan" has occupied my time today. Weather tolerably warm.

Sunday, August 23. Our regiment being detailed on "post duty" in town, we today moved our camp into town, camping in the streets at the crossing of Locust and Fayette streets. Weather very warm. We are expecting new tents.

Monday, August 24. Most of our regiment (including myself) is on guard today in town. Weather very warm until late in the evening when a passing shower made the atmosphere quite cool.

Tuesday, August 25. This morning we again changed our camping place and are now ensconced on a ridge near the City Hospital. A cool north wind commenced blowing last night, and the weather has been very pleasant today. We drew three new tents for the company today.

Wednesday, August 26. A very pleasant day—weather quite cool. Luther Carey (one of the best men of our company) died at the City Hospital today and was buried with military honors by the company this evening. Another gone!

Thursday, August 27. A pleasant day, which I spent in my tent writing letters and muster books. We received a mail this morning.

Friday, August 28. I have been busy today making out muster rolls. A heavy rain fell this afternoon.

Saturday, August 29. This forenoon I was employed in making out muster rolls. This afternoon in company with Lieut. Porter of the Brown county cavalry, I rode around and visited the rebel works, particularly the river batteries above and below town. Weather pleasant. Alfred Dodge, a deserter from our company, returned yesterday.[16]

Sunday, August 30. I attended divine service in town this morning. This afternoon I was engaged in reading. Weather very cool—the thermometer standing at 57 after sunrise this morning.

Monday, August 31. On duty, in town, as officer of post guard. Weather very pleasant. We were mustered this morning.

Tuesday, September 1. I was relieved from guard at 8 o'clock this morning.

Before returning to camp, I had a *negative* for some photographs taken. Quite a number of the furloughed men of our regiment returned today. I drew a new tent this afternoon.

Wednesday, Sep. 2. Our regiment, the 4th Minnesota and 63d Illinois, constituted a detachment under command of Col. Banbury to do "post guard" duty in town. This arrangement was just made on the 23d ult. and still continues. The citizens of Vicksburg, are repairing their houses and going to work as if they considered matters "settled" at this point, and the streets of the city present quite a busy appearance. I have spent the day in camp reading and writing letters. Weather warmer than it has been since August 23.

Thursday, Sep. 3. Poor and Fouts of our company (who have been home on furloughs) returned today. [Adam] Ritter & [William] Adamson started home on furlough this evening. Weather pleasant.

Friday, Sep. 4. Weather warmer than it was yesterday, but still pleasant. I went to town and got my photographs this afternoon. I made some appointments of non-commissioned officers in the company today.

Saturday, Sep. 5. This forenoon I visited the 10th Iowa. I have written several letters today and made out some company papers. Capt. Dumgan called to see us today.

Sunday, Sep. 6. On guard today in town. I attended and participated in the communion services at the Presbyterian Church this forenoon—the first opportunity I have had to partake of "the Lord's Supper" since I have been in the service. Weather warm.

Monday, Sep. 7. I was relieved from guard at 8 o'clock this morning and, procuring a horse from John Woodward, rode out to visit the 13th Iowa. On returning from the 13th, I found that our Division had orders to be ready to march with 10 days rations. Weather warm with indications of rain. Rain is much needed as the roads are very dusty.

Tuesday, September 8. This is about the warmest day we have had this year. The thermometer indicated 99 in the shade! We have heard nothing about marching today. I wrote to the *Free Press* and Register today.

Wednesday, September 9. Another very warm day.

Thursday, September 10. Weather warm. Our regiment was detailed this afternoon to unload boats to carry us up the river. A meeting of the regiment to express the views of the old 5th, on the candidates and issues now before the people of Iowa, was thwarted by our being detailed on duty and we lost the opportunity of letting General Tuttle know what a poor opinion we have of him.[17] We had made preparations to have a "good meeting." Speakers and music had been secured and all arrangements made to have a creditable meeting.

Friday, September 11. This morning we received notice that we would leave today and I made preparations accordingly. At sundown, the regiment moved down to the river and after unloading a lot of freight, we marched aboard the steamer *Adriatic*. Weather warm. Our whole Division is embarking on steamers and our destination is said to be Little Rock, Arkansas.

Saturday, September 12. We slept aboard the boat at the levee last night. At noon today we started up the river[;] our boat is a very slow one and has poor fuel and we had made poor time. At sundown we stopped at a Government wood yard at Island 102 to "wood." After "wooding" our boat started again and ran all night. Soon after going to bed I was startled by a crash that made nearly every man on the boat jump to his feet, and which I thought was some explosion. The hull of the boat had run onto a sand bar, and the crash was caused by the cabin's attempt to go ahead. The river is very low.

Sunday, September 13. Our boat reached [Lake] Providence [Louisiana] this morning about 8 o'clock and our boat stopped and took on a lot of planks for fuel. During the day, the boat stopped again and took on a lot of rails. Nothing of interest has transpired today. The Mississippi is a poor river to travel on for pleasure. Nothing can be seen from a boat in low water, for the banks, and nothing can be seen at a high stage, *for water*. Weather warm.

Monday, September 14. Our boat ran all night again and we found ourselves a short distance below Gaines' Landing this morning. We have stopped several times today to take in rails. All of our fleet, excepting one boat, have passed us and are "away head." We passed several boats of the Marine Brigade lying at Cypress Bend. We reached Napoleon [Arkansas] at dark and entered the mouth of the Arkansas river, and from it entered the "cut off" and made our way into the Mississippi again. Our boat stopped "for the night" a short distance above the mouth of the White River. Generals Desertion and Destitution are in command along the banks of the Mississippi at present. Weather warm with appearances of rain.

Tuesday, September 15. Our boat started before day this morning. At sunrise we stopped for rails. At 11 o'clock A.M. our boat landed at "Hunting Wild" near Island 67 for wood. The wood yard is kept by some darkies. From them we learned of the occupation of Little Rock by our forces.[18] They also informed us that the guerrillas had fired into one of our fleet as it passed their wood yard yesterday evening. The fire was returned from the boat and the guerrillas fled. We lay at Hunting Wild until 3 o'clock P.M. At night our boat stopped 20 miles below Helena. Weather warm with indications of rain.

Wednesday, September 16. Our boat reached Helena at 10 o'clock this morning and we immediately disembarked. We had Brigade Review this afternoon. We have orders to be ready to march at 4 o'clock in the morning. I have been on guard today.

Thursday, September 17. I made my bed on the river bank last night and slept very well, till morning. During the night our Colonel received orders countermanding our "marching orders." At 8 o'clock this morning our regiment marched to the brigade camp above town. This afternoon, our Division changed camp to a position on the river bank a mile below town. The weather "changed" today and is growing quite cool. Health good.

Friday, September 18. Last night was a very cold night and I slept poorly although I had two blankets over me. I got up this morning with a sore throat. We had Battalion and Brigade Drill this afternoon. Weather clear and cold. We were fortunate enough this evening to *borrow* some tents which belong to Steele's forces. Enough were borrowed for our whole Division.

Saturday, September 19. Another cold night—another clear, cool day. This is the anniversary of the Battle of Iuka—an anniversary that will ever be remembered by our regiment. Battalion Drill this forenoon—Brigade Drill in the afternoon. General Buford, our old Brigade commander, called on our brigade this afternoon and was given a fitting reception.

Sunday, September 20. Some of the officers of our regiment disgraced themselves & dishonored the dead of Iuka by celebrating the anniversary of the battle of Iuka by *getting drunk* last night. Weather clear and cool. Our Chaplain preached to a very slim audience this forenoon.

Monday, September 21. Weather pleasant. Quite an "occurrence" happened in our camp last night. When we left Vicksburg our Quartermaster drew ten days *"marching rations"* which consist of flour, crackers, coffee, sugar, and side meat. On a march, this would have been sufficient as *"foraging"* would have made up all deficiencies. But we did not march, and a brigade guard has been kept around camp so that "foraging" has been an impossibility. The side meat drawn was a *very inferior* article. The consequence of all this is what I am about to relate. The boys did not get enough to eat and grew hungry and discontented. The Quartermaster said he could not draw again until the "ten days' rations" were gone. Last night, at a late hour, when all honest people were abed, a company was organized (by getting a few men from each company in the regiment)—a Captain was chosen—and the crowd started for town. Having procured the *countersign,* they passed the pickets between camp and town as a "fatiguing party." On reaching town, they marched down to the levee where a negro sentinel was guarding a lot of commissary stores. Marching up close to him, the *Captain* halted his company and told the sentinel he had come for a lot of stores for the purpose of carrying them down to the steamer *New Kentucky.* He then sent one of the boys up town (ostensibly) to see the Quartermaster. This messenger soon returned flourishing a *requisition* and saying it was all right—all perfectly proper. The darkey, having no reason to doubt the word of the Captain (who wore a sword) and seeing the *requisition* said it was *"all right"*—he *"hoped they would take them all."* The party then went to work and carried off about thirty sacks of potatoes and onions and made their way back to camp. The darkey "Sergeant of the guard" came around soon after their departure and learning what had transpired, had his suspicions aroused and forthwith reported to the Quartermaster. The Quartermaster immediately started in pursuit and, tracing the boys through the pickets, came upon them in camp as they were dividing their plunder. His debut caused a general "scatterment" and the "spoils" were left in his hands. He waked up our Lt. Colonel and had the camp searched and succeeded in finding all but one or two sacks. A guard was established over them till this morning when they were hauled back to town. The *"Captain"* of the party and several of the "privates" were found out and had to pay for the missing sacks. *Moral:* Two wrongs will not make one right. There is a general feeling of discontent among the boys at staying in our present camp and a strong desire to get back to Vicksburg.

Tuesday, September 22. Weather beautiful. Orders have been issued prohibiting the quantity of any passes to leave camp. We had squad drill today. Fishing is getting to be quite a business with us. Many large catfish have been drawn from the "Father of Waters" in a few days past.

Wednesday, September 23. Weather very pleasant. Passes are "good" today. This forenoon, the tents of our regiment were re-arranged and the camp laid off in regular style. This forenoon, a wagon, six-mule team, and five men from our brigade were captured by guerrillas about five miles from camp while out after wood. A squad of cavalry started in pursuit but succeeded only in re-capturing the wagon. The mules and men were run off into the interior.

Thursday, September 24. We received news today of a battle between Rosecrans and Bragg in Northern Georgia—result doubtful.[19] We are anxious for further news. Drill as usual.

Friday, September 25. This morning we had to give up our borrowed tents, as they were going to be shipped to their *owners.* We are again left out in the cold. We received news today of Rosecrans' second day's fighting. Old Rosey seems to have been overpowered by superior numbers and compelled to fall back, after a gallant fight, with considerable loss. The enemy, however, seems to have been too badly punished to follow up their advantage. Among the thousands of good and brave [men] who fell on our side, I was deeply pained to find the name of "Adjutant John Shepherd, of the 9th Kentucky"—an old school-mate and ultimate friend. We have "orders for Memphis."

Saturday, September 26. Last night was another cold night and being without tents, we slept but poorly. This morning as the St[eame]r. R. Campbell, jr., stopped a few moments at the landing *John King* of Foster's Cavalry stopped off and brought me a package from home, containing kind remembrances from the near and dear friends of home. Several boat loads of troops passed up the [river] today, from (Sherman's Corps) Vicksburg. We received an order today announcing that our Division had been changed to the Second. Drill, as usual. Gen'l Matthies seems determined to keep us stirring.

Sunday, September 27. A beautiful day. Our Chaplain preached to a very slim assemblage forenoon. More troops from Sherman's Corps passed up today. I have spent the day reading.

Monday, September 28. Weather pleasant. We have been in readiness to leave today for Memphis but our boat has not yet arrived. This is my "birth-day"[—]a Quarter of a Century old! Over a third of the days allotted to man I have already passed and yet life seems to have just begun.

Thursday, September 29. We have been waiting anxiously all day for our boat. About three o'clock in the afternoon she hove in sight, but grounded on a sand bar just above Helena, where she remained for "two or three hours." In the evening we marched aboard our boat (the New Kentucky) and about 8 o'clock P.M. we started for Memphis. Weather warm and cloudy.

Wednesday, September 30. On the way to Memphis. It has rained all day. We arrived at Memphis about sundown. Being officer of the guard, I went down on to the bow of the boat when she landed to post the guards to keep the men from getting out into town. I was greatly and very agreeably surprised when the boat struck the landing to see Angus standing on the levee looking anxiously up into the crowd on the boat, to see JQA. I soon jumped ashore and shook his best paw and escorted him on the boat. He is on his way to take the vote of the 40th Iowa. Our destination is unknown to us whether will remain at Memphis or go to Rosecrans can only conjecture. Troops here and along the railroad are under marching orders.[20]

Thursday, Oct. 1. Weather clear & pleasant. Our regiment moved out to camp 2 miles north of town this morning. After going out to camp I came back to town to see Angus. We are still ignorant of our destination.

Friday, Oct. 2. In camp, Weather cool.

Saturday, Oct 3. Weather cool. Our baggage came up from Vicksburg today. At 5 o'clock this evening our brigade "packed up" and marched down to the Depot of the Memphis & Charleston R.R., where we stacked arms and waited for the 1st train. By half past nine, our baggage and teams were loaded on the cars and we got aboard and started for Lagrange. Our wagons were loaded on platform cars—our baggage was loaded on and around the wagons, and we were loaded (30 to a car) on the baggage. In this way we had to ride. The night was very cool and we had to sit up and almost froze, till we got beyond Moscow where the train, proving too heavy for the locomotive, was divided and we were left behind, while the Locomotive took the first half of the train on to Lagrange. We improved the opportunity by building big fires and warming our chilled and benumbed limbs. When we left Memphis, there were rumors of fighting at Lagrange.

Sunday, Oct. 4. The locomotive returned for our half of the train about sunrise this morning. At Lagrange, our train was united and a Locomotive hitched on to the other end. We then started on for Corinth. At Grand Junction our extra locomotive left us. At Saulsbury our train stopped an hour or more, for the *down train.* With several others, I walked ahead and had quite a little chase to catch the train as it came along on a heavy "up grade." We reached Corinth at 4 P.M. All the bridges along the R.R. are guarded—forts and stockades being built at all the principal bridges. At Corinth, our train was again divided and we remained in Corinth while the locomotive took the forward half of the train on to Glendale. At Corinth I met several Newton boys. The train came back from Glendale at 12 oclock, with orders for us to remain till morning.

Monday, Oct. 5. I slept very well last night under a shed in front of a bakery. This morning our train was again divided and we did not reach Glendale till noon. After unloading the cars we marched out 3/4ths of a mile to camp and erected our habitations. Weather cool. Glendale is merely a station, no town. We arrived in Corinth, just one year from the day of the battle—October 4th.

Tuesday, Oct. 6. Weather cool. I have been writing and "fixing up."

Wednesday, Oct. 7 On picket. Weather cool.

Thursday, Oct. 8. On being relieved from picket I went to camp and found our regiment marching out. Part of our brigade marched to Burnesville (7 miles from Glendale) a day or two ago. The balance of the brigade marched there today. We reached the town about noon.

Friday, Oct. 9. Five companies of our reg't (B.C.F.A. & K.) were roused up this morning at 3 o'clock and ordered to be ready to move at 6 1/2 o'clock. At sunrise, we got aboard a train and moved out east 2 miles to Walker's Station. We have our tents along and our business is to guard the Engineering regiment while they repair the R.R. We are to move along with them as they advance. Weather pleasant.

Saturday, Oct. 10. The engineers having completed the building of three bridges, we moved forward a mile to Dean's Mill. This evening Co. B. was detailed for picket. Weather pleasant.

Sunday, Oct. 11. Last night we stood picket at a bridge near Widow Jocelyn's. This morning we were thrown forward to a bridge about 2 1/2 miles from Iuka, where we have stood today. I sent a squad with dispatches to Gen. Osterhaus to Iuka today. Osterhaus' Division marched to Iuka yesterday.

Monday, Oct. 12. The balance of our regiment moved up and camped near Dean's Mill yesterday. As we were not relieved from picket till dark, we did not get our tents up, and I have been busy today building a bunk, fixing up desk, &c. Weather pleasant.

Tuesday, Oct. 13. Company on picket at Widow Jocelyn's. This is election day and we cast our vote before coming out. It has rained most of the day.

Wednesday, Oct. 14. We had quite an alarm on picket last night caused by the sentinel firing at some object supposed to be a man on the R.R. track. Four others fired at the object as it ran, and we (we were on the advanced post) thought the inside post was attacked, and started to reinforce the boys when we met them, coming to inform us of the cause of the disturbance. The result of the election in our regiment, yesterday was as follows: Stone 302; Tuttle 12— Total vote 318—four voted for no candidate for governor.[21] This evening I had a talk with Col. B., which did me some good, but agitated *him* considerably— "facts are stubborn things."

Thursday, Oct. 15. In camp, writing letters. Rain.

Friday, Oct. 16. A beautiful day. I have been on picket with the company today at Walker's Station. My Mulatto servant boy, a bright, intelligent fellow, died this afternoon of some disease, the Surgeon could not name. He was taken sick last evening and thought he had the ague. After I went on picket this morning he was taken suddenly worse and died about the middle of the afternoon. The physician, being ignorant of the nature of his disease, could do nothing for him. He is supposed to have been bitten by some insect and poisoned. While on picket this evening, four refugees from Tuscaloosa County, Alabama, came in, bound for Union lines. They had been conscripted and forced into the rebel army, but being Union men, they deserted.

Saturday, Oct. 17. On being relieved from picket this afternoon, I had my servant's body buried near camp. A sad burying the funeral of the downtrodden African is.

Sunday, Oct. 18. A heavy rain fell last night. Our Chaplain preached two good sermons today. Weather pleasant. This afternoon I spent two or three hours in the woods reading. This evening we received orders to prepare for a march. Gen. Sherman is about to start on an expedition with the following force: 2nd Division—[Brig. Gen.] Morgan Smith. 1st Division—J.P. Osterhaus. 3d Divison John E. Smith. 4th Div. [Brig. Gen. Hugh] Ewing. We expect to march Tuesday. Part of the force had already gone to Iuka.

Monday, Oct. 19. I walked down to Burnesville this morning and got there just in time to see our Divison moving out on the road to Iuka. My business being thus "knocked in the head," I took the first train and came back. Weather very pleasant. This afternoon, we were paid for July & August. At dark we received marching orders and loading our "traps" on the cars, we marched to Iuka where we arrived about 11 o'clock P.M. The cars did not arrive till nearly morning and my blankets being on them, I got but very little sleep. We stopped in the streets all night. The Army is jubilant over the Election news from the North.[22]

Tuesday, Oct. 20. Early this morning we moved out to the Brigade camp southeast of town. Soon after getting our tents "up" we received orders to be ready to march by noon, but noon and night came, but we did not march. Weather cloudy.

Wednesday, Oct. 21. At 9 o'clock this morning we "struck tents" and loaded our wagons. It commenced raining about the time we got our wagons loaded and continued till after noon. Before the regiment moved out of camp, company B was detailed to go to town on fatigue, where we reported to the Divison Quartermaster. After loading 13 wagons with grain, we "waited for orders" until about 3 o'clock when we [grew] tired of waiting, we started for our regiment, but before we got out of town, "orders" overtook us, and we had some more fatiguing to do. At 3 o'clock we started to overtake our regiment. Our division started in the forenoon for Bear Creek, but owing to the rain and mud, made but poor progress. We overtook our regiment after marching about 5 miles at a point where it remained during the night. Weather cloudy in afternoon with appearances of rain.

Thursday, Oct. 22. At day-light this morning we started on the march and reached Bear Creek about 8 o'clock. At 10 o'clock we camped 2 miles east of Bear Creek—having marched 4 miles in all. Weather clear.

Friday, Oct. 23. Some very stringent orders were read last-night on Dress Parade from Gen. Sherman with regard to the conduct of our army on the march. Rain commenced falling about the middle of the last night and continued during today. At nine o'clock A.M. we struck tents and loaded our wagons and at 10 o'clock we started through rain and mud for Dickson, Alabama 4 miles about. At noon we reached Dickson and camped on or around a "knob" in a most beautiful valley. By the time we camped the wind had shifted to the north and was blowing very cold. We heard today that the Divisions ahead of us (Osterhaus' and Morgan L. Smith's) have had a fight with the enemy.[23] The R.R. between Dickson and Bear Creek is very badly damaged.

Saturday, Oct. 24. In camp at Dickson. Weather cold and windy and getting "more so." I have been busy today, writing and posting books.

Sunday, Oct. 25. Company B was detailed for escort this morning and reported at Division Hdqrtrs, at 8 A.M. and escorted a forage train to and from a plantation 2 miles north of camp. Weather moderating. No divine services today, our Chaplain being absent.

Monday, Oct. 26. In camp. Weather warm and cloudy.

Tuesday, Oct. 27. On camp guard. I have employed my time today making out muster rolls. Osterhaus and Smith's Divisions which have been camped 2 miles in advance of us, moved ahead yesterday morning—having only skirmishing with the enemy. Weather clear and pleasant.

Wednesday, Oct 28. Boats were heard on the Tennessee last night. The R.R. being repaired up to this point, two trains came up today. I have been employed on the muster rolls today. [John] Huffman of Co. H has been assigned to duty in camp.

Thursday, Oct 29. At 3 1/2 o'clock this morning we had reveille and at 6 o'clock our Division (the 5th Iowa in advance) started for Chickasaw on the Tennessee River, 12 miles due west of Dickson's Station. Soon after starting we heard very brisk artillery firing in our rear, which continued for half an hour. It proved to be Osterhaus shelling some rebel cavalry who were threatening his train as he moved out of camp to follow us. The road today runs through (or over) a very hilly and rocky country to one or two valleys of very pleasing appearance to our weary eyes as we neared Chickasaw, which we reached about 1 o'clock P.M. One or two of our gunboats now lie on the river at Eastport which is in sight about one mile below. As we expected to cross the river we did not put up our tents till evening, when it commenced raining. The Tennessee is at a good stage for navigation. Chickasaw is a "one horse town."

Friday, Oct 30. We had reveille at 5 o'clock this morning and struck tents and loaded our wagons as soon as we got our breakfasts. It commenced raining soon after we struck tents and continued at continually through the day. The 93d Ills. crossed on the gunboat and barge today, to open a road on the other side of the river. At 3 o'clock we got orders to stay till morning and again "pitched our tents." The 1st and 2d brigade are crossing the river this afternoon. Ewing's Division is here. Osterhaus' is crossing here. Morgan L. Smith's Division will cross at Tuscumbia where it is reported to be. All four Divisions are to report *towards* Chattanooga by order of Genl. Grant. The R.R. east of Iuka will probably be abandoned. I have been busy all evening making out "returns."

Saturday, Oct 31. A bright pleasant day. The first and second brigades of our Division crossed the river today. Our regiment was mustered this afternoon. I found John, Ed, & Harry Patterson on the "Anglo-Saxon" at the river crossing this afternoon.[24]

Sunday, Nov 1. I was on duty with the company last night till midnight loading the Division train on the boat. Soon after getting asleep, after the "fatigue work" was over, I was awakened by heavy skirmishing on our picket line. I got up and got ready for action thinking we were about to be attacked. It proved to be only an attack on Osterhaus' Division pickets which was soon "*over.*" This morning at daylight we struck tents and marched to the crossing where we "stacked arms" and awaited for our turn to cross the river. Most of the day was accompanied in getting our trains over the river, and we did not cross until about 4 o'clock P.M. I spent the day aboard the boat with Harry Patterson from whom I gathered many items of *Ripley News.* After crossing the river we marched out about a mile to Waterloo (a small village) where we camped for the night. Weather clear and pleasant. Ewing's Division has crossed the river at Eastport and is now on the road to Stevenson, Ala. Morgan L. Smith's and Osterhaus' Division are at Chickasaw ready to cross and follow us, and one Division ([Brig. Gen. Grenville] Dodge's from Corinth will be at Eastport by the time Osterhaus and Smith cross) to follow them. Our corps will thus consist of *five* divisions. Gen. Sherman has already started for Stevenson with the cavalry. Our first and second brigades have been on the road today. I saw Charley Bramble on the Anglo-Saxon today. Until we reached our destination we will be cut off from all "mail communication." "Farewell vain World!"

Monday, Nov. 2 At 6 1/2 o'clock A.M. our brigade started eastward—our regiment being rear guard. Our route for about 8 miles lay up the Tennessee valley, from there we bore more into the interior, passing through the village of Gravel Springs. At 6 1/2 o'clock P.M. we camped on Cypress Creek, 25 miles from Waterloo and from Florence. The roads today have been very good. Grading and bridging is all that is necessary to make a first class gravel road from Waterloo to this point. The country we passed through on the first half of the route was broken and hilly. The hills and valleys are covered with gravel, but the soil in the valley is very rich. Good springs and clear streams are numerous. The inhabitants are poor and ignorant. The country along the latter half our route was less broken and better cultivated. The timber through this country is very good.—Pine, Oak, Gum, Poplar, and Hickory. Weather pleasant.

Tuesday, Nov. 3. Started this morning at 7 1/2 o'clock and around Cypress Creek near the ruins of some Cotton Mills. These mills were taken from a Union man and run for the benefit of the Confederacy. They were consequently burned by our cavalry some time since. About 100 men from the mills are now in the loyal Alabama cavalry regiment which is near Corinth as we passed by this morning a lot of young ladies had gathered by the roadside and cheered for the Union as we marched by. We marched through Florence with colors flying and music playing. Florence is a pretty place of about 1000 inhabitants. We passed through without halting. About the middle of the after noon, we crossed Shoal Creek (a very pretty stream) on a covered bridge, 450 ft. long. We camped at sundown, 13 miles east of Florence—16 from Cypress Creek. Country we have passed through today has been rolling and well suited for cultivation. Most of it has been under cultivation. The timber is about the same as yesterday. Weather is clear and pleasant.

Wednesday, Nov. 4. Started at 6 1/2 o'clock A.M. and reached Rogersville at noon, where we overtook the balance of our Division. We crossed Blue Water, Clear Creek, and Second Creek, three beautiful streams, on the route. These streams are generally shallow and we cross them by making bridges on rafts of rails. Soon after reaching Rogersville, the first and second brigades started out on a road heading N.E. from the village. The rebels are said to have burned the bridge over Elk River, 4 miles E. of Rogersville, and thus changed our course. After half an hour we started out on the same road the other brigades had taken. At Sundown, we stopped at Anderson's Creek, 7 miles from Rogersville—having marched 18 miles during the day. Country and timber are the same as yesterday. There is a considerable sprinkling of the male population at home in this region. On the first day of our march some of these "citizens" gobbled a sutler's goods that were left behind on a wagon that broke down. They might have done more. Weather clear and pleasant.

Thursday, Nov. 5. Started at 7 o'clock A.M. marched in a N.E. direction through a very hilly region. Halted 2 hours at noon on Sugar Creek. Camped after dusk, at Gilbertsboro on Shoal Creek, 14 miles from our camp on Anderson's Creek. It has rained nearly all day and is still "at it." The roads have been very bad. The soil along the route is very rich and the timber excellent—Oak, Gum, Poplar, Hickory, Hackberry, Beech, and Walnut—Pine has disappeared. Near Sugar Creek we passed through Ewing's slaughter yard where his men had captured and killed a lot of fine *porkers* which some guerrillas were driving South.

Friday, Nov. 6. Started at 8 o'clock A.M.—crossed Shoal Creek and marched in a N.E. direction—passed through Bethel, (a small village) 2 miles from

Gilbertsboro—reached the Nashville and Decatur R.R. at a point six miles N.E. of Bethel—marched 2 miles North, alongside the R.R. and then turned on in a N.E. direction—marched half mile, over a high hill and camped on its side at 9 o'clock P.M. We have been delayed today by one of the trains of the other brigades, the roads being very bad. The country we have passed through today is one of the finest regions for farming I ever beheld. We passed from Alabama into Tennessee, just before reaching Bethel. We passed quite a number of fields of "winter wheat" today and saw some excellent stone fences. Just before reaching the R.R. we crossed a small creek. The R.R. is a first class road. Distance travelled today 10 1/2 miles. Weather clear and pleasant.

Saturday, Nov. 7. Started at 9 o'clock A.M.—marched 3 miles to a ford on Richland creek, where the men forded the stream which was four feet deep at the ford. I was fortunate enough to ride across on a horse. After crossing the creek, we marched 1 1/2 miles in a N.E. direction, where we struck the Nashville and Huntsville pike—we marched 5 miles on the pike in a S.E. direction—we then took the road to Fayetteville and marched 7 miles in a N.E. direction, over a rough road, and camped near a creek. The country along the pike was well adapted for farming and is well improved. Since we left the pike the country has been rough and hilly although the soil is good. Weather clear and pleasant. While we were resting after fording Richland Creek this forenoon, one of the boys in the company fired a charge of damp powder out of his gun, for which he was arrested by the Colonel and I was arrested by the same *power* because I did not arrest the man who fired the gun. Not being in command of the company, I didn't consider it my business. Lieut. Huffman and the "Officers of the Day" both saw the gun fired and took no notice of it, but not a word was said to either of them. I may have deserved censure but "faulting this and that together," it looks much too much like *spite* work. All I have to do is "grin and bear it." Timber about same as yesterday excepting "more beech."

Sunday, Nov. 8.—Started at 8 o'clock—marched in eastern direction crossed Short Creek, Swan Creek, and several small branches—country hilly roads bad. We have been delayed today by teams of the brigade in front of us. At Swan Creek, cedar made its appearance among the timber. We camped at sun-down on the North bank of the Elk River 3 miles from Fayetteville in a fertile region of country. Weather clear and cool. We marched 14 miles today.

Monday, Nov. 9—Started at 8 o'clock and marched one mile when we were ordered into camp at the bridge over Cane Creek—2 miles from Fayettsville. The first and second brigade and Ewing's Division are camped near. The cause of our halting here has not yet been made known to us. Last night was a cold night and today the weather gives promise of getting "no better fast." I am still "under arrest." We have various rumors of fighting at Chattanooga. We have received no mail since leaving Chickasaw.

Tuesday, Nov. 10. Last night was a clear cold night, the coldest we have had this season. I slept but poorly. At 11 o'clock A.M. we started again on the march. A march of two miles brought us to Fayetteville, an ordinary "country town" of about 800 inhabitants. We passed through the town and crossed to the south bank of Elk River on a bridge built entirely of limestone, supported by six arches—the whole structure being a credit to the county and the state. It was erected by an Indianian. After crossing the bridge, we continued our march in a serpentine course for five miles over hills and through valleys, when we ascended a high hill, when we reached what appeared to be a piece of table-land. We marched eastward, on this up-land for five miles and camped. Distance marched 12 miles. Weather pleasant and moderating. Morgan L. Smith's Division is marching close behind us today. Rations getting scarce.

Wednesday, Nov. 11. Weather clear and cool. We started at 7 o'clock this morning—marched 10 miles on the "upland" road and then descended into the valley of the foot of the Cumberland mountains. We then marched North East 3 miles to the village of Salem and 4 1/2 miles up the valley towards Winchester when we camped. The country for the first ten miles we travelled today was poor, barren, and uninhabited. The valley at the foot of the mountains is only moderately fertile and is now perfectly desolate, having suffered the ravages of war at the hands of both parties. Salem is almost deserted—it is a small village 10 miles S.W. of Winchester and north of the Winchester and Fayetteville R.R. Rations were brought to us on the cars from Winchester this evening. We received a large mail today.

Thursday, Nov. 12. Started at 7 o'clock A.M.—marched 3 miles towards Winchester and camped. I have employed myself today to writing letters. We will probably start for Chattanooga tomorrow. Gen. Grant is evidently gathering a large army at Chattanooga, and a big battle will doubtless be fought in Northern Georgia within 30 days. It is useless to speculate as the result. While I *believe* that it will result in a great victory for our army, I cannot tell what the *result* will be, if even we should be victorious. Every day my conviction becomes firmer that the hand of *God* is in this and that in spite of victories and advantages he will deny us Peace unless we grant to others the liberties we ask for ourselves—"break every yoke and let the oppressed go free." The difficulties of this war have proved knotty questions to our Belshazzars and our "wise men" but in a generation from this time, every child will be a Daniel—able to interpret the handwriting of God, telling us that we have not been faithful to the charge he committed to our trust.[25] My earnest prayer to God is that we may have mercy and not judgement. I believe that our Nation will yet emerge from the conflict, entire and triumphant but it will only be after she has been purged with fire. Weather pleasant. Sent a squib [i.e., letter] to C[harley, (Campbell's younger brother)].

Friday, Nov. 13. Marched 20 miles. 2 miles to Winchester the country seat of Franklin Co. and a town of some 800 Inhabitants thence E. 2 miles to Dechard, a station on the Nashville and Decatur R.R. then S. 8 miles to Cowan, a station on same road, then S.E. over the mountains to an old camp of

Rosecrans forces on the mountain 8 miles from Cowan. From the base to the top of the mountain (some two miles by the road) the road was very bad, being rough and rocky, it being about impossible at times for the horses to get a footing. After getting on top of the mountain the road has been very good. These mountains are not much more than a *big hill* the highest being but 500 ft. We left camp this morning at 7 o'clock and camped this evening about five. We passed two farms after getting on top of the mountain. Timber on the mountain—hickory, oak, ash, sugar, chestnut, etc. on the side of the mountain among the rocks, where there is good soil—red cedar. We are living on scant rations. Still *"under arrest."*

Saturday, Nov 14. Our brigade has been the advance of the Division today for the first time since we crossed the Tennessee. We started at 7 o'clock A.M. Until 10 o'clock A.M. we marched through the rain. The clouds then "dried up." From camp to the foot of the mountains, some ten miles, the road was about the same as yesterday. We descended from the mountain into *"Sweet's Cove,"* a narrow valley in East Tennessee (in Marion county). We marched down the valley along *Sweet's Creek* some 4 miles and camped in a fertile valley, which is divided into small farms and has been well cultivated. The population is loyal almost "to a man." Most of the adult males are in our army. Weather clear this evening. There are no negro cabins, and I suppose, no slaves in *"Sweet's Cove."*

Sunday, Nov. 15. Started at 9 o'clock—marched down Sweet Creek to the Tennessee (around 6 miles)—then down the Tennessee six miles to Bridgeport—12 miles in all. Camped on the hill-side above the bridge. We received a large mail after getting into camp. The *town* of Bridgeport is *wanting.* The R.R. bridge is not yet completed. A pontoon bridge spans the stream under the R.R. bridge. The bridges from the main shores to an island in the center of the stream. The river is in good navigable condition. "Our folks" have built three transports here which are now plying the river and an *iron-clad* is now under process of construction. Weather pleasant. A large fort frowns upon us from the opposite side of the river but it is on "friendly terms" with us. We have marched 195 miles since we crossed the Tennessee river—13 miles a day for 15 days. We are now in Jackson County, Alabama.

Monday, Nov. 16. In camp at Bridgeport. Weather cloudy. We have heard firing at Chattanooga today. I have been busy writing.

Tuesday, Nov. 17. In camp at Bridgeport. Weather clear.

Wednesday, Nov. 18. Ewing's Division crossed the rivers on the pontoon bridge yesterday. Morgan L. Smith's Division arrived at B[ridgeport] today. We have reveille at 5 o'clock this morning and fixed to march by 7 A.M. We did not move, however, until 10 A.M. when we marched down to the bridge where we remained until 2 o'clock, P.M. when we crossed the river on a pontoon, some 480 yards in length. There are some light earthworks on the island. After crossing we marched 9 miles—crossing from Alabama into Georgia and from Georgia into Tennessee. Near Shell mound we passed *"Nigga-Jack"* cave—a large cave, which extends some 15 miles into the mountain and [contains] some nitre beds which the rebels formerly worked. A large clear stream—about a solid yard of water—issued from the mouth of the cave. We marched 10 miles to day and [I] was released from arrest this morning without trial or request.

Thursday, Nov. 19. Marched 20 miles—camping at sun-down in the bend, opposite Chattanooga. Brigade marched in the advance of the Division and our regiment in front of the brigade. We have beheld some splendid mountain scenery today. Our route has been up the valley alongside the Memphis & Charleston R.R. At Falling Waters we passed a brigade of troops in camp. While resting at one point I saw Will Parker (formerly of the *Bee* offices) now a captain in 75th Ills. Regt. The last 8 or 10 miles of the route we marched was down the Lookout Valley along the base of Lookout Mountain in plain view of the rebels, but we were not molested. We passed Hooker's battle-ground and also his headquarters and saw the veritable *"Fighting Joe"* himself, as he stood in front of this tent taking his first view of troops from the Army of the Mississippi.[26] He is a fine looking man. His camp is well fortified. We crossed the pontoon at Browns Ferry and camped in the bend on the north bank of the stream. Ewing's corps yesterday occupied the town of Trenton, Georgia, driving the rebels out. Weather pleasant. The arrival of "Sherman's Army" is hailed with pleasure by the troops here.

Friday, Nov. 20. We were waked this morning at 2 o'clock and ordered to be ready to march in 20 minutes. We had no time to eat breakfast. We however did not start until 3 1/2 o'clock when we "pushed out" with only one team to the regiment. We got on the wrong road (which led to Chattanooga) and by the time we had found our mistake and got back on the right road, it was 4 o'clock. We marched 3 miles northward and halted in a valley, where we cannot be seen by the enemy. The object in moving before day was to keep such movements concealed from the enemy. The first and second brigades are with us—they having marched nearly all night. Our train came up, today, the trains are constantly moving up and down the valley. The movement of the train in day time would not attract attention. From the best class I can gain, I judge that the design in sending us here is to conceal us until Sherman's whole force comes up, when we will throw a pontoon across the river above here and establish ourselves in positions on the enemy's right flank—threatening his R.R. communication. I ascended a peak near our camp this morning from which I obtained a view of Chattanooga and our batteries (on Moccasin Point) shelling the rebels on Lookout Mountain. This afternoon I ascended another peak (much higher than the one this morning) on which our Signal Corps has a station. From this peak I obtained a view of the "scene of conflict" and the surrounding country—the positions of both armies—Bragg's headquarters, etc. The right of our line (Hooker) rests in Lookout Valley. The rebel left rests on Lookout Mountain, which juts out into the river and lies between Lookout Valley and Chattanooga. The rebels lines extend from Lookout Mountain, along Missionary Ridge, parallel with and about 2 miles from the river, to a point some five miles above Chattanooga where the Atlanta R.R. passes [through] the mountains. Missionary Ridge extends to Chickamauga Creek some 7 miles above Chattanooga. Our main army lies in and close around Chattanooga, where we have some strong works. A small part of our force lies in the bend opposite Chattanooga, on the north side of the stream. Rain this evening. Deserters are coming into our lines every day—about 100 every 24 hours. A captain and 89 men came in one squad a few nights since. The rebels pickets and ours are stationed within 10 yards of each other at the base of Lookout Mountain. They live on amicable terms with each other but do no shooting.

Saturday, Nov. 21. It rained nearly all night and all this forenoon. This afternoon is cloudy and getting cool. All our tents (excepting one to the company) were left at Bridgeport[;] some of the boys had to sleep out in the rain last night. Gum blankets were above *par.* Morgan L. Smith's Division came up last night and camped in one of the mountain coves. Gen. Sherman came up today. We will probably remain here until the Corps all come up when we will probably cross the river on a pontoon bridge (which is being prepared) above the mouth of the Chickamauga Creek. "Then comes the tug of war" *Later!* We have orders to be ready to march at a moment's notice, with one blanket, three day's rations, and 100 rounds of cartridges to the man. Gen. Thomas' [*Entry ends here.*]

Sunday. Nov. 22. We did not move last night as we anticipated we should. Weather clear. Dodge Porter of Foster's Cavalry called to see me today. He came from Vicksburg with dispatches from Genls. Smith and Sherman. Went with him to headquarters. I heard Gen. Smith state that we would cross the river tonight, and have a fight or a foot race tomorrow. I saw Gen. Grant, [Maj. Gen. David] Hunter, [Brig. Gen. Montgomery] Meigs, [Maj. Gen. Francis Preston] Blair, Ewing, Smith, & [Brig. Gen. John] Corse at headquarters. I attended preaching in camp this afternoon.

Monday, Nov. 23. We did not cross the river last night although the batteries and part of the infantry force started down to the crossing last evening. Orders postponing movement for 24 hours were received from Gen Grant about 9 o'clock P.M. Weather cloudy today. This afternoon Gen. Thomas' forced attacked the enemy near Chattanooga and drove them from a line of rifle pits. One could hear the firing (which was every heavy at time) quite plainly. We do not know particulars.[27]

Tuesday Nov. 24. At 12 o'clock last night we were called up and our Division started for the river. After marching 1 1/2 miles we arrived at the river and began crossing. Morgan L. Smith's division passed over ahead of us and captured all of the enemy's pickets but one. We crossed in pontoon boats (30 men to a boat) and landed just below the mouth of Chickamauga creek. Our Division was all across by daylight. Ewing's Division crossed next and Jeff Davis' Division (of

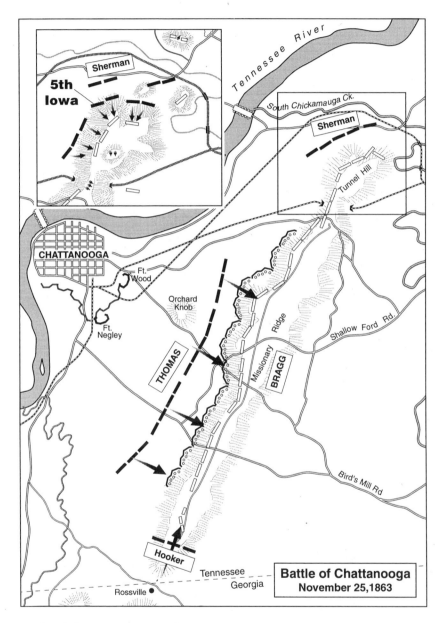

Battle of Chattanooga, November 25, 1863.

Thomas' army) after Ewing. As soon as a regiment landed it began entrenching, and by daylight we had a long line of works thrown up along a low ridge just below the mouth of Chickamauga creek in an open field. We expected the enemy to attack us every moment, but for some unaccountable reason they did not molest us. After getting suitable works thrown up, we waited the crossing of our artillery. It could not be brought up until a pontoon bridge was laid. By noon, the bridge was done and the artillery commenced crossing. Early in the morning a small steamer came up from Chattanooga and assisted in ferrying troops over. When our artillery had crossed, our army was instantly put in motion for the north end of Missionary Ridge—moving in three columns of "battalions closed in mass"—Ewing's Division on the right, John E. Smith's in the center, and Morgan L. Smith's Division on the left. After marching 2 miles across the bottom (through timber and under-brush, most of the way) we struck the foot of Missionary Ridge. Morgan L. Smith's Division, having better ground to march over, reached the top of the ridge first—and as his skirmishers ran up the ridge they saw a rebel regiment coming up the other side of the ridge, snapping caps to clear their guns for action. The rebs were intending to occupy the ridge but they were *a little too slow.* As each Division ascended the ridge each regiment deployed into a line of battle. Ewing's Division formed a line up and down the west side of the ridge facing south. Morgan L. Smith's Division occupied the crest of the ridge. The rebels soon opened fire on us from a gun farther along the ridge, and threw shell over us until one of Ewing's batteries "hushed it up" by a shot from a 24-pounder. As soon as our troops got into position they began fortifying and continued it during the night. At sundown the 1st and 2d brigades of our division were marched down into the bottom to guard the ridge and Jeff Davis' division still was at the river. Weather (last night and today) cloudy and smoky. Thomas' forces have been doing some heavy fighting today on Lookout Mountain.[28]

Wednesday, Nov. 25. At one o'clock this morning our regiment was deployed as skirmishers on alone stretching from Ewing's line at the foot of the ridge to Jeff Davis' line, near the river. We were thrown out as pickets and had to keep a close watch. About sunrise Morgan L. Smith's and Ewing's Division moved southward along Missionary Ridge and found the enemy in force on the ridge, just over the Railroad Tunnels. Some fierce fighting was done, but without driving the rebels from their position. Our army appears to have been poorly handled. From our position in the woods we could hear, but could not see, the conflict going on. About noon we received an order to "assemble on the left." As soon as we could we assembled, and were immediately marched to our brigade. Our brigade was then marched southwards between the Ridge and the East Tennessee Railroad, until we reached a point nearly opposite the Tunnel. We then marched by the front into a meadow, in plain view of the rebels and within a mile of their batteries. We lay down on the edge of the field and "waited for something to turn up." We had not long to wait. We soon had one rebel battery (on our right flank) throwing shells at

Confederates defend Tunnel Hill against Sherman's assault. From a wartime sketch by A. R. Waud.

us, and in a few minutes another battery could be seen moving into position in our front. This battery soon made our position too hot for comfort. One shell killed one man and wounded two in the 10th Iowa. Then Matthies, seeing that we were getting into "business" moved us by the left flank behind a low ridge where were shielded from the enemy's fire. We had been in this position but a few moments when an officer rode up to Gen. Matthies and commanded him to move is brigade up to "that white house" (which lay just below the tunnel and under the rebel batteries—3/4ths of a mile from our position). The general instantly started us in line, on "double quick" for the point designated. As we crossed the field the rebels swept the field with the batteries, and solid shot, shell, and grape flew about us in a most unbecoming manner over our heads, and but few in the ranks were struck. However, their shell[s] fell very close to our heads, just missing us. One exploded so near us that I felt the heat of it very plainly, and the smoke of it curled around Sergeant Pennywitt's head (he was just behind me) making him (as he expressed it) "feel the queerest kind." On arriving at the "white house" Gen. Matthies saw that it was a position too much exposed and he moved the brigade farther up the hill. Our regiment was on the right of the brigade as we entered a piece of timber (about 250 yards from the rebel lines) a minie ball struck me on top of the head and knocked me down. Here my connection with the regiment for the time ceased. The brigade moved on up to the brow of the ridge and engaged the rebels, our regiment was moved by the flank to the right and engaged the rebels above the tunnel. All but two companies were deployed as skirmishers, the ground the regiment had to hold being so extensive. The other two companies were about being ordered out as skirmishers, when the rebs made a *bulge* on our line, and came *swarming* out of the tunnel and going around in rear of our line.[29] The order was then given for the boys to "save themselves and get out of here." The boys threw their blankets, haversacks, and canteens and "ran for dear life," the rebs firing at them as they ran and calling on them to "halt," "stop," and "surrender." Quite a number of the boys were "gobbled" there going to far up the hill to get out before they were surrounded. Corporals [Silas] Copper, [Isaac] Loudenback and [John] Volk, and privates, [Dan] Bixler, Courtwright, [David] Loudenback, and [John] Sparks were captured. Bixler had previously captured one of the Sixth Texas and sent him to the rear. Our major, adjutant, colors, and 80 men were captured—2 were killed and 24 wounded.[30] General Matthies was wounded in the head. Colonel Putnam of the 93d Ill. was killed while sitting on his horse holding the colors of his regiment. The 2nd brigade was moved up the support of ours, but only succeeded in losing a great many of the men. The design in sending our brigade into the position it was ordered to take is a mystery to us. I suppose it was "ordered" and that was sufficient. We were whipped, but it was the fault of our generals, not of the men. Our charge is highly spoken of by lookers on. Gen. Sherman has certainly not improved his reputation by operations today. He has not gained a single position and his army has lost heavily. I am not now (nor ever was) an admirer of Gen. Sherman for he has only succeeded at failing.[31] In every expedition and undertaking he has tried during the war he has sacrificed more lives than any other general in the Western Army. When the rebels marched their troops on their right to meet our attack this afternoon General Thomas pierced their center and drove them from Missionary Ridge at that point.[32] Our dead and wounded are in the hands of the enemy. When I was knocked down, I was somewhat confused and lay for some minutes where I fell. I then got up, and left the field. After getting out of the reach of the rebel shell, I stopped and bathed my head which was smarting and swelling from the wound. The ball had glanced off the top of my head cutting a gash about the size of the ball. I found on examination of the wound that I was "worse scared" than hurt. "Better luck next time."[33] Weather clear and cool.

Thursday, Nov. 26. This is National Thanksgiving Day and we have new cause for returning thanks. Last night, under cover of the darkness, Bragg withdrew his army and is now on the skedaddle with our forces after him. Our forces started in pursuit some two or three hours before day. The rebels left our dead and wounded and their own dead on the field. They stripped our dead

Contemporary photograph of the railroad tunnel at Tunnel Hill, on the north end of Missionary Ridge. Library of Congress.

of all but their underclothing. At sun-rise our Division moved down to the river for rations. At noon, we joined in the pursuit in crossing Chickamauga creek and moving up its right-bank. At 9 o'clock P.M. we halted for the night—2 miles east of Chickamauga Station. At Chickamauga Station, we saw large piles of corn and meat burning which the rebels had set fire to. Large piles of corn were left untouched much to the gratification of our stock, which has been literally starving. We do not know the full results of our victory yet. Several thousand prisoners have been taken and "still they come." Weather pleasant.

Friday, Nov. 27. Weather pleasant. We started at an early hour this morning. After marching five miles we are arrived at Pigeon Gap and halted for two hours. At this Gap, Osterhaus' force captured a rebel battery this morning. At this point—Thomas' Army, which had been pursuing on another road, came on the road we have been traveling and has "taken the lead." After resting two hours we were informed that we would not move till morning. In the afternoon, I visited the 70th Ohio and saw some old acquaintances. Deserters and prisoners are still coming in. Longstreet's Corps of the rebel army, which started for Knoxville, a week or two ago, may get in a very tight place if it does not hastily retrace its steps.[34] Our army will soon be in its front, flank and rear, if it does not skedaddle.

Saturday, Nov. 28. Soon after retiring last night, rain commenced falling and disturbed our slumbers since we were all "out in the weather." The rain continued till noon today. At seven o'clock our Division started on the back track through mud and rain and at 4 o'clock P.M. we arrived in our old camp in the bend, north of Chattanooga. We had a very tiresome march but we are satisfied to get back to our blankets and tents. We do not know the reason of our being sent back.

Sunday, Nov. 29. Last night was cold and disagreeable and today the weather is improving for the worse. Nothing doing.

Monday, Nov. 30. In camp. Weather cold but more agreeable. Rations scarce, and we are having a pretty tough time.[35]

Tuesday, Dec. 1. Weather clear, cold and pleasant. Our Division was reviewed this evening by Genls. Grant and Hunter, accompanied by Gen. Logan, Meigs, and Smith. Our army pursued Bragg as far as Ringgold and after tearing up the R.R. track for 12 or 15 miles returned. On their return they buried our dead whom the rebels had left unburied since the battle of Chickamauga. Gen Sherman, with a heavy force, is now after Longstreet.[36]

Wednesday, Dec. 2. Weather clear and cool. We were paid for September and October today. Rations are very scarce. Some of the boys had no bread today.

7

———◦◦◦◦———

"What Can't Be Cured, Must Be Endured"
In Garrison and on Furlough, December 3, 1863–May 13, 1864

Winter was generally a season of quiet for Civil War armies. The cold temperatures and more frequent rains further complicated the already arduous business of active campaigning. Offensive action was not out of the question—in February 1864 Sherman launched a 150-mile raid from Vicksburg against the Confederate supply center at Meridian, Mississippi—but it was certainly unusual. Campbell's experience with the Fifth Iowa was typical. He and the regiment spent the winter of 1863–64 mainly engaged in guarding the railroads supplying the Union army at Chattanooga.

During this period, both sides prepared for the coming campaign of 1864—a campaign that would be waged on the political as well as the military front. Seeking to capitalize on the decline in Confederate morale that accompanied the defeats at Gettysburg, Vicksburg, and Chattanooga, Lincoln on December 8 issued a Proclamation of Amnesty and Reconstruction. It combined generous terms for pardon and amnesty to those who would take the oath of allegiance to the United States with an equally lenient plan whereby if 10 percent of the number of 1860 voters within a given state took the oath, they would be permitted to form a state government and send representatives to Congress. Campbell saw numerous Alabama citizens take the oath of allegiance and also attended a meeting in which the citizens of Huntsville considered the possibility of returning to the Union, but only in Louisiana and Tennessee did Lincoln's "10 percent" plan make real headway.

Instead, most Confederates pinned their hopes on the fact that 1864 was a presidential election year in the North, and Northern war weariness might result in the repudiation of Lincoln and the elevation of a candidate willing to accept a negotiated peace. They might also have pondered the fact that the term of service for Union soldiers who had enlisted in 1861 was about to expire, and that the Northern war effort was poised to lose its most experienced reservoir of military manpower. Unlike Confederate soldiers, who by law had to serve for the duration of the war, the term of service for most Union soldiers was three years. The enlistments of the first 1861 volunteers were due to expire in April 1864. After that, the priceless pool of veterans would drain steadily away—unless the veterans themselves forestalled it by enlisting for a second three years.

In a powerfully real sense, then, soldiers like Campbell held the fate of the Union in their hands during the winter and spring of 1864. Would they agree to face yet again the threat of disease, wounds, and death, as well as the loneliness, boredom, and petty indignities of military life, or would they avail themselves of a well-earned right to go home to family, friends, and loved ones?

Unable to force the veterans to remain, federal, state, and local officials did everything possible to persuade them to reenlist. The basic tactic was twofold. First, it played heavily on the desire of many veterans to "see the job through" by assuring them that if three-quarters of the men in a given regiment reenlisted, the unit could both retain its identity and add "Veteran" to its official title (as in the "Fifth Iowa Veteran Volunteer Infantry"). Second, it exploited the yearning for home by providing that soldiers who reenlisted could immediately go home on "veteran furlough" rather than await the expiration of their terms of service. Returning veterans would also receive a federal bounty of four hundred dollars as well as varying amounts from state and local governments, but the "veteran regiment" and "veteran furlough" gambits were by far the most effective. Ultimately 136,000 Union veterans—slightly over half—decided to reenlist. Campbell and most of his comrades were among them, though the Fifth Iowa narrowly missed the 75 percent threshold necessary to become a "Veteran" regiment. Still, to those who reenlisted came the priceless veteran furlough, and on April 1, 1864, Campbell headed north—for home.

Thursday, Dec. 3. We were "roused" at 5 o'clock this morning and ordered to be ready to march for Bridgeport by 7 o'clock A.M. At 7 o'clock the 1st and 2nd brigades marched out but we had to wait for teams. We "waited" till noon and still no teams came. Our brigade commander (Col. Banbury) then ordered us to load what wagons we had and leave the rest of our baggage to be brought up afterwards. We then started and on reaching the Chattanooga road near Brown's Ferry we found Osterhaus's Division passing—it having got in between us and the balance of our Division. We were thus delayed for several hours and did not get across the Ferry till after night. After crossing the Ferry we marched two miles up Lookout Valley and camped. Many of the boys have had no bread today and numbers of them have had nothing but parched corn to eat. Parched corn and half a hard cracker is all I have had since an early breakfast. We are a hungry set. Weather clear and pleasant. Distance marched today, 5 miles.

Friday, Dec. 4. We started at an early hour this morning but after marching two miles were stopped by Osterhaus' train which delayed us until 11 o'clock. We then left our teams and "took the railroad" and thus passed Osterhaus' Division. We reached Whiteside Station at 3 o'clock and there obtained a few crackers. We then marched on about a mile and camped in the woods. Our mess had a good breakfast this morning—the Colonel having furnished us enough flour to make some biscuits. Most of the boys, however, have had nothing and a great many started ahead "on their own hook" for Bridgeport and are now well on their way to *grub*. We have marched 11 miles today.

Saturday, Dec. 5. The teams did not catch up last night and I had no blankets, but the night was warm and I managed to sleep very well before a fire. One of our cooks came up from Bridgeport with some grub and we are again supplied where we expected to go hungry. We started this morning at 9 o'clock and 10 minutes and arrived at Bridgeport (13 miles distant) before 3 o'clock. We marched on the R.R. It rained lightly this morning just after crossing the bridge (at Bridgeport) I had the pleasure of meeting Major Chambers Baird. After getting into camp I was very agreeably surprised by a visit from Wm. McNickel and James Bradford. We are camped on the river a mile below the bridge.

Sunday, Dec. 6. Our teams came up this morning. We went into camp today where we have the promise of remaining at least three weeks. It is a beautiful camp, on the river, not more than 1 1/4 miles below the bridge. As my tent is "back" at Chattanooga, I will have to live out doors for a few days. Weather pleasant, but cool.

Monday, Dec. 7. Weather clear and cool. I have been busy writing letters and attending to company duties.

Tuesday, Dec. 8. Raining all day. As I have no tent, I have spent most of the day trying to keep out of the rain.

Wednesday, Dec. 9. Weather clear and pleasant. I went to town this afternoon. While there I saw Harvey Espey, formerly of Ripley.

Thursday, Dec. 10. Weather cloudy in forenoon, but clear and pleasant in afternoon. Company on picket. Our tents and baggage, "left back," came up today.

Friday, Dec. 11. Weather warm. In camp, writing & reading.

Saturday, Dec. 12. Raining. Kept close to my tent.

Sunday, Dec. 13. Cloudy in forenoon—clear at noon—raining in afternoon. I attended preaching in 10th Iowa in forenoon & preaching in camp by a preacher from the North in the afternoon. This preacher (from Indiana) preached to a squad of gamblers yesterday.

Monday, Dec. 14. On duty, in "Board of Survey" examining damaged clothing.[1] We had a stone chimney built to our tent today. Capt. Pennywitt received his discharge and was sworn in today. The long looked-for [change] has come at last. Of course, I do not relish the new state of affairs. But "what can't be cured, must be endured." "Better luck next time." I have considered the question of resigning and have come to the conclusion that it would only "make it worse." Seven months, at farthest, will end my term of service. I can "grin and bear it" for that length of time.

Tuesday, Dec. 15. I have been busy today "squaring my accounts" to turn over "the books" to Capt. Pennywitt. Weather clear.

Wednesday, Dec. 16. Busy "squaring accounts." Weather warm and cloudy. The officers and men throughout the camp are building chimneys, mud huts, and otherwise "fixing up," as if they intended to stay here *a week or two!*

Thursday, Dec. 17. Busy "squaring accounts." Last night we had a thunder storm. The river is rising steadily.

Friday, Dec. 18. Busy on "Board of Survey." Weather clear and cool. Wrote home today.

Saturday, Dec. 19. Last night was "the coldest night of the season." Today the weather is clear and cold. Played a few games of chess today.

Sunday, Dec. 20. Weather clear and cold. I attended Divine Services in the 10th Iowa, our Chaplain still being absent.

Monday, Dec. 21. Weather clear and cold.

Tuesday, Dec. 22. Having received marching orders, we struck tents and started "on the jog" again at 8 o'clock this morning. Our Corps is to be stationed, the remainder of the winter, along the Memphis & Charleston R.R. from Huntsville to Bridgeport. Our Division will be stationed near Larkinsville. Our first brigade has already gone to Larkinsville. Our brigade and the Second started thither today. We had a vexatious and tedious march, being detained by the teams and at sundown we camped having marched but *six miles.*

Wednesday, Dec. 23. Started at 8 o'clock A.M.—marched 4 1/2 miles "right along" reached Stevenson, a *very* "one horse" village, and camped in the suburbs! Weather cloudy and cool.

Thursday, Dec. 24. Started at 8 o'clock, marched 8 miles in a *circular* direction and camped at 4 o'clock P.M., 4 miles west of Stevenson. Weather clear and pleasant, roads very bad. After getting into camp we had a good supper and at 9 o'clock P.M. had a "Christmas" Eve *Oyster Supper.*

Friday, Dec. 25. A dry Christmas this has been. We were aroused at daylight—but our brigade had not yet started till 10 o'clock. We marched about 12 miles and camped at dark, 2 miles west of Bellefonte. The roads for the first half of our route were very bad, but of the latter half were excellent. Bellfonte is the county seat of Jackson county. It *has been* a nice little village of some 500 or 600 inhabitants. It is now almost entirely deserted. Hardly a half dozen families live in the place. The best buildings have been burned and all have been sacked. No town I have seen since I have been in the service has presented the desolate appearance that Bellefonte does. Weather cloudy.

Saturday, Dec. 26. It rained nearly all last night and has rained and drizzled by spills all day. At 8 o'clock this morning we struck tents but our regiment being rear guard, we did not get started until 10 o'clock A.M. and did not get into camp until after dark. We marched about ten miles during the day over the roughest road we traveled. When we were not marching along the base of the mountains (where the roads were almost rendered impassable by big stones) we were marching through swampy bottoms, where the teams were constantly "sticking." We camped in the suburbs of Larkinsville. Our march this day has been a fit counterpart of our march this day last year. In fact, the weather for the past five days has been just such as it was the same days last year. Our brigade was in advance of the Second today and it did not get through to Larkinsville.

Sunday, Dec. 27. Raining again this morning. The boys have been busy putting up their habitations. Everything looks dismal. Rained all day.

Monday, Dec. 28. Last night, the weather made a change for the better, and although we have not seen a clear sky today, yet there has been no rain and the weather is getting cooler. I have spent the whole day laying a floor in my tent and building a bunk. I sit down satisfied that I have done a good day's work. Larkinsville is a small village of some 200 or 300 inhabitants. Near our camp is a large creek, which runs mostly under *terra firma,* appearing "on top of ground" every half mile or so to "air itself."

Tuesday, Dec. 29. Reveille at 6 o'clock with orders to be ready to march at 9 o'clock A.M. for Gross' Mills, 5 miles south of Larkinsville, to take charge of and run the mill. At 9 o'clock, we started and reached the mill at noon. We passed though some tolerably fair country coming out. We camped in the woods near the mill. I was, this morning, appointed Adjutant of the Regiment, *pro tem.,* by order of Lt. Col. Sampson. Weather clear and cool.

Wednesday, Dec. 30. Weather clear and pleasant. In camp, attending to duties.

Thursday, Dec. 31. Raining nearly all day. About fifty citizens come in today to take the oath of allegiance. They were all sent to the Provost Marshall at Larkinsville.

Friday, January, 1. 1864. Just after dusk, last eve., the Weather "kicked up a breeze" and

> The Old Year went out with a rain and a rustle
> And the New Year came in with a terrible bustle.

This morning, everything is frozen up "tight." Today has been very cold—the natives say it is the coldest weather that ever visited these parts. Our mess had a New Year's Dinner, Roast Goose and Goose Roasted! More citizens came in today to take the oath—all anxious to "swear."

Saturday, Jan 2. Weather *very* cold. Citizens still come to trade and "swear" themselves into the Union. "Our Mill" is grinding. A large saltpetre cave near our camp has been visited by some of our boys and found to [be] very interesting. I was very busy yesterday and today in the office.

Sunday, Jan 3. Weather moderated during the day and by night, rain began to fall. No preaching today although our Chaplain has returned.

Monday, Jan 4. Weather wet. I have been busy in the office. "Marching orders" came this evening. Oh! for a tramp through the mud tomorrow.

Tuesday, Jan. 5. This forenoon, our regiment marched from Gross' Mill to Larkinsville, over a very bad road. On arriving at Larkinsville, we occupied the deserted huts of the Pioneer Corps which has gone to Huntsville. The weather has been very cold all day. This afternoon we had Dress Parade, J.Q.A. Campbell officiating as adjutant. *He performed very well!* There has been considerable excitement in our regiment today on the "Veteran" subject. An effort is being made (with good promise of success) to get three-fourths of the regiment to re-enlist, that the regiment may go home in a body to recruit. As goes Company B, so goes J.Q.A. Campbell.

Wednesday, Jan. 6. Weather still very cold. The *"Veteran"* excitement has continued today with about the following result. Three-fourths of the regiment have not reenlisted by 21 men. More than half of the regiment (present) have re-enlisted and the regiment is a *Veteran Regiment,* although it cannot go north in a body to recruit. Companies A., C., D., E., F., and G. have reenlisted the requisite 3/4ths and can get to go north to recruit, as companies. Company B came within *one* of the 3/4ths, but one man backing down, spoiled the 3/4ths, and only 10 of the company re-enlisted. We have orders for marching at 8 o'clock in the morning.

Thursday, Jan. 7. At 8 o'clock this morning, our Brigade started for Huntsville, the 5th Iowa "in the lead." The roads have been very rough and slippery but we find ourselves this evening in camp, 4 miles west of Woodville and 16 from Larkinsville. A light rain or mist, has been falling most of the day, and freezing as it fell, covering everything with ice. We passed the camp of Osterhaus' Division near Woodville. We crossed Paint Creek (a very pretty stream) late in the day. Weather cold.

Friday, Jan. 8. Our Division train (which started from Larkinsville, with our Brigade) did not get into camp last night and we were detained (waiting for it) until noon today. We marched 11 miles, camping at dark near Maysville on [the] Flint River. The road today has been much better that it was yesterday. The country is improving as we march westward. Weather bitter cold.

Saturday, Jan. 9. Starting at 8 o'clock (5th Iowa in advance) we marched down to Flint River, a stream some 50 yards wide. This we had to *ford* on horseback, mule-back, in wagons, and in one small flat. We were delayed in crossing by the Second Brigade, which we came up with at Maysville, and which crossed ahead of us. Our regiment crossed in the "flat." By 10 1/2 o'clock we were all safely "over." By three o'clock P.M. we reached Huntsville and camped on the pike 1/2 mile S. of town. Huntsville is the prettiest town I have seen in the South. It has numbered 8,000. The surrounding country is beautiful to behold—fair and fertile—and well improved. Our whole Division is now camped at and near Huntsville. Gen. Sherman's Head Quarters are in town. Weather very cold.

Sunday, Jan. 10. Weather moderate and cloudy. A "chain guard" has been put around camp and no officer nor man is permitted to leave camp except on duty. We have had no preaching today.

Monday, Jan. 11. Weather moderate and cloudy. I have kept close to my tent attending to my duties posting my Diary, &c., &c.

Tuesday, Jan. 12. I visited Huntsville this forenoon and rode through the different streets and made a "survey" of the town, and the more I see of the place the better I like it. The grounds about many of the private residences are *very* tastefully ornamented. The "water-works" of the town are far ahead of anything of the kind I have ever seen. The whole town is supplied with water from a large Spring, the stream from which furnishes the power to work a force-pump, which sends the water all over town. This stream is 45 ft. wide by 2 ft. deep, and is the clearest water I ever saw. "Clear as crystal" is no name for it. The whole "machinery" of the water-works can not occupy more space than 20 feet square. In the stream long waving fingers of green moss, beckon one to taste of the bright and sparkling water. Weather moderate.

Wednesday, Jan. 13. I have [been] busy all day in the office making out Reports of various kinds. Weather moderate.

Thursday, Jan. 14. I visited town this afternoon and procured some photographs of J.Q.A.C. Weather pleasant.

Friday, Jan. 15. In camp, busy in the office. Weather pleasant. Inspection this afternoon.

Saturday, Jan. 16. This morning I went to town and attended Sabbath School at the New School Presbyterian Church.[2] After Sabbath School was over I attended Divine services at same place, and heard Dr. Ross of "New School" notoriety preach a very sensible sermon. At only one point did he intimate anything that might be understood as leading to Secession[;] that was a remark that "we had gone astray after the Democratic idea of *equality.*" His congregation was composed of two-thirds soldiers and one part citizens. The citizens were almost all females, not more than ten males in the congregation. There was no apparent coldness towards *nor* contempt for the Yankees manifested but they were very politely treated. The church itself is a magnificent edifice—equal to any I have seen anywhere. My "leave of absence" came today. Don't want it.

Monday, Jan. 18. Last night we had very heavy winds and some rain. Today the weather has been cloudy with occasional sprinkles of rain. This afternoon the weather is getting cooler. This forenoon I visited town on business.

Tuesday, Jan. 19. I visited town again this morning and succeeded in getting a pair of boots. Weather clear and pleasant.

Wednesday, Jan. 20. Weather clear and pleasant. A number of citizens of Huntsville, who refused to take the oath of allegiance, were sent "beyond the lines" today.[3] One captain, two lieutenants, and eight privates, from Longstreet's cavalry came in and gave themselves up today.

Thursday, Jan. 21. This day has certain[ly] abstracted from the month of May—such weather in the middle of winter makes me have a *hankering* for Dixie. I went to town this morning for business.

Friday, Jan. 22. A second edition of yesterday. I began reading "Blair's Rhetoric," today.[4]

Saturday, Jan. 23. Weather "salubrious," "splendid", "magnificent," &c., &c., &c. In camp, pitching quorts—writing &c., including studying "Rhetoric."

Sunday, Jan. 24. Weather "ditto" to yesterday. I attended divine services in town, this morning and hear a very able sermon (on the atonement) from Dr. Ross. I received three letters today.

Monday, Jan. 25. Weather *"more than ditto"* to yesterday. I am fearful of the appearance of that terrible malady "Spring Fever!" Battalion Drill.

Tuesday, Jan. 26. Weather still "ditto." Alarm today.

Wednesday, Jan. 27. The alarm, which caused orders to be sent to us yesterday to hold ourselves ready for an emergency, was caused by the appearance of Roddy's Rebel Cavalry, on this side of the river, southwest of town.[5] Wilder's Mounted brigade was sent out and attack Roddy's force near Athens, whipping them and driving them back across the river.[6] They returned today bringing three officers and seven men as prisoners. Weather continues "delightful." I had a game of ball this afternoon. The *iron-horse* now pays us daily visits from Stevenson.

Thursday, Jan. 28. Weather "ditto." I have been busy today arranging the "papers" in the office. This evening I took a stroll through town.

Friday, Jan. 29. I have been in the office all day arranging the "papers." Weather beautiful. The 10th Iowa and 93rd Ills., have gone to Mooresville on a scout.

Saturday, Jan. 30. Weather cloudy but pleasant—a slight sprinkling of rain during the day. I have been busy in the office today.

Sunday, Jan. 31. I have been busy the greater part of today making out the "monthly return." The 10th Iowa and 93rd Ills returned today. Weather cloudy.

Monday, Feb. 1. We had quite a *"blow"* last night and today, the weather is clear and pleasant. The Monthly Returns have kept me busy today. Our Division is doing a great deal of *"foraging"* in the surrounding country. The 59th Indiana *"Veterans"* are preparing for "Home Sweet Home."

Tuesday, Feb. 2. Busy in the office all day. Weather windy. The 59th Ind. Veterans started for home today. Success to them.

Wednesday, Feb. 3. Weather clear but windy—busy in the office all day. "Our" veterans were *mustered* today.

Thursday, Feb. 4. Weather clear but windy. Busy in the office most of the day.

Friday, Feb. 5. Rain today. Busy in the office.

Saturday, Feb. 6. Slight rain this morning. Gen. Matthies has returned to take command of the brigade and Col. Banbury has returned to the regiment. The general did a good thing on the first morning after his return—make Gen. Smith modify one of his orders, which he had issued instructing pickets to let no contrabands inside our lines. The Gen. made a speech to the boys of our regiment to induce them to join the "Veterans." His effort was not attended with much success. Company H is a stumbling block in our way.

Sunday, Feb. 7. I attended church in town this forenoon and heard a very good sermon. This afternoon, I read one of Henry Ward Beecher's sermons in the *Independent.*[7] Weather very pleasant.

Monday, Feb. 8. Weather pleasant. I went to town this morning on "mess business." This afternoon, I read a chapter in "Blair's Rhetoric."

Tuesday, Feb. 9. Weather pleasant. Reading Rhetoric.

Wednesday, Feb. 10. Weather very pleasant. I have been busy in the office. Went to town on Reg. business. Went to Soldier's Meeting in town, in evening.

Thursday, Feb. 11. A beautiful day. Busy in the office all day. The 10th Iowa and 93rd Ills of our brigade leave today on some expedition—going *via* Chattanooga. Gen. Matthies goes with them—he is assigned the command of the force constituting the expedition, which consists of 14 regiments and 2 batteries—quite a compliment to our "Dutchman." In the absence of the General, Col. Banbury commands the brigade and J.Q.A.C. is Ass't Adj.-Gen'l of the brigade! Weighty honors! Hasten, O! General! to ease my burdened shoulders, by a speedy return!

Friday, Feb. 12. Weather very pleasant. I bought a volume of "debates in the Alabama Convention of secession" today.

Saturday, Feb. 13. Weather very pleasant. I was busy in the office this forenoon. This afternoon I went to town and called on Dr. Ross to make some inquiries concerning Father's brother Samuel and his family. The old Doctor received me very cordially but could not give me the information I sought. My health for a few days past has been "absent without leave." I have had a bad cold and sore throat.

Sunday, Feb. 14. My cold is "no better fast." It has rained nearly all day. I did not go down to Church.

Monday, Feb. 15. My cold is a *"leetle"* better. A heavy rain fell last night and it rained during this forenoon. This afternoon, the clouds "dried up." I have been very busy in the office today.

Tuesday, Feb. 16. Health better. Weather clear, windy, and cool. I have been busy in the office most of the day. I rode down to town to see paymaster this eve.

Wednesday, Feb. 17. I have been pretty busy in the office today. Weather quite cool. I rode down to town to see [the] Paymaster this afternoon.

Thursday, Feb. 18. Weather very cold with a sprinkle of snow this morning. We were paid today for months of November and December.

Friday, Feb. 19. Weather clear and cold. I have been busy in the office today.

Saturday, Feb. 20. Weather clear and pleasant. I went to town and purchased some Clothing this morning.

Sunday, Feb. 21. A remarkably pleasant day. I heard Dr. Ross preach a very good sermon this morning.

Monday, Feb. 22. A pleasant day. I have been very busy in the office. There will be a ball in town tonight in honor of Washington's Birthday.

Tuesday, Feb. 23. Weather pleasant. Busy in the office. The ball last night was a "stag dance."

Wednesday, Feb. 24. Weather very pleasant.

Thursday, Feb. 25. Weather very pleasant. We have orders to remain in camp today to "be ready for emergencies." The rebs are said to be crossing the river south of here.—Later! "The cavalry have come back *with their hats on!*" The danger is past.

Friday, Feb. 26. Weather pleasant. Some of our "boys" disgraced themselves today by getting beastly drunk. Oh that *men* should barter their manhood for the gratification of their appetites.

Saturday, Feb. 27. Weather pleasant but atmosphere very smoky. I rode round the picket lines this afternoon with Col. Sampson.

Sunday, Feb. 28. Weather very warm with a sprinkle of rain. I attended Divine Services in town this forenoon.

Monday, Feb. 29. Rained most all day. I have been busy making out Monthly Returns. No mail today.

Tuesday, March 1. It has rained nearly all day. I have been busy making out Monthly Returns. Received three letters today.

Wednesday, March 2. A clear, bright day. I went to town on business, this forenoon—did considerable business in the office and played "some" chess. We are waiting anxiously for news from Gen. Sherman's expedition into Mississippi and Alabama. The news from the cavalry expedition that left Memphis is favorable.[8]

Thursday, March 3. Weather "mixed." — have spent the day in the office—read a chapter or two in Blair's Rhetoric.

Friday, March 4. Rain. Part of Gen. Matthies' Expedition returned today. They have been at Cleveland [Tennessee].

Saturday, March 5. A very pleasant day. This evening, in company with Col. Banbury, Captain Merrill, and Capt. Lee, I took [a] ride up the mountain east of town. The view from the summit of the mountain was most beautiful. At our feet lay Huntsville, with its pleasant surroundings. Here and there near the suburbs of the town, the white tents of the soldiers could be seen. Stretching far away, for fifteen or twenty miles, the meadows and fields swelling and falling like the undulations of the sea could be seen dressed in their russet hues and the dark lines of evergreens furnished bordering away in the distance, the beautiful Tennessee could be seen, reflecting the glories of the setting Sun. I was satisfied but not satiated with the view.

Sunday, March 6. I attended preaching at the soldier's church in town this morning and partook of the Lord's Supper at the same place this evening. Weather beautiful.

Monday, March 7. We have had rain and thunder today. I was relieved of my duties as A.A.G. today—turning over the documents to Lieut. McKee.

Tuesday, March 8. Rain in forenoon—afternoon clear and pleasant.

Wednesday, March 9. Col. Banbury took command of Brigade today. Gen'l Matthies is commanding the Division in the absence of Gen. Smith. Weather clear and pleasant. Battalion Drill this afternoon.

Thursday, March 10. A heavy rain fell last night. Today the weather has been very warm—clear in forenoon, and cloudy in afternoon. The Regiment was inspected today and the men, clothing, quarters, arms, &c. found to be in the best condition. The men are better "housed" and clothed than they have been since we entered the service.

Friday, March 11. Weather very pleasant. In the afternoon, I rode around the Picket lines with Col. Sampson.

Saturday, March 12. Weather "fine." I attended a "citizens" meeting in town this forenoon, which was called for the purpose of taking initiatory measures towards "bringing Alabama back into the Union" as expressed by the words of the call. The meeting was rather small but very respectable. Resolutions were adopted denouncing secession, deploring the results of the rebellion, and favoring a return to the old flag. Short addresses were made by a Mr. Humphreys and Hon. Jerry Clemens (President of the meeting.)[9]

Sunday, March 13. Weather beautiful. I have heard two good sermons today—one by Dr. Ross in town, and one by the Chaplain of the 10th Iowa in camp. I also attended Sunday School in town this morning.

Monday, March 14. A pleasant day—a portion of which I spent in town viewing among other objects of interest, some statues of fine finish at our post hospital. After dusk this evening I made "the rounds" for the picket officer.[10]

Tuesday, March 15. This has been a rather disagreeable day. This afternoon I called on Hon. Jerry Clemens in town, and although cordially received by him, I found that he was not sober enough to be himself and I soon made it convenient to leave.[11] Mrs. Clemens, an intelligent and very agreeable lady, was evidently mortified at his conduct, though manifestly it was not a new thing to her. She humors him as a child and rules him like a mother.

Wednesday, March 16. Weather cold and blustery.

Thursday, March 17. Weather clear and cool. We received no mail today— the rebs made a raid on the R.R. between Stephenson and Nashville and captured a train or two. I am afraid they have got some of my letters.

Friday, March 18. Weather pleasant. This afternoon I rode around the picket lines with the "officer of the day". We rode about nine miles.

Saturday, March 19. Weather pleasant. I rode out west of town this afternoon and viewed Huntsville from Russell Hill. I was well paid for my trouble.

Sunday, March 20. Weather pleasant. I attended Divine services in town this forenoon and afternoon and read a *dry* sermon of Beecher's in the evening.

Monday, March 21. Weather raw, cold, and disagreeable. A magnificent sword was presented to Colonel Sampson this afternoon by the officers of the Regiment. The money for the sword was contributed while we were at Vicksburg last Summer. The present was made in consideration of the gallant services of the Lieut. Colonel during the "Vicksburg campaign," when he commanded the regiment. The sword was presented by Capt. [Daniel] Lee in a neat speech and Colonel Sampson made a few very happy remarks in accepting the sword.

Tuesday, March 22. Last evening Col. Sampson gave a supper to the officers of the Regiment. After supper liquor was brought out and many of the officers became intoxicated and behaved with all the simpleness, foolishness, and disgust that drunk men generally do. Some of these same officers have had their men punished for getting drunk and making a disturbance in camp. Oh! consistency, thou art a jewel. This morning, on rising, I found five inches of *snow* on the ground and the "feathers" still falling! The day has been raw, cloudy, and disagreeable.

Wednesday, March 23. A bright, pleasant day which I have spent in camp. In the evening, I took a walk into town.

Thursday, March 24. Weather clear and pleasant in forenoon—afternoon, cloudy, and towards night, windy and disagreeable.

Friday, March 25. Commenced writing a history of our Regiment for the State. Weather wet and windy. I have kept close to my tent.

Saturday, March 26. Cloudy in the morning—the afternoon clear and pleasant. I took a stroll into town in the evening.

Sunday, March 27. Weather clear and pleasant. I heard Dr. Ross preach an able sermon in the forenoon. In the evening I attended services at the Soldier's church.

Monday, March 28. Weather disagreeable and "blustery" with heavy rains. I have spent the day in my tent.

Tuesday, March 29. Weather windy and cloudy. I have spent the day in my tent.

Wednesday, March 30. Weather clear and pleasant. I went to town in forenoon—spent the afternoon in my tent preparing for tomorrow's work.

Thursday, March 31. I have been as "busy as a bee" all day and have very nearly finished all my reports. This afternoon the order came to our Regiment to report as a Veteran Regiment to the Governor of Iowa and we have turned over our property and are ready to start at an early hour in the morning for "America!" Weather cloudy with some rain falling.

Friday, April 1. At five o'clock this morning we took the cars at Huntsville and tonight we find ourselves in Nashville, having come over the Decatur R.R. *via* Athens, Pulaski, and Columbia. The country we have passed through today is broken and rolling—well timbered and watered and is as good as any I have seen in the South. We had the pleasure of riding part of the distance today with Gen. McPherson and a noted guerrilla named Moore who was wearing "anklets."[12] On our arrival at Nashville, the Regiment was quartered at Zollicoffer Barracks—that "horror" of Nashville.

Saturday, April 2. We remained in Nashville until 4 o'clock A.M. today and I had a chance to look over the city. Last night I visited the "Orphan's Fair." I slept in the Depot with the baggage. This morning I took an outside and inside view of the State House, a magnificent structure, built almost entirely of gray limestone. From the capitol I had a splendid view of the city and the surrounding country. I visited the tomb of James K. Polk during the day. Nashville is a place of considerable importance but could never be called a pretty city—its streets are too narrow. At four o'clock we left Nashville on the train for Louisville. The country we passed through before dark was gently rolling and was in all respects a beautiful farming country. Weather clear and pleasant.

Sunday, April 3. We traveled all night and arrived at Louisville at six o'clock this morning. The Regiment was quartered in the "Soldier's Home," a filthy place provided for the reception of traveling soldiers.[13] This forenoon, I called on Mr. and Mrs. Baird & Mr. & Mrs. Johnson of Ripley and attended church with Mr. Baird.[14] Some of the boys of our Regiment became intoxicated and got into a difficulty with a K[entuck]y Regiment near the "Home" this morning.

Monday, April 4. The officers of the Regiment were paid this forenoon and this afternoon we made some purchases, preparatory to going over into "*America.*" At 4 o'clock P.M. we started from the "Home" for the Louisville and Jeffersonville ferry. As we were marching through the city a heavy rain came up and we got completely "soaked." At 7 1/2 o'clock P.M. we took the cars for Chicago *via* Indianapolis.

Tuesday, April 5. We arrived at Indianapolis at day-light this morning and remained there until noon and I had an opportunity to view the city. Although a very pretty place, it does not rival Louisville which far surpassed my anticipations of it. The State-House at Indianapolis is an old, dingy, ugly, dilapidated structure. Leaving Indianapolis about noon, we "sailed" for Chicago *via* Lafayette. We passed through some excellent farming country and over some prairies that were very beautiful but too flat to suit my eye. Weather cool and cloudy.

Wednesday, April 6. We arrived at Chicago at 4 o'clock this morning and left for Davenport at 10. The Regiment was furnished an excellent breakfast at the "Soldier's Rest." Before we left the city, I called to see Harry Boss. We arrived at Davenport at 6 o'clock this evening and were furnished free suppers at the Hotels by the citizens.

Thursday, April 7. We have all been busy today making out furloughs, getting transportation, turning over arms, and making other preparations for starting home in the morning. This evening I took a stroll over the city with Jim Patterson. I am very much pleased with Davenport and would like to make it my place of abode *after the war.* Weather very pleasant.

Friday, April 8. At 8 o'clock this morning I took the train for Grinnell. At Iowa City the train was detained by a "land slide" on the track. We arrived at Grinnell at 3 o'clock in the afternoon. On making our way through mud and rain to the stage office, we found that there were no stages "in port," and no beds "empty" at the hotels. But fortunately for us, two stages came in about an hour after our arrival and at 5 o'clock we started for Newton. The roads were bad and the stages were overloaded and we had to get out and walk through mud and rain up all the hills. At nine o'clock we arrived at Kellogg's farm, 8 miles from Newton. Our stage stuck in the mud in sight of the house, and the drivers unhitched both teams and expressed their intention of waiting there till daylight. We accordingly took refuge in the farm house and spent the night. As I had neither bed nor blanket, I slept sitting up on the floor.

Saturday, April 9. After getting a good breakfast this morning and taking a survey of the roads and the mud-hole our stage was in, Lt. McKee and I and a fellow soldier concluded to make the rest of our journey on foot. We accordingly "struck out" and reached Newton at 11 o'clock A.M. I "dropped in" on the folks rather unexpectedly and found Bell in deep meditation—considering where she would find the next patch for her carpet! In the afternoon I went down town to see old acquaintances and found a host of them. As a result of getting wet yesterday, I am very hoarse today. Weather cloudy, cool, and windy.

Sunday, April 10. Weather clear and pleasant. I attended church this forenoon. My hoarseness is "no better fast" today.

Monday, April 11. Weather wet and pleasant *in the house by a good fire.* I am not quite as hoarse today as yesterday. Capt. Harry Skiff of the 13th spent the evening with us.

Tuesday, April 12. Weather cloudy and cool. I took dinner at Mr. Blair's today—spent the evening at home with Nerve, Bell, and Angus.[15]

Wednesday, April 13. On my way to Ripley. At 8 o'clock this morning I took my valise down town to get aboard the stage but it was "full to overflowing" and I had to pay $3 to get a ride to Grinnell in a road wagon. I arrived at Grinnell in time to get my dinner before the cars started for Davenport. We arrived at Davenport at 8 P.M. and at 8 1/2 P.M. I took the cars for Chicago. Weather cloudy and cool. The Spring is, in Iowa as in Dixie, very backward. The farmers are just sowing their wheat which should have been in the ground a month since.

Thursday, April 14. On leaving Davenport last night, I took a sleeping car and this morning when I awoke we were within fifteen miles of Chicago. We arrived at Chicago at six o'clock A.M. I stopped at the Matteson House and got my breakfast. After breakfast, I called on Uncle Lowry Rankin's family and in the evening took dinner at Harry Boss'.[16] At 9 o'clock P.M. I took the cars for Cincinnati via the "Cincinnati and Chicago Air Line Road."

Friday, April 15. Taking a sleeping car last night, I threw myself into the arms of "Murphy" where I remained until morning. On lifting up my eyes at early dawn, I found myself a short distance east of Anderson, Indiana. About 8 o'clock we reached Richmond, a very pretty town. The section of country we passed through this morning was a fine farming region. Many large fields of excellent looking winter wheat greeted our eyes. Our train arrived at Cincinnati at 10:40 A.M. and I took up "quarters" in the Henry House. Being disappointed in some *"business"*(?) matters, I "jumped aboard the Telegraph" at 5 o'clock P.M. and started for *home*. Weather cloudy.

Saturday, April 16. At 4 o'clock this morning the boat arrived at Ripley wharf and I conveyed myself to the Bank Hotel where I remained for an hour and then started for *Third Street*. On making a survey, I found "nobody up" but the "natives" were soon aroused and I was "detained in a hostile manner." After breakfast I started out to see old acquaintances and spent the balance of the day in saying "how-are-yous" and shaking hands. In the evening I attended church. I find a number of improvements in the town and many changes in the people but Ripley still looks more like home than any other place on this terraqueous globe. Weather cloudy and cool.

Sunday, April 17. I attended Sunday School this morning and preaching

Ripley, Ohio, c. 1846. Courtesy of the Ohio Historical Society, Columbus.

in the forenoon and afternoon. In the forenoon the sacrament was administered. Weather cloudy and cool.

Monday, April 18. This morning I finished my "Monthly Return" for March and started it to Washington. This afternoon I made some calls and took tea at "Uncle Tom's."[17] Weather wet.

Tuesday, April 19. I spent the forenoon "downtown"—the afternoon "up town," making calls. Weather clear in forenoon, but cloudy in afternoon.

Wednesday, April 20. Weather clear and pleasant. I spent the afternoon, very pleasantly, at Rankin's. In the evening, I called on the *Shepherdess*, and passed away a few hours very agreeabl[y].[18]

Thursday, April 21. Weather clear and pleasant. This afternoon I enjoyed myself at A.O.'s expense. I spent the evening on the "eminence."[19] In the early part of the evening, I attended a called meeting of our old Debating Society. Three butternut members were expelled and their names expunged from the records of the Society by unanimous vote.[20]

Friday, April 22. Weather cloudy, with some rain. I spent part of the morning writing.

Saturday, April 23. Last night—or rather at 2 o'clock this morning, I "jumped aboard the Telegraph" with Sister to make a trip to Hanging Rock to pay a visit to Mag. Coles. At the dinner-table today, a "she-rebel" who sat opposite me took occasion to "blurt out" or hint a little treason. I placed her *hors du combat* by a *sympathetic sneer*. We arrived at the "Rock" at 5 o'clock this evening where we were taken up and kindly cared for by Mag. and her Father, Mother, &c.

Sunday, April 24. It has rained most of the day. We attended preaching in the forenoon, and partook of the *Sacrament* in the afternoon.

Monday, April 25. After breakfast this morning, I took a ride on horse-back around the village. This Afternoon Mag., Sister, and I drove to Ironton and took a survey of that town. I express my opinion of that place when I say that I never want any acquaintance of mine to live there. This evening, Mag., her Sister Martha, Sister Neth, and I (principally "I") gave a concert in the parlor. "Great Applause" but "small proceeds"—owing, I suppose, to "the inclemency of the weather." Weather "drizzly" in forenoon, but clear in afternoon.

Tuesday, April 26. Weather cloudy, with occasional glimpses of sunshine and some occasional drizzles of rain. Mag., Sister, and I had a pleasant drive out to Pine Grove Furnace where we spent a few very pleasant hours with the family of "Cousin John Peebles," having a good dinner "thrown in" by way of *interlude*.

> May "Cousin John" and "Cousin Joe"
> And "Cousin Thomas" never,
> From "Cousin Mag." "Martha" nor "Aunt"
> "Lucy" nor "Legion" sever.

After getting back from the furnace, Mag., Martha, Sister, and I went up on to the "Rock" where we had a splendid view of the river valley, for a number of miles. It is seldom I have viewed more beautiful scenery. At 8 o'clock P.M. we got aboard the Ohio, and started for home.

Wednesday, April 27. At 10 o'clock this morning, we arrived at the Ripley wharf and I find myself at home again, after one of the most pleasant visits that fall to the lot of "mortals" here below. Weather clear and warm during the day. This evening we had rain.

Thursday, April 28. Weather pleasant. Went to Felicity—walked 4 miles.

Friday, April 29. Weather pleasant—I came back from Felicity today.

Saturday, April 30. Weather warm and cloudy. I spent a good part of the forenoon at home, writing. Spent the evening at W.B. Campbell's on the hill. Slight rain in afternoon.

Sunday, May 1. Attended preaching at First Church in forenoon—Second Church in afternoon—and Methodist Church in the evening. Weather cool and clear.

Monday, May 2. We have had considerable rain, much hail, and a little sunshine today. The "National Guard" for Brown county has been assembling here today.[21] I took supper at Uncle Hayden's and spent the evening at Mr. D. B. Evans'.

Tuesday, May 3. At 7 o'clock this morning, I started with Father for Georgetown. We arrived there at 9 o'clock A.M. where I remained two hours. I then bid Father "good-bye" and started for Winchester *via* Russellville and Carlisle. I arrived at Winchester at 3 P.M. and spent the afternoon with Aunt Mag. and Alma. The weather has been rather cool today to be pleasant. The roads are in bad condition.

Wednesday, May 4. At 8 o'clock this morning, Mag., Alma, and I started for Ripley *via* North Liberty. We arrived at North Liberty where we stopped and took dinner with Cousins Victor & Adaline King. At 2 1/2 o'clock P.M. we started for Ripley where we arrived at 6 1/4 P.M. This evening I spent pleasantly at home with several of the Ripley girls.

Thursday, May 5. After spending three weeks at home, on "Veteran Furlough," I started (to join my regiment) today for Davenport, Iowa. The weather is very pleasant and I have a prospect of pleasant traveling. I left home at noon on the packet and arrived at Cincinnati at 7 P.M. and took lodging for the night at the Broadway Hotel. My visit home was of a very pleasant nature and I cannot but regret its briefness. After an absence of over three years from my native place, I found that "home" still had its attractions and that my short stay of three weeks did not give me opportunity to see all my friends nor permit me to enjoy the company of those I did see as I would like. I kept my spirits up as best I could in parting. After enjoying myself among friends for a few weeks, I again find myself *"enroute"* to "Dixie," to fight for Uncle Sam.

Friday, May 6. At 7 o'clock this morning, I took the train for *Lockland* where I arrived at 7 1/2 A.M. I was met at the Depot by friend Miss Hat Burkhalter, with whom I spent the day very pleasantly. "May I spend many as pleasant days" is making as good a wish for myself as I can imagine. At 7 o'clock P.M. I took the train on the Air-Line Road for Chicago. I did not get to bed until we reached Richmond, Indiana, where a sleeping car was attached to our train. Weather during the day warm and pleasant.

Saturday, May 7. At 8 1/2 o'clock A.M. I reached Chicago and at 9 1/2 I left for Davenport on the "Rock Island Road." This road, after reaching Joliet, runs for a considerable distance down the beautiful Valley of the Illinois River. After it leaves this Valley it runs through a very level prairie country until it nears the Mississippi where the country is more rolling. I reached Davenport at 6 o'clock P.M. On my arrival, I found Lt. Col. Sampson and a number of the "boys" already in town. I took lodgings at the "Pennsylvania House." Weather pleasant. Slight rain in forenoon.

Sunday, May 8. I attended service at the Baptist Church this morning and heard a very good sermon. In the evening I heard an excellent discourse at the Methodist Church. Weather warm with slight rain.

Monday, May 9. This forenoon I spent in writing and attending to various little matters of business. This afternoon I walked out to Camp McClellan (two miles) to witness the payment of Co. D. While at the camp I visited the quarters of some Sioux Indians who are confined there. These Indians were captured by Gen. Pope in Minnesota. They are much more intelligent looking than I expected to see them. Their heads are remarkable for their largeness.[22] On my return from the camp I was caught in a rain and got somewhat *dampened.* At 8 o'clock this evening, our Regiment took the Rock Island train and started for *"Dixie."* Weather very warm in the forenoon. Rain in the afternoon and evening.

Tuesday, May 10. The weather got considerably cooler during the night, and we found it very uncomfortable riding in the cars. We arrived at Chicago about 9 o'clock this morning—too late to "make connections"—and we had to remain in the city all day. The Regiment stayed at the "soldier's rest." I called on some friends in the city. Quite a gale visited the city last night and a number of vessels were wrecked on the lake. Today the weather is very cool and the wind "high." The sight of the Lake in turmoil is a new and interesting one to me and was to most of the boys of the Regiment. At 8 o'clock this evening we took the cars on the "Cincinnati Air-Line Road" for Indianapolis.

Wednesday, May 11. At 3 o'clock this morning we changed cars at Kokomo and at daylight we reached Indianapolis. At 9 o'clock we left Indianapolis for Louisville where we arrived at 6 P.M. Being unable to get off on the evening train, we "put up" for the night at the "Soldier's Home." Having slept the two nights previously sitting up in the cars, I retired at an early hour this evening to cultivate the acquaintance of "Old Morpheus." Weather cool.

Thursday, May 12. At 7 o'clock this morning, we started for Nashville where we arrived at 5 1/2 o'clock P.M. and took quarters in the "Zollicoffer." (The distance from L[ouisville] to Nashville is 180 miles). Some of the country we passed through today is very beautiful. From Bowling Green, Ky. to Nashville, the land lies beautifully and is as far as appearances indicate as good a farming country as I ever saw. Weather very pleasant. The contrast between the state of vegetation here and at Chicago is very considerable. Here Nature has put on her livery. There, hardly a bud has swelled. The news from the Army of the Potomac still continues favorable. Gen. Grant is pressing Lee back to Richmond and I hope we may soon hear of a decisive victory by our army.[23] The news from Gen. Sherman is meager but favorable.[24]

Friday, May 13. Being unable to secure transportation to the front, our Regiment has been compelled to remain at Nashville today. I improved the time by writing letters, visiting the Capitol, &c., &c. From the top of the dome of the Capitol, I had an excellent view of the surrounding country. Nashville is certainly situated in a delightful region of country. To little *Udora Hatton* of Michigan, I am indebted for my view from the dome and for a visit to the State Library. This evening, I called on Miss Mary Knapp of Nashville, a classmate of my Sister at Oxford, Ohio. I found her to be an intelligent, well-informed and agreeable lady. Although she is a native of the South and has always lived there, yet she is *radically Union* in her political principals. Hating the rebellion she strikes at its cause, and is an "immediate emancipationist." Not withstanding her friends and relatives have been in the rebel army, yet she has, from the beginning, been true to the Stars and Stripes. All honor to Mary Knapp of Nashville.

8

⸻ ⦿⦿⦿ ⸻

Yankee Vandals and Rebel Guerrillas
Guarding Sherman's Rear, May 14–September 14, 1864

The spring campaign of 1864 got underway while Campbell was still enjoying the familiar sights of Ripley. In Virginia, the Army of the Potomac began its march south on May 4, crossing the Rapidan River and becoming embroiled almost at once in a grueling struggle with the Army of Northern Virginia under Gen. Robert E. Lee. Now general-in-chief of all Union armies, Campbell's erstwhile commander, Ulysses S. Grant, accompanied the Army of the Potomac as it grappled with Lee's forces in a month-long campaign that resulted in over fifty thousand Union casualties. In Georgia, the combined Armies of the Tennessee, Cumberland, and Ohio—over one hundred thousand men under Maj. Gen. William T. Sherman—advanced against the much smaller Army of Tennessee under Gen. Joseph E. Johnston. Sherman took fewer casualties, but by midsummer he had neither beaten Johnston's army nor captured his objective, the industrial center of Atlanta.

The result was a full-blown crisis for the Union. The month of August found the major Union armies stalled in front of Richmond-Petersburg on the Virginia front and Atlanta in Georgia. At those points, as elsewhere, the Confederacy was holding its own. The Democrats proclaimed the war a failure and urged the repudiation of emancipation and the opening of negotiations for peace. In Washington, Abraham Lincoln seriously pondered the thought that the autumn elections would repudiate his administration and that his likely successor, George B. McClellan, would find it politically impossible to continue the war.

Quincy Campbell viewed these developments from deep in the rear of Sherman's army, in a region of Alabama, Georgia, and Tennessee corresponding to what military men would one day term the "zone of communications."

This area saw no pitched battles between Union and Confederate armies, only a constant, wearing effort to shuttle adequate supplies to Sherman's army while defending the railroads and wagon trains against marauding Confederate cavalry and guerrillas. As his diary makes clear, such duty could be as arduous, as dangerous, and if anything more frustrating than on the battle lines.

Saturday, May 14. At 7 o'clock A.M. we started for Decatur, Ala., on the "Nashville and Decatur R.R." We arrived at the "Decatur Junction" at 5 o'clock P.M. The principal towns we passed through were Franklin, Columbia, Pulaski, and Athens. The railroad runs through a beautiful country and as nature has put on her livery, adorning the forests and carpeting the earth the scenery was perfectly enchanting. The "cleared land" along this route (which is considerable) is nearly all under cultivation—about an equal extent being planted in corn and cotton and sowed in winter wheat. The wheat is not very good—will not produce an average crop. On arriving at the "Junction" our Regiment got off the cars and marched to Decatur about 3 miles distant. We crossed the Tennessee on the pontoon bridge, which by "stepping" I found to be some 635 yards in length. We arrived at Decatur about dark and as our camp equipage is still at Huntsville, we "took up quarters" just where we could find them. The weather for the past two days has been very pleasant.

Sunday, May 15. This morning we find ourselves again "at the front." The rebs have been making demonstrations on the picket line of our forces every few days since this place has been occupied. The have kept the "*yanks*" on the *qui vive,* and have given the "commanding general" considerable uneasiness. A large force has been reported as hovering round, but I think that if the truth were known, it would reveal the fact that there are not 500 rebels within 100 miles of here. I think Joe Johnston needs all the troops he can muster. He has not extra strength to "fritter away" on "side-shows." The force here consists of two brigades numbering together 1500 or 2000 men. Gen. Stevenson was in command up to last Friday. Gen. Matthies now commands the post. A strong line of earthworks, about a half or three quarters of a mile in extent, have been thrown up around part of the town—the ends of the line resting on the river. Nearly all of the town outside this line of works has been demolished to give range to our guns that the houses may not afford shelter to the enemy in case of an attack. I listened to a very good sermon preached by the Chaplain of the 10th Iowa this afternoon. Weather very pleasant.

Monday, May 16. Reveille at 4 o'clock according to orders issued by Gen. Stevenson. I contend that such early rising is deleterious to health and I protest against it in the name of Comfort, Convenience, Health, and the Sanitary Commission. Decatur "as it was" was a pleasant little town, well situated and if it had been in a free state, would have become a place of some importance. From the town there is a view of the beautiful Tennessee for about eight miles. None of our Regiment, but the returned Veterans, is here. The detachment we left at Huntsville when we started home is still there and there is a probability of our remaining separated. I hope, however, it may not be so. Weather very pleasant. The news from the Army of the Potomac still continues favorable to our cause.

Tuesday, May 17. Our Colonel returned from Huntsville last evening where he received orders for the following dispositions of our Regiment. Head Quarters, and one fourth of the Regiment at Madison Station, on the Huntsville and Decatur R.R.—one fourth at Indian Creek on same road—one fourth at Beaver Dam—and one fourth at Limestone on same road. At 8 o'clock this morning, we started for our various destinations. We had just reached Decatur Junction (3 miles from Decatur) and were loading our teams when a frightened bluebacked Alabamian came dashing up with the intelligence that a large force of rebel cavalry had captured our forces at Madison Station and burned the Depot. Col. Banbury immediately telegraphed the fact to Gen. Matthies who immediately sent an order back for Col. B[anbury]. to remain at Decatur Junction and hold that place if it should be attacked. Our regiment and two companies of the 25th Indiana Infantry (which were stationed at the Junction) were at once ordered into the earthwork near the Junction, pickets were thrown out—ammunition issued and every preparation made for a fight. Messengers kept coming in for several hours with intelligence of the capture of Madison Station and also reporting the capture of our forces at Beaver Dam and Limestone. In the afternoon (the enemy not having made his appearance near the Junction), Gen. Matthies sent the 25th Indiana Regiment towards Madison Station on a "scout." The day wore away without any further alarm and about 9 o'clock in the evening a "reconnoitering train" arrived from Huntsville, bringing the intelligence that the rebels, about 600 strong, with three or four pieces of artillery, had driven the 13th Illinois Infantry out of Madison this forenoon, had burned the station and captured some 50 or 60 of the Illinois Regiment. Some 8 or 10 of our Regiment (who had come up from Huntsville yesterday evening) were in town at the time of the fight. They were all unarmed and some of them were sick. One of them was killed, two escaped, and the remainder were taken prisoner. The Illinois Regiment numbered nearly 300 but did not have a man killed. They seem to have taken great umbrage at the enemy's using artillery and skedaddled in a manner not very praiseworthy. Their flight was stopped by a detachment of our Regiment at Indian Creek or they might have been running yet. The rebels did not destroy the R.R. but left in a great hurry. The Illinois Regiment returned to the Station after the departure of the rebs. They had all their baggage burned. The Adjutant's and Quartermaster's desks of our Regiment were burned with all the Regimental papers. They were put off the cars at the station last night. Weather warm today, with rain this evening.

Wednesday, May 18. At 9 o'clock this morning we received "marching orders" and started again for Madison Station. At Limestone, Companies A., G., & E. relieved two companies of the 93d Illinois. C, I, and F relieved two

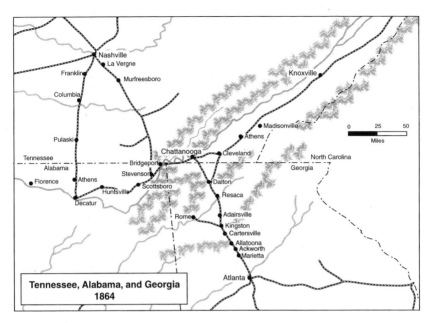

Tennessee, Alabama, and Georgia, 1864.

companies of the 26th Missouri. Company D stopped at Madison Station and Companies B and K are stationed at Indian Creek. Head Quarters of the Regiment at Madison Station, 15 miles from Decatur and 10 from Huntsville. Weather clear and warm.

Thursday, May 19. Weather clear and warm. In company with the Colonel and others, I rode to Huntsville today. We did not get back till after sundown. I found Huntsville more beautiful than ever. On my way to H[untsville]., I stopped at Indian Creek to see Company B. I found the boys in good health and spirits.

Friday, May 20. I had no breakfast this morning—*kase why:* there was none cooked for me. I asked to be relieved from my position as Adjutant that I might return to my company, but my request was refused. I got permission, however, to spend the day with the company and availed myself to the privilege. Weather clear and warm. On returning to Madison, I found that, I had missed a *"scare"* caused by the 13th [Illinois] pickets firing on some negroes and giving the alarm that the rebs were coming.

Saturday, May 21. "Headquarters" and Company D moved today to Beaver Dam. Our camp at Beaver Dam is a much more pleasant one than that at Madison Station. The creek is excellent for bathing in. Our camp is on high ground. We are well supplied with milk and butter by the citizens. For the purpose of defense, we have a good block-house. Weather very warm.

Sunday, May 22. Weather very warm. We have no chaplain with us, and consequently have no preaching. I will have to spend my Sabbath by reading Beecher's sermons, &c.

Monday, May 23. Weather warm. I went to Decatur on the Morning train and returned this afternoon. While there, I ate a 75c dinner at the hotel, having as part of my meal *green peas* and *straw-berry* pie. The Colonel is having our camp fortified by surrounding it with a line of breastworks and abattis.[1] A. L. from M.

Tuesday, May 24. A pleasant shower this morning has improved the atmosphere greatly. I have spent a good part of this day in writing letters.

Wednesday, May 25. Weather quite pleasant. Part of the 17th Army Corps passed our camp today under command of Gen. Frank Blair. The troops came from Huntsville and are marching to Rome *via* Decatur. They camped for the night in the vicinity of our camp. The head of the column reached here at 3 o'clock P.M. The rear did not get in until after 6 o'clock P.M. The 13th Iowa was in the rear Division and after they halted for the night, I called on the boys of Co. B. and spent an hour or two very pleasantly with them.

Thursday, May 26. Weather *airy* and pleasant. I have been busy most of the day on "official business"—making out my Regimental Returns of the Month of April. I received *two letters* from home today, the first since I returned to *Dixie.*

Friday, May 27. Weather pleasant. I have spent the day in camp, writing letters and attending to business.

Saturday, May 28. Weather pleasant. In camp at Beaver Creek Bridge. Beaver Creek is a stream some 16 ft. wide by 2 ft. deep. It heads about one mile above our camp where a large spring is located.

Sunday, May 29. Weather warm. No Chaplain—no Preacher—no sermon today.

Monday, May 30. Weather warm. I have been busy today on "Monthly Returns" and other "public documents" due at the last of the month.

Tuesday, May 31. Weather warm. "Busy" with my "Returns." At 3 o'clock this afternoon, we received orders to prepare to move to Decatur. At 10 o'clock P.M. we were relieved by part of the 12th Indiana Cavalry and, getting on the train they came on, we traveled "by rail" to Decatur Junction, arriving there at 12 1/2 o'clock Wednesday morning.

Wednesday, June 1. After reaching the "Junction" this morning, we marched over to Decatur. On arriving there I *burglariously* entered the room of the Chaplain of the 10th Iowa and got in bed with him. This, at 2 o'clock this morning. At 5 o'clock A.M. I "arose from my *couch*" and took breakfast at the McCartney Hotel. This forenoon the Regiment camped just outside of and at the south-east angle of the line of fortifications which surrounds the town. At eight o'clock this morning, the 10th Iowa Infantry and the 9th Ohio Cavalry, with two pieces of Artillery went out south-west of town on a reconnaissance. About the middle of the afternoon, four or five reports of cannon were heard from the direction our forces had gone in the morning. Of course, men dropped their work, their writing and their reading, and gathered outside of camp to look, listen, and speculate. Soon a cloud of dust was seen coming, whirling up the road. Presently, as it approached us, a horseman could be seen through the cloud of dust, "hurrying in hot haste" to Head Quarters—an orderly with dispatches no doubt. In a few moments the "long roll" was sounded in the other regiments and an orderly came dashing up with orders for us to "fall in," "to fight." Our Regiment was soon in line and joining the rest of the brigade, we moved out (on the road our forces had gone out on) with the purpose of seeing *"fair play."* Our Regiment was assigned the position of "support" for two pieces of Artillery which moved out with our brigade. While marching out we learned that our force went out six miles on their reconnaissance when they came upon the enemy in strong force and were compelled to fall back. The reports of cannon which we had heard were from our artillery which was shelling the pursuing enemy. We marched out about one mile when we met the reconnoitering force and learned that the enemy were on the retreat. We immediately returned to camp, our regiment bringing up the rear with the loss of a great deal of *sweat!* Weather excessively hot. In the evening we had a shower.

Thursday, June 2. Reveille at 4 o'clock A.M. according to "orders." Weather very warm during the day with some rain.

Friday, June 3. Reveille at 4 o'clock A.M. Weather warm with rain. Dress Parade in the evening. I have been reading "Hans of Iceland, or, The Demon of the North" by Victor Hugo. The news from Sherman and Grant still continues cheering.

Saturday, June 4. Weather warm with frequent showers. I finished reading "Hans of Iceland" today.

Sunday, June 5. Weather clear and pleasant. The Chaplain of the 10th preached to an audience of about 40 in an old mill above town this afternoon.

Monday, June 6. Some "intelligent contraband" having informed the commander of the post, that Roddy was going to make an attack on the place this morning, we had reveille at 3 1/2 o'clock A.M. Weather clear and warm. I have been writing on the history of the Regiment today.

Tuesday, June 7. Weather clear and very warm. I have been writing "history." Reveille this morning at 4 o'clock.

Wednesday, June 8. Reveille at 4 o'clock. After the Regiment was formed on the color line, it was moved into "Fort No. One," where it remained until 5 o'clock P.M.

Thursday, June 9. A clear, pleasant day. Battalion Drill in afternoon. News came this afternoon of the nomination of Lincoln and Johnston [sic] by the Baltimore Convention. Fremont and Cochrane were nominated by the Cleveland Convention a few days ago. McClellan will be nominated by the Chicago

Convention.[2] Neither of the three is my choice but Lincoln will certainly get my vote, if I live to cast one. I am loyal, and cannot vote for McClellan. I am in my right senses and cannot vote for the Cleveland faction nominations. Mr. Lincoln is the choice of the great majority of the *loyal* people of the North, and *I* will endorse the nomination by my vote.

Friday, June 10. Weather pleasant with a short shower. I am kept busy in the "office."

Saturday, June 11. Weather pleasant with slight showers.

Sunday, June 12. It has rained steadily all day and we have been kept in our tents. The 18th Michigan Regiment arrived here from Nashville this evening. The are part of a force that is coming here to relieve our brigade. They have been in Nashville for 14 months—have never been in a fight—and yet we are to go to "the front" and they are to stay back. Nevertheless, I don't envy them, their history, or reputation.

Monday, June 13. Rain in the evening. During the day, clouds "dried up" or "give out" and the weather turned cool. It has rained or sprinkled every day but one since we came here.

Tuesday, June 14. Weather clear and warm. We received "marching orders" today.

Wednesday, June 15. At six o'clock this morning our Brigade took up its line of march for Huntsville—the 5th Iowa being in advance. The 18th Michigan and 134th Indiana (100-day Regiment) will garrison the works at Decatur.[3] The Brigade of the 16th Corps will leave Decatur for Huntsville today. At noon, we camped near the railroad about one mile from Madison Station having marched 15 miles. The men marched on the railroad track while the trains, under escort, came by the wagon-road. The weather has been clear and warm. Our camping place this evening is a very pleasant one. May we see many similar ones on our coming march.

Thursday, June 16. Weather clear and warm. We marched 12 miles, starting at 6 o'clock A.M. and arriving at Huntsville at 10 1/2 A.M. We camped about one mile S.E. of town. On getting into camp we were informed that we would probably remain here 3 or 4 days. The brigade of the 16th Corps marched back to Decatur today. We had not been gone from Decatur two hours when the rebels drove the Michiganders and Hundred Day Indianians into the works and captured two of their outposts. Hence the brigade was ordered back. Our present camp is a very pleasant one—"may we *stay with it.*"

Friday, June 17. Weather clear and warm. This forenoon I visited town on business and to look around. This afternoon I have spent in camp writing letters, &c.

Saturday, June 18. Weather cloudy and more pleasant than yesterday. I have spent the day in camp.

Sunday, June 19. Weather warm with a shower in the forenoon. I attended

Episcopal church in town this forenoon. I can't say that I approve of their form of worship. This afternoon I spent some time reading the *"Independent."*

Monday, June 20. Weather clear and warm. I have kept myself employed in camp today.

Later! Weather warm with rain late in the afternoon. I rode down to town in the afternoon and my horse ran away with me, much to my chagrin and peril. I have been busy with my Ordnance accounts.

Tuesday, June 21. Rain last night followed by rain today. I have been busy in camp.

Wednesday, June 22. Reveille at 3 1/2 o'clock this morning. At 5 o'clock the 1st Brigade of our Division moved out of Huntsville on the Road to Stevenson. The 2nd Brigade followed the First and at 9 o'clock A.M. the 3d Brigade moved out. The fair dames of Huntsville were out "in force" to see us leave, glad to get a *last* look at us. The weather which had been quite *"wet"* for 36 hours, changed for the better this morning and we had a pleasant day for marching. We marched 12 miles and camped on Flint River. Our Brigade being "rear-guard" did not get into camp until 3 o'clock P.M.

Thursday, June 23. Reveille at 3 1/2 o'clock. At 5 o'clock the 2nd Brigade moved out and were followed by the 3d—our Regiment being the advance of our Brigade. Weather clear and warm during the day. We marched 15 miles during the day—camped at 3 P.M. on Paint Rock Creek.

Friday, June 24. Reveille at 20 minutes before 3 o'clock. At 4 o'clock our Brigade moved out—our Regiment being rear-guard of the Brigade. We marched 18 miles and camped near Scottsboro. The advance got into camp at 2 o'clock P.M. The weather has been very hot and numerous cases of sunstroke have occurred—one in our Regiment. One man in the 63d Ills. accidentally shot and killed himself after getting into camp. The roads have been very bad and in repairing them at one place, one of the Pioneer Corps cut his foot nearly off. The 2nd Brigade (being in the rear) did not get up this evening but camped at Larkinsville, 5 miles from Scottsboro.

Saturday, June 25. Reveille about 4 o'clock. At 6 o'clock our Brigade moved out following the 1st Brigade. We marched 17 miles and camped within 3 miles of Stevenson, at 6 o'clock P.M. The weather has been extremely hot today but as we were longer on the road and did not march as far as yesterday, there were fewer cases of sunstroke. We passed through Bellefont.

Sunday, June 26. This, I think, has been the warmest day I have seen in the South. We have remained in camp but have suffered much from the heat. Orders have been received indicating that we will take the cars at Stevenson for Kingston, Georgia. We have received no mail since we left Huntsville. The news from Grant and Sherman is not as encouraging as we had expected it would be. Gold has been up to $2.35—now stands at $2.17!!. These are "blue days."

Monday, June 27. The weather is *not quite* as hot today as it was yesterday. At one o'clock P.M. the "assembly" was sounded and about two we started for Stevenson. On the way to town (3 miles distant from camp) one of the 93d Illinois was sun-struck. On our arrival at Stevenson we were "loaded" on box cars and shipped to Chattanooga where we arrived at *some time* in the night.

Tuesday, June 28. At 9 o'clock this forenoon our train left Chattanooga for Kingston, Georgia. As the trains on the road to Kingston run by Telegraph, we were delayed at different points along the road and did not reach Kingston until 9 o'clock P.M. At Dalton we were delayed three or four hours. A train that started North, from Dalton, a few moments after our arrival at that point, ran into the train of the 93d Ills., about one mile north of Dalton. About 35 of the 93rd boys were injured—17 so severely that they were sent back to Chattanooga. The Conductor jumped off the train and motioned to the boys to do likewise. No one was hurt who remained on the cars. The county we have passed through today has been rough and mountainous and is a poor section. The towns are not worthy of the name. Dalton (the largest) is a very ordinary place, of some 800 or 1000 inhabitants in time of peace. Kingston is not so large by one fourth.

Wednesday, June 29. Our Regiment being the only one of the Brigade that got to Kingston last night, Col. Sampson marched us out to an old camp this morning and the boys soon built themselves habitations of the ruins left behind by the *previousers.* Our tents were left behind to be brought up by our wagon train. The 93d Ills. and two Regiments of the 2nd Brigade arrived today. Weather warm with indications of rain.

Thursday, June 30. Brigade Head Quarters and our horses and private baggage arrived on the train last night. All of the 2nd Brigade is now here. The 26th Missouri of our Brigade is bringing in a drove of cattle through from Chattanooga. The news from Sherman's army is conflicting. I judge that we have not gained much in the fighting this week. Trains of wounded pass North every few hours. I have been busy making out Returns and Reports this afternoon. This forenoon we changed our camping place.

Friday, July 1. I have been very busy making out Returns and Reports today. A heavy rain fell this evening. The 2nd Brigade left for Resaca about sundown.

Saturday, July 2. Weather very warm with heavy showers in forenoon and afternoon. At noon, our Regiment (agreeably to orders) marched from Kingston for Wooley's Bridge on the Etowah river 2 1/2 miles west of Kingston. The boys got considerably *wetted* by the rain on the way. My gum-blanket played for me the part of a "friend in need."

Sunday, July 3. Our Regiment is quartered in the houses on Wooley's plantation and are very comfortably situated. "Wooley's Place" has been one of the finest in the South. The dwelling, barns, and outhouses are all of Northern style and a tact is displayed in the surroundings that we seldom see in

"Dixie." Mr. Wooley is a South Carolinian by birth. Near his house, a covered bridge of 122 yards span has been built over the Etowah at his own expense. Mr. Wooley "took wings and flew away" from his riches on the approach of the "yanks." The river here is a clear, swift stream, one hundred yards wide. It is called by the whites of this country "High-tower." It was called "E-*tow*-ah" by the Indians. (Like *tow* in tower) Our Regiment maintains a guard at Reynold's ford, 2 1/2 miles up the river and at Murchison's ford 1 1/2 miles down the river and at Wooley's Bridge. We yesterday received the very unwelcome intelligence of the resignation of Secretary Chase. Today we received news of the appointment of Senator Fessenden as Chase's successor—a good appointment.[4] News came in the Nashville paper today of the death of Gen. Hooker. I hope this is a mistake. Weather very warm.

Monday, July 4. "The glorious Fourth." Won't they have a gay time up in "America" today? I began a celebration of the day by going to work. I then took a short rest to pick huckle-berries. I then took another pull at my work. I then make a *big* pull at a rather ordinary dinner. I then took another "pull" at my work—then played a few games of chess—then worked awhile—*then ate a big* portion of a very good supper—then had Dress Parade—then rode around the picket lines. About the time I was going to bed, an orderly came out from town with the intelligence that the rebels intend [on] destroying the bridge at this point tonight. Of course, the pickets had to be notified and I rode out to one post. At 10 o'clock P.M. I "retired." Weather hot.

Tuesday, July 5. Owing to the information brought from town last night, we had reveille at 3 o'clock this morning. The Regiment was formed and "stood to arms" until after sun rise. No rebels made their appearance and the bridge was not burned. "ditto" the "fords." I received three letters today—the first for two weeks. This evening I rode to town on business.

Wednesday, July 6. Weather hot. I spent a good part of my time today in writing. This evening after Dress Parade, I took a ride on horseback to Murchison's Ford. The news of the evacuation of Kennesaw Mountain by the rebels is confirmed.[5] Hooker is not dead.

Thursday, July 7. Weather hot. I have remained in camp. Nothing going on to excite or interest.

Friday, July 8. "Ditto" to yesterday.

Saturday, July 9. Weather hot. This evening in company with Dr. Carpenter, I rode out three miles out the Rome road—found a poor country, poorly settled by a poor people.

Sunday, July 10. I read three of Spurgeon's Sermons today and heard our Chaplain (who has returned to the Regiment) preach another. Weather hot with a slight rain in the afternoon.

Monday, July 11. Weather hot, with slight rain in the afternoon—heavy rains "passed around" us. I was "out black berrying" this afternoon.

Tuesday, July 12. Last night the Colonel received orders to relieve the 93d

Illinois Regiment which was guarding the fords above us and at 5 1/2 o'clock this morning, the Colonel started with the "left wing" to carry out the order. I accompanied him "by order." Companies A. and D. were left at "Island Ford" about 4 miles from our Head Quarters. Companies B. and G. were left at Gillam's Bridge 2 1/2 miles farther up the river and Company "H" was stationed at Caldwell's Ford, 4 miles above Gillam's bridge. We reached Caldwell's Ford at 10 1/4 o'clock. On our return the Colonel and I stopped at a Dr. Gillam's and got our dinners. The "bill of fare" consisted of Graham bread—bacon—fried chicken—chicken gravy—good butter—young Irish potatoes—snap beans—summer squashes—cucumbers—pickled beets—and apple and blackberry pie with "sop," and cream to drink. We stopped an hour at Kingston and reached camp on our return at 4 o'clock P.M. Our Regiment is now stretched along the river for twelve miles. Brigade Head Quarters are at Kingston. Division Head Quarters at Cartersville, 12 miles South of Kingston. Weather very hot with a slight sprinkling of rain.

Wednesday, July 13. Weather hot. I have done a little writing, a little reading, and some loafing today.

Thursday, July 14. This is the last day of my three years' service. I have busied myself making out my Ordnance Return. This afternoon, in company with the Chaplain and Lieut. [Spencer] Getts, I "went a berrying." We got our vessels full of the nicest blackberries I ever saw. We also procured some rare flowers at a "natives" house.

Friday, July 15. Weather hot. I rode to town this morning—gathered huckleberries this afternoon.

Saturday, July 16. I have spent the day writing, gathering blackberries and reading Parton's "Butler in New Orleans."[6] Weather dry and hot. Lieut. Col. Sampson received a dispatch this afternoon, stating that the veterans and Recruits of our Regiment had been transferred to the 5th Iowa Cavalry by order of Gen. Sherman. This is in accordance with a petition of the men, which was forwarded a week or two since. This disposition having been made, the officers and non-veterans expect to be mustered out in a very few days.

Sunday, July 17. Weather hot. Our Chaplain preached an excellent sermon this forenoon. This afternoon I read two of Spurgeon's sermons. About sundown this evening, word was sent out from Brigade Head Quarters that two Regiments of rebels with *"right smart"* artillery were reported to be within a few miles of us on the other side of the river. Necessary precautions were taken and we retired for a sound sleep.

Monday, July 18. No rebels came last night and the weather being very propitious we enjoyed a night of excellent slumber. Weather today much more pleasant than for a week past. I rode to town this morning. This afternoon I was out gathering huckleberries.

Tuesday, July 19. Weather warm. I rode out to Hargis' this afternoon and to town this evening. I wrote two letters today which I will not mail until we get orders "disposing of the 5th Iowa. Lt. [Samuel] Sample started to Gen. McPherson's Head Quarter today with a *"prayer"* from Lt. Col. Sampson, asking that the non-veterans be sent home to be mustered out of the service.

Wednesday, July 20. An eventful day! Several of the non-veterans, feeling aggrieved at the injustice of not being mustered out when their time expired, this morning refused to do duty and were sent to Kingston under arrest. Their treatment has certainly not been just nor merited but their action in refusing to do duty only adds to their misfortunes or injuries. Col. Sampson has used his every endeavor to secure the boys their rights and their conduct has caused him great mortification. There has been no reason given why the men are not mustered out and we are all "doubt and uncertainty." Fifty men of the 8th Iowa Cavalry came out to re-inforce us this afternoon. This afternoon, a party under command of the Provost Marshal of Kingston crossed the river and burned all the buildings on a plantation 2 miles below our camp—turning a family "out into the weather." The occasion of this proceeding was so follows: A week ago, a man, belonging to a government "corral" was captured at said plantation. He escaped from his captors and returned to Kingston where he reported that "the lady of the house" gave the information to the guerrillas that led to his capture. Hence the "retribution." I rode to town this forenoon. Weather hot. About dark this evening a force of 18 men crossed the river on a scout. At nine o'clock this evening, I was sent by the Colonel, with the Lieut. of the 8th Iowa and two of our boys, out to Murchison's to bring in two boys living there who were thought to be meditating an escape to the other side of the river. The man who escaped from the rebels (as above mentioned) reported that Murchison's son was among his captors and that a line of communication was kept up, through the Murchison family, with the other side of the river. Today, the Murchison family were ordered to pack up, to go North.

Thursday, July 21. After bringing the boys from Murchison's last night, I "retired" and had been asleep about an hour and a quarter when I awakened by a volley of musketry. Jumping up and dressing, I found others, similarly engaged for the firing still continued and it was evident "something was up." This was about 11 1/2 o'clock. After getting out, I ran down and roused the 8th Iowa boys, who were all sound asleep, and the Colonel formed the boys in line down near the Railroad. The firing (which was in the direction of our picket post at Murchison's Ford) was kept us up constantly during all this time—sounding much like skirmishing—about one shot a minute being fired. About this time, the scouting party came in from across the river and one of the boys from the Ford arrived "in hot haste." He reported they had been attacked in front and flank and that they had escaped by falling back without firing—all the firing we had heard having been done by the enemy. Col. Sampson sent Lt. Peck with Company E out on the road to the Ford and marched the rest of the force up to the grove about Head Quarters. Soon after Lt. Peck started out the firing ceased and on his return, we learned that he marched to the ford and found that the enemy had all recrossed the river. They fired their last shots at our pickets from the Railroad 1/3 of a mile this side of the ford. Their design was evidently to "gobble" our picket post—perhaps in retaliation for the "house burning" yesterday. Part of them crossed the river below the Ford to surround the boys but their companions on the other side of the river opened fire too soon and frustrated their plans. After learning that [all] was again quiet on the Etowah, we lay down (at 3 o'clock) for a few hours rest. This morning I rode down to the ford and reconnoitered the bank for a mile below but failed to make any astounding discoveries. I found *"tracks"* but couldn't assert that *"ex pede Herculem."*[7] I have not yet learned the difference between the track of a yankee vandal and southern *"gorilla."* A company of mounted men from the 93d Ills. came out to reinforce us during the "battle" last night. This afternoon, three of Murchison's daughters were sent North, being considered dangerous characters in this region. The rest of the family will "follow suit" if they don't carry themselves very straight. We had a good rain this afternoon. The weather was extremely hot.

Friday, July 22. A pleasant day. I finished reading Parton's *"Butler in New Orleans"* today. This evening, I rode to town. While there, word was received from Gillam's Bridge that Wm. Anderson of Co. B. had been killed and John Hall of the same company had been wounded by guerrillas. The boys had gone to a house about a half a mile from, and in sight of, the bridge. Just as they reached the house the man of the house drove up with a load of wheat—stopped his team—and started back, without saying a word to the boys. His daughter (who claims to be Union) told the boys to run for their lives. They started but had run but a few paces when they were fired at. After running a short distance, Anderson was shot in the shoulder and fell. Hall was also shot but ran (firing his revolver over his shoulder) till he reached the Bridge. Capt. Pennywitt immediately crossed the river with about twenty men, and the guerrillas (some 25 in number) fled. After Anderson fell, they shot him through the neck and beat him about the head till life was extinct. Hall was wounded in the hip. His life was saved by his revolver (it being then in its scabbard). A "squirrel rifle" ball struck the barrel of his revolver and lodged against the hinge of the rammer. A piece of the ball passed on and entered his hip. Capt. Pennywitt burned all the houses on Johnston's place. We received news of the capture of Atlanta by our forces this morning.[8] The papers today contain a call for 500,000 more troops. So mote it be.

Saturday, July 23. A very pleasant day. I rode to Kingston on business this morning. News was received this morning that Gen. McPherson was killed yesterday.[9] The report has caused a deep gloom to settle over the minds of all. No better officer can be found in our army. Our order to go home has not arrived yet. There will be much trouble in the Regiment if the orders does not come soon.

Sunday, July 24. Weather pleasant. Our Chaplain went to town this forenoon to preach at the hospital. I took my Sunday reading from "Spurgeon's Sermons." This afternoon word was received that the mustering officer would be here to muster out our non-veterans tomorrow and that the officers would be held in the service. The news of the death of Gen. McPherson is confirmed. He was so well loved by his men and so honored by the nation, that deep grief will pervade the army and the loyal North at the news. So young, so intelligent, so kind, so modest, and so brave—all who knew him loved him. The news of the capture of Atlanta was premature. There has been very hard fighting and heavy losses within the last day or two. At eight o'clock, I received word from "Perry" that the 7th Ohio Cavalry was at Kingston and would leave in the morning.[10] I jumped on my horse and rode to town instanter. On arriving at town, I hunted the cavalry camp and soon found Capt. [Cal] Rankin. His company all being in bed, I accepted the Captain's offer to "bunk" with him and soon talked myself to sleep.

Monday, July 25. At 2 1/2 o'clock this morning, the cavalry had reveille and I got up and began to stir about to find old acquaintances. My search was not in vain, as the following list will show. I had the pleasure of shaking hands with: Ed. Gaddis, Howard Johnson, Tom. Coulter, Ben. Durstine, Tom. McCayne, George Cradit, Andy Espey, Archie Dixon, Will Jones, and others. Their regiment started for Marietta at daylight. I rode into town after the cavalry left and remained there until about seven o'clock, when I started for Wooley's Plantation acting as guide for four companies of the 26th Missouri which relieved our regiment. After being relieved our regiment marched into Kingston and we are now camped just east of town. This forenoon, Col. Banbury was relieved of command of the Brigade and orders were received transferring the 5th Iowa Infantry Regiment to the Army of the Cumberland and directing the Colonel to report to Gen. Thomas for instructions. Col. Banbury accordingly started to the front this evening. This afternoon, a mustering officer came from Head Quarters of the 3d Division to muster out the non-veterans but on seeing the order transferring our Regiment to the Army of the Cumberland, he concluded we were out of his jurisdiction and he returned to Div. Hd. Qrs. We are now awaiting "the next thing that is turn up." Weather pleasant—nights cool.

Tuesday, July 26. Our teams and camp and garrison equipage were "turned over" today. Weather pleasant but warmer than yesterday.

Wednesday, July 27. Col. Banbury got back from Dept. Head Quarters this afternoon with orders. The non-veterans start to Chattanooga tomorrow morning to be mustered out. The officers, veterans, and recruits are temporarily assigned to the 5th Iowa Cavalry for duty.[11] The recommendation for the transfer to the cavalry has been approved by Gen. Thomas and Gen. Sherman and has been forwarded to the War Department. Weather warm with rain in the afternoon.

Thursday, July 28. The non-veterans started for Chattanooga at six o'clock this morning. We are left "desolate and lonely" but hope to hear soon from the 5th Cavalry and learn our fate. Weather warm.

Friday, July 29. Col. Banbury started to Nashville for orders today. Weather very warm.

Saturday, July 30. The news came from the "front" is encouraging. Hood seems to be determined to butt his men's brains out against our works.[12] He seems to be devoid of that "better part of valor"—discretion. Capt. Thompson returned this evening from Chattanooga bringing news that the boys were probably mustered out today. Weather hot.

Sunday, July 31. The 10th Iowa Veterans returned from furlough today. They bring word that our boys were mustered out yesterday afternoon. Capt. Pennywitt started to Chattanooga this morning with a detachment of the recruits of the Regiment who expect to be mustered out. Weather hot with a light shower of rain. The Regiment was payed to day for May and June. Although we have only about 175 men present, the pay master paid us over $10,000. I received my pay last night.

Monday, August 1. Weather hot with a sprinkle of rain. Most of our Regiment was on duty today while the 26th Missouri was being paid.

Tuesday, August 2. Our Regiment was detailed as escort for a train and reported at Brigade Head Quarters at 6 1/2 o'clock. We proceeded to Collister's Mill 11 miles South of Kingston and returned (by 5 o'clock P.M.) with 28 bales of cotton belonging to Collister, who is a "refugee." This cotton will be paid for after the war if Collister continues loyal. In the meantime, Uncle Sam'l pockets the proceeds. We were able to bring only about half of the lot. The country on the other side of the river is much better than on this. Collister's Mill is in the center of the best pine region I ever saw. We crossed the river at Island Ford as we went out and at Gillam's Bridge coming back. We saw four guerrillas on the route. The Colonel refused to let the boys fire at them, thinking they were not in range. I, in common with others, thought they *were* in range and I was anxious for the boys to fire on them. *They* seemed to think they were in range of our pieces for they were in much of a hurry to place a hill between themselves and us. Weather warm.

Wednesday, August 3. Weather very warm with slight rain. The old 3d Brigade, 3d Division, 15th Army Corps has been broken up, since the transferring of our Regiment to the Army of the Cumberland. The 93d Illinois has been assigned to the first brigade and the 26th Missouri and 10th Iowa to the second. May the leaven that is thus introduced into the First Brigade, leaven the whole lump and make a *fighting* brigade of it.

Thursday, August 4. Weather very oppressive. We have heard nothing from Col. Banbury yet. We had a big watermelon treat this P.M.

Friday, August 5. Weather very warm. We are having a very lonesome time—have but little to do and the officers get no letters worth noting and Kingston is as "dry as a chip." Slight rain this P.M.

Saturday, August 6. This forenoon, in company with Lieut. Barrett, I rode out to Reynold's Ford on the Etowah [River] and got about twenty dozen ears of green corn for the mess. This afternoon we had a very heavy rain.

Sunday, August 7. I listened to a sermon by the Chaplain of the 10th Iowa this morning. Weather very warm. We have heard nothing from Col. Banbury yet.

Monday, August 8. Weather very warm. Col. Sampson received a dispatch from the commanding officer of the 5th Iowa Cavalry stating that he daily expected an order for us to go to Nashville. Slight rain this afternoon.

Tuesday, August 9. Weather warm with showers in the afternoon. I received a letter from home this morning.

Wednesday, August 10. Weather tolerably warm with heavy rains. I received two letters today written last May.

Thursday, August 11. Weather pleasant with hard rain in the evening. Waiting for orders.

Friday, August 12. Weather warm with rain. No orders received yet.

Saturday, August 13. Weather warm. I went to Rome this morning on the R.R. and came back this afternoon. Rome is a tolerably pretty place for this Southern country but would be a very common looking town at the North.

Sunday, August 14. I was quite unwell last night and this morning and am not in a perfect state of health yet. I have had a slight attack of bilious fever. Weather warm.

Monday, August 15. Weather warm. A squad of our recruits left for Chattanooga yesterday to be mustered out. A rebel cavalry force attacked and captured a large part of a drove of cattle near Adairsville yesterday evening. They also tore up the R.R. track near Dalton. At noon today our regiment received orders to be ready to embark on the cars with two day's rations and 100 rounds of ammunition. At eight o'clock this evening our regiment and the 10th Iowa embarked on the cars for Resaca. Two trains preceded ours on which were two regiments from Rome, two regiments from Alatoona, and two from Marietta. I spread my blanket and went to sleep soon after getting on the cars and slept till morning.

Tuesday, August 16. At Resaca. At 7 o'clock A.M. we debarked from the cars and at 9 o'clock we moved out of town to a convenient shade. Lieut. Col. Sampson has been placed in command of a brigade of four regiments—the 5th and 10th Iowa, the 93d Illinois and 48th Indiana. There has been no communications with Chattanooga by rail since Sunday afternoon. The rebel cavalry force that cut the road is reported to be at Spring Place, 16 miles east of Resaca

Wednesday, August 17. At sunrise this morning our force moved out the Spring Place Road in the following order: 1st—the Cavalry Regiment. 2nd—the two Regiments from Marietta under Col. Logan. 3rd—two Regiments from Rome under Lt. Col. Hurlbut. 4th Lt. Col. Sampson's brigade. The order to move this morning was sent round last night but failed to reach Col. Sampson and we had to start out without breakfast. Brig. Gens. John E. Smith and Ed. McCook are with our expedition. Smith in command. One mile N.E. of Resaca we crossed the Conesauga river—two miles from Resaca we stopped and took a lunch. We marched 11 miles from Resaca and halted near a creek till evening. Gen. Smith and the cavalry went on to Spring Place, the rebels having left yesterday afternoon. The country we passed through on the march is in Northern Georgia—*ergo* is very poor. The rebel cavalry force is said to number from 8,000 to 10,000 and is commanded by Wheeler and Morgan.[13] The men live principally on green corn. Wheeler held the *town* of Dalton Sunday evening for a short time but a force of black troops came down from Chattanooga and soon drove them out. Two companies of the 17th Iowa were captured on the R.R. near Tilton. It is reported today that they have ben released. At dark, we started back to Resacca [*sic*] marching left in front. Our brigade arrived at town at ten minutes past midnight after a very fatiguing march.

Thursday, August 18. About sunrise this morning, the other two brigades came in, they having stopped on the road last night. At one o'clock P.M. our brigade embarked on the cars for Kingston where we arrived at 3 o'clock P.M. A heavy rain fell this afternoon. Owing to the deficiency in the supply of cooks, cooking utensils, and eatables, I have fared rather rough on this trip but my health has been good. At 8 o'clock this evening Col. Sampson received a dispatch from Col. Banbury stating that the order consolidating our regiment with the 5th Cavalry had been issued by the War Department and that we will be sent to Nashville in a few days.

Friday, August 19. At 10 o'clock last night we were "scared up" by an order from Post Head Qrs. to "prepare for action" immediately. A telegram has been received stating that Cartersville is attacked. This regiment was formed just in time to stack arms and go to bed. Another order came which stated that the telegram was incorrect—that Acworth and not Cartersville was attacked. We were not long in getting back to bed. Weather warm this forenoon with rain in the afternoon. A train came through from Nashville this evening.

Saturday, August 20. Weather warm with heavy rains.

Sunday, August 21. Weather warm and clear.

Monday, August 22. Weather ditto to yesterday. We have orders to be ready to move out at a moment's notice.

Tuesday, August 23. Left camp at 2 o'clock this morning and got aboard the cars and started for Chattanooga. At 4 o'clock P.M. we arrived at the "Junction" 7 miles from Chattanooga where we found Gen. Steadman with a force from Chattanooga awaiting our arrival.[14] On starting this morning, our regiment (90 men) was consolidated with the 10th Iowa, our Lieut. Colonel not being able to accompany us on account of sickness. I accordingly left my horse at Kingston. As soon as we arrived at the "Junction," our train was switched off on to the Cleveland track and we started for East Tennessee to look after

Wheeler. At dusk we reached Cleveland and stopped an hour and then started for Charleston. Weather clear and warm.

Wednesday, August 24. At daylight this morning our force got off the cars at a point where the road was torn up two miles east of Charleston. We started for Athens at sunrise and reached there after an easy march of 12 miles. After resting an hour or two, we marched four miles farther east on the Loudon road and camped for the night. Athens is a very pretty little village full of pretty girls and loyal people. The rebels have torn up the R.R. track, (without destroying any bridges of any size) for a distance of 14 miles. Our march today has been, for the first nine miles, up "Dry Valley"—so called from its lack of any stream larger than a rivulet. Gen. Steadman's force numbers about 4,000 men—including one negro regiment—as good soldiers as any in the force.[15]

Thursday, August 25. Starting at sun-rise, we marched seven miles on the road to Madisonville and halted for two hours. Here Gen. Steadmen learned that Gen. Wheeler had crossed the Tennessee river and we turned back. After marching 2 miles in return, we camped for the night on a farm belonging to a rebel conscript agent and at a hint from the General, the boys literally stripped the farm of fruits of vegetables and other eatables.

Friday, August 26. Starting at daylight, we marched back to Athens and camped east of that place. Weather warm with slight rain in the evening.

Saturday, August 27. Starting at 9 o'clock this morning, we marched back to a point four miles east of Charleston and there camped for the night. Weather clear and warm. I today met some Ripley boys in the 2nd Ohio Heavy Artillery.

Sunday, August 28. Getting on the cars at 2 o'clock P.M. we started for Chattanooga where our train arrived at 8 o'clock P.M. and we got off the cars and "bivouacked" on the "commons" near the Depot. The train in rear of us ran off the track and is not in yet. I have seen something of East Tennessee and am well pleased with both the country and people. I have seen no such loyalty anywhere else in the South. The inhabitants are as loyal as the people of Ohio and even more so. The country is undulating and hilly and very pleasant to the eye. When near Madisonville, we were within 18 miles of, and in sight of, the mountains of North Carolina.

Monday, August 29. We expected to go to Kingston today but have been disappointed. I have spent my time today making purchases and attending to Regimental business. I learned this morning from Col. Banbury (who came up from Kingston on business) that I am one of six officers to be transferred to the 5th Iowa Cavalry with the veterans of our Regiment. Weather clear.

Tuesday, August 30. Lying around in the dust and dirt near the Chattanooga Depot, we still find ourselves Disappointed again. A number of the boys went down today "on their own hook." Weather clear and warm.

Wednesday, August 31. Learning that we would not get off for Kingston today, I took a trip on to Lookout Mountain and feel well repaid for my walk of eight miles. The view from the top of the mountain is magnificent. I saw Dr. Carpenter on the mountain and was the recipient of a present from him. Our Regiment moved outside the picket lines and bivouacked in an orchard this morning.

Thursday, September 1. At 5 o'clock this morning (and agreeably to orders) we left our bivouac and marched to the cars, preparatory to making another chase after Wheeler. At 7 o'clock we started for Murfreesboro where we arrived at eleven o'clock P.M., and debarked from the cars. Weather clear and warm.

Friday, September 2. At three o'clock this morning, we were called up and started for Lavergne where Wheeler was reported to be tearing up the Railroad. We marched on the Murfreesboro pike through the battlefield of Stone River and arrived at Lavergne about 10 o'clock A.M. having marched 15 1/2 miles *before breakfast.* We rested about a half mile North of Lavergne until 5 o'clock in the morning when we formed a line of battle and moved into position south of Lavergne. A body of rebels were reported to be near and we prepared for action but they failed to come to time. At dark, we lay down in line of battle for a night's rest but about eight o'clock P.M. we were called up and started towards Murfreesboro. After a wearisome march of seven miles, we halted and lay down to rest along the pike. The weather today was pretty warm but during the night march it was very sultry and oppressive. Our night march was for the purpose of looking after a force of rebels which was reported to be in camp at the point where we halted. We failed to find them.

Saturday, Sept 3. At sunrise this morning we had breakfast. About 8 o'clock a few mounted rebels were seen near a skirt of timber a mile east of us and force of 200 or 300 of them was reported in that neighborhood. About 9 1/2 o'clock a force of cavalry (which had been sent by Gen. Steadman) under command of Gen. [Robert] Milroy arrived and they were immediately sent around, while we formed a line of battle and moved on the rebels from the front. After an advance in line-of-battle for a mile, we found the rebels (200 cavalry) had made good their escape and we were again formed in column and after a rest, marched four miles farther east and halted on Stone River. The weather was excessively hot when we were moving in line-of-battle and I never suffered as much from heat at any time in my life with one exception. At 5 o'clock we marched back 3 miles to the Railroad where we halted for the night. Our force is of about equal strength with the force we had in East Tennessee but composed of different regiments. The negro regiment is still with us. I never saw any Regiment move in line-of-battle in as good order as they did when we were expecting a fight. They are an excellently drilled and disciplined Regiment.

Sunday, September 4. At sun-rise this morning, we started on the *cars* for Murfreesboro. Wheeler having burned considerable wood and burned several miles of the R.R. track near Lavergne, was chased away by a force of cavalry under Gen. [Lovell] Rousseau on the evening of the 2nd. He has gone west towards Franklin. On arriving at Murfreesboro we got off the cars to get breakfast. At ten o'clock A.M. our brigade was marched south along the R.R. half a mile and then marched west on the Lebanon Pike for a mile. The rebels were reported to be two miles west of town. After marching a mile we halted to rest, and news came that Gen. Milroy's cavalry had driven the rebels northward. We could distinctly hear the cannonading. The weather was more intensely hot this forenoon than yesterday and during the march of a mile and half the suffering was extreme. Numerous cases of sun-stroke occurred. After a rest of half an hour, we started back to Murfreesboro where we remained in the shade the balance of the day.

Monday, September 5. Murfreesboro is a very pretty town—is intensely secesh—and is the most strongly fortified place I have ever seen. The country between Murfreesboro and Nashville is rolling and is the finest looking I have seen anywhere in the South. It is well timbered, has a good soil, is well improved but is not very well watered. It is the greatest "peach region" in the South. At 10 o'clock this morning we got on board the cars and started for Pulaski *via* Stevenson, Huntsville, and Decatur. Owing to delays we did not reach Stevenson until near midnight and our train stopped a few miles west of Scottsboro till morning.

Tuesday, September 6. Starting at sun-rise, we reached Huntsville about 11 o'clock A.M. Our whole force debarked and marched out to the big spring near town where we drew rations and got dinner. We then got aboard the cars again and started for Pulaski, where we arrived about 11 o'clock P.M.

Wednesday, Sept. 7. Pulaski is one of the prettiest towns in Tennessee. We lay at the depot on the cars until eleven o'clock A.M. when we started back for Athens, Alabama. Wheeler having been driven from the neighborhood of Pulaski by our cavalry towards Florence, Alabama. Arriving at Athens we debarked and camped in the suburbs of the town. Late this evening, one brigade of our force moved out on the Florence road. Weather pleasant.

Thursday, Sept. 8. Most of Rousseau's and [Brig. Gen. Robert] Granger's cavalry came in today for rations and ammunition and having their wants supplied, started for Wheeler again. Athens is a very respectable looking village.

Friday, Sept. 9. We had quite an alarm last night caused by an attack on the pickets at a block-house south of town. No blood spilt. At 6 o'clock this evening, our brigade (commanded by Lieut. Col. Dunne, of the 29th Indiana) started for Elk River, where we arrived at one o'clock A.M. Saturday morning. We had to ford the river immediately and did not get to lie down until 2 o'clock A.M. The distance we marched was 16 miles. We had moonlight until eleven o'clock. When I lay down, I was pretty well "tuckered." Night marching don't agree with me, or I don't agree with it—one of the two—or both.

Saturday, Sept. 10. This morning, I found myself tired and sore, and felt as if I had been rolled through a sugar mill. We lay all day on the banks of Elk River. The other two brigades of our Division have gone on after Wheeler.

Sunday, Sept. 11. We lay in the woods on the banks of Elk River until 5 o'clock this evening. We then received orders to march to Athens. Wheeler has crossed the Tennessee and we are to return to Kingston. We again forded the river and started at 6 1/4 o'clock for Athens. Our Regiment being "advance guard" we "led out" in a style calculated to keep a man from going to sleep. We marched four miles in one hour during the march. We arrived at Athens at 12 1/2 o'clock.

Monday, Sept. 12. We got aboard the cars at Athens at 11 o'clock A.M. and after a quick run of 12 hours, arrived at Chattanooga. We were detained one hour at Larkinsville by the train which preceded ours running off the track. On arriving at Chattanooga, we got off the cars and took our old position near the Depot.

Tuesday, Sept. 13. We remained at Chattanooga until 6 o'clock P.M. when we started for Kingston.

Wednesday, Sept. 14. At 2 o'clock this morning we reached camp, glad, very glad, to get back once more to our camp and valises. We have been on a "wild goose chase" and we rejoice that it is ended. This has been the hardest campaign I have ever passed through—owing to short rations, long night marches, constant exposure, suffering from heat, from inconveniences arising from a lack of cooking utensils, from heat and from cold, and from the fact of being unable to change clothing for three weeks. The weather only has been favorable to us. We had no heavy rains during the whole time—only when we were under shelter (in the cars or elsewhere). We have been out three weeks and traveled over 900 miles—marching over 120. Wheeler's raid (considering his opportunity and force) has been a failure. *Our* pursuit has been a farce.

This morning I was the recipient of the sad, sad news of Father's death. Our family is without a head—our hearthstone is desolate. God has given us to drink of the cup of affliction and oh! how bitter are its waters! May He enable us to say "thy will be done." This is our first family affliction and oh how crushing the blow. I cannot doubt the sad intelligence, yet I cannot realize that *Father is no more*—that I shall never hear his kind voice nor see his loving face again. Death robs us of our friends and crushes our hearts, yet death only teaches us how much we love each other. Oh! the bitter hours that Mother, Sister, and brothers are spending. God grant them comfort.

9

―――⊰◦◦◦⊱―――

"THERE IS HOPE YET FOR AMERICA"
Final Days in Service, September 15–November 24, 1864

The death of Campbell's father in mid-September 1864 coincided with the dissolution of the Fifth Iowa Infantry, whose demise had been assured back in March, when the requisite three-quarters of its veterans failed to reenlist. Both developments made Campbell reevaluate his continued military service. His final diary entries suggest a man who feels the press of responsibilities at home and has also become disillusioned—not with the war, but with the prospect of achieving any further sense of personal satisfaction and accomplishment from army life.

He could scarcely have had reason for dissatisfaction with the war. The Union navy's seizure of Mobile Bay, Alabama, in late August, coupled with Sherman's capture of Atlanta in early September, electrified the North, as did a series of autumn victories in the Shenandoah Valley by Union forces under Maj. Gen. Philip H. Sheridan. For those dismayed by the military stalemate during the spring and summer, here was positive proof that the North was winning. The result, Campbell wrote, was "the greatest victory of the war": Lincoln's reelection in November 1864.

Thursday, Sept. 15. In camp. Weather pleasant. The Veterans and Recruits of our Regiment today received orders to report to the 5th Iowa Cavalry, 1st Brigade, 3rd Cavalry Division, at Long Pond, Georgia. They form Companies I and G of that Regiment. The officers transferred are as follows: Company G—Capt [Albert] Ellis, 1st Lieut [Jerry] Limbocker, 2nd Lieut [William] Peck. Company I—Capt. [William] McElrea, 1st Lieut. [Robert] McKee, and 2nd Lieut. Campbell.

Friday, Sept. 16. Weather pleasant. I today bought a horse from Lieut. Jones of the 8th Iowa Cavalry. I gave $150 for the horse and equipments. I also take Adjutant Byers bay mare at $75.[1] I today borrowed $80 [from Thomas] Tracey. I owe Wm. Rattican $25. We leave for Long Pond tomorrow morning.

Saturday, Sept. 17. We did not get off this morning as we expected. Weather pleasant.

Sunday, Sept. 18. At midnight we had reveille. At 2 o'clock A.M. we marched down to the depot and loaded our baggage and horse[s] on the cars, preparatory to starting at 3 1/2 o'clock A.M. Before that hour arrived, a telegram came announcing that the train from Chattanooga had been thrown off the track at Adairsville by guerrillas tearing up the track. Of course, our departure was delayed. The track was repaired and several trains arrived about 11 o'clock A.M. Most of the men got on one of these trains and started for Atlanta. A few more remained with the cars (containing our baggage and horses) which the trains would not take along. I remained with the boys and we did not succeed in getting away from Kingston until the evening train arrived. Weather warm with occasional showers.

Monday, Sept. 19. Our train made very slow progress last night and at daylight this morning, we had only arrived at the Chattahoochie river. The grade from the river to Atlanta is very heavy and our train moved at a slower rate than a man's walking pace. On arriving at Atlanta, we disembarked at the depot where we found the rest of our regiment. The men got breakfast at the soldier's home. I breakfasted out of my own grub pile. We remained at the depot until eleven o'clock A.M. when, having procured wagons to haul our baggage, we started for the camp of the 5th Iowa Cavalry eight miles west of Atlanta. Before leaving town, I had occasion to walk around three or four squares. My impression of Atlanta is not very favorable to the place. A better look at the place *might,* however, change my impressions. On our way to camp, we passed through the enemies' works, which are the strongest I ever saw. Heavy earthworks form the base. On top of these, large logs are laid to protect the men when firing, an opening left under the logs to fire through. In rear of the works, the men had thrown up works to protect themselves while off duty. In front of the works, rifle pits were dug for sharp shooters. In front of these were a row of abattis, several rows of stakes driven into the ground—the ends of the stakes sharpened and leaned from the works—and a line of "*devils*" formed by inserting sticks into a piece of timber so as to form an X—the ends of the sticks being sharpened. These "*devils*" if rolled over and over, even presented a row of sharp sticks to the unlucky man who might attempt to charge over them. We arrived at "Camp Crooks" at 4 o'clock P.M. having gone out of our way a mile or two, on the route. We found our regiment *without horses* and our prospect for serving as *dismounted* cavalry for some time is very good. Weather clear and warm.

Tuesday, Sept. 20. Having cleared off our camping ground and drawn "shelter tents," we this evening camped in line with the regiment. On arrival yesterday evening, we received quite a large mail which had been sent to the cavalry for us. Today we occupied a good part of our time answering the letters. Weather cloudy with rain in the evening.

Wednesday, Sept. 21. We have been occupied today in fixing up our camp. A very heavy rain fell this afternoon. We were called up at 3 o'clock this morning and "stood to arms" until daylight. *Cause*—the enemy is reported in our immediate front and an attack was apprehended on some part of our line.

Thursday, Sept. 22. Weather cloudy, with rain in the afternoon and evening. I have been employed a good part of the day, assisting in the building board habitation for myself and Lieut. McKee. A detail was called for from our company for picket this morning. The pickets are required to stay on duty three days without being relieved. The country between our camp and Atlanta and around our camp is broken but not hilly. The soil is very thin and very poor. The timber is principally oak and pine. Georgia, as far as I have seen it, is the poorest of the States.

Friday, September 23. Weather warm with rain. The news of Sheridan's victory is quite cheering.[2] This, the taking of Atlanta and the successes at Mobile, will have a great influence on the elections.[3] McClellan will get but few votes in the army of the west.

Saturday, Sept. 24. The weather "cleared off" this morning and this afternoon the sky is clear and the atmosphere cool. Lt. McKee is acting as Qr. Master.

Sunday, Sept. 25. Weather clear and cool. I had no opportunity to attend Divine services today and there has been little indication about camp of this being Sabbath. I have not yet received any letter from home since Father's death.

Monday, Sept. 26. Weather clear and cool. Nights quite cool. This afternoon I rode around the picket lines with Capt. Ellis.

Tuesday, Sept. 27. Weather warm with indications of rain. I got a pass this morning and started for the camp of the 7th Ohio Cavalry at Decatur, Georgia to see friends and acquaintances. On my arrival at Atlanta, I found all the officers of my old regiment (the 5th Infantry) at the Trout House, they having been ordered to Atlanta to be mustered out of the service. After a short stay in Atlanta, I started on for Decatur. I found the camp of the 7th Ohio Cavalry 1 1/2 miles beyond Decatur. I arrived there at 2 o'clock P.M. I found but few of my acquaintances and at 3 o'clock I started for Atlanta to find cousin Will Thompson. I failed to find him and continued on to camp, where I arrived at 7 o'clock P.M. having traveled 31 miles during the day without dinner or supper for "man or beast." I received a very welcome letter from Aunt Mag. today in which she gave some particulars of Father's death, which were very comforting to hear.

Wednesday, Sept. 28. Twenty-six years old today! One year nearer my grave. Am I one year nearer Heaven and happiness? I cannot hope to live as many days as I have lived but may I not be more useful than I have been. I will *strive* to be. The officers of our old regiment were mustered out this forenoon. Two of our Regiment who were captured at Mission Ridge last fall, escaped from the enemy and arrived in Atlanta yesterday. They were a pitiable looking sight. They report that 35 (out of 72 that were captured) have died. We are under orders to go to Nashville to be armed and mounted. Weather warm with rain.

Thursday, Sept. 29. In camp awaiting orders. Our baggage has been sent to Atlanta preparatory to our moving.

Friday, Sept. 30. This day I have spent visiting friends and old acquaintances. I rode to Atlanta and dined with Surgeon Dixon. I then made useless search for Will Thompson and found he was not in the State. In the afternoon, in company with Doctor Dixon, I visited the camp of the 89th Ohio and saw Major [John] Jolly and George DeBolt. I afterwards visited Department Head Quarters (Gen. Howard's) and saw Col. Wilson, Capt. Gilbert, John Woodward, and other Brown County boys. After this, I visited the camp of the 13th Iowa and saw Capt. Skiff and others. I then returned to camp. On my way to camp I was caught in a rain and slightly dampened. On my arrival there, I found Lt. Col. Sampson there.

Saturday, Oct. 1. At five o'clock this morning our Regiment started to Atlanta to take the cars for Nashville. Heavy rains during the night had rendered the roads very bad. I rode to town with Col. Sampson in advance of the Regiment. After getting to town the regiment bivouacked on the outskirts until 7 o'clock P.M. when we got aboard the cars. Between 8 and 9 o'clock P.M. we started for Nashville. The weather during the day has been clear and pleasant.

Sunday, October 2. At 12 o'clock last night, we reached Marietta where we were detained by the non-arrival of a train due from the North. Soon after we crossed the Chattahoochie bridge last night, it was washed away. Rain last night and today. We were detained at Marietta until 4 P.M. when our train ran on to Big Shanty where the down train ran off the track last night. Soon after our arrival at the scene of the catastrophe, the road was cleared of obstructions and repaired, but we could not proceed by reason of the track not being clear—a band of guerrillas having thrown a train off the track between Acworth and Big Shanty this morning. About dark, the road was again repaired and the Locomotive that had been thrown off was got on the track and arrived at Big Shanty. Major [J. Morris] Young (commanding our regiment) refused to travel after night and we "put up" at Big Shanty. About 8 o'clock P.M. we were visited by a heavy rain and hail storm.

Monday, October 3. At six o'clock this morning we again started on our journey. About 10 o'clock A.M. we arrived at Kingston where we stopped for about 3 hours. I got off the cars and took dinner with Uncle William. During the forenoon and until two o'clock this afternoon, the rain has fallen almost constantly and heavily. On arriving at Resaca we found the bridge across the Oustananula quite unsafe and learned that the R.R. was torn up below Dalton. On arriving at Tilton, we could learn but little about the break in the R.R. but

Wartime photograph of Lt. Col. John M. Young. Courtesy of the State Historical Society of Iowa.

procured some "section hands" and tools, [and] we proceeded on our way. About four and half miles below Dalton, we found the R.R. torn up and the telegraph wires cut. Our train, of course, "halted" and a reconnaissance was made which showed that the road was torn up for over a mile. The Regiment was ordered off the cars—pickets were thrown out and parties set to work immediately to repair the R.R. The road had been turned "up side down," but no rails or ties had been burned. All who were not on picket were set to work turning the ties and rails back into their places. I was engaged with the party that worked at this business. We were kept hard at work until 1 o'clock P.M. Tuesday morning by which time we had the road all "right side up" on its proper bed. It rained all night and we got the benefit(?) of the water's cooling influence. At 1 1/2 o'clock I got to bed.

Tuesday, October 4. After we had "turned" the road last night, details were kept at work levelling, gaging [*sic*] and spiking the road. But only a few could work at a time (owing to a scarcity of tools) and at daylight this morning not more than half of the spiking and gauging was done. About sunrise a party of workmen arrived from Dalton (having been sent for by Major Young) and at noon we had repaired all the damaged portion of the road and started for Dalton. After arriving at Dalton we were delayed by an accident on the track and by being compelled to await the arrival of a construction train coming South from Chattanooga. While at Dalton *rain fell!!* At 5 o'clock P.M. we started for Chattanooga where we arrived at 10 o'clock P.M. (I forgot to state in the proper place that the officers of the 5th Infantry came from Atlanta to Kingston with us.)

Wednesday, Oct. 5. At midnight I was called up to change my horse to another car. The one they had been in having been broken down. At one o'clock and thirty minutes A.M., our train started for Nashville. This morning, on awakening, I found our train with several others on "Hooker switch" 10 miles from Chattanooga. We were delayed there at Whiteside Station and Stevenson several hours and dark came upon us just as we got through the tunnel South of Cowan. We ran after night till we reached Aramanda Station when we "tied up" for the night.

Thursday, Oct. 6. Weather clear and pleasant. This has been the only day since we left Atlanta that it has not rained. The men had to ride on top of the cars and it has rained every day and night. They have had a tough time. I was fortunate enough to get inside of a box car but was much crowded. Besides a full allowance from our own regiment in our car, we had a number of officers who had resigned & who were going home on leaves of absence whom we took into our car as a favor to them. Owing to heavy rains, the streams all along the route we came [to] are very high. We were delayed today by the crowded state of the R.R. and did not reach Nashville until 4 o'clock P.M. Our train ran out to our camp on the Franklin road and we soon disembarked and bid farewell to car No. 389 and betook ourselves to camp. About the time we left Atlanta, Forrest made a raid on Decatur and Nashville R.R., captured Athens, and burned Elk River bridge. Although he has been compelled to retreat, the road is not yet in running order—Hence the crowded state of the Stevenson road.[4] On arriving at camp this evening, I received a number of letters from Sister & one each from Mother, Frank and Archie. They were truly welcome. From them I learned many painful yet consoling particulars of Father's sickness and death. Before retiring this evening I took a wash and changed clothes. Feel better.

Friday, October 7. We are camped on an elevated piece of ground in a woods pasture about two miles south of town. Our camping place is certainly pretty. Last night and today the weather has been clear but quite cool. I have remained in camp all day. Wrote to Sister.

Saturday, October 8. I walked to town this morning and returned in the afternoon. While in town, I saw Major Baird, Mary Knapp, James King, and other acquaintances. Weather cool.

Sunday, October 9. The weather is quite cool and as I have had no tent since we arrived here, my slumbers have been quite uncomfortable. We had company inspection at ten o'clock this morning.

Monday, October 10. Weather cool. Captain and I got a new wall tent today. Company, squad, and regimental drill was commenced today and will be continued till further orders. Studying tactics and drilling will keep me busy. After supper this evening I rode to town and returned before tattoo.

Tuesday, October 11. This is election day in some of the states. I look for Union victories.[5] Drill and Dress Parade today. This afternoon I rode to town and made some purchases and saw a number of old acquaintances—among them Thed. Collins. Weather a little warmer.

Wednesday, October 12. Drill three times a day. I sent my horses to town this forenoon for Mr. Baird and Mr. Blanchard but they had received orders to report at the front and could not come. Weather cloudy. No news from the election in the morning's papers. Extras this afternoon—report great Union victories in all the States.

Thursday, October 13. Weather clear and pleasant. News today from the Northern elections is not so cheering. While Ohio has done well and Indiana gloriously, Pennsylvania has done poorly. It is doubtful whether she is Union or Copperhead. Shame on the State! I went to town this evening and saw a new regiment (43d Wisconsin) coming in.

Friday, October 14. In addition to my drilling and other duties, I am now detailed on a Board of Survey which will occupy my spare time for a week or more. There is quite a strife in our regiment between the two Majors and their friends about the position of Lieutenant Colonel, which is vacant. I today made out and signed a recommendation in favor of Major Young, whom I consider best qualified for the position. My health is as good as usual. My letters from home are not as frequent as I would like. Letters from dear Father, letters always full of affection—I never can receive again. Alas! the thought. But such is earth.

Saturday, October 15. This forenoon, I was busy on Board of Survey. This forenoon I rode into town and visited the Government Printing office. Rain this afternoon. News from the front indicates that Hood is making a bold strike to cause the evacuation of Atlanta by Sherman. At last accounts he was on the R.R. below Chattanooga moving North with Sherman following him with his army—the 20th Corps occupying Atlanta. Sherman is not to be *Hood-winked* by one man, and the Confederacy may hear some *bad* as *well* as good news.[6]

Sunday, October 16. Weather clear and cool. Our chaplain preached a very sensible sermon this forenoon.

Monday, October 17. Employed the forenoon in drilling & on Board of Survey. This afternoon, in company with Lieuts. Peck and Hays, I visited the Acklin place, two miles from our camp. I found it the best improved place I ever have seen. A million of dollars is said to have ben expended in improving it. The most attractive features are the statues, the evergreens, the fountain, tower, and green-houses. My visit was very entertaining and profitable. I received Mag. C's miniature in a letter today—looks quite natural. Weather pleasant but cloudy.

Tuesday, October 18. Weather pleasant and clear. I have put in the day drilling and writing.

Wednesday, October 19. Weather clear in forenoon—cloudy in afternoon. Drilling and attending to my duties on Board of Survey occupied most of my time. I wrote a letter to the *Bee* this evening.

Thursday, October 20. Weather pleasant. Drill, Dress Parade, and Board of Survey.

Friday, October 21. Weather cool and windy. I rode to town on business this morning. News of Sheridan's third victory came today.[7] "Bully for Little Phil." No drill this afternoon.

Saturday, October 22. Weather cool, cloudy, and *clear.* I rode to town for rations this morning and while in town, I met Capt. Cal. Rankin and Cousin Will Thompson. I took dinner with them and then took a stroll about town with Will Thompson and returned to camp about 4 P.M. with the headache.

Sunday, October 23. Weather cool and very windy. We got a stove for our tent last evening and I have kept close at home all day. I have been considering, for a week or so past, the propriety of resigning after the Presidential election. I will stay till then, to get to vote. I have not yet been able to decide as to whether I had better resign (i.e. be mustered out) by reason of expiration of term of service under late orders) or not. So many arguments present themselves, *pro* and *con* that I have not yet been able to make up my mind.

Monday, October 24. Weather very pleasant. I rode to town this afternoon to see the Mustering officer. Saw Capt. Rankin, Will Thompson, John Kirk and a son of "Jim Bramble."

Tuesday, October 25. Weather pleasant with indications of rain. We received orders today to start tomorrow for Louisville to get horses. The mounted portion of our Regiment started on a scout this morning. We were payed this evening for July and August.

Wednesday, October 26. Owing to the bad state of the weather, we did not start to Louisville today. Rain all day.

Thursday, October 27. The weather "cleared up" last night. At noon today we started for the depot. About 3 o'clock our train crossed the river and "laid over" at Edgefield until 5 1/2 o'clock P.M. when we started for Louisville.

Friday, October 28. At daylight we reached Cave City—breakfasted at Elizabethtown—and arrived at Louisville at 2 P.M. On arriving at the Soldier's Home (where we were assigned quarters) I was detailed as "officer of the day." The men were allowed to go out in town as they choose and I expected to have a hard turn of duty but I managed to get along without much trouble, although a number of the men came to quarters very drunk during the evening. I ate my supper at the Soldier's Home table. About seven o'clock, orders came from Hd. Qrs. Mil. Div. of Ky., ordering our Regiment to Paducah—to leave at 8 P.M. I carried the orders to the Hotel but failed to find the Major. I gave the orders to the Senior Captain, who repaired to Military Hd. Qrs. with the orders to represent the fact that our Regiment was only partially armed and was in the city on special duty. I returned to quarters and waited till 11 o'clock P.M. for "marching orders" when (no orders coming) I went to bed. Weather windy and cold today.

Saturday, Oct. 29. On being relieved this morning, I called on John Shepherd, who is on duty at Military Head Quarters of the Post. I found him in bed having crippled himself a week or so since by spraining his ankle. I took supper with him this evening and will stay with him tonight. Our Regiment will not have to go to Paducah—the order has been revoked. Weather clear and cold.

Sunday, October 30. Weather clear and cold. I started to church this forenoon and met John Hopkins on the way. I returned with him to Shep's room where we stayed a short time and then went to church. After church, I went with him to his boarding house where I met Mr. and Mrs. Johnson and Sarah. After dinner I returned to Shep's Boarding house and put up with him for the night.

Monday, October 31. I engaged boarding this morning and will stay with Shep while our Regiment stays in the city. At the boarding house I have made the acquaintance of Lieut. Love of Maysville, Ky., Capt. McArthur, Adjutant of Post, Major Plessner, Post Provost Marshall, Mrs. Plessner and little Nellie, Col. Humphreys, Medical Inspector of the District and others—military and civilian characters. This evening, Capt. McArthur, his guitar and I had some music in Shep's room. Weather today clear and cool. Our Regiment still stays at the barracks near Soldier's Home.

Tuesday, Nov. 1st. This morning I met Capt. Thed. Bratten, formerly of Ripley. Our Regiment still lingers in the Fall's City.[8] I visited the great Artesian Well, drank of its waters, and took a bath in them this forenoon. I also visited the Paper Mills near the well and witnessed the process of paper making.

Wednesday, Nov. 2nd. Our Regiment drew 500 horses this morning at a Government corral about two miles from the city this morning. A cold rain commenced falling soon after we started out and continued till about two o'clock P.M. I was in command of Company I (the Captain being temporarily absent) and I drew 73 horses. By the time I got back to quarters I was pretty well dampened and considerably chilled. This afternoon our company rode out on a "trial trip." When returning from this, I met cousins Joe and Henry Reynolds on their way home.

Thursday, Nov. 3d. At eight o'clock this morning our Regiment left Louisville for Nashville. I have no regrets to make at our departure, for the men have behaved shamefully while we have sojourned in the city and some of the officers have behaved no [better] than the men. We marched through three or four streets of the city and then took the road to Shephardstown. Soon after leaving the city, a cold rain began falling and continued during the day. We marched 17 miles and camped in an open field at 5 o'clock P.M. I made a nest in a fence corner with my gum blankets as soon as we got into camp. All the other officers (excepting Capt. McElrea) stayed at a farm house near camp.

Friday, November 4. I slept about ten hours last night. The weather cleared up during the night but clouded over again before morning. At eight o'clock A.M. we resumed our march. Before starting our company had a little practice in "fence building." We passed through Shephardstown about noon and camped at Belmont furnace about 2 P.M., having marched 12 miles. Before we camped, rain commenced falling again and it "still comes." We crossed a branch of Salt River at Shephardstown.

Saturday, Nov. 5. Our horses got only about half rations of forage last night. I got supper and breakfast with a Mr. McAfee, a native of Missouri, who moved to Kentucky about a year since. The Major and several other officers stayed at the same house. I *slept* in a small house with some of the company. Having torn one of my boots I was unable to get it on and off and slept with it on. This morning at the breakfast table, we had a little grub, some wit, considerable laughing, and a strong hint to the landlord. Our fare consisted of coffee, biscuits and corn bread, roast mutton, and milk (sweet and butter-milk). Mr. McAfee remarked that he would make a poor soldier as he used neither tea nor coffee and could not get along without milk. I remarked he could get little milk in the army as the "milk of human kindness" could not even be found there. The Major remarked that if there had ever been any of the "milk of human kindness" in the army, it had soured or been churned into buttermilk. I then remarked that if it had been churned, I had not been able to see the butter! Considering the fact that there was buttermilk and *no* butter on the table, Mr. McAfee *might* have taken this as a broad hint, but I hope he did not! as he only charged us $1.50 for two meals! We marched fourteen miles today and camped at Colesburg, a small village on the R.R. The weather today has been clear and pleasant.

Sunday, Nov. 6. I slept with the Captain in a hay mow last night. We got our meals at a "poor white" Kentuckian's, who wanted to know if there was general in our army by the name of *Sheridan!* Weather cloudy again today but no rain until 6 o'clock P.M. The country we have passed through since leaving Louisville has been generally hilly and our course has lain through the valleys principally. Today we marched up out of the valleys and gained the high ground at Muldraugh's Hill. We passed through Elizabethtown about 11 o'clock A.M. and Nolin about 2 P.M. The road from the former to the latter place was very good, being mostly gravel road. We marched 17 miles and camped at Red Mills on Nolin Creek.

Monday, Nov. 7. I ate supper and breakfast at a Mr. Bell's where I had a very good fare. Mrs. Bell told a good joke on a dutch soldier who took a plate of biscuits that was passed to him and passed back his own plate amid the laughs and jeers of the other soldiers—himself laughing at he did not know what. P.S. he ate all the biscuits. I slept last night in the woods. I made my bed by throwing cornstalks on two logs which lay together. I kept the rain off by spreading my gum blanket over my others. In this way, I managed to sleep pretty well, notwithstanding my bed was rather hard and confining. My horse bothered me some by trying to steal my bed from under me. We started at the usual hour (8 o'clock) this morning. We marched 22 miles and camped at Munfordsville on Green River. The road today for the first ten miles was very muddy, the rest was pike.

Tuesday, November 8. Rain yesterday evening, last night, and today. I stayed at a hotel last night—the men in barracks. This morning, we started for Bowling Green *via* Mammoth Cave.[9] The road to the cave lies through a very rough country. We reached the cave about 3 P.M. Soon after our arrival, the polls were opened at the Hotel and our Regiment proceeded to the ballot. I was appointed one of the Judges of Election. After the election, the officers paid $2 apiece and procured a guide and lanterns to go into the cave. The men got in "scott free." We went 3 miles into the cave in one direction and traveled 10 miles in all while in the cave. We came out about midnight. We visited Lake Lethe, Bacon Chamber, Gothic Chamber, Star Chamber, and other notable places in the cave. The Hotel is the only building near the cave. It is in a wild country and is reached only by traveling over the roughest of roads. The mouth of the cave is near the top of a high ridge. The rain today has been very steady and at times very hard.

Wednesday, Nov. 9. A strong South Wind was blowing this morning when we started and before we had traveled many miles, rain began falling and continued till we entered camp in the afternoon. This has been the roughest day's march we have had. It rained very hard at one time and most of the day it blew in our faces. We marched 14 miles, passing through a little town called Dripping Springs where we again struck the pike.

Thursday, Nov. 10. I stayed the night at a citizen's house where I was very well entertained. I was engaged with the other judges till eleven o'clock P.M. counting the votes of our Regiment. It stood 235 for Lincoln and only 10 (ten) for *Littlemac.*[10] Bully for the 5th Iowa Cavalry! The weather cleared up soon after we got into camp yesterday afternoon and the men spent a very pleasant night. The weather today has been clear and cool. We have traveled on the pike all day. We have marched 20 miles. We passed through Bowling Green about one o'clock P.M. I was left behind with 24 men as escort for our train, which stopped to get rations. While in town, I saw and concurred with Rev. Mr. Garrison, formerly of Mason co. Ky., and father of Robert and Samuel— two of Angus' classmates with whom I was acquainted. I received a pressing invitation to stay with him all night. The Regiment was camped seven miles South of Bowling Green and I did not reach camp till sundown. At the town procured late papers from which I learned of Mr. Lincoln's overwhelming triumph.[11] There is hope yet for America. God grant that our nation may ever be as wise. Thanks to Him who ruleth over nations for this glorious triumph should be offered up by every loyal heart.

Friday, Nov. 11. Weather clear and pleasant. We marched 14 miles to-day and camped at Franklin. Last night I stayed with a very ignorant family near camp. One of the boys kicked our landlord during the night for prowling around his own house and told him to go to bed. The landlord thought it was rather rough but had to laugh at the soldier's impudence.

Saturday, Nov. 12. I stayed last night at a hotel in Franklin. I was employed till bed-time filling out the poll books. Weather cloudy and cold today. We travelled 21 miles. On stopping, I was appointed officer of the day. I was assigned to a house to get meals and lodging but failed to get accomodation. I accordingly took supper with one of the men who kindly shared with me his meal.

Sunday, Nov. 13. I slept in the woods by a fire last night and got along pretty well. I got a little coffee and a cracker from one of the boys for my breakfast. Weather clear and pleasant today. We passed through Gallatin, Tenn. at 11 o'clock A.M. I procured some crackers and cheese there and satisfied my hunger therewith. We marched 14 miles today.

Monday, Nov. 14. I gave one of the men some money to buy bread with and I ate my supper last night and breakfast this morning with them. I slept in the camp by a fire. We started at the usual hour this morning and after 16 miles travel on the pike, reached Nashville and got back to our old camp about 4 o'clock P.M. having been on the way from Louisville 12 days.

Summary of the trip.

We had a very rough trip owing to the bad weather. Our horses were in bad condition when we got them, many of them diseased with sore tongue, distemper, &c., and quite a number of them are unfit for service. The towns along the route traveled by us are mostly insignificant places. Elizabethtown, Munfordsville, Bowling Green, Franklin, and Gallatin are very respectable towns. We crossed Salt, Green, and Barren Rivers. The country from Bowling Green to Nashville is fertile and lies very well. My health during the trip has been rather poor. I have suffered from colds and [a] bowel complaint. The boys have stood riding very well. The inhabitants of the country we passed through are an ignorant class generally.

Tuesday, Nov. 15. I have been busy today writing and attending to various duties. I have been unwell all day. I took some medicine this evening.

Wednesday, Nov. 16. I was quite unwell last night and don't feel much better today. I threw up some medicine the Dr. gave me today and don't think I will trouble him for more. Weather wet. Trains loaded with troops have passed down the road towards Decatur every few hours for several days past. Gen. Thomas is evidently gathering a strong force to meet Hood.[12] Gen. Sherman, according to reports, has left Thomas to take care of Hood, while he has gone to capture Augusta and Savannah and cut the Confederacy in twain.[13] If I am not mistaken, Gen. Hood will find that by withdrawing his army from Sherman's front and marching it into Northern Alabama, he has committed the (to the South) fatal blunder of the War. Amen! and Amen!

The Presidential election is over—the smoke of the contest has cleared away and we can see the result: *a glorious victory* for Loyalty, Liberty and Union. Mr. Lincoln has carried every state but Kentucky, Delaware, and New Jersey—and has a majority of the popular vote of about 400,000! The people, with an unanimity unparalleled, have declared that this war is *not* a failure, that Slavery must die, that treason must be punished and traitors hung, and that this war must continue till the old flag floats in proud supremacy over every foot of Uncle Sam's dominions. The day for conciliation is passed. The day for subjugation is at hand. In my judgement, the victory of November 8th, is the greatest victory of the war. A Congress has been elected with a majority of two-thirds passing a Constitutional amendment prohibiting slavery and the doom of the institution is sealed.[14] It is well that the question has been decided now. If the issue had not been made till the close of the war, I am afraid that self interest, love of ease, prejudice, and political chicanery, might have gained the victory over justice and liberty. I believe 'tis well that the decision has been made while the nation is suffering from its chastisements. My earnest prayer and hope is that the doom of slavery may be irrevocably fixed, that there may be no chance to go back to the wallowing in the mire.

Thursday, Nov. 17. Weather cloudy with rain in the afternoon. I have felt considerably better today. We had an inspection of the Regiment today by a Captain of the 2nd U.S. Cavalry.

Friday, Nov. 18. It rained all the forenoon and quit about noon. After dinner I rode over to the camp of the 173d Ohio and saw Frank Cole. I rode thence to town and just as I started back to camp, it began raining and I got pretty wet before I got back to camp.

Saturday, Nov. 19. I made up my mind (after I retired to bed last night) to leave the service and go home. After a *six weeks'* consideration of the subject, I suppose I may say that I arrived at a *deliberate* conclusion. Since Father's death, Mother has been solicitous that I should come home and I have hardly spent a day nor a night during the past six weeks that I have not earnestly considered the propriety of yielding to her solicitations. A desire to continue in the service of my country and to remain a soldier of Uncle Sam till this war closes has been a strong motive for my continuing a soldier. Having made up my mind, I this morning rode to town and procured some blank muster-out rolls, and instructions for filling them. It rained again this afternoon. Our Regiment drew new sabres and 500 Spencer Rifles this afternoon.[15]

Sunday, Nov. 20. Weather cloudy and disagreeable. In camp.

Monday, Nov. 21. Having sold my bay mare for $75, I this morning "squared my accounts," gave my extra blankets away, packed my valice, shook hands with the boys, bid them good-bye and started to town to be mustered-out. Capt. McElrea and Tracy (one of the members of the company) rode into town with me. Soon after we started it commenced snowing quite briskly, and blowing directly in our faces made it very disagreeable riding—the snow continued to fall till about noon, and the weather was very disagreeable during the day. After getting into town and putting my valice in the Commercial Hotel baggage room, I started out to sell my horse. After several hours ineffectual trial, I came across Lieut. [William] Ketterman of the 7th Ohio Cavalry and he kindly took my horse and promised to sell him for me and forward me the money. About 4 o'clock P.M. I was mustered out of the service of Uncle Sam, *honorably* agreeably to a late order of the War Department, that permits any officer to be mustered out who has served three years in one Regiment. I have, therefore, become a private citizen. Counting three weeks in the State Service, I have served three years and five months and one day. At eight o'clock this evening, I procured transportation and will start for Louisville in the morning.

Finis

Thus ends my *"War Diary"*

Addenda

November 22, 1864. At 7 o'clock this morning, I took the train for Louisville. The weather today has been pretty cold. Among the passengers in the car I rode in was a Captain who had just made his escape from a rebel prison. He gave quite an interesting account of his adventures. We arrived at Louisville about 6 o'clock P.M. and I "put up" at the Louisville Hotel. Before going to bed, I met Capt. Cal. Rankin of the 7th Ohio Cav., he being on his way from Ripley to Nashville.

November 23, 1864. This morning I called at Post Head Quarters to see John Shepherd and while there John Woodward came in. I had the pleasure of having the company of both at dinner. At 3 o'clock P.M., I started for Cincinnati on the Steamer Rebecca.

November 24, 1864. At 8 o'clock this morning, our boat reached Cincinnati. I immediately secured passage on the Bostonia for Ripley where I arrived at 7 1/2 o'clock P.M. Part of the 40th Kentucky was on the Bostonia, going home on 20 days furlough. One of the boys fell overboard and was drowned as the boat touched at the Ripley wharfboat. I took the folks at home considerably by surprise, they having had no intimation of my coming.

APPENDIX

Letters to the *Ripley Bee,* 1861–1864

Letter 1. Published August 15, 1861; Dateline Keokuk, Iowa, August 7, 1861

Dear Charley:

I have but little time to write and will have to scribble fast. We left Burlington last Friday Evening and came down the river on a little stern-wheel steam boat— our company occupying the hurricane deck. I slept very well. Monday morning we received our belts, cap pouches, cartridge boxes, bayonet scabbards and gun slings. At 10 o'clock the same day we got our muskets and were ordered to repair to the depot in *twenty minutes.* We went without baggage or blankets. At the depot we received 40 rounds of cartridges each. We left in a hurry and were cheered loudly by the crowd at the depot. The cause of our leaving was this. About 1,500 Secessionists attacked a little town named Athens on the Desmoines road west of here.[1] The home guards of Athens and other towns in Missouri and Iowa gave them battle, but they only had about one third the number [of] the secessionists and they sent down for help. Five companies of the sixth [Iowa] Regiment and five picked companies of our Regiment were sent to their aid. Just as we were starting we heard that the rebels had been whipped. We went out on the R.R. to within 4 miles of Athens when we (five companies got off the cars, "fixed bayonets," loaded and then forded the river, pulling off our boots and rolling up our breeches) marched about eight miles intending, if possible, to get in rear of the seceshers. But they were all mounted and had retreated far beyond our reach, although we did not know it at the time. The weather was awful hot and one or two men in other companies gave out. We stopped just at dark and pitched our camp. We then stacked our guns and (after the sentinels were stationed around the camp) lay down without supper to sleep on the grass, having nothing under or over us and nothing on us but our woolen shirts and our pants, boots and caps. We slept with our munitions buckled around us. I slept very well. After midnight, one of our sentinels fired his gun and the cry of "fall in" soon had us, guns in hand, in the ranks. Flanking parties and skirmishers were thrown out and every man got ready for a fight. It was soon evident, however, that it was a false alarm and we again stacked arms and dropped asleep. Some of the boys were frightened but the majority were cool and ready. The Colonel complimented us for our promptness and good order. Individually I can say that I was not in the least frightened and that I was perfectly cool and ready for them. Next morning, we made a good breakfast on pilot bread and raw and half raw ham. We learned while breakfast was getting ready, from a prisoner who had escaped from them and come into our camp, that the Missourians had camped 15 miles off and as we were afoot and they mounted, we marched back to Athens. On the way back, our Surgeon extracted a big ball from the neck of a wounded secessionist who had been left at a house on the road-side. At Athens we found hundreds of armed men who had come in (after the fashion of Lexington and Bunker Hill) to whip the rebels. We camped on the battlefield of the previous day. I could see bullet marks in the trees all around. Near our camp was the grave of one secessionist who was shot in the action. In the hospital I saw a number of wounded. We came back on the cars yesterday evening. I expect we will go to St. Louis today or to-morrow and go from there into the interior of Missouri.

J. Q. A. Campbell

Letter 2. Published August 29, 1861; Dateline "On Board Steamboat 'Satan,'" August 17, 1861

Dear Charley:

I have now been on the Mississippi, the Missouri, and the Ohio rivers, and I like the Ohio better than either of the others.

Half of the way to St. Louis from Keokuk, there is scarcely a mile of the Mississippi of clear channel. It is all cut up into small channels by the numerous islands and the consequence is that the boats have to be throwing out the "lead" every mile or two. You might think that the islands would add to the beauty of the scenery, but it is "too much of a good thing." The boat is running so continually through these narrow channels that one forgets almost that he is on the "Father of waters." The first half of the distance from Keokuk, the scenery of the river is uninviting. There are no hills and you can merely see the woods on the banks.

The latter half of the journey is more inviting but there is not the beauty of scenery there is on the Ohio. There are however, some beautiful stone bluffs along the banks, extending on the Illinois side for several miles.

The Missouri is more like the Ohio. It has fewer islands than the Mississippi and more sandbars than the Ohio and is very difficult to navigate. It is but very little wider than the Ohio. The scenery along its banks reminds me some of the Ohio. Neither the Missouri have as high banks as the Ohio. The soil [is] loose and sandy and is continually washing away which accounts for the water being so muddy.

I have told you something about the rivers, now for something else.

Thursday night we stopped at Hermann, a German town. Last night we stopped at Jefferson City, where we could see the Capitol the traitors of Missouri hold their legislature in. We could see cannon placed all around it.[2]

We are now going on up the river. I don't know how far we are above the city or where we will stop tonight. Our company and the other flank company have rifled muskets—the rest of the regiment have smooth-bore muskets. We have got our blankets—they are rather thin.

Our company stood "picket guard" night before last—the "Orderly" don't have to stand guard.

The boat we are on is the one the battle of Boonville commenced on between Lyon and Jackson.[3] There are several shot marks on the spars.

SUNDAY 18 Last night we stopped at an island about 20 miles below Boonville. Two boats with a regiment of St. Louis 3 mos. volunteers aboard stopped at the same place. They were coming down the river, their time having expired and they were going home to reenlist again. They have lost only six men since they enlisted—one yesterday. They have been stationed at Lexington. They say that they have been fired on every day since they left Lexington. Yesterday they had one man killed and several wounded about 3 miles above Booneville [*sic*]. They have several prisoners aboard their boat. This morning our Col. turned our boats down the stream and we are now enroute for Jefferson City. The Col. of the Missouri Regiment said it was not safe for us to go up without artillery and we are going back to Jefferson City to telegraph to Fremont to see if we can't get more ammunition and the cannon and the howitzer the Missouri Regiment have with them.[4] Yesterday afternoon, about four miles below where we laid up for the night, a crowd of men (about 20) gathered on the bank at a small village as we passed. Upon some of our boys waving their hats, one of the pukes hallowed "Hurrah for Jackson" twice.[5] The Major ordered the boat backed up and some of the boys who were on top drilling went through the motion of "loading." Immediately the crowd began to disperse and in a few minutes we could see them on the mules making 2:40 time out of town. The boat then went on and the boys had a good laugh. At the same place the stars and stripes were hung out from a back door so we could see them but they could not be seen from the town. We supposed that some Union man was surrounded by Secessionists and he dare not show his colors publicly.

This morning we all had orders to "load" and keep our guns beside us. Last night we slept with "our armor on" and our guns close at hand. Most of our company went out scouting.

AT CAMP, JEFFERSON CITY, Mo. Aug 22

I have a little time before drill and I will try and finish this letter. We got back to Jefferson City at 10 o'clock Sunday morning. We remained on the boat until Tuesday morning when we got our tents and went into quarters about 200 yards from the river. Monday night a report came in that the Secessionists were marching upon this place in force. About midnight 3 companies of our reg. and three of the "Irish Brigade" (a Chicago regiment that has been stationed here from some time) went on the R.R. to Osage to defend the bridge. The troops have been kept there ever since. The remainder of our regiment were marched up to a piece of ground near the penitentiary where we spent the night intending to take refuge in and fight from the Penitentiary if attacked by a superior force. I spread my blanket in the road (newly McAdamized) and slept very soundly. We slept in ranks on our arms. The alarm was groundless, as I was certain it would be from the first. Next morning we marched to the boats at daylight.

"Our bill of fare" for dinner was as follows: Pilot bread, fried beef and side meat, potatoes, pickles, and peaches. We have occasionally tomatoes and beets. While we were on the boats we did not fare so well. Hundreds—thousands—of Home Guard Cavalry, driven from their homes, are coming in here every day.

Part of our regiment is quartered in "contraband" houses—we have plenty of "contraband" apples and peaches. The owners and proprietors ran off with Jackson.

J. Q. A. Campbell

Letter 3. Published February 13, 1862; Dateline Boonville, Missouri, February 3, 1862

Dear Bee:

I have no ink convenient but I have a pencil that is, perhaps, as sharp as my ideas and I will venture to impose upon you a short letter. A copy of the *Bee* which I received by last mail, suggested the idea.

I was forcibly struck with the wise and patriotic action of the ladies of Ripley in forming a "Soldier's Relief Society." Now, I would not advise, but merely suggest that nothing gives so much relief after a day's fatigue or a round of guard duty as a letter from home. Apropos to this I would compliment the relief society for their exercise of wisdom, in appointing a "corresponding committee" as an effective branch of their body. Dun. P[eregrine]. suggests that the committee is "honest, faithful, and competent" but thinks they will be busily employed if they correspond with all the soldiers who have left Ripley.

Our regiment (the 5th Iowa) is at present, camped at Booneville [*sic*] but we expect to start Wednesday for New Orleans. If I am not grievously mistaken, we are en route for Leavenworth to join Jim Lane's expedition.[6] There are several Brown county boys in our company and quite a number in the 39th Ohio, which forms part of our brigade. So you see that old Brown is not only to be represented in the army in Virginia and in Kentucky, but in that branch of the army which proposes to take care of the Union and let slavery take care of itself!

Secession is scratched, if not killed, in Missouri. Their reverses at Knob Knoster, Mount Zion, Silver Creek, &c, have considerably depressed the spirits of the rebels. The late victory in Kentucky is also having its influence.[7] Hereafter, I think the state militia, with the aid of a few U.S. regiments will be able to keep "all quiet in Missouri." More Anon, (perhaps).

Letter 4. Published March 6, 1862; Dateline Camp Defiance, Cairo, Sunday, February 23, 1862

From Syracuse to Cairo

We left Syracuse at 10 o'clock A.M., Jan. 31. Our camp, after we had our tents struck, was worth seeing and would have presented a very interesting spectacle to you. The cords of men, wagons, horses, mules and the chimneys standing alone with big fires rolling the bright blazes out of their tops presented a truly novel spectacle. We marched 14 miles the first day, and camped in barns at night. Next morning our company was placed in the lead and we led off in Company B style making Boonville by noon—marching 12 miles over a road glazed with ice. It is an easy matter to walk 12 miles in four hours by one's self, but for a battalion to do it marching in ranks is an entirely different performance. About a mile from Boonville, we found the remainder of our regiment drawn up to receive us. We were placed in two store rooms for our quarters. We found our new quarters quite different from our comfortable quarters at Syracuse, which we left (in one sense) reluctantly. On one of the chimneys left standing there after the tents were pulled down was found the following "Ode to our Chimney."

Old Chimney, I love thee for what thou hast done
To cheer us, and warm us, and keep us in fun.
Without thee, I fear lest the merciless storm
Had beat on our poor pates and done us much harm.
Like man, thou wert made of the dust of the earth
But thy nature detracts not one whit from thy worth.
Like woman, our helper thou always hast been.
How can we forsake thee, and yet have no sin?
I love thee, old chimney, for well thou hast drew—
Without thee, old chimney, what, what shall we do?
Without thee, I fear lest we'd frozen our toes,
And perhaps brought our days to an untimely close.
Farewell then, old chimney! Adieu! We must part—
But thy mem'ry shall linger fore'er in my heart.
See! The blest little water-drops steal from my eyes;
Curs'd, curs'd, be the hand that thus severs dear ties.
Adieu.

We were joined at Boonville by five companies of the 39th Ohio, and the 47th Illinois regiments and also Constable's Ohio Battery. In this battery, I found Fred. Kramer and George ———, the german boy that used to clerk for Jos. Brafford. The evening before we left Boonville, we had a very heavy rain. Thursday morning, 6th inst., we crossed the river—the weather having turned very cold. We marched 2 miles and camped near Franklin, a small village on the river bottom, opposite Boonville. We pitched our tents—digging through the frozen ground with axes so as to drive the tent-pins. My bedfellow failing to cross the river, I had to sleep Thursday night alone with only two blankets. About midnight, I was frozen out and had to get up and sit by the camp fire till daylight. The night was very cold. Saturday morning at 8 o'clock we started on the march—marched 12 miles over the icyist road I ever saw. I could have skated half the way very conveniently. I took the precaution before starting to fill my haversack with biscuits, sausage, and cheese so that I did not suffer from hunger. Saturday night we camped on a field of ice. We kept our straw off the ice by covering the ice with a lot of twigs. Sunday morning our brigade was drawn up in line and witnessed a novel scene. Four artillerymen the night before were caught bringing a stolen pig into camp. They were compelled to stand guard over it, until we were ready to start in the morning when they had to carry it along in front of the whole brigade amid cheers, taunts, and laughter, that would have abashed an imp of Satan. Sunday, we marched only eight miles in a south-easterly direction. In all our marching, we aimed to camp at 2 P.M. —Monday, 10th, we marched fifteen miles passing through Columbia and camping about 4 miles southeast of it. Tuesday, 11th, we marched 12 miles in a southeasterly direction camping as usual in timber. Wednesday, 12th, marched 12 miles, passing through Fulton. The march this day was very fatiguing; owing to the mud which was deep and tough. The anxiety during the march, was not how fast we could travel, but whether the teams could make the trip. We all had our knapsacks hauled during the march by teams which we hired at $3 a day.

Letter 5. Published June 5, 1862; Dateline Camp near Corinth, Mississippi, May 24, 1862

Dear Bee:

While the blows fall "thick and fast"—while fighting is the programme, minor matters are looked over and only the details of "brilliant naval engagements," "terrible bombardments" &c, &c. are considered worthy a glance. But while there is a lull in the storm of war, the rustle of a leaf may attract attention. Ergo, I will venture an intrusion into the presence of your readers. While Halleck and Beauregard are playing "won't and dare not" I will seize the propitious moment and tell what I dare and what I fancy.[8]

I suppose that by this time you have all given up any expectations of any engagement "within a short time" and that news of a fight, here, would strike the tympanum of the public ear with startling surprise. As with you, so with us. We have prepared for "a fight today" so often that we would likely consider it all a joke, if, after a victorious conflict, we should be told that the fight had come off. Our camp is within 3 miles of Beauregard's nest, but the only realization we have of it, is an occasional *spat* with some battery of the enemy or the more frequent exchange of compliments between the pickets. True, we have a line of earthworks thrown up along our front, the whole extent of the army but I am positive that *Yellow Jack's* army will cross them long before Beauregard will, and they are no reminder to us of the presence of the South's last hope.[9] It is a puzzle to us (the uninitiated) to understand these defences. If we are going to take Corinth, we can't take them along—why then were they constructed? Are we to wait here till Beauregard attacks us? I hope not.—All they ask, "is to be let alone." But perhaps this may be the policy and it may prove wise. The mass of Beauregard's army is composed of new recruits—men who have been drafted, enlisted for sixty days &c.—and these men must suffer greatly from disease as all new recruits do, especially in the summer season. And again, this army was got up for *action*, and will die of *ennui*. Thousands could come and fight or stay a month but vital interests at home will not permit a lengthy stay. Perhaps then Halleck will wait for them to come out of their entrenchments and fight them on equal terms. Halleck's army *can* stay here until all this may be accomplished. There is no danger of Yellow Jack or any of their pestilences here. A more healthy position for the army, could not well be found. Situated in a region whose waters flow into the Tennessee, Mississippi, and the Gulf, the altitude of our camps above the regions of swamps and cane brakes, renders us secure from the fevers and plagues of the lower country. We have abundance of water and Uncle Sam has plenty of bread.

But these conjectures may almost be needless. Perhaps ere this is finished and sealed doubts may be banished and the riddle solved.

Let us take a look at the army. Tishomingo county, Mississippi, has at present, a very large population—just how large I suppose Halleck and Beauregard both would be glad to know. This population is mostly German, Irish, and American, a great many of the former and *considerable* of the latter. The county formerly had a floating population of Africans but they have given way before the superior race of Northmen. But I was to speak of the army. Well, the average distance between the armies is about 2 1/2 miles. On the left wing (Pope's Division) we are 3 miles above Corinth. In the center (Buell's Division) they are within 1 1/2 miles of the rebels. While, on the right they are probably hold a similar position to the left wing. The county is hilly and wooded and although we are near neighbors, we rarely get to see each others faces. Occasionally our men will cut down a strip of timber to enable them to get a squint at their backward neighbors or as if we were ashamed of ourselves or our works, we will plant a grove in front of some battery of Parrott guns or big mouthed howitzers hiding them from the *friendly* gaze of some o'er curious rebel. Not content with this, we even hide ourselves in the bushes, pitching our tents among the oaks and hickories on the *safe* side of the hills. From the secretive disposition that has been manifested, I should not be surprised that, if we should be attacked, many of our riflemen would hide themselves in certain pits which have been dug all around the batteries. I am almost suspicious that even the cannoniers would screen themselves behind some sand-bags which are piled up on the brow of the hill. Gen. Pope seems to be the most curious man we have. He has a great desire to see the rebels and what they are at. On the top of a hill stands a big tree. This tree Pope has rigged up for his "look out." By means of a rope-ladder, he ascends to the platform in the top of the tree where by the use of his sight-helper, he tries to "spy out the fat of the land," (in and around Corinth). What great sights he has seen, I can't tell, as he has not divulged.

One would naturally suppose that in a county having so large a population as this, there would be plenty of groceries and provision stores, but it is true as strange that we have to get all our grub from Hamburgh on the Tennessee river. As the roads have preserved their Adamite (not McAdamite) condition in this region, transportation of food "for man and beast" is no small job. To render it more feasible, Uncle Sam has been improving on nature by making his boys dig down the hills and fill up the hollows—in many places, making extra jobs, by putting in patches of the everlasting *corduroys.*[10] Owing to this fact, of our having to get our supplies all from one source, we have to take just what we can get. True, Uncle Sam makes provision for feeding us *well* but between rascally contractors and stupid Quartermasters, we are cheated out of a good portion of our dues. It is not a rare thing for crackers to have a green lining or beans to look muddy and smell musty. Fresh beef is generally protected from the flies by a lining of mud and filth that would turn most anybody's stomach but a soldier's. Of potatoes, we get hardly half rations. Our salt (generally good) is not the coarse sack salt used in packing houses. Thus Uncle Sam's good intentions are thwarted by the rascality and incompetency of officers. Were it not that the rations of bread, rice, and coffee are over large, we would suffer from the shortcomings. As it is we have barely sufficient.

The health of the army is good—the prospects better.

With best wishes to all, I remain

Yours   Q.

Letter 6. Published June 26, 1862; Dateline Camp Beautiful, Mississippi, June 17, 1862

Dear Bee,

I have dated my letter in camp but I am not certain that the word "settlement" should be substituted for "camp." Everything indicates that we have settled here, or, as expressed in Bostona lingo, "We have come to stay." The officers believe it and the privates believe it. The prevailing impression is that we will remain here at rest during the hot and sickly months (including September) unless Beauregard should assume the offensive and threaten us at some point in our line of posts.[11] After waiting for the enemy to leave Corinth, Halleck now has determined to wait for them to come back! After letting the bird out of the cage, he has concluded to wait for it to come back to its prison, thinking that the poor thing will die of starvation if it doesn't. Perhaps, (like Noah), he will find out in the course of time that the bird has found a place to set its foot and has no notion of returning.

After the evacuation of Corinth, we pursued (?) the enemy 25 miles southward. You have no doubt seen in the papers accounts of Pope's Division "pushing hard upon the fleeing rebels," "taking more prisoners than they knew what to do with," &c., &c. There is a grain of truth in these reports. We marched the 25 miles in five days! So hard did we push the enemy that they came very near falling into the last ditch! The reason that Pope had "more prisoners than he knew what to do with" was because he hardly knew what to do with his own men. Before the evacuation, he wanted to use his men in caging the rebels but he was not heeded and had to wait until the proper time was passed and he then had no doubt "more men than he knew what to do with." The prisoners taken by Pope (excepting a few stragglers) were 2,000 taken by the 2d Iowa Cavalry, when they burned the train at Boon[e]ville. Being in an enemy's country, without any support, and being compelled to use celerity in their movements, of course they had "more prisoners than they knew what to do with" and they released them "on parole."[12] So much for "official reports" of our doings.

After remaining in the neighborhood of Boonville, a few days, drinking putrid pond water, a change came o'er the mind of Halleck and the whole force were ordered back, to go into camp on the headwaters of Tombigbee river. On the 9th, Gen Ammen's brigade passed our camp on the way to new camping. The general looked hearty as if he was blessed with good health again.[13] On the 11th, we shouldered arms and started for water. Our regiment was rear-guard of a division and as the dust was three inches deep, we got our share of Mississippi soil. Some of the boys thought they swallowed their 160 acres! If you ever travel all day on a road where the dust flew so thick that you could roll your tongue and spit out a good sized marble every eight or ten steps, you may have a faint idea of the ordeal we had to pass through!

On the 12th, we camped about 5 miles southwest of Corinth on the Mobile and Ohio R.R. Saturday the 14th, we came to our present camp one mile east of the old one. I have dubbed it "Camp beautiful," for it is admired by all and declared to be "a lovely place" by men who scarcely ever see beauty in anything. The country is very broken and wild and partakes of the romantic. We are camped on a series of ridges which are barely wide enough to stick our tents on. From these ridges, innumerable spurs jutting out interlock each other and present that irregularity which constitutes one of the beauties of nature. The "majestic oak," and "the lofty pine" are our forest friends and they are "friends indeed." Under their welcome shade, we can find comfort and pleasure, despite the fierceness of Old Sol's rays.

In the ravine are innumerable springs from which the clearest and coolest water flows to add to the soldier's comfort and health. All of these springs are good but there is one near Gen. [Charles S.] Hamilton's headquarters which deserves special attention. Fatigue men have been laboring for the past two days in placing it in order and sinking reservoirs for it flood[s] of water. Gen. Hamilton's civil engineer calculated that this spring runs seventy gallons of water a minute! And that it would supply one whole army! What a blessing to Ripley this spring would be located on the hill!

In our travels south of Corinth, we got a glimpse of a little farther South and some things we deemed worthy of attention. First, the inhabitants. Like Southerners generally, (so far as we have seen) they have just enough improvement on their farms to remind one of the absence of them. As there are but few men at home, it would hardly be fair to judge them by the specimens at home, else we might be tempted to say a few things about the "butternuts." The women (widows) are at home, however, and as their natural curiosity was too strong for their prejudice against the yankees, we had abundant opportunities of seeing them. If I didn't dislike to say anything derogatory to the sex, I would express my opinion of them. Suffice to say, that the soldier boys will take their hearts home with them when they return to the North. Haller had quite an amusing chat with one of the Southern belles, who, it is said, wears a finger-ring make of a yankee's jaw bone, sent to her from Manassas. Haller amused and enlightened the young lady and her mother, no little, and they no doubt found him to be a live yankee—such a one as would be desirable for a "pet."

The amount of corn that is planted was a matter of attention with us. As far as we went, all the cotton fields were planted in corn. Not a solitary field of cotton did we see. Cotton presses stood on almost every farm but only as indices of the past. At almost every farm, we could see the work of the Confederacy in the destruction of cotton which is burned and "scattered to the four winds of heaven." From the nature of the soil and the appearance of the country here, I would judge that good "upland cotton" would thrive in Brown county.

Wishing all a good time on "the Fourth," I remain,

Q.

Letter 7. Published July 17, 1862; Dateline Camp near Rienzi, Mississippi, July 9, 1862

Dear Bee:

Thinking that your readers have not entirely lost interest in military movements in the West, I have concluded to give you an account of "our visit to Ripley," including matters and things by the way.

On the morning of the 27th ult., the major part of General [William S.] Rosecrans' (formerly [John] Pope's) Division left camp near Corinth and commenced a march for Holly Springs, Miss. The line of march lay southward to Rienzi, (a small town, 15 miles south of Corinth) thence west on the State road through Ripley to Holly Springs. Owing to the dusty state of the roads and the hot weather, we marched slowly. On the morning of the 30th we passed through Ripley which is 27 miles west of Rains. As we entered the town our flags were unfurled and the bands struck up "Dixie" and Yankee Doodle, while the men, "catching the step," marched with a steady trump into the county town of Tippah county, Mississippi—the former residence and birthplace of Gen. [Thomas C.] Hindman of the C.S.A. Having some knowledge of the characteristics of Ripley, O., I determined to note the points of resemblance in the two, but found soon that I could more easily observe their dissimilarities. First, our reception convinced me that we were not among the loyal people of your place. The morning was very warm and our reception correspondingly cool. Almost every house was closed and but few faces were to be seen. The streets were deserted, window-blinds closed, and dogs and children shut up, while the "darkies" were the only individuals that seemed to have liberty to show themselves and make observations of the "Yanks." The only business houses open were the drug store, the barber shop, and the hotel—left open, I suppose, in hopes that we would take their drugs, cut our throats, or put up at their tavern—either of which is certain to kill. Not fancying our reception in the town we passed through without stopping and camped one mile beyond. Ripley contains in peace times about 1200 inhabitants and is a pretty place. Some of the residences are beautiful and display skill and taste in their surroundings. The town contains some of the finest dwellings I have seen in any city in the south. There are evidences of former thrift but none of present. The men are mostly "off to the wars"—serving in Beauregard's and Johnston's armies—and the slaves are the principal business men of the place now. The character of the people in and around Ripley is intensely secesh. Charleston, South Carolina cannot, probably, boast a population more devoted to the cause or more hostile to the "Yanks." How their countenances betrayed their feelings! The few we saw, as we passed through town, looked as if they had lived on vinegarstews for a fortnight!

There was one class of the population, however, that welcomed us and manifested sympathy for our cause. Of course, I mean the slaves. Universally, we find them loyal, ready to aid us by word or deed. NO love of master holds them back, but they give us any desired information they can. While every other one around him is plotting destruction for our Union, he declares to sympathize with and act for it. Is it anything but fair that our government should lend a helping hand to these Union men of Mississippi? One of this class of Union men joined our regiment on the way out and is cooking for one of the captains. His master joined us on our return. He was captured at home by Gen. Hamilton's body-guard—dragged from under the bed where he was concealed and compelled to join our army pro tempore. He was a member of the Mississippi Legislature and voted for the ordinance of secession. He will be sent North for his health. His brother was killed in the battle of Fair Oaks.[14]

On the morning of the 1st inst., we received orders to countermarch and instead of going on to Holly Springs, turned back to our old camp.

The county we passed through between Rienzi and Ripley is hilly and wooded. The soil is poor and the people poorer. Occasionally a tolerable farm greets the eye but they are as oases in the desert. The almost universal style of the houses is like the old fashioned log corn-cribs, with crib in each end and an open space in the centre for driving the wagon in. Window-glass seems to be a luxury that most don't indulge in—a wooden shutter serving to close the hole the carpenter(?) left for the window. I suppose that these people have no daylight in their houses during the cold season of the year—like the inhabitants of the frigid zones, they probably have six months of day and six months night. This class of dwellings is inhabited by the non-slaveholder—men who are as much dependent on the slaveholders as the slaves themselves. Whenever I saw a respectable house, I saw slaves.

We are now camped near Rienzi—or I suppose, we are rather bivouacked here, as our camp (tents and all) is back near Corinth. There are rumors afloat that the enemy in considerable force, is in the neighborhood of Boonville south of here. If he is, he will either have to evacuate or take a drubbing. I believe, however, that the rumors are false—that the enemy has the same desire to lie idle, this hot weather, that we have.

Hoping that you may find more pleasure in reading, than I do in writing this, I remain,

Yours,

Q.

Letter 8. Published October 9, 1862; Dateline Camp Near Jacinto, Mississippi, September 24, 1862

Dear Archie,

In the note, I wrote a few days ago, I said I would send a full account of the part of our regiment played in the battle of Iuka, as soon as I could. I just procured some paper and will try and scribble it over.[15]

Tuesday, the 16th inst., our tents and baggage were all sent to Corinth. Wednesday, the 17th, we stayed in camp and were treated to a heavy rain all day. At night we were ordered to cook three day' rations and be ready to march by three o'clock in the morning. At one o'clock the next morning (Thursday) we were called up and at half past three, we started through the rain, mud and darkness, for Iuka, where [Confederate major general Sterling] Price was reported to be with his army having driven out our forces (three regiments belonging to [Gen. David S.] Stanley's Division) a few days before. We marched about 8 miles and then halted in the road and moved no farther that day. Thursday night, we camped in a field near where we halted. We were joined that night by Stanley's Division, from Corinth. Our force then consisted of Hamilton's and Stanley's divisions—about 20 regiments, or nearly 10,000 men. Friday morning, we started on, our regiment (5th Iowa) in the van. About 8 miles from Iuka, our cavalry drove in the enemy's mounted pickets. Six miles from Iuka, we encountered their infantry pickets and our cavalry fell back. Three companies (E, G, and D) of our regiment were thrown forward as skirmishers. They immediately pressed upon the enemy's pickets and drove them back. But it was a slow job, for the pickets fought stubbornly. Our regiment (the balance of it) moved by the flank along the road, close behind the skirmishers, in order to support. One or two of the skirmishers were wounded and two or three of the pickets killed while the skirmish continued. A very nice frame house, containing piano &c. was burned by Gen. Rosecrans' order as we passed along. From that house, one of our skirmishers was shot and badly wounded—whence its destruction. About sundown when the pickets had been driven in four and half miles (within 1 1/2 miles of Iuka) and just as the road ran along a timbered ridge, our skirmishers got into a hornet's nest. The skirmishers, then were from the 26th Missouri regiment, they having relieved our skirmishers but a few moments before. The head of our regiment was beginning to descend the road at the point of the ridge, when our skirmishers fired a few shots and were answered by a volley that said nixcumerous![16] Gen. Hamilton was then at our head, Gen. Rosecrans having left us but a few moments before to examine another road. Our skirmishers had to come upon the enemy in force and they soon reported to us that the enemy were flanking us on the right. At the same time a rebel battery opened on us in front but with little effect. Our regiment was thrown in line across the road at the same time the enemy fired the first volley. When the skirmishers reported the that the enemy were flanking us on the right, Col. [Charles] Matthies (the General being at that instant absent) whirled his horse and remarked "I see about dat." In a moment he was back and changed our position to meet the flankers. The 11th Ohio Battery which was immediately in our rear, took its position on the point of the ridge and prepared for action. Four companies of the 26th Missouri took position on our left in rear of the battery. These preparations were made in a short time and we then awaited (but only for a moment) the appearance of the enemy. They came. We were ready for them. They opened with buck and ball, we replied with Minies. We were not to exceed fifty yards apart and you may readily imagine that the balls flew thick and fast both ways. Our boys loaded and fired rapidly and kept a constant blaze along our lines. But although our fire was heavy it did not by far come up to that of the enemy. Beside the regular fire, which they constantly kept up, they every few moments would fire a volley that would almost make the earth quake. Every one of these volleys would sweep through our lines with a besom of destruction and we had naught to oppose but our steady firing. They managed thus. One regiment or more was stationed on top of another on a small ridge opposite us and this line kept up a steady fire upon us. The volleys were fired by other regiments that would come up to the brow of the ridge and fire and then fall back out of danger to load and return again to riddle our ranks. Thus we were opposed to no less than three regiments at a time and to five different ones during the fight—the 11th and 37th Alabama, 3d Louisiana, 5th Missouri, and 38th Mississippi. Of course our loss was terrible—fighting against such odds, how could it be otherwise. Our regiment lost full half its number in killed and wounded during the fight. But notwithstanding the carnage, the boys did nobly. For a full hour and a quarter, they faced the storm of lead and beat back the foe. Several times the enemy charged upon us, but every time they fell back before our steady fire. Standing over their dead and dying comrades, the boys fought with a determination and enthusiasm that was an honor, even to the name of Iowa. Once we made a charge and the enemy fell into confusion and broke before us, but owing to the darkness and our ignorance of the nature of the ground, we were not able to follow up our advantage, but paused at the edge of the ridge and again fell back to our old line. After fighting over an hour and when half our force was placed hors du combat and when the majority of the other half had shot away the last cartridges, we fell back and the 11th Missouri (which had been drawn up in our rear) check[ed] and firmly held at bay the rebels. Our regiment formed in rear of the 11th and moved off the field to procure cartridges but our services were not needed again. For the enemy were shortly after driven back and our forces held the field. The left wing of our regiment and the four companies of the 26th Missouri suffered the most severely during the battle. The battle was principally fought by Buford's brigade. Only about half of [Brig. Gen. Jeremiah C.] Sullivan's brigade (Hamilton's Division) was actively engaged in the fight. Excepting the 11th Missouri, none of Stanley's Division fired more than one round and some of them were not on the field. While we were fighting the enemy on the right of the ridge, the 48th Indiana, 4th Minnesota, the 16th and 17th Iowa, and 8th Wisconsin were respectively engaged with the enemy on the left. The brunt of the battle fell on the Fifth and well she played her part—officers and men all did nobly and they have received the highest praise from all the generals and their comrades in arms of the other regiments. The Ohio Battery did excellent service for a short time but it was in a very bad situation and it was soon silenced—half its number being killed or wounded. During the fight, the rebels captured the battery but were driven back from it afterwards. They carried off two pieces with them as they fell back but they were found the next morning near the field. The result of the battle was this: The enemy chose their own ground and attacked us in their own time with superior numbers but were driven off the field and skedaddled under cover of the night. After the fight, I lay down on two rails with my gum blanket over me to sleep but after sleeping a few minutes, I got up and went to the hospital. I there found that Lieut. Mateer (very badly wounded) was waiting his chance to be taken in an ambulance to another hospital a mile and half further down the road.[17] With several others of our company I carried him down on a litter and then returned. I then lay down but was hardly asleep when the regiment was called up and I got no more sleep. We did not then know that Price was gone. We were making preparations to attack him at daylight. After we found he was gone, our regiment was permitted to visit the battleground and details were made to bury the dead. A few wounded were found who could not be found by the litter bearers the night before. After looking over the field, the details were left behind to bury the dead and we started back for Jacinto, [Maj. Gen. Ulysses S.] Grant having commenced the pursuit of Price. We marched about five miles and camped overnight. At one o'clock the next day, we (Rosecrans' Army) started for Jacinto and arrived here about 7 o'clock. We are still here. You will get the particulars of the battle (as to killed and wounded and prisoners on both sides and the forces engaged) from the papers, whence we must glean them. Lieutenant Mateer was alive the last we heard from him. Nothing from Dun Peregrine. I have no doubt he is a prisoner (as he was wounded) in the hospital at Iuka. The rebel's left some of our wounded (whom they had taken prisoners) there. All our wounded, who could bear to be moved, have been sent to Corinth. I have no envelopes or stamps yet—plenty in my trunk at Corinth. I understand that our baggage will be here to day. I hope it will. Perhaps you would like to know something of my conduct and feelings during the battle. I felt a little of what is called a peculiar feeling—that is a fear of consequences and an anxiety as to results—but no thought of doing anything but my duty. This was before the fight had really begun. When the firing commenced, I lost all this peculiar feeling—lost all consciousness of danger and was anxious only that the boys should show themselves true sons of Iowa. I did not lose my caution or present of mind but I felt an enthusiasm that to me is unaccountable. I don't understand myself. Some of the boys told me afterwards (referring to my cheering and exhortations) that I would make a good Methodist. This feeling, however, was not confined to me—others felt the same electric current. As the fight progressed, I assisted the boys in loading—enabling them to fire with more rapidity. I would take cartridges from their boxes and tear them, ready for loading, and hand them to the boys as they needed them. I supplied two or three in this manner at a time. As one of the boys was taking a cartridge from me he was struck in the back of the neck with a buckshot and knocked flat—wounded in the big leader of the neck. About the second volley that was fired, one of our company, who was standing immediately in front of me was shot in the head. He dropped dead at my feet. I said nothing to the boys for fear it might have an effect on them and not a word was said by anyone. Afterwards another fell dead by my side, grasping hold of me as he fell. He also was shot dead. As we returned from our charge, I saw another of our company fall dead a short distance to my left. I saw a number wounded close to me. But what is a matter of greatest wonder to me, I felt no emotion—not the least at these sights and stood over these dead men as if life had never existed in their bodies, instead of having been my daily companions. During the fight, one of the boys asked me for cartridges—he had run out. I supplied him from the cartridge box of one of the dead men who lay by me. Such are a soldier's feelings during a battle. It is well it is so. Even the next morning when we visited the battlefield none of its horrors moved me. It was only after we had left the scene and I began to miss those who had constantly been with us, that my feelings came back to me.

One thing more and I am done. I have read accounts of correspondents about the horrible appearance of the countenances of those who die in battle. I will say that I saw none of this. Some countenances were distorted, but the majority looked natural, as if death had come in its slower and less violent forms.

Quincy

Letter 9. Published December 18, 1862; Dateline "Camp on Tal[l]ahatchie River [Mississippi]," December 4, 1862

Messrs. Eds: Grant's army commenced moving South, from Memphis and Grand Junction on the 28th ult—Sherman commanding the right wing, McPherson the center and Hamilton the left wing. Being with that part of the army which marched from Grand Junction; I propose to give you a few lines about matters which have come under my observation.

The first day's march was uninteresting. The second day we passed through Holly Springs where we found but a few people and they with long faces and sour countenances. They very coolly informed us that we would be showing our heels before the sun set on the morrow, but I rather guess that they changed their notion before the last of the blue coats passed through town—at least they have changed it ere this. Holly Springs has been "a business place"—numbering perhaps 4,000 inhabitants. It boasts many elegant residences and some fine business houses.

Passing through Holly Springs, we continued on our course southward over a very broken, barren country—barren because the soil is so sandy and the country so broken that the fields was filled of deep gullies and are rendered unfit for cultivation. After passing through Holly Springs, our cavalry skirmished with the rebel pickets, with slight loss on both sides.

Seven miles South of Holly Springs we came to "Lumpkin's Mill," where the rebels had been camped making good use of the mill during their sojourn. The country about the mill afforded the rebels a good situation for making a stand but they merely paused to skirmish with our cavalry.

Between Lumpkin's Mill and the Tallahatchie River, our cavalry had considerable skirmishing with the rebels but the butternuts invariably gave back.

Sunday evening last, the rebels "packed up" and left their fortifications on the Tallahatchie in hot haste. The next morning our cavalry were after them and succeeded in capturing a party who had been left behind to burn the railroad tresslework. Our infantry was not slow in following our cavalry and the pursuit is still kept up. The secesh with soon find "the last ditch" in the west.

Two or three divisions of Grant's army are still on this (North) side [of] the river, waiting for the repairing of the roads and bridges, and a supply of rations.

Prisoners

Squads of prisoners are taken by our cavalry daily. Besides these, numbers straggle away from the rebel army and come into our lines. They represent Price's army to be much down-hearted.

Condition of the "Rebs"

I have heard it stated again and again—have heard it iterated and reiterated—have seen it in print and heard it "proclaimed from the house tops," — that the rebel army is in a naked, starving condition,—one-third of them have no shoes, no blankets, no bread, &c, &c. Now I wish to enter a protest against all this. I have seen, (since I have been in the army) thousands of dead, wounded, and captured secesh, and I have never seen one who was barefooted or who had not comfortable clothing. They are not dressed in uniform, nor are they as well clad as Uncle Sam's boys but they are far from being destitute. I judge that they have plenty of food because we always find plenty when we glean where they have been. From what I have seen I judge the whole: "Expede Herculem."[18]

The Rebel Fortifications

The rebels talked loudly about the stand they intended to make here on the Tallahatchie river, and they made preparations to make their boasts good. They threw up works here superior to but not so extensive as those at Corinth. To give their guns full sweep they "cleared" quite a "patch" of ground and to keep the Yankees from coming to close quarters they burned the bridges. But "the best laid plans of mice and men gang aft aglee." A flank movement by Sherman and Steele proved to the rebels that the danger was not all in front and they left for a more hospitable clime—leaving their works as monuments to their folly.[19] They had heavy works on both sides of the river, but those on this side, were in a position that we could command from a neighboring hill and were therefore a mere cipher.

A Novel Sight

"And Linkum saw another sight." My eyes were greeted by a strange, an unusual, an interesting sight yesterday. "What was it?"—"A beast of the earth, a fowl of the air, or a fish of the sea?" Neither! Was it a Secesh General? Not that. "A Union man in Mississippi?" No. "What then, was it, a ghost or hobgoblin?" No. It was—(though it may be doubted)—it was a secesh nigger! Let John Van Buren, Fernando Wood, and Chilton A., rejoice that there is one, at least, who will not listen to the voice of Abraham, and "go out FREE," on the first day of next January, I say again, let them rejoice.[20]

An Earthquake

Last Sunday morning we felt a slight shock of an earthquake. If we had been given to superstition, we might have imagined that the Goddess of Mississippi was angry at our invasion of her fair land, and the people of Holly Springs might have witnessed a fulfillment of their prophesies.

The Weather In Dixie

During the entire fall, the weather has not been so pleasant as a soldier desires. Three days out of four have been rainy. We would have the proportion the other way. Yesterday was clear and bright and a bracing North wind blew all day. "Old Boreas," however, does not blow with us as with you—he looses much of his asperity from his frequent kissings of a Southern sun.

"Contraband" Information

A great many lies that are written for the Northern papers about our army are said to be based upon the statements of intelligent contrabands.[21] In this way, Mr. Intelligent Contraband has almost, if not quite, lost his character for veracity. Now it may be that the untutored African has in some instances "taken in" his more cultivated white brother—he may be given to telling big tales when asked for them. It is probable that in some cases he is so afflicted. But I can say in defense of his character, that I have often interrogated them about matters, where I afterwards had an opportunity of testing the truth of their statements and I always "found it so—just like the darkies told me, Oh."[22]

Yours,

Q.

Letter 10. Published January 22, 1863; Dateline Germantown, Tennessee, Jan. 9, 1863

Dear Bee:—I wrote a few (?) Lines for your columns, from our camp on [the] Tallahatchie river. We were then after Price. "But since that time how things have changed." We followed the fleet-footed rebels to the Yacona river, some ten miles south of Oxford. Stopping there to get [our] breath, (or provisions) the rebels took advantage of our halt and making a circuit, dashed upon Holly Springs with a strong cavalry force (mounted infantry) and through the incompetency or cowardice of the commander of the post, succeeded in capturing the place [and] burning our stores there. Our communications being thus cut off, we had to start back for subsistence. Grant withdrew his whole army to the North of the Tallahatchie River burning all bridges and mills as he fell back.[23]

A train of 400, or 500 wagons was then sent to Memphis for rations. [Brig. Gen. Isaac F.] Quinby's Division acting as escort. The train was loaded with provisions at Memphis and returned to the army by way of the "State-Line Road," meeting the Locomotive (from Holly Springs and Grand Junction) at Lafayette, Tenn. The army was put upon half and three quarter rations until the provision train returned from Memphis, but the boys made their rations more than full by pressing potatoes, pulling chickens, and drawing hogs from the citizens. There is no such thing as starving a soldier while the good things of life stare him in the face. "Tantalus" never sojered or he never would have been "taken in" as he was.[24]

Grant's New Base of Operations

Gen. Grant has opened the Memphis & Charleston Railroad and now has Memphis as his base of operations. Two Divisions (twelve regiments and eight batteries) are required to guard the road (50 miles) from Memphis to Grand Junction. There is no portion of the south more infested with guerillas than this section, and the utmost vigilance is required to keep them from destroying the track. When the attempt was made to open this road last summer, they threw a train off the track and destroyed it within a mile and a half of this place. A member of our company was upon the train at the time and with others, escaped by "taking to timber." The guerillas pursued them with blood hounds but failed to catch them. Since we came here our boys have made it a special business to kill every hound in the country they came across. "Every dog has its day."

Poor Whites

I have read much and heard much about "the poor whites of the South" and while in Mississippi I saw sufficient to satisfy me that all I have heard is true. From conversation with many of them, I have learned (what I before believed) that they were a mere cipher—having no voice or vote in determining the status of their State. Many of these men were torn from their helpless families and forced into the rebel army, while in many cases, the leaders in the Secession movement remained at home, either by hiring substitutes or under pretense of watching the blacks and raising supplies when they find our army has got between the rebel army and their homes. "They would shoot me quicker than they would any of you," said one of them to me, "if they could catch me. I have deserted from the army twice. The last time they tied me and carried me off." He procured a free pass to Cairo for himself and family from Oxford. "I have staid [sic] in the swamp and would have been there yet if you had not come," said one of the regular tow-headed poor whites to me, "I never was tired of the Union" said a venerable gray headed man "but my seven sons have ben conscripted." Three of his sons deserted and went home when the rebels skedaddled out of Oxford. Every one of these men recognized slavery as the cause of the war and heaped their imprecations upon slavery and slaveholders for bringing them and their families to misery. The Abolitionists don't all live outside of Mississippi. When the South is once subjugated and free speech and free press established there, the revolution in sentiment in favor of the old Union and a free country is not as far distant as even many ardent patriots suppose. Slavery has bred ignorance and treason. Freedom will breed light and loyalty.

Winter Quarters

While the army in other quarters is going into winter quarters, the army of the West has no such intentions or desires. One month of winter has passed and it has been very favorable for military operations. True, we have had rain, on an average, once a week but owing to the sandy nature of the soil, the roads are in good condition most of the time and the weather is just cool enough to make marching profitable exercise for man and beast.

Our Mode of Living

At present, the 3d Brigade of Quinby's Division is stationed here in a section of country that has never before been "staid with" by the Yankees. The soil being fertile, forage is abundant and Uncle Sam's boys "fare sumptuously every day." Our Quartermasters make requisitions on the guerilla commissaries and draw potatoes, yams, fresh meat, &c, from the plantations of this vicinity.

A Correction

In my last letter, through a mistake of yours or mine (more presumably yours) I was made to say that it had rained there days out of four during the fall. I merely intended to say that it had rained three out of the first four days of winter. "Uncle Sam's till the war ends."

Q.

P.S. Jan. 10. Dun Peregrine joined the regiment last night with good health.

Letter 11. Published January 29, 1863; Dateline Germantown, Tennessee, January 19, 1863

Dear Bee—It is a fact, patent to all, that on the first day of this year, ABRAHAM LINCOLN, President of the United States issued a War Proclamation emancipating the Slaves in most of the rebellious states. What will be the effect of that proclamation is a question of dispute. The true Unionist welcomes it as an effective agent in crushing out the rebellion. The rebels and their sympathizing friends of the North, profess to have a great contempt for it and attempt to laugh at it as an harmless measure that will not affect the institution of Slavery and only bring contempt on its author. But behind this laughing mask, they wear a serious, anxious face. Despite their wish that it may be harmless, they "believe and tremble" that Slavery is doomed and the Union is saved.

"I looked anxiously over the Proclamation" said a Dr. Hall of this place, "to see if it included Tennessee and I found that it did not—that we are all right."

"But it wouldn't have made any difference," chimed in his wife, "it won't amount to anything."

"No, it won't amount to anything—of course it won't," said the doctor who had been so anxious to see if Tennessee was all right.

Inadvertently, he had spoken from his heart, and his wife, more wary, came to his rescue.

While we were at Oxford, Mississippi, in December, a squad of butternuts assembled there to elect a Congressman in order that their District might be exempted from the effects of the Proclamation. While their brothers and sons were in the army fighting to save slavery, they marshaled their force at home to fight for Slavery with other weapons. The proclamation is to be a "harmless measure," nevertheless, it causes many anxious thoughts and where it is possible, the lovers of the "peculiar institution" were desirous of going through the forms of electing a Congressman to prevent the disasters that a "harmless proclamation" would bring upon them. The "cloven foot" shows through it all.

Do the Slaves Desire Freedom?

I do not intend to deny that the slaves are well fed and well clothed—that they are happy—that they love slavery—nor will I deny that they love their masters. Perhaps they do. Perhaps they don't. But do they desire to be free? I answer emphatically, they do. Nothing but the innate love of liberty in man could have caused the wide spread desire for freedom that is manifested among the slaves wherever our army goes. In regions where an Abolitionist was never heard of, the Yankees are hailed by the darkies as their deliverers. And their masters as far as they are able (though they talk loudly about the happiness and contentment of their slaves) keep shoving them farther south as our army advances. The darkey is not to be trusted (contented or discontented) where Freedom is in question. They often travel for days to meet us, "running" the enemy's pickets, risking their lives for freedom. Two shoemakers came into our camp, 15 miles north of Holly Springs bringing us information from the enemy. They were three days and nights coming that distance, having to avoid the enemy's cavalry which was scouring the country. These slaves belonged to a Mr. Watt of Holly Springs who had been making shoes for the Confederate Government. His shoemakers (some dozen or more) "came over" to our lines and Mr. Watt's tanner and shoe-manufactory "went under." A Mr. Porter who lived near Oxford, gathered his "boys" together and started for Alabama when the yankees approached Oxford. The "boys" had experienced enough of Slavery and they left their master at the half-way house and came into the yankee lines. For the privilege of staying with us, they piloted the yankees to Mr. Porter's cotton, by which Uncle Sam realized some $25,000 or $30,000 dollars.

It may do, to tell those who do not know, that the slaves are contented, but it won't go down with one who has been with our army and seen for himself. He has seen too many "goin' Norf" to think that much contentment exists among the slaves of the South.

Slavery Must Die or Rule

It is admitted, frankly and unhesitatingly, by the rebels wherever we find them that Slavery is the "bone of contention" and that the slave question must be settled by this war—meaning by this, that either the South will succeed in her rebellion and establish slavery on a National basis or the North will whip them and slavery die. Most of them believe that they will win. But some see only failure for them. A Mr. Green, of this place, a firm, outspoken Secessionist—a man of mind and of strong Southern proclivities—frankly admits that he believes the end of all this will be that "the Stars and Stripes will float in triumph over all this land." So mote it be.

> The Star-Spangled Banner in triumph shall wave,
> While the land of the free is the home of the brave.

Yours,

Q.

Letter 12. Published April 2, 1863; Dateline from Gen. Quinby's Division, near Helena, Arkansas, March 12, 1863

Dear Bee:

As announced by the telegraph, "Quinby's Division left Memphis for Lake Providence, on the 3d of March.[25] Quinby's is one of the three Divisions that constitute the 18th Army Corps—commanded by Major General [James B.] McPherson.

By the way, "Foster's Cavalry" are McPherson's body guard. As McPherson is a fighting general, his selection of the Brown County boys as body guard is a compliment which that excellent company has well merited.

Quinby's Division, as I have stated, started for Lake Providence but our destination was changed and the boats "rounded to" a short distance below Grand Lake, Arkansas within two miles of the Arkansas line. We camped on what was said to have been once a plantation belonging to John C. Breckinridge but which is now little more than a "wild waste of waters."[26] A few dry spots here and there afforded ground to pitch tents on. The deserted cabins furnished boards to make bunks of to keep the boy's beds out of the mud and Breckinridge's rails made very good fires for cooking beans and bacon!

Our stay at Grand Lake was short. The design of cutting a canal at that point, from the Mississippi to bayou Macon (pronounced Mason) was abandoned and our Division was ordered up the river to join the "Yazoo Pass Expedition." We were landed in Arkansas nearly opposite the mouth of the pass and about four miles below Helena. The transports that brought us up have gone down to bring up another Division. [Brig. Gen. Andrew J.] Smith's Division arrived here yesterday from Memphis. The troops in Helena (some 50,000 or 60,000) are "under marching orders" and expect to form part of the Yazoo Pass Expedition. About 20,000 troops have already gone into the pass. Putting this, that, and the other together it will be seen that the expedition to operate on the Yazoo is one of no little importance. The only thing that puzzles me is "how are all these troops to get transportation?" None but small boats can go through the pass and it will be a difficult to get enough to convey the whole force. We have been waiting here over a week for transports and as yet only one brigade (out of three) has been forwarded—perhaps Grant "knows what is what."

The work of cleaning out the pass before the first troops entered was quite difficult. It was performed by the troops stationed at Helena. The rebels had felled large cypress trees across the pass and they had to be removed by man power. It was a heavy job but the boys had a merry time over it. At first, they were rather shy of the mud and water but they soon got used to it. The modus operandi was simple. They would tie a large cable to a tree and as many a could would take hold and walk off with the tree.

Large cypress trees—measuring three feet at the butt and carrying their thickness for eighty feet were hauled off with perfect ease—large limbs snapping off like twigs before the tremendous power applied to them.

The pass was navigated by flat-boats and some steam boats about fifteen years ago.

Helena

I had an opportunity of visiting the noted city of Helena a few days ago. Permit a short description of the place.

Helena is a mud hole.

I thought when I saw Cairo that I had seen "the lowest deep;" the ultima Thule of muddom but Cairo must give up the ribbons to Helena. I will not particularize but state one fact that will illustrate Helena in wet weather. In the streets of Helena the mules often push the slosh before them with the breasts. The Georgetown road is nowhere compared with the streets of Helena. The county back of Helena (extending 35 miles westward) is very broken and hilly—rougher than any I have seen.

The Weather in Dixie

For the past week we have had regular May weather. The roads are improving rapidly and will soon be in good condition for military operations.

Yours,

Q.

Letter 13. Published June 11, 1863; Dateline "Bivouack, Near Vicksburgh, [sic] May 22, 1863"

Dear Folks at Home:

I wrote home last from Black River.[27] We left there on Saturday, 9th inst. We passed through Utica and arrived at Raymond just as Logan's division finished whipping the rebels there. The next morning (13th) McPherson's corps started for Jackson via Clinton and Sherman's corps via Mississippi Springs (There went two shells from the rebel fort within 20 feet of me!) Our regiment was in the advance and skirmished all the way to Clinton. The 5th Iowa were thus the first to cut the communication between Jackson and Vicksburg—or, the first regiment on the railroad. On the 14th, our division and Sherman's corps attacked Jackson on two sides. We had the hardest fight. Our 2nd brigade charged the rebels and made them skedaddle. They (the rebs) were mostly South Carolinians. Our company was thrown out as skirmishers and we were about the first yankees in Jackson. Our regiment lost only four wounded. On the 15th we left Jackson and started for Vicksburg. On the 16th we fought a big battle at Champion hills and whipped the rebels badly. Our regiment lost 20 killed and 74 wounded—out of 350. The 10th Iowa lost 37 killed and 130 wounded out of 375. Our brigade lost 500 killed and wounded—about 125 of whom were killed.[28] The loss in our brigade was heavier, I think, than in any other on our side. We have only four regiments in the brigade (the 5th and 10th Iowa, 26th Missouri, and 93d Illinois) and they did not average over 400 to the regiment. Our company lost only four—wounded. I have not received a scratch yet. We were in a hot place at Champion Hills—our boys fought nobly. Particulars in another letter. Uncle William Kephart is in good health—he has been doing good service among the wounded.

On Sunday, 17th, [Maj. Gen. John C.] McClernand's Corps whipped the rebels badly at the bridge at Black river—taking 3,000 prisoners. We have taken at Jackson, Champion, and Black River 6,000 prisoners and nearly 100 pieces of artillery. We have been banging away at Vicksburg for four days. We are in sight of and within rifle range of the rebel forts. We, the infantry, lie in close behind the bluffs—out of danger while our batteries, mortars, and gunboats shell them. Our sharpshooters are keeping up a continual firing at the rebel gunners and keep them from firing except occasional shots. Health good as usual.

Sunday Morning, May 24th, 1863.

This is the sixth day of the siege of Vicksburg and it is the first day our brigade has not been under fire. We lay, one day, within 300 yards of the rebel forts. I understand we will have chance to send letters today and I send this note to let you know that I am still safe and well, but very dirty and nearly eaten up by chiggers. We have had no tents for four weeks, and have had to lie out in all sorts of weather. The chiggers are small (almost invisible) wood lice that are worse than fleas and gray backs combined.

Our company had one man killed and two wounded Friday. I saw Henry Crozier yesterday. He was in good health.

This is very little firing going on this morning.

Capt. Poage was killed at the battle of Champion Hills.

Quincy

Letter 14. Published December 10, 1863; Dateline "3 Miles North of Chattanooga, November 21, 1863"

Dear Charley,

We crossed the river on the pontoon bridge at Bridgeport on the 18th at one o'clock P.M. We marched 10 miles (9 after crossing) and camped. We marched out of Alabama into Georgia—out of Georgia into Tennessee. We camped at Shell Mound. A mile or two below Shell Mound we passed the mouth of "Nigga Jack" cave, which I must tell some things about. (In the first place, you must remember that this country is full of mountains.) This cave opens on the north side of the mountain in the river valley. The mouth of the cave is about 20 wide by 30 feet long. The cave is 15 miles deep—so say the "natives"—it is about 100 yards wide and 30 feet high. A stream of clear water (about a cubic foot) flows from the mouth of the cave. In this cave is a nitre bed and the rebels had 1,000 men working in it, before Rosecrans chased them away. The cave was discovered by a negro who chased a bear into it—hence its name. On the 20th, we started at daylight for Chattanooga—our regiment being the advance of the Division. Our route lay up the Tennessee valley for a few miles—then up Running Water valley, past Whiteside mountain—then up Racoon valley, and then down Lookout valley, along the base of Lookout mountain—then across the pontoon bridge at

Brown's ferry and camped in the bend north of and within 1 1/2 miles of Chatta-nooga. We marched 20 miles during the day. It looked dangerous marching down Lookout valley, alongside the mountain on the side of which we could see rebel camps and where we knew rebel batteries were planted. It looked like some of our moves under the guns of the rebs at Vicksburg. There was this difference however. At Vicksburgh they didn't dare to expose themselves long enough to use their guns. Here the distance is greater than it seems and they couldn't much more than reach us with the best pieces (24 pounders). They had tried it on trains before we came along and failed to do any damage. We passed Hooker's battle-ground where he whipped [Brig. Gen. Micah] Jenkins' brigade ([Lt. Gen. James] Longstreet's Corps) when he first opened up Lookout valley to our forces. I saw "Fighting Joe [Hooker]." He stood in front of his tent taking his first look at Mississippi troops as the 5th Iowa passed. He is the finest looking Major General I have seen. He is over 6 feet high—well built—good looking—florid complexion—"Presbyterian whiskers"—and looks "every inch a soldier." His hair and whiskers are very gray—nearly white. His forces are very strongly fortified—nothing short of double their number can drive them from their position. The arrival of Sherman's army is hailed by the troops here with a great deal of pleasure. Some of the Potomac boys remarked as we passed "there goes Sherman's army—they have never been whipped." Our regiment being in the advance we had to answer a great many questions. "What regiment is that?" "The 5th Iowa." "Bully for Iowa." &c., &c. Our regiment is the first Iowa regiment that ever came to these "diggings." Lookout mountain is a very high range (with the north end jutting out close to the river) running S.W. It lies between Lookout valley and Chatta-nooga. We crossed the pontoon at Brown's ferry and camped in the bend 1 1/2 miles North of Chattanooga. The next morning (the 20th) we were waked up at 2 o'clock and marched out 3 miles to our present camp where we are secreted among the mountains. The object in moving before day was to keep the enemy from seeing where we would go. We will probably remain where we are until Sherman's whole force gets here, when I think we will cross the river at some point above Chickamauga creek and get on the right flank of the rebels. If we do, we will probably have some hard fighting. Gen. Sherman came up today. Morgan L. Smith's Division came up last night and hid in the valley close by. (We have orders not to make any loud noise) [Brig. Gen. Hugh B.] Ewing's Division drove the rebels out of Trenton, Ga, on the 18th and still holds the town. I think, however, that it will join us yet. For I have an idea that it was sent there to draw the attention of the rebels that way and to protect our flank while we marched from Bridgeport to Chattanooga. You can see the position of Trenton on the map. A railroad runs from Chattanooga to Trenton. [Maj. Gen. Peter J.] Osterhaus' Division was at Bridgeport when we left and will probably be up tonight. We will probably be ready to move in three or four days. Deserters are coming in from the rebel army to the number (on the average) of 100 a day. Five came down and delivered themselves up to the pickets as we came down Lookout valley. A captain and 89 men came in the night before in one squad. The rebel pickets are stationed along the base of Lookout mountain and only a small creek separates them from ours—some 10 or 20 feet from our line to theirs. There is a mutual understanding between them and they will not shoot at each other and they have traffic and conversation every day.

Company B has been short of tents during this whole march and I gave the boys my tent. I have slept "out" half the time—the other half (bad weather included) in the tent with Captain of Co. K. When we left Bridgeport we were ordered to take only one tent to the company. Last night it rained most of the night and some of the boys got soaked. Most of them, however, had gum blankets which they sheltered themselves with. I had about 6 inches by 6 feet of terra firma in the tent to lie on. It rained all this forenoon. This afternoon it is cloudy and getting cool. The army has been living on rather slim rations. Since Lookout valley was opened, rations have been more plenty but the dumb brutes don't get quarter rations yet. It is pitiable to hear them whinny for something to eat. Our teams are in splendid order compared with the teams of the Cumberland army. "40 rounds of ammunition" are to be issued—that looks suspicious. I must stop writing and see "what's up."

Monday morning, 23d—Saturday night passed without any movement. The general impression is that General Grant did not want to fight on Sunday. About noon yesterday, Dodge Porter (of Foster's Cavalry) called at my tent. He had just arrived from Vicksburg with dispatches for Gen. Smith and Gen. Sherman. I went with him to head quarters. While there I heard Gen. Smith say we would cross river last night and have a fight or footrace this morning. I also saw a map on which I saw the positions of our Divisions after crossing at the mouth of Chickamauga creek. We [are] to cross on the pontoon bridge which was ready to be thrown across and then march to and occupy the north end of Missionary Ridge, where we were to intrench ourselves before day. This morning a general attack was to be made. Late in the afternoon, our batteries (10 or 15) moved down close to the river to be "on hand" and every preparations was made for moving across after dark. We lay down with our clothes on expecting to cross about midnight. [Maj. Gen. Oliver O.] Howard's Corps of Hooker's army crossed from Lookout valley into Chattanooga—one Division of Hooker's army was reported to be a part of our force, and would arrive in time. About nine o'clock, however, an order arrived from Gen. Grant postponing the movement 24 hours. We know of no reason for it—as the night was very moonlight, this might have interfered. This morning the weather is cloudy. While at Sherman's Headquarters, I saw Major Gens. Grant, [Francis P.] Blair, and Hunter (David)—Brig. Gens [Hugh B.] Ewing, [John M.] Corse, and [Montgomery C.] Meigs. We may cross tonight.

While I am anything but anxious for a fight, I cannot but wish the suspense was over. No one who has ever been in battle can tell the feelings of a soldier on the eve of an engagement. The feelings are aroused and the men realize the critical position they hold and you will hear them speaking one to another the possibilities and probabilities which include the questions of life and death [and] while they each and every one determine to do their duty on the battlefield, they cannot forget that many who enter the battle never return from it. The feelings of the soul are aroused when the gambler throws away his cards, the profane ceases his profanity, the jester forgets his humor, and they all march together in silence to the field, thinking, fearing, and hoping but remembering it is necessary and right, they should thus take their lives in their hands and stand in the breach of death. You may think you can imagine the feelings of a soldier on the eve of a conflict, but no, you cannot. Not even the soldier himself can, 24 hours after the battle is over. It is this terrible waking up of the feelings of a man's soul that makes him so daring in battle and makes him welcome his comrade after the conflict with feelings more fervent than ever he welcomed a brother. It is not everyone, it is true, who is thus affected, for there are men whom it appears nothing can move. But it is a very common thing to see cards strewn along the road to the battle-field and to hear men who themselves are profane swearers, speak disapprovingly of the practice on such occasions.

Sunday, Nov. 29. Monday night, last, at 12 o'clock, we were waked up according to previous notice and our Division moved down to the river to cross. On arriving at the river, we found that Morgan L. Smith's Division was crossing not on a pontoon bridge, but in pontoon boats. By day-light, our Division was across and we had thrown up a line of works along a low ridge just below the mouth of Chickamauga creek and about 500 yards from the river. When the first brigade of Morgan L. Smith's Division crossed, they captured all of the rebel pickets but one, who escaped. He fled and gave the alarm, and we expected the enemy down on us in force. But daylight arrived and found two divisions over and intrenched and still no enemy had made his appearance. Just after daylight, a small steamer came up from Chattanooga and assisted in bringing Ewing's Division across. No batteries were brought across until the pontoon bridge was laid, which was noon. As soon as the batteries got across, we started for the north end of Missionary Ridge—moving in three columns— Each Division moving in column closed in mass—Morgan L. Smith's Division moving up the creek—our Division about 1000 yards to his right and Ewing's Division about the same distance to our right.

We marched about two miles through a piece of timber land, thick with underbrush, when we reached the foot of the ridge and immediately started for its summit forming into line of battle as we moved up the hill. Morgan L. Smith's Division first reached the summit—they having the end of the ridge to ascend. When his skirmishers reached the summit of the ridge, they found a rebel regiment coming up the other side of the ridge, snapping caps to clear the tubes for action. The rebs were a little too slow and we gained the hill and held it. They soon got a gun into position farther up the ridge and began shelling us but did no harm. One of our guns was brought to the top of the ridge and the first shot from it silenced the rebel gun. Our forces immediately began fortifying, laboring till daylight next morning. [Maj. Gen.] Jeff C. Davis' division of Thomas' army crossed the river where we did but did not move out from the river. At 1 o'clock Wednesday morning our regiment was deployed as skirmishers in the bottom between the landing and ridge. We were to act as pickets and watch the movements the enemy might attempt up the bottom. I should have stated in the proper place that Thomas and Hooker were fighting the rebels on and around Lookout Mountain, firing Monday and Tuesday—having some heavy fighting and gaining important advantages. We remained on picket till noon Wednesday. Early in the morning, Ewing's and Morgan L. Smith's Division, moved down (Southward) along the ridge—Smith on the East and Ewing on the West side—to attack the enemy. As we were in the woods, we could not see the fighting but could hear very plainly. At noon the order came for us to "assemble on the left." We knew the meaning of that very well. We were going into the fight. After assembling, we joined our brigade and immediately moved forward in line until we reached an open field on the west of the ridge, in plain view of the enemy. We were there ordered to lie down. The enemy had no intention of letting us taunt them, by lying in plain view of them and within easy range of their guns. So we soon had the pleasure(?) of seeing one of their batteries on our right flank open on us, and of seeing them bring up a battery in our front and place it in position to shell us. The shells from the battery on our right, fell short, but the battery in our front sent them whizzing over and about us in a very uncomfortable manner. The third shell struck in the ranks of the 10th Iowa, killing one man and wounding two. Gen Matthies saw that the rebs were getting too good [of] range of us and he moved our regiment and the 10th Iowa, by the left flank to the rear of the left half of our brigade, where we were shielded by a slight elevation in the field. We had been in this position but a few moments when an officer came galloping up to Gen. Matthies, and ordered him to "move his brigade up to that white house." This house lay at the foot of the ridge, just under the rebel batteries, near the tunnel. To reach it we would have to cross an open field, over 3/4 of a mile wide, under a cross-fire of the enemy's artillery and infantry. As soon as the General received the order, he put his brigade in motion and we went across the field, in line, at the double-quick. As soon as the rebs saw us start, they opened on us from three batteries, two in front and one on our right flank. Their shell and shot hissed, whizzed and whirred around us thick as hail, comparatively speaking. Fortunately, however, few, if any, were killed by the enemy's batteries while we were crossing the field, although we were subject to a cross-fire and the enemy served their batteries splendidly. Most of their missiles just missed our heads and struck the ground or exploded behind us. One shell exploded so near my head that I felt the heat of it plainly and Sergt. Pennywitt, who was just behind me, said the smoke curled about his face and made him have the "queerest kind of feelings." It is a fact, which all may not know, that the momentum of a shell is greater, for the distance shell are generally thrown, than the explosive force of the shell and when a shell explodes after having passed one, no danger is to be apprehended from it. A few shot and shell struck in front of us but they luckily bounded over us. It appeared to me that the artillery men would bring their guns to bear on us but before they could fire we would pass out from under their range and the missiles would thus pass over our heads. It was either this, or the difficulty of depressing their guns, that saved us many lives. After reaching the house where we were ordered, the General saw that it would not do to stop the brigade there and he moved it farther up the ridge where it would be less exposed. After we had got out of the cleared field our regiment entered a patch of timber while the regiments on our left still moved through clear ground. Here my connection with the regiment ceased for the time. A minie ball coming from the top of the ridge, on my left, struck me on top of the head, glanced, and passed out of my hat—knocked me down—somewhat confusing me. The regiment soon after moved to the right and opened fire. Our general ordered several companies forward as skirmishers—he soon sent out more, and finally all but two companies, B and K, were ordered forward as skirmishers. These two companies were finally ordered forward, but before they could move, an order came to retreat. The retreat came about in this way: the rebels seeing our regiment all deployed reinforced their line (according to their own statement) and made a dash on our skirmish line. At the same time they sent a force through the tunnel, which succeeded in getting to the rear of our boys before they knew it. When the rebs were seen coming out of the tunnel and swinging around to "take in" the boys—the order was given for the boys to "skin themselves and get out of that." All who could immediately threw away their blankets, canteens and haversacks, and "ran for life." "Such a getting down hill, you never did see." Some of the tallest running was done then that has ever been seen on [this] continent, for the rebs were close on to the boys and were firing at them at every jump they made and calling on them to "halt," "stop," or "surrender." It was "Hobson's choice with the boys." Libby prison on one side and a poor chance for life on the other. One of our company was shot in the ear as he ran and another had his shoulder grazed. If they had level ground to run on, many of them would not have lived to tell the tale but as they were getting down hill "faster than lightning," the rebs could not take aim and had to shoot at random. Many who were not in position to run were captured. Seven were captured from our company—as brave men as we had. Eighty were captured from our regiment. Nearly all the color company (K) were captured and our colors were taken. Three of the color guard were wounded, one escaped, and the rest were taken. When the color bearer was told to run with his colors he refused saying that these colors should not be carried back; 24 were wounded in the regiment and two killed. The other regiments suffered considerably more than ours in killed and wounded; they retreated before ours and had but few captured. The second brigade of our Division came to the relief of ours and succeeded in losing a good many men. No one can tell the design of sending us where we were sent. Gen Smith knew nothing of the order and did not know that it was his brigade that he was watching fighting until word came to him for reinforcements. It is said the man who ordered our brigade is only a colonel commanding a brigade in Ewing's Division. About 230 are now in the hospital from our two brigades. Many more were slightly wounded. The Colonel of the 93d Ill. was killed while sitting on his horse holding the colors of his regiment, two color bearers having been killed. Gen. Matthies was wounded in the head; skull cracked; will probably not get well enough to take the field for some time.

All who witnessed the charge of our brigade say it was "splendid." Some Eastern battery men said there was no use talking about the fighting of Eastern and Western troops; they never saw such fighting—this is not a flying rumor but a statement made to a Lieutenant of the 70th Ohio from Adams Co. A batteryman told me it was the hottest place he every saw troops in. We were whipped but it wasn't our fault.

I lay where I was knocked down for a few moments when I got up and started back—after getting off the field, I washed my head which was smarting and swelling and went to camp. The ball cut through to my skull, but glanced off or I would have received my quietus. I was aware that it was pretty hard to get anything into my head but didn't think it was minie-proof. I didn't know at first how badly I was hurt but when I saw two holes in my hat, I knew the ball had "passed on" instead of in.

Wednesday night, the rebels skedaddled and Thursday and Friday we followed them—our Division going as far as Graysville Station (17 miles from Chickamauga). Yesterday we came back to our camp. One of our company, who rushed forward of our skirmish line during the fight and brought in a prisoner, was himself afterwards taken.

Your brother,
Quincy

Letter 15. Published March 24, 1864; Dateline Huntsville, Alabama, March 14, 1864

Dear Bee:

A meeting of the citizens of Madison county was called to meet at the Court House in Huntsville on the 12th inst., "to consult as to what action shall be taken to restore civil government, and through it, peace and order, and secure protection for ourselves and families, and immunity for our posterity."[29]

Seeing a notice to the above effect, posted in Huntsville and being in Alabama on a "law and order" errand, I marked the day and hour of the meeting in my memory and made it convenient to be near at the Court House at 11 o'clock A.M. last Saturday when Col. Humphries of Huntsville called the citizens together to organize their meeting.

As a spectator and an eager listener, I joined the crowd which assembled at the North East corner of the Court House.

Ex. U.S. Senator, Jerry Clemens was called to the chair and on taking his place, set forth the object of the meeting in a few happy remarks.[30] After which a committee was appointed who retired to draft resolutions.

The committee soon returned and reported a set of resolutions, which were adopted without a dissenting voice. These resolutions denounced the rebellion, deplored its result, and expressed an earnest desire for the restoration of civil government under "the old flag." They set forth that the rebellion was wrong in itself and would have been wrong even if it had been successful. They called upon the Governor of Alabama to convene a convention to adopt such ordinances as would bring their state back into the Union and invited their fellow citizens in other counties to join them in their appeal to the governor.

Their resolutions had been adopted at a preliminary meeting and Mr. Clemens in his opening speech referred to them and the action they contemplated. He said he did not know whether the Governor of Alabama would listen to their appeal—"In fact," said he, "I have no idea that he will pay any attention to it, but we will thus avoid the charge of precipitation which otherwise might be preferred against us."

Mr. Clemens said that it should be remembered to the credit of Madison County that she gave 1800 votes against secession and that she was forced out of the Union—"taken out by falsehood, and crime"—that "we were unarmed and cut off from all succor, and the President (Buchanan) a man whom we had every reason to believe would and assist our enemies."[31] "We were told that Cotton would be king, and that we would have money in every pocket and it would grow on all the trees. And how is it now? The man who can get 5 cents on the dollar for this Confederate currency accomplishes a miracle in trade. We were told that we would secure protection for our slave property. And what has been the fruits of this promise? In fifty years before the war, Madison county had lost half a score of slaves. Now, no man in North Alabama can say that he has a title to a single slave. "But," said Mr. Clemens, "I do not know, but in the end, this will be for the best." We were told that by secession, we wold secure State Rights—and nearly the first act of the Confederate congress, deprived us of the right to designate the commanders of our own forces. Their Congress has passed a law exempting from service a man who owns ten slaves, but ten famished children will NOT exempt the poor man from the merciless conscription.

Speaking of the "firing of the first gun on Sumter," Mr. Clemens stated that one day, soon after the establishment of the Confederate Capital at Montgomery, he stepped into the Capitol Building, where he found Mr. President Davis, Mr. Meminger, Mr. Gilchrist, Secretary of War Walker and others, earnestly conversing in an undertone.[32] As soon as Mr. Clemens entered, the conversation was dropped but three or four of the junta gathered in one corner of the room and continued the discussion of their subject, which, evidently, was the propriety or impropriety of opening fire on Sumter. Secretary Walker urged delay, but the others argued that delay was death, and one in the argument exclaimed "We must sprinkle blood in the faces of these people, or, in two months, Alabama will vote herself back into the Union." Such were the measures used to force the South into this war and such was the cause of the firing on Sumter. Woe, woe be to the men whose shoulders bear the burden of their guilt—whose hearts are steeped with these crimes—against whom the blood of this nation cries out in anguish to a God of Justice.

Mr. Clemens stated that as for others, they might choose their own course, but he had determined to accept the amnesty proffered by the President and to take shelter under the stars and stripes.

Mr. Clemens is a fascinating speaker and compels the closest attention of his audience. His words do not come forth in a torrent like the waters come down at Lodoré, but rather with the graceful flow of the waters of the blue Juniata, soothing with their smoothness, enchanting with their brightness, and convincing by their power. Although he made but a few remarks, they were sufficient to enchain the attention of his audience and leave them, when he took his seat, longing and hungering for more.

After the adoption of the resolutions, Col. Humphries took the stand and delivered an address of an hour's duration.

Col. Humphries is a lawyer, and he has been one of the prominent politicians of this county—having been in the Legislature several terms and having had the honor to vote for Stephen A. Douglas in the Charleston Convention. Although originally a strong Union man, he followed the fortunes of the South when his State went out and was in the first battle of Manassas. After that battle, he returned to this county and raised a rebel brigade, and failing to get a Brigadiership (on account of his political standing), he left the army and returned "to his first love." After I had looked once at the man and heard one sentence from his lips, I lost all confidence in his integrity and listened to his speech only to pick up the facts he might drop, and to see how a "trimmer" would sail through a heterogenous crowd of Yankees and Alabamians. His whole speech was a studied and labored effort—every word dropping from his lips as if it had been weighed in the balances and nicely adjusted to the sentiment of his hearers. And often trembling in their utterance as if he were fearful he was dropping a word too many or was holding back the important monosyllable of his sentence.

In his manner and style and his nervous "limber-jack" gestures, he very much resembled Chilton A. White.[33]

About the only points he made was that "every man of the South, who went into the rebellion, expected assistance from foreign powers and believed that without it, they could not succeed."

The meeting was not large, but was respectable in point of numbers and character. When we consider the enemy holds the territory within 13 miles of Huntsville, and that a reverse to our arms, this spring, would probably bring them in possession of the place—and when we consider the fact that the citizens of Madison have no guaranty that the union forces will permanently occupy this place—we are rather surprised that a few could be found, bold enough to initiate this important movement. May we not hope that this is the "cloud about the size of a man's head," that is to o'erspread the whole political sky of Alabama?

Yours,

Q.

NOTES

Introduction

1. Quoted in Earl J. Hess, *The Union Soldier in Battle: Enduring the Ordeal of Combat* (Lawrence: University Press of Kansas, 1997), 83. The range of soldier responses is ably explored in several sections of the book, but see especially 73–93.
2. Chapter 4, diary entries for September 19 and 20, 1862.
3. "J. Q. A. Campbell," in *Memoirs of the Miami Country* (Chicago: Robert O. Law, 1920), 3:99–100; "Charles Fenlon Campbell," in *The History of Brown County, Ohio* (Chicago: W. H. Beers, 1883), pt. 5, pp. 56–57; 1860 Brown County Census, Union Township, microfilm roll #939, vol. 6, Dwelling No. 689; Family No. 689, Brown County Historical Society, Georgetown, Ohio.
4. An undated press clipping (c. 1907) in the Campbell Family File, Logan County (Ohio) Public Library, states that Angus and Frank moved to Iowa in 1858, where they edited the *Jasper Free Press.* It adds that John Q. A. Campbell moved to that state in "the latter part of 1859," but this is incorrect. According to Campbell's pension records, he resided in Ripley, Ohio, until December 26, 1860.
5. *History of Jasper County, Iowa* (Chicago: Western Historical, 1878), 411–16.
6. The other was Cold Harbor, Virginia, on June 3, 1864. U. S. Grant, *Personal Memoirs of U.S. Grant,* 2 vols. (New York: Charles L. Webster, 1885), 2:276.
7. Chapter 6, diary entry for November 25, 1863.
8. "Death Summons Is Answered by J. Q. A. Campbell," *Bellefontaine (Ohio) Daily Express,* March 2, 1922; "J. Q. A. Campbell," in *Memoirs of the Miami Country* 3:100–101.
9. Gerald F. Linderman, *Embattled Courage: The Experience of Combat in the American Civil War* (New York: Free Press, 1987).
10. Bell Irvin Wiley, *The Life of Billy Yank, the Common Soldier of the Union* (New York: Bobbs-Merrill, 1951), and Bell Irvin Wiley, *The Life of Johnny Reb, the Common Soldier of the Confederacy* (New York: Bobbs-Merrill, 1943); Pete Maslowski, "A Study of Morale in Civil War Soldiers," *Military Affairs* 37 (December 1970): 122–26.
11. James M. McPherson, *What They Fought For, 1861–1865* (Baton Rouge:

Louisiana State University Press, 1994); Charles P. Roland, review of *What They Fought For, 1861–1865*, by James M. McPherson, *Journal of Southern History* 61 (November 1995): 813. See also James M. McPherson, *For Cause and Comrades: Why Men Fought in the Civil War* (New York: Oxford University Press, 1997), which expands his thesis concerning soldier motivation. Also very helpful is Hess, *Union Soldier in Battle*.

12. Chapter 1, diary entry for July 9, 1861.
13. Chapter 4, diary entries for September 25 and 26, 1862, and chapter 5, entry for July 4, 1863.
14. A good recent work that explores this dynamic is Reid Mitchell, *The Vacant Chair: The Northern Soldier Leaves Home* (New York: Oxford University Press, 1993).
15. See Letter 11, Appendix.
16. Chapter 4, diary entry for February 11, 1863.
17. Chapter 3, diary entry for April 17, 1862.
18. Chapter 4, diary entry for December 12, 1862.
19. See Letter 11, Appendix.
20. Chapter 4, diary entry for February 22, 1863.
21. Chapter 6, diary entry for October 14, 1863.
22. Chapter 5, diary entry for June 24, 1863.
23. Chapter 6, diary entry for July 28, 1863.
24. Chapter 6, diary entry for November 7, 1863.
25. Chapter 9, diary entry for November 19, 1864.
26. The regiment's colonel was accidentally shot to death on May 21, 1862; Frank Johnson died on February 22, 1863, when his weapon discharged as he was cleaning it. A third soldier, James Shelledy, accidentally shot himself in the foot on September 9, 1862, but survived, while yet a fourth, Ewing Reynolds, was discharged after receiving an accidental gunshot wound on September 7, 1863.
27. Since published as Mark Grimsley, *The Hard Hand of War: Union Military Policy Toward Southern Civilians, 1861–1865* (Cambridge: Cambridge University Press, 1995).

Chapter 1. Buckling on the Harness of War: Sojourn in Missouri, July 9, 1861–January 30, 1862

1. It did not end the fighting in Missouri, however. A savage guerrilla struggle wracked the state until the end of the war, and Confederate armies invaded again in September and October 1864. James M. McPherson, *Battle Cry of Freedom: The Civil War Era* (New York: Oxford University Press, 1988), 784–88.
2. Poultney Loughridge founded the United Presbyterian Church of Oskaloosa and was the father of one of the men in Company B. W. A. Hunter, "History of Mahaska County with Its Cities and Towns," *Annals of Iowa* 6 (October

1868): 289–90. A havelock was a piece of light colored or white cloth made to fit over the forage cap or kepi. It was designed to keep the sun off one's neck, but soldiers usually found them stuffy and hot.

3. Cpl. Samuel H. M. Byers, twenty-four, later wrote a memoir, *With Fire and Sword* (New York: Neal Publishing, 1911), detailing his time in the Fifth Iowa Infantry as well as his subsequent capture and escape from a Confederate prisoner of war camp.

4. Sometimes called the "soldier's disease," Campbell's diarrhea was probably caused by contaminated water or a change in diet.

5. A maternal uncle of Campbell, William Kephart later became the chaplain of the Tenth Iowa.

6. A "mess" was typically a group of four to five men grouped together for the purpose of sharing cooking duties.

7. A hawser is a heavy rope used for towing or tying up a boat or ship.

8. New School Presbyterianism was a pro-revivalist version of nineteenth-century Presbyterianism with strong ties to New England Congregationalism. Originating during the Second Great Awakening, it combined pietism with a cultural emphasis on making the United States a Christian nation. Daniel C. Reid, ed., *Dictionary of Christianity in America* (Downers Grove, Ill.: Intervarsity Press, 1990), 819–21.

9. Martin E. Green, a native of Missouri, served under Gen. Sterling Price at Lexington, Missouri. He was wounded on June 25, 1863, while in command of the Second Brigade at Vicksburg and was killed two days later by a sharpshooter. Ezra J. Warner, *Generals in Gray* (Baton Rouge: Louisiana State University Press, 1959), 116–17.

10. About 1,000 pro-Confederate Missourians under Col. Martin E. Green attacked Athens on August 5, hoping to drive beyond the town and capture a stockpile of arms, ammunition, and other supplies in nearby Croton, Iowa. They were driven off by 333 Union Home Guardsmen under Col. David Moore, a local grocer who had served as a captain during the Mexican War. Although the Fifth and Sixth Iowa were dispatched to Moore's assistance, they exerted no influence on the skirmish, arriving only after the combat had ended. Union losses in this minor action were 3 killed and 20 wounded. Colonel Moore estimated Confederate losses at 31 killed and wounded. Contrary to what Campbell heard, only a small portion of Green's force was mounted. Details of the Athens fight are in Dave Page, "A Fight for Missouri," *Civil War Times Illustrated* 34, no. 3 (August 1995): 34–38.

11. Hard crackers, or hardtack, was a staple of soldier's rations. It was approximately three inches square and was made of flour, water, and salt. Rather than soft bread, these crackers would keep for months without spoiling.

12. Although Campbell does not mention it, on this date he penned his first surviving letter to the *Ripley Bee*. See the Appendix.

13. William H. Worthington served as the first colonel of the Fifth Iowa Infantry.

He was appointed its commander on July 15, 1861. Addison A. Stuart, *Iowa Colonels and Regiments* (Des Moines: Mills, 1865), 125–30.

14. Jefferson Barracks was, and still is, a regular army post downstream from St. Louis on the Mississippi River.

15. William Hicks Jackson served on the frontier and in Indian fighting before resigning on May 16, 1861, when he was commissioned as a second lieutenant of Confederate artillery. He was wounded at Belmont, Missouri, and named colonel of the First (later Seventh) Tennessee upon recovery. Warner, *Generals in Gray*, 152–53.

16. See also Letter 2, Appendix.

17. Macadamized roads were roads paved with layers of compacted, broken stone. "Sleeping on arms" meant literally sleeping with weapon and accouterments at one's side. This enabled the soldier to be ready in the event of a surprise attack.

18. Charles Leopold Matthies was a native of Prussia, where he served in the army there. In 1849 he emigrated to the United States and settled in Iowa. Stuart, *Iowa Colonels and Regiments*, 125–30.

19. "Double quick" means that soldiers lengthened their stride from the "common time" of twenty-eight inches to thirty-three inches and increased their pace from 90 steps to 165 steps per minute.

20. "Secesher" (or "secesh") was a slang term for anyone supporting secession.

21. That is to say, the colonel commandeered a wagon, presumably from a local civilian.

22. Presently the university is the University of Missouri at Columbia.

23. Campbell probably means Brig. Gen. Thomas A. Harris of the Missouri State Guard, who operated with a significant cavalry force in the area around Jefferson City, Missouri. *War of the Rebellion: A Compilation of the Official Records of the Union and Confederate Armies*, 128 vols. (Washington, D.C.: Government Printing Office, 1880–1901), ser. 1, vol. 3, pp. 189–90. (Cited hereafter as *Official Records*. Unless specified, all citations are to series 1.)

24. Archie is no doubt Campbell's brother Archibald. The identity of "Bill" is unknown.

25. Soldiers assigned to picket duty were posted along the camp perimeter. They kept out unauthorized individuals and warned the camp in the event of an attack.

26. Col. Benjamin Brown commanded a regiment of Missouri State Guard Cavalry.

27. Nathaniel Lyon was a captain in the U.S. Army when the Civil War broke out. He was instrumental in securing St. Louis for the Union and was appointed brigadier general on May 17, 1861. In the summer of 1861, he led an army into southwestern Missouri but perished in the Battle of Wilson's Creek on August 10. Ezra J. Warner, *Generals in Blue* (Baton Rouge: Louisiana State University Press, 1964), 286–87.

28. Nicknamed "Old Pap," Gen. Sterling Price took command of the Missouri

militia in May 1861. He joined the Confederate side in response to the actions of Nathaniel Lyon and Congressman Francis P. Blair in St. Louis, and rose to the rank of major general. Warner, *Generals in Gray*, 246–47.

29. "Flying artillery" was a synonym for horse artillery.

30. New Orleans would not be captured until April 29, 1862.

31. Blue mass pills were a common "cure all" for afflictions of all types in the 1860s. As the name implies, these were small, blue pills containing, among other things, mercury.

32. "Sister Bell" was the wife of Angus Campbell, his brother.

33. As Campbell suspected, the rumors were unfounded.

34. John C. Frémont, largely through political friends, was appointed major general on July 3, 1861, and placed in command of the Department of the West with headquarters in St. Louis. He proved inadequate to the task and created a crisis for the Lincoln administration when, on August 30, 1861, he imposed martial law in Missouri and peremptorily freed the slaves of all who were in rebellion. Lincoln asked Frémont to modify the order but Frémont refused, whereupon Lincoln nullified the emancipation provision of Frémont's order. Mark Mayo Boatner III, *The Civil War Dictionary*, rev. ed. (New York: Vintage, 1991), 314–15.

35. The soldier in question was James B. Van Horn, who died of disease. William Thrift, *Roster and Record of Iowa Soldiers in the War of the Rebellion* (Des Moines: E. H. English, State Printer, 1908), 1:673–782.

36. Having received false information concerning the movement of Confederate troops across the Mississippi River from Columbus, Kentucky, to Missouri, Brig. Gen. Ulysses S. Grant attacked Belmont, Missouri, on the morning of November 7, 1861. With 3,114 troops under his command, he attacked six Confederate regiments and pushed them back to the Mississippi River. While his men were looting the Confederate camps, the Rebel commander ferried 10,000 troops across from Columbus and attempted to cut Grant off from his transports. Grant, however, was able to make his way back to the transports and safely evacuate the area. Confederates lost 642 out of 4,000 engaged, and the Federals lost 607 out of the 3,114 engaged. Boatner, *Civil War Dictionary*, 57–58.

37. Adm. Samuel Francis Du Pont led a naval force that included 12,000 troops under Brig. Gen. Thomas W. Sherman in an attack on Confederate Forts Beauregard and Walker on November 7, 1861. This victory gained the Union a base for operations against the coasts of South Carolina, Georgia, and Florida. E. B. Long, *The Civil War Day by Day: An Almanac, 1861–1865* (Garden City, N.Y.: Doubleday, 1971), 135–36.

38. The skirmish at Piketon, Kentucky, occurred on November 8–9, 1861. Humphrey Marshall to Samuel Cooper, November 11, 1861, *Official Records* 4:538.

39. Although officially designated the Fourth Ohio Independent Company of Cavalry, Campbell refers to it as the Brown County Cavalry or Foster's Cav-

alry. The unit would have been of interest to Campbell because his home town, Ripley, was located in Brown County. Whitelaw Reid, *Ohio in the War: History of Its Regiments* (Cincinnati: Moore, Wilstach, & Baldwin, 1868), 795.

40. Issued on November 20, 1861, General Order No. 3 barred fugitive slaves from entering Union lines. Ostensibly issued because such slaves posed a security risk, the order was really designed to avoid the thorny political complications of slavery. Like Campbell, many interpreted General Order No. 3 as evidence that Halleck had pro-slavery convictions. Halleck denied this. For the order, see *Official Records* 8:370.

41. Richard Calvin "Cal" Rankin, Campbell's cousin, was a member of the Fourth Ohio Independent Cavalry Company. Later Rankin would transfer to the Seventh Ohio Cavalry, in which he would rise to the rank of captain. Reid, *Ohio in the War*, 795, 929. See also *History of Brown County* (Chicago: W. H. Beers, 1883), biographical section, 174–75.

42. The reference here is to the "*Trent* Affair," a diplomatic incident that briefly threatened war between the United States and Great Britain. The episode began with the stopping of the British mail steamer *Trent* by the Union warship *San Jacinto*. The U.S. warship then removed two Confederate diplomats, James Mason and John Slidell, who were imprisoned in Boston. The seizure was illegal under international law and drew a sharp response from the British government. The situation was defused when Secretary of State William H. Seward ordered the two men released. McPherson, *Battle Cry of Freedom*, 389–91.

43. The Battle of Rose Hill occurred on December 18, 1861. Campbell inflates the number of captives. Pope in fact captured only 150 prisoners. John Pope to Henry W. Halleck, December 18, 1861, *Official Records* 8:442.

44. Walker Ellis came to visit his son, Albert Ellis, who was the captain of Company C. Thrift, *Roster and Record of Iowa Soldiers*, 673–782.

45. In the King James Version, Proverbs chapter 25, verse 17 reads, "Withdraw thy foot from thy neighbor's house; lest he be weary of thee, and so hate thee."

46. The game is now known as soccer. It was played in American colleges as early as 1820; the first organized league was formed in 1862.

47. Town's ball was an early form of baseball, or "rounders," as it was sometimes called.

48. President Abraham Lincoln removed Simon Cameron from his cabinet following a brief but scandalous tenure as secretary of war. He was replaced by Edwin M. Stanton, a prominent Pennsylvania attorney who had previously served in the cabinet of President James Buchanan. Although a Democrat, Stanton was hardly "conservative," as Campbell feared. Instead he became one of the fiercest proponents of a more vigorous war policy toward the Confederacy. Benjamin P. Thomas and Harold M. Hyman, *Stanton: The Life and Times of Lincoln's Secretary of War* (New York: Alfred A. Knopf, 1962), 132–39.

49. Senator James H. Lane of Kansas was an outspoken proponent of emancipation and the arming of slaves. Boatner, *Civil War Dictionary*, 471.

50. Confederate brigadier general Felix Zollicoffer was killed in the Battle of Mill Springs, Kentucky, on January 19, 1862. The Union victory there, by forces under Brig. Gen. George H. Thomas, broke the eastern anchor of the Confederate defenses in the western theater. Warner, *Generals in Gray,* 349–50.

Chapter 2. "Our Turn to Send Compliments": The Island No. 10 Campaign, January 31–April 16, 1862

1. For details of the campaign, see Larry J. Daniel, *Island No. 10: Struggle for the Mississippi Valley* (Tuscaloosa: University of Alabama Press, 1996).
2. For the letter to the *Ripley Bee,* see Letter 3, Appendix.
3. By "contrabands," Campbell meant runaway slaves who had fled their masters to join the advancing Union armies. The term originated with Maj. Gen. Benjamin F. Butler, who used it in May 1861 to justify the retention of several escaped slaves who had labored on Confederate fortifications. Although the Lincoln administration then had an official policy of noninterference with slavery, Butler argued that because the Confederates had used the slaves for military purposes, they were contraband of war. The First Confiscation Act, passed in August 1861, made Butler's distinction official Union policy. Use of the term soon expanded to include almost any fugitive slave in Union hands. Ira Berlin et. al., *Slaves No More: Three Essays on Emancipation and the Civil War* (New York: Cambridge University Press, 1992), 20–22.
4. Edward Bates, a Missourian, served as attorney general in Lincoln's cabinet. Boatner, *Civil War Dictionary,* 50.
5. A huckster was a slang term for a traveling peddler.
6. A sutler was a private merchant who possessed War Department authorization to set up shop within military encampments and sell goods to soldiers (frequently at exorbitant prices).
7. Campbell's pension record indicates that he suffered permanent injury from this incident.
8. Fort Donelson, a Confederate bastion on the Cumberland River near the Kentucky-Tennessee state line, was captured by Union general Ulysses S. Grant on February 16, 1862. Together with the fall of Fort Henry, Donelson's counterpart on the Tennessee River, the victory cracked open the Confederate defensive line in Tennessee and allowed Union forces to overrun much of the state within weeks. Long, *Civil War Day by Day,* 171–72.
9. A reference to Halleck's General Order No. 3. See chapter 1, note 40.
10. A butternut in the jargon of the day was anyone from the south or supported southern secession. The term derived from the butternut color of some Confederate uniforms.
11. Union forces under Maj. Gen. Don Carlos Buell captured Nashville on February 24, 1862. Long, *Civil War Day by Day,* 174.
12. See also Letter 4, Appendix.

13. Brig. Gen. M. Jeff Thompson commanded troops in the Missouri State Guard. Boatner, *Civil War Dictionary*, 837–38.

14. Brig. Gen. John Pope took command of the Army of the Mississippi on February 23, 1862. Boatner, *Civil War Dictionary*, 659.

15. The soldier who was killed was William Beaver. Thrift, *Roster and Record of Iowa Soldiers*, 673–82.

16. The grand guard was a group of men, usually in company strength, whose duty it was to support the picket posts in case of trouble. They would be kept several hundred yards to the rear of the picket posts, and while pickets could not cook or build fires, men on grand guard could. See Dennis Hart Mahan, *An Elementary Treatise on Advanced-Guard, Out-Post, and Detachment Service of Troops, and the Manner and Posting and Handling Them in Presence of an Enemy* (New York: John Wiley, 1861), 83.

17. If there was a danger of a cannon getting captured, the crew could "spike" the cannon by driving a barbed nail into the touch hole. This would render the cannon useless until the touch hole was repaired, something that typically could not be done in the field.

18. Constructed by the Confederates to command the Mississippi River about fifty miles north of Memphis, Fort Pillow was evacuated on June 3–5, 1862. Garrisoned thereafter by Federal troops, in April 1864 it became the scene of an infamous massacre of African American and white Tennessee Unionist soldiers by Confederate forces under Maj. Gen. Nathan Bedford Forrest. Long, *Civil War Day by Day*, 221, 484.

Chapter 3. "Upholding Uncle Sam's Authority": The Siege of Corinth and After, April 17–September 17, 1862

1. A Confederate bastion near the Tennessee-Kentucky state line, Fort Henry protected the Tennessee River and was captured by Flag Officer Andrew Foote on February 6, 1862. Long, *Civil War Day By Day*, 167.

2. Brig. Gen. Napoleon Bonaparte Buford commanded the Second Brigade, Third Division, comprised of the Fifth Iowa, Tenth Iowa, Twenty-sixth Missouri, Fifty-ninth Indiana, and Sand's Eleventh Ohio Independent Battery. *Official Records*, vol. 10, pt. 2, p. 147.

3. The Parrott rifled cannon, easily identified by the wrought-iron hoop that reinforced its breach, was one of the more common rifled artillery pieces employed by the Union army. The cannon that Campbell saw were likely heavy twenty- or thirty-pounder Parrotts used for siege operations. *Official Records*, vol. 10, pt. 2, p. 122.

4. Samuel H. M. Byers supplies some additional details regarding the death of Col. Worthington: "One incident of great importance, however, happened to my regiment here. It was the death of our colonel. One night when he was going the roads of the picket lines out in the woods he was shot dead by one

of our own men. The sentinel who did the killing declared that Rebels had been slipping up to his post all night, and when he would hail with 'Who goes there?' they would fire at him and run into the darkness. He resolved to stand behind a tree the next time and fire without hailing. By some accident Colonel Worthington and his adjutant were approaching this sentinel from the direction of the enemy. Suddenly the sentinel held his gun around the tree and fired. The bullet struck the colonel in the forehead, killing him instantly. As he fell from his horse, the adjutant sprang to the ground and cried 'Who shot the officer of the day?' 'I fired,' exclaimed the sentinel, and he then told of his experiences of the night. He was arrested, tried, and acquitted. Yet there were many among us who believed that the colonel had been intentionally murdered. He was one of the most competent colonels in the army, but among his soldiers he was fearfully unpopular. He was, however, a splendid disciplinarian but this was something the volunteers did not want. In their minds the colonel had been only a petty tyrant, and not even wholly loyal. With a different disposition he certainly would have been a distinguished soldier. He was one of the most military looking men in the whole army, but friends he had none. More than once his life had been threatened by soldiers who regarded themselves as having been treated badly by him. . . . After his death numbers of the men of the regiment were indignant, when they found among his papers warrants and commissions intended by the governor for them, commissions that had never been delivered. Their promotions had never come about. Now they knew why." Byers, *With Fire and Sword*, 26–27.

5. See Letter 5, Appendix.
6. The commander of the Union army during this period, Maj. Gen. Henry W. Halleck, was anxious to avoid being caught by a surprise Confederate counterattack, as had occurred at Shiloh the previous month.
7. Fearing the besiegement and destruction of his army if he remained in Corinth, Beauregard evacuated the town on the night of May 29–30, 1862. Long, *Civil War Day By Day*, 190.
8. The Whitney Plymouth Navy rifle was a .69-caliber rifle originally designed, as the name implies, for use aboard warships. It utilized a twenty-seven-inch saber bayonet. *Arms and Equipment of the Union* (Alexandria, Va.: Time-Life Books, 1996), 51.
9. Brig. Gen. Jacob Ammen was a native of Brown County, Ohio, where Campbell evidently knew him before the war. Warner, *Generals in Blue*, 6–7.
10. In a brief but savage naval battle near Memphis, Tennessee, on June 6, 1862, five Union ironclads and four rams commanded by Commodore Charles Davis destroyed seven much inferior Confederate vessels and drove off an eighth. Thousands of Memphis civilians watched the action from bluffs overlooking the river. When it was over, the mayor surrendered the now-defenseless city. Long, *Civil War Day By Day*, 222–23.
11. See also Letter 6, Appendix.

12. Maj. Gen. John Pope was ordered to the east to take command of the Army of Virginia on June 26, 1862. Long, *Civil War Day by Day*, 231.

13. The rumors concerned the Seven Days' Battles (June 26–July 1, 1862), in which Confederate general Robert E. Lee's Army of Northern Virginia forced McClellan away from Richmond. Long, *Civil War Day By Day*, 230–35.

14. See Letter 7, Appendix.

15. On July 2, 1862, Lincoln issued a call for three hundred thousand new three-year volunteers, ostensibly in response to a demand from northern governors for renewed recruiting to "follow up" the supposed recent Union victories. In reality, Lincoln's secretary of state, William Seward, had engineered the demand to avoid the appearance of a panicked administration response to the recent defeat in the Seven Days' Battles. McPherson, *Battle Cry of Freedom*, 491–92.

16. The Second Confiscation Act, signed into law on July 17, 1862, provided for the confiscation of property of persons found guilty of aiding the rebellion and the emancipation of their slaves. Lincoln briefly threatened to veto the legislation until its language was changed to avoid certain constitutional difficulties. McPherson, *Battle Cry of Freedom*, 500.

17. This loosely refers to a dramatic cavalry raid by Brig. Gen. John H. Morgan that drove deep into Kentucky. For a time it was feared that Morgan would cross the Ohio River, but he did not. The story of his reaching Indiana was a rumor. Long, *Civil War Day by Day*, 237–44.

18. "The Judge" in question is Campbell's father, Charles F. Campbell, who served as a judge before taking over as editor of the *Ripley Bee*. *History of Brown County*, biographical section, 56.

19. Col. Charles Matthies. "Dutch" or "Dutchy" (deriving from *Deutsch*) was a common term for German Americans.

20. Campbell refers to a collection of essays entitled *Chamber's Miscellany of Useful and Entertaining Tracts*, edited by William and Robert Chambers.

21. Led by Col. Charles R. Jennison, the Seventh Kansas Cavalry Regiment—known as "Jennison's Jayhawkers"—had a well-deserved reputation for unauthorized foraging, vandalism, and arson. Stephen Z. Starr, *Jennison's Jayhawkers; a Civil War Cavalry Regiment and Its Commander* (Baton Rouge: Louisiana State University Press, 1973). During the summer of 1862 such acts, especially foraging, became increasingly widespread among Union troops. See Grimsley, *Hard Hand of War*, 85–91, 98–105.

22. On August 4, 1862, the War Department issued a call for 300,000 nine-month militia in addition to the 300,000 three-year volunteers summoned in July (see note 15). In practice, the militia levy became a way to encourage states to exceed their quota of three-year men, since every three-year volunteer recruited beyond the quota would count as four nine-month militiamen. Together the two calls eventually produced 421,000 three-year volunteers and 88,000 militiamen. McPherson, *Battle Cry of Freedom*, 492–93.

23. Although the U.S. government did not adopt a formal conscription act until March 1863, the August call for three hundred thousand militiamen announced that if the states could not mobilize this number on their own, the War Department would intervene and do it for them: a de facto draft. McPherson, *Battle Cry of Freedom,* 492.

24. The term means "not of sound mind." Jon Stone, *Latin for the Illiterati* (New York: Routledge, 1996), 33.

25. Campbell refers to one of the Waverley tales by Sir Walter Scott.

26. Another of Scott's Waverley tales.

27. In the Second Battle of Bull Run (August 29–30, 1862), General Pope's Army of Virginia was defeated by Robert E. Lee's Army of Northern Virginia. Long, *Civil War Day by Day,* 257–58.

28. Gen. Sterling Price, with fifteen thousand men, had orders from Braxton Bragg to prevent Maj. Gen. William S. Rosecrans's two divisions from reinforcing Buell in Tennessee. Herman Hattaway and Archer Jones, *How the North Won: A Military History of the Civil War* (Urbana: University of Illinois Press, 1983), 250.

Chapter 4. "Nobly the Boys Stood Up to the Work": Fighting in Mississippi, September 18, 1862–March 1, 1863

1. These engagements are detailed in Peter Cozzens, *The Darkest Days of the War: The Battles of Iuka and Corinth* (Chapel Hill: University of North Carolina Press, 1997).

2. The Fifth Iowa suffered 3 officers and 34 enlisted men killed at Iuka, as well as 10 officers and 169 enlisted men wounded. One enlisted man was listed as captured or missing. *Official Records,* vol. 17, pt. 1, p. 78. Although the strength of the Fifth Iowa during the battle is not known, 500 would be a likely estimate. Total Union losses were 790 out of 4,500 engaged (though 17,000 Union troops were in the general area), against 1,516 out of 3,200 engaged for the Confederates (with 14,000 in the area). Long, *Civil War Day by Day,* 269.

3. 1st Lt. Alexander Mateer died of his wounds on October 14, 1862.

4. See Letter 8, Appendix.

5. Issued on September 22, 1862, Lincoln's preliminary Emancipation Proclamation, declared that unless the rebellious states returned to the Union by January 1, 1863, the slaves within those states would be "thenceforward and forever free." The final proclamation exempted the border states, Tennessee, and several occupied districts in other parts of the Confederacy. McPherson, *Battle Cry of Freedom,* 557–58.

6. The Fifth Iowa suffered no casualties at Corinth, but Union losses were serious: 2,520 out of about 23,000 engaged. Confederate losses were 4,233 out of about 22,000 total troops. Long, *Civil War Day by Day,* 274–75.

7. Military records conflict with what Campbell read and report that Edmonds did not die until November 1, 1862.

8. The "Mahony clique" were supporters of Dennis A. Mahony, editor of the *Dubuque Herald,* acknowledged leader of the Peace Democrats in Iowa and a candidate for the seat in the Third Congressional District. Mahony was so outspoken in his opposition to the war effort that he was arrested and imprisoned without trial by the Lincoln administration. The vote in the Fifth Iowa anticipated the outcome of the election: the Republican candidate, William Boyd Allison, won the contest. Republicans won all six of Iowa's congressional seats in the 1862 election, partly on the strength of the soldier vote. Instead of simply receiving absentee ballots, soldiers were visited by election commissioners who unabashedly urged them to "vote as they shot." Leland L. Sage, *A History of Iowa* (Ames: Iowa State University Press, 1974), 163–64.

9. Rosecrans was transferred to take command of the Army of the Cumberland on October 30, 1862. Long, *Civil War Day by Day,* 282.

10. In some respects, the 1862 elections were a sharp disappointment for the Republicans. The lost the governorships of New York and New Jersey as well as their legislative majorities in New Jersey, Illinois, and Indiana. The Democrats won a net gain of thirty-four seats in the House of Representatives. On the other hand, as James M. McPherson points out, the Republicans actually gained five seats in the Senate and they retained their working majority in Congress. McPherson, *Battle Cry of Freedom* , 561–62.

11. The Battle of the Hatchie Bridge on October 5, 1862, was an attempt to cut off the retreat of Gen. Sterling Price's force after the Battle of Corinth. Long, *Civil War Day by Day,* 275.

12. This particular rumor was untrue, although Burnside's army soon suffered a serious defeat at the Battle of Fredericksburg on December 13, 1862. Long, *Civil War Day by Day,* 295–96.

13. See Letter 9, Appendix.

14. These lines are part of the refrain of a contemporary song entitled "Kingdom Comin'," a popular wartime song describing the actions of slaves and their white masters at the approach of the Union army. For the lyrics, see Leon F. Litwack, *Been in the Storm So Long: The Aftermath of Slavery* (New York: Alfred A. Knopf, 1979), 111–12.

15. Victor Hugo's novel *Les Misérables,* published in 1862.

16. Campell probably refers to any one of the many works by Marius, an early scientist.

17. Gen. Earl Van Dorn led thirty-five hundred mounted troopers on a raid against Grant's secondary base of supply at Holly Springs on December 20, 1862. Van Dorn destroyed $1.5 million worth of supplies and captured fifteen hundred men. The raid forced Grant to abandon his overland offensive against Vicksburg and fall back from Oxford, Mississippi, to La Grange, Tennessee. Long, *Civil War Day by Day,* 298; Hattaway and Jones, *How the North Won,* 311.

18. Campbell probably refers to the private school run by abolitionist John Rankin, which at any given time had a large number of the local children enrolled. *History of Brown County,* biographical section, 174–75.

19. See Letter 10, Appendix.

20. Acting on his own initiative, Maj. Gen. John McClernand undertook an expedition to capture Arkansas Post, which fell on January 11, 1863. Long, *Civil War Day by Day,* 310–11.

21. See Letter 11, Appendix.

22. Frederick Marryat, *Japhet in Search of a Father.*

23. Maj. Green L. Blythe commanded an irregular cavalry battalion of Mississippi State Troops during the Vicksburg campaign. *Official Records,* vol. 24, pt. 1, p. 27.

Chapter 5. "Glorious Victory": The Vicksburg Campaign, March 2– July 12, 1863

1. There is as yet no standard treatment of the Vicksburg campaign. The most detailed work is Edwin C. Bearss, *The Vicksburg Campaign,* 3 vols. (Dayton, Ohio: Morningside, 1985–86). A good account from the Union perspective is Bruce Catton, *Grant Moves South* (Boston: Little, Brown, 1960), 304–490.

2. "Even from Dan to Beersheba" is a common Old Testament expression meaning the entirety of Israel. See, for example, Judges 20:1.

3. See Letter 12, Appendix.

4. Kedging was a slow, back-breaking means of moving a ship when other means of propulsion were unavailable. An anchor was dropped into the water some distance ahead of the vessel, after which the crew hauled in the anchor line, causing the ship to glide to the point directly above the anchor. The anchor was then retrieved and the process repeated.

5. Fort Pemberton, located near Greenwood on the Yazoo River, guarded the approach to Vicksburg. Long, *Civil War Day by Day,* 328.

6. Brig. Gen. Lorenzo Thomas became adjutant general of the U.S. Army in May 1861 and held that position until March 23, 1863, when he was given the specific assignment of supervising the organization of the U.S. Colored Troops. Part of this duty involved explaining to white soldiers the Lincoln administration's new policy of actively recruiting African Americans.

7. Confederate guns turned back nine Union ironclads under Adm. Samuel Francis DuPont during a naval attack on the defenses of Charleston, South Carolina, on April 7, 1863. Long, *Civil War Day by Day,* 335–36.

8. The allusion is to a contemporary song, "Richmond is a Hard Road to Travel."

9. The Union victory at Port Gibson on May 1, 1863, allowed Grant to launch the main phase of his Vicksburg campaign. Long, *Civil War Day by Day,* 344–45.

10. Grand Gulf was a Confederate fortification on the Mississippi River about

twenty miles below Vicksburg. Grant originally planned to land his army there, but Union gunboats under Adm. David Dixon Porter proved unable to defeat the garrison with a six-hour bombardment on April 29. Accordingly, Grant decided to land farther south at Bruinsburg, Mississippi. As Campbell notes, the Confederates abandoned Grand Gulf on May 3. Long, *Civil War Day by Day*, 343, 347.

11. Campbell's summary is correct. At the Battle of Raymond on May 12, a Union division under Maj. Gen. John A. Logan was attacked by a Confederate brigade under Brig. Gen. John Gregg. After several hours of combat, the Confederates withdrew, each side having lost about five hundred men killed, wounded, or missing. Long, *Civil War Day by Day*, 352.

12. Although Campbell could not know it, the Confederates made scant effort to defend Jackson. Gen. Joseph E. Johnston, the Rebel commander in charge of the Department of the West—which included Pemberton's army as well as the force at Jackson—had reached the town only the day before. After a brief study of the situation, he reported to Richmond, "I am too late" and soon ordered an evacuation of the Mississippi state capital. *Official Records*, vol. 24, pt. 1, p. 215. His passivity during the Vicksburg earned him the undying enmity of President Jefferson Davis. Craig L. Symonds, *Joseph E. Johnston: A Civil War Biography* (New York: Norton, 1992), 204–48. The brief rear guard action at Jackson, which Campbell recounts, cost the Union side about 300 casualties. Confederate losses totaled 845. Bearss, *Vicksburg Campaign* 2:555–59.

13. The Battle of Champion Hill was the most severe of the campaign. It cost the attacking Union forces 2,441 out of about 29,000 engaged, and the Confederates 3,851 out of approximately 20,000. Long, *Civil War Day by Day*, 354. Campbell's casualty totals for the Fifth Iowa are correct. The unit went into action with 350 men. *Official Records*, vol. 24, pt. 2, p. 316. His figures for the other regiments in his brigade coincide almost exactly with official returns, except for the Ninety-third Illinois, which suffered fewer dead (36) and wounded (113) but also lost 11 men captured or missing (ibid., 10). A detailed account of the battle is in Bearss, *Vicksburg Campaign* 2:559–642.

14. At the Battle of Big Black River, Lt. Gen. John C. Pemberton's last opportunity to delay Grant's move toward Vicksburg, Confederate forces numbering four thousand were overwhelmed by an assault of ten thousand men under Sherman. The way to Vicksburg now lay open. Long, *Civil War Day by Day*, 354.

15. Campbell heard the artillery fire that accompanied Grant's first assault on the Vicksburg fortifications. This attack, made hastily in hopes that one quick smash might rout the supposedly demoralized Confederate army, failed miserably. Union casualties totaled 942 against Confederate losses of about 250. Bearss, *Vicksburg Campaign* 3:753–73.

16. This second assault on Vicksburg, albeit on a larger scale than Grant's May 19 attack, was no more successful. In part this owed to the strength of the Con-

federate works, but a significant factor was the failure of two Union corps commanders—Maj. Gen. William T. Sherman and Maj. Gen. James B. McPherson—to make more than token assaults, notwithstanding Grant's plan for a concerted all-out attack. Campbell's regiment had the poor luck to be one of the few units in McPherson's corps to be seriously engaged. (Ironically, Maj. Gen. John C. McClernand, the one corps commander who did mount a strong attack, was sacked shortly afterward.) Grant's second—and last—assault on the Vicksburg fortifications is detailed in Bearss, *Vicksburg Campaign* 3:787–862.

17. See Letter 13, Appendix. The Fifth Iowa entered the fight with 250 officers and men; it lost 2 killed and 17 wounded. *Official Records,* vol. 24, pt. 2, p. 316. Union casualties in the assault totaled 3,199 out of about 45,000 in Grant's army. Confederate losses were fewer than 500. Long, *Civil War Day by Day,* 356.

18. The word "minies" refers to the hollow-based, cylindroconical lead bullet fired by rifle muskets. Designed by Capt. Claude E. Minié of the French army, the Minié ball was adopted by the U.S. Army in 1849.

19. On June 7, Confederate forces attacked the Union garrison at Milliken's Bend, Louisiana, Grant's main base prior to the spring phase of his Vicksburg campaign. They pressed the defenders almost to the river bank before Union gunboats helped drive them back. The "African Brigade" of newly recruited black troops received considerable praise for its conduct during the fight. Union casualties were 652 against Confederate losses of 185. Long, *Civil War Day by Day,* 363. Sgt. Thomas Keisler had been discharged from the Fifth Iowa on July 31, 1862, to accept a commission as lieutenant in the Eleventh Louisiana Colored Infantry. Thrift, *Roster and Record of Iowa Soldiers,* 673–782.

20. "Logan's car" was the nickname of a railcar used to protect Union soldiers digging a trench, or sap, so as to provide a covered approach to the Confederate entrenchments. Packed with about twenty cotton bales to absorb bullets and shell fragments, it was pushed forward by hand as work on the sap advanced. Confederate troops eventually destroyed it by ingeniously daubing cotton wads with tow and turpentine, wrapping them around bullets, and then firing them using light charges. The cotton wads ignited when fired and set "Logan's car" ablaze. Bearss, *Vicksburg Campaign* 3:908, 910. See also *Official Records,* vol. 24, pt. 2, pp. 200, 371.

21. Grant's army, which numbered about forty-five thousand troops when it crossed the Mississippi River in May, was heavily reinforced during the siege to ensure Vicksburg's capitulation. By mid-June its strength was about seventy-seven thousand.

22. The rumors were sparked by a minor skirmish on June 9 at Macon Ford on Big Black River. Johnston never made a serious attempt to relieve Vicksburg. Long, *Civil War Day by Day,* 364.

23. Campbell refers to a trench, or sap, dug from the position of Logan's division toward the Confederate works, then extended by a "parallel," a second

trench perpendicular to the first and roughly parallel to the line of Confederate fortifications.

24. Commanded by Maj. Gen. Ambrose E. Burnside, the Ninth Corps was at one time part of the Army of the Potomac in the eastern theater. It was sent to Kentucky in March 1863 and subsequently to reinforce Grant in June.

25. The capture of Vicksburg on July 4 came after a forty-seven-day siege. Union losses during the entire period totaled 4,910. Confederate losses prior to the surrender came to 2,872 killed, wounded, and missing. The capitulation of Pemberton's army encompassed about 30,000 Confederates, most of whom were simply paroled, that is, released after a written promise not to fight again until exchanged for Union soldiers similarly circumstanced. The Federals also took possession of 172 cannon and nearly 60,000 stand of small arms. Hattaway and Jones, *How the North Won*, 411–12.

26. Port Hudson capitulated on July 8, 1863; the formal surrender occurred the following day. Helena, Arkansas, was the scene of a failed Confederate attack on July 4, 1863. Braxton Bragg was forced out of central Tennessee and driven across the Elk River through Tullahoma, Tennessee. Reports of a victory at Jackson, however, were a bit premature. The town did not fall into Union hands until July 16. Long, *Civil War Day by Day*, 379, 381, 386–87.

27. Paroled prisoners were seldom allowed simply to go home but were usually held by their own side in parole camps—what Campbell here terms camps of instruction.

28. Robert E. Lee's Army of Northern Virginia was forced to retreat after battling George Meade's Army of the Potomac at the Battle of Gettysburg on July 1–3. Long, *Civil War Day by Day*, 374–78.

Chapter 6. "The Hand of God Is in This": Vicksburg to Chattanooga, July 13–December 2, 1863

1. Entry for October 24, 1863, in Tyler Dennett, *Lincoln and the Civil War in the Diary and Letters of John Hay* (1939; rpt. New York: Da Capo, 1988), 106.

2. The best overview of the Chattanooga campaign is James Lee McDonough, *Chattanooga: A Death Grip on the Confederacy* (Knoxville: University of Tennessee Press, 1984). The most detailed tactical study is Peter Cozzens, *The Shipwreck of Their Hopes: The Battles for Chattanooga* (Urbana: University of Illinois Press, 1994).

3. See chapter 5, note 27.

4. On Brig. Gen. William Hicks Jackson, see chapter 1, note 15. Campbell's summary of the engagement is substantially correct. For details, see *Official Records*, vol. 24, pt. 2, pp. 535, 654.

5. This was a considerable overestimate. Gen. Joseph E. Johnston commanded approximately twenty-three thousand men in the days following Vicksburg. Symonds, *Joseph E. Johnston*, 219.

6. See chapter 5, notes 26 and 28.

7. The post-Vicksburg fighting at Jackson was less a battle than a short-lived partial siege. On June 22, Maj. Gen. William T. Sherman received orders to move east to the Big Black River area in order to block any attempt by Confederate forces to relieve Vicksburg. Shortly after the garrison's capitulation on July 4, Sherman continued east, reached the outskirts of Jackson on July 10, established a siege line west of the town, and opened fire on the Confederate forces with artillery. Confederate general Joseph E. Johnston chose to evacuate the town on July 17. Sherman promptly gave orders to destroy Jackson's war resources, as well as the railroads forty miles north and sixty miles south of the capital. John F. Marsazalek, *Sherman: A Soldier's Passion for Order* (New York: Free Press, 1993), 229. As Campbell's account indicates, the role of his regiment was confined to guarding Sherman's line of communications back to Vicksburg. *Official Records,* vol. 24, pt. 2, p. 525.

8. Sherman reported the capture of 764 prisoners. *Official Records,* vol. 24, pt. 2, p. 538. His chief of artillery noted the capture of only three fieldpieces, but a large quantity of artillery and small arms ammunition. *Official Records,* vol. 24, pt. 2, pp. 541–42.

9. Between July 2 and 26, 1863, twenty-five hundred Confederate cavalry under Brig. Gen. John Hunt Morgan made a dramatic but militarily insignificant raid into southern Indiana and Ohio. Most of the force was killed or captured at the Battle of Buffington Island, Ohio, on July 19. Morgan himself was captured near Steubenville, Ohio, on July 26. "The attack on Charleston [South Carolina]" refers to the naval bombardment of Fort Wagner and several land assaults against this key component of the Charleston harbor defense. The most famous of these assaults was the July 18 attack by the African American Fifty-fourth Massachusetts Infantry Regiment. Long, *Civil War Day by Day,* 376, 387–88, 391.

10. Officially called the Ninth Army Corps, it was then under the command of Maj. Gen. John Parke.

11. Unfortunately, there are a number of books by that title written during the time leading up to the Civil War, so it is impossible to say to which one Campbell is referring.

12. On July 15, 1863, President Abraham Lincoln issued a "Proclamation of Thanksgiving" in gratitude for the recent Union victories at Gettysburg, Vicksburg, and Port Hudson. As Campbell notes, this Thanksgiving day was slated for August 6, 1863. Roy P. Basler, ed., *Collected Works of Abraham Lincoln,* 8 vols. and index (New Brunswick, N.J.: Rutgers University Press, 1953), 6:332–33. At the urging of Sarah Josepha Hale, the editor of *Godey's Lady's Book,* Lincoln proclaimed a second day of Thanksgiving for the last Thursday in November 1863, thereby inaugurating the modern Thanksgiving holiday. David Herbert Donald, ed., *Lincoln* (New York: Simon and Schuster, 1995), 471.

13. *Chronicles of the Conquest of Granada,* by Washington Irving.

14. The destruction of the *City of Madison* was later blamed on the work of Confederate saboteurs. Federal authorities considered it the first of thirteen such acts committed by these agents in August and September 1863. See *Official Records,* vol. 48, pt. 2, pp. 194–96.

15. *Mabel Vaughan,* by Maria S. Cummins.

16. Alfred Dodge deserted before the Fifth Iowa left for the Vicksburg campaign. See chapter 5, diary entry for March 3, 1863.

17. Brig. Gen. James Madison Tuttle commanded the Third Division, Fifteenth Corps. The reference is to James Tuttle's election bid for governor of Iowa (see chapter 6, note 21).

18. On September 10, 1863, Federal forces under Maj. Gen. Frederick Steele captured Little Rock, Arkansas. Long, *Civil War Day by Day,* 407–8.

19. Campbell refers to the Battle of Chickamauga on September 19–20, 1863. Having cleared southeastern Tennessee of Confederate forces and captured the strategic rail center of Chattanooga, Maj. Gen. William S. Rosecrans's Army of the Cumberland was suddenly attacked and defeated by Gen. Braxton Bragg's Army of Tennessee. Rosecrans then withdrew his army to Chattanooga, where it endured a six-week quasi-siege. Long, *Civil War Day by Day,* 411–12.

20. As Campbell would presently learn, Sherman's corps was being transferred to reinforce Rosecrans's beleaguered army at Chattanooga. Maj. Gen. Henry W. Halleck, the Union general-in-chief, had urged Grant to take this step even before the Battle of Chickamauga. See William T. Sherman, *Memoirs of General William T. Sherman,* 2 vols. in 1 (1874; rpt. Westport, Conn.: Greenwood Press, 1974), 1:350.

21. In the 1863 Iowa gubernatorial election, Republican William M. Stone faced War Democrat James M. Tuttle. Since both men staunchly supported the war effort (Stone was a Union colonel and Tuttle a brigadier general), the election issues tended to revolve around charges of personal immorality and malfeasance while in office. Stone won the election by a margin of thirty thousand votes.

22. The 1863 gubernatorial and legislative elections in several Northern states resulted in the repudiation of Peace Democratic candidates. McPherson, *Battle Cry of Freedom,* 687–88.

23. Confederate major general Stephen D. Lee, the officer responsible for harrying Sherman's army as it advanced to Chattanooga, attacked the Union division under Maj. Gen. Peter J. Osterhaus on October 21 and drove it back to Cherokee Station, Alabama, where the Federal retreat stopped. Lee then withdrew the following day. *Official Records,* vol. 31, pt. 1, pp. 26–27.

24. John Patterson commanded the "Anglo-Saxon." See chapter 5, diary entry for March 9, 1863.

25. The passage in quotes approximates Isaiah 58:6: "Is not this the fast that I have chosen? to loose the bands of wickedness, to undo the heavy burdens, and to

let the oppressed go free, and that ye break every yoke?" Belshazzar was a Babylonian king who, in the midst of revelry at his court, was confronted by strange handwriting on the wall that greatly troubled him. No one could decipher its meaning save Daniel (Daniel 5:1–31).

26. Maj. Gen. Joseph Hooker commanded the Union Eleventh and Twelfth Corps, recently transferred west from the Army of the Potomac. Like Sherman's corps, they had been sent to reinforce the Army of the Cumberland. The battleground to which Campbell refers was Wauhatchie, a minor station on the Memphis and Charleston Railroad linking Chattanooga and Bridgeport, Alabama. On the night of October 28–29, Hooker's troops repelled a Confederate attack at Wauhatchie and, by so doing, ensured the reopening of a regular line of supply into Chattanooga. Cozzens, *Shipwreck of Their Hopes*, 78–100.

27. Campbell refers to a preliminary engagement at Orchard Knob, where the Confederates had their outposts. The Union victory here paved the way for a direct attack against Missionary Ridge. Cozzens, *Shipwreck of Their Hopes*, 128–31.

28. This was the Battle of Lookout Mountain, fought on the lower slopes of that elevation just south of the Tennessee River. The Union success here enabled Hooker, with the Eleventh and Twelfth Corps, to move into a position from which to attack the southern end of the main Confederate line on Missionary Ridge. Cozzens, *Shipwreck of Their Hopes*, 159–98.

29. At Tunnel Hill, Sherman's troops received a sharp counterattack from a Confederate division under Maj. Gen. Patrick Cleburne. During and after the battle, a story arose that the attack had succeeded so well because the Confederates had come pouring through the railroad tunnel. No Confederate reports mention such a stratagem, however.

30. Official returns differ slightly from Campbell, placing the Fifth Iowa's loss at two men killed, twenty-two wounded, and eighty-two captured. *Official Records*, vol. 31, pt. 2, p. 58.

31. Peter Cozzens, the closest student of the Tunnel Hill fight, concurs with Campbell's assessment. It was, he writes, "one of the sorriest episodes in this or any other battle of the war. . . . In his assault on Tunnel Hill, Sherman exhibited an egregious lack of imagination." Cozzens, *Shipwreck of Their Hopes*, 241.

32. Thomas's successful assault on the center of Missionary Ridge won the battle and became one of the most famous tales of the war. Cozzens, *Shipwreck of Their Hopes*, 244–342.

33. Out of 56,359 men, the Union suffered 5,824 casualties, while the Confederates suffered 6,667 out of 64,165 men involved. Long, *Civil War Day by Day*, 437–38.

34. On November 4, Maj. Gen. James Longstreet led a force of ten thousand infantry and five thousand cavalry to oppose Burnside at Knoxville. Long, *Civil War Day by Day*, 430.

35. Probably on this date, Campbell completed a lengthy letter-journal describing his experiences in the Chattanooga campaign. See Letter 14, Appendix.

36. Answering Ambrose Burnside's pleas for assistance, Grant sent Sherman's Fifteenth Corps and Maj. Gen. Gordon Granger's Fourth Corps to Knoxville. However, with Sherman's force a day's march away, Longstreet withdrew his army towards Virginia, and Sherman returned to Chattanooga after leaving two divisions with Burnside in Knoxville. Long, *Civil War Day by Day*, 439–40, 442–43.

Chapter 7. "What Can't Be Cured, Must Be Endured": In Garrison and on Furlough, December 3, 1863–May 13, 1864

1. A board of survey inspected army equipment to determine its serviceability.

2. For New School Presbyterianism, see chapter 1, note 8.

3. Around this date a scout for Confederate major general Joseph Wheeler reported that "the enemy has compelled all the citizens in North Alabama to take the oath, and the people are both whipped and cowed." *Official Records*, vol. 32, pt. 2, p. 539.

4. Campbell refers to a collection of essays by Hugh Blair.

5. Confederate brigadier general Philip D. Roddy led a number of cavalry raids in Tennessee, Mississippi, and Alabama. Warner, *Generals in Gray*, 262.

6. Named in honor of its commander, Col. John Wilder, the brigade consisted of mounted infantry armed with Spencer seven-shot repeating rifles. Boatner, *Civil War Dictionary*, 919.

7. Henry Ward Beecher was a prominent abolitionist clergyman.

8. Between February 3 and March 4, 1864, twenty-five thousand troops under Maj. Gen. William T. Sherman made a major infantry raid against the Confederate supply and railroad center of Meridian, Mississippi. A force of seven thousand cavalry under Maj. Gen. William Sooy Smith left Memphis with orders to meet Sherman's column at Meridian, but—Campbell's diary entry notwithstanding—Smith's column was defeated by Maj. Gen. Nathan Bedford Forrest at West Point, Mississippi, on February 21. Long, *Civil War Day by Day*, 460–72.

9. Judge D. C. Humphreys of Madison County, Alabama, had been in the Confederate army but resigned. Some time after this meeting, he was arrested by Confederate brigadier general P. D. Roddy and imprisoned. In January 1865, Federal authorities seized a number of Confederate sympathizers in Huntsville as hostages for Humphreys's safe treatment. For Jeremiah Clemens, see chapter 7, note 11. Nothing of consequence resulted from the Unionist meetings in Huntsville, but they were indicative of a growing disaffection among the people of northern Alabama (and, for that matter, much of the Confederate South).

10. See Letter 15, Appendix.

11. A member of the Alabama secession convention in 1861, Jeremiah Clemens commanded the state militia but turned against secession in 1862. As Campbell saw firsthand, he was a heavy drinker. When the secessionist fire-eater William L. Yancey asked him not to drink so much, Clemens allegedly replied that "he was obliged to drink his genius down to a level with Yancey's." Walter L. Fleming, *Civil War and Reconstruction in Alabama* (New York: Columbia University Press, 1905), 125 note 1.

12. On March 31, 1864, Brig. Gen. Grenville Dodge sent the following dispatch to Maj. Gen. James B. McPherson: "We captured the celebrated Captain Moore, also Colonel Mead and 30 men." *Official Records* 32:538.

13. Organized by the U.S. Sanitary Commission, a quasi-public relief association, "Soldiers' Homes"—also known as "Soldiers' Rests"—were maintained in numerous cities in the North and the occupied South for the use of Union soldiers in transit. William Quentin Maxwell, *Lincoln's Fifth Wheel: The Political History of the U.S. Sanitary Commission* (New York: Longmans, 1956), 189.

14. Chambers Baird was a prominent local attorney and state senator from Ripley, Ohio. Carl Thompson, *Historical Collections of Brown County, Ohio* (Piqua, Ohio: Hammer Graphics, 1969), 424, 647–48.

15. Nerve, short for Minerva, was the wife of Campbell's brother, Frank. Olive Porter, *Jasper and Marshall County Marriage Records* (Des Moines, Iowa: Daughters of the American Revolution, 1936), 19.

16. Lowry Rankin was a son of Ripley abolitionist John Rankin. *History of Brown County,* biographical section, 175.

17. This almost certainly refers to John Rankin's house, which was fictionalized in Harriet Beecher Stowe's novel, *Uncle Tom's Cabin.*

18. Very likely this would be the sister of John Shepherd, another boyhood chum of Campbell's who was serving in the Ninth Kentucky.

19. The "eminence" is most likely another reference to the Rankin house, which stood on a high bluff overlooking Ripley.

20. The "butternut members" were clearly Southern sympathizers or Peace Democrats—"Copperheads" in the parlance of the day.

21. With their volunteer forces on active duty with the Union army, many Northern states reactivated compulsory militia systems. Ohio designated its militia the National Guard. Such units were mainly responsible for the preservation of public order, but they also turned out in response to invasion scares and furnished short-term troops to the Union forces in the field. Jerry Cooper, *The Rise of the National Guard: The Evolution of the American Militia, 1865–1920* (Lincoln: University of Nebraska Press, 1997), 21.

22. The Indians were taken prisoner by the U.S. Army after the failure of a major Sioux uprising in Minnesota in 1862. Maj. Gen. John Pope led the forces assigned to defeat the uprising. Alvin M. Josephy Jr., *The Civil War in the American West* (New York: Alfred A. Knopf, 1991), 95–140.

23. Campbell refers to Grant's spring offensive. On May 6–7, 1864, Grant and Lee fought a bloody battle known as the Wilderness. It was the beginning of al-most continuous fighting that would not stop until Robert E. Lee surrendered to Grant at Appomattox Court House on April 9, 1865. Long, *Civil War Day by Day*, 493–95.

24. With orders from Grant to destroy Joseph Johnston's army (Bragg had been relieved in December), get into the interior of the state, and do as much dam-age as possible to the South's war-making resources, Sherman began his ad-vance south toward Atlanta on May 7, 1864. Long, *Civil War Day by Day*, 495.

Chapter 8. Yankee Vandals and Rebel Guerrillas: Guarding Sherman's Rear, May 14–September 14, 1864

1. An abattis (or abatis) is a form of field fortification in which trees are felled with their branches pointed in the direction of the enemy so as to impede an attacking force.

2. An assortment of radical abolitionists and German Americans met in Cleve-land, Ohio, where they nominated John Frémont for president. This new party, calling itself the Radical Democratic Party supported a constitutional amend-ment to end slavery and called for the absolute equality of all men. Nominated for vice president was John Cochrane of New York. Two weeks later in Balti-more, a convention nominated Lincoln for a second term. Calling itself the National Union Party to attract Southern Unionists and War Democrats, the party's platform supported an amendment to end slavery and continuation of the war until the South agreed to unconditional surrender. Nominated with Lincoln was Andrew Johnson of Tennessee. Finally, in Chicago at the end of August, the Democrats nominated George McClellan for president. The Democrats supported a platform calling for peace to be the first priority and restoration of the Union as the second. They also adopted language that called for the continuation of slavery. Nominated with McClellan was Congressman George Pendleton from Ohio. Philip Shaw Paludan, *The Presidency of Abraham Lincoln* (Lawrence: University Press of Kansas, 1994), 270–74, 283–85; McPherson, *Battle Cry of Freedom*, 713–17, 771–73.

3. As the designation implies, these were units of national guardsmen, called to active duty for one hundred days and employed mainly in rear-area garrison duties.

4. Salmon Portland Chase was Lincoln's secretary of the treasury until July 1864, when Lincoln forced him to resign after a series of political conflicts between the two men. Senator William Pitt Fessenden was appointed secretary of the treasury upon Chase's resignation. In December Lincoln named Chase to be chief justice of the Supreme Court, knowing that Chase's strong abolitionist sentiments would support favorable interpretation of federal antislavery laws. Paludan, *Presidency of Abraham Lincoln*, 286–87, 302.

5. Kennesaw Mountain, a four-hundred-foot ridge northwest of Marietta, Georgia, was one of several defensive positions occupied the Confederate Army of Tennessee during the Atlanta campaign. Sherman unsuccessfully attacked the Rebel defenses on June 27 and remained in the area for several days before maneuvering to turn the position. In response to Sherman's attempt to get around his flank, Confederate general Joseph E. Johnston ordered a withdrawal from Kennesaw Mountain on July 2. Albert Castel, *Decision in the West: The Atlanta Campaign of 1864* (Lawrence: University Press of Kansas, 1992), 285, 329.

6. James Parton, *General Butler in New Orleans.*

7. Literally translated as "from the foot of Hercules," the phrase means "from a part we may divine the whole." Stone, *Latin for the Illiterati,* 33.

8. This news was erroneous. Atlanta would not fall until September 2, 1864. Long, *Civil War Day by Day,* 565.

9. Well loved by his men and respected by his peers, Maj. Gen. James B. McPherson was killed during the Battle of Atlanta on July 22, 1864. Warner, *Generals in Blue,* 306–8.

10. The Seventh Ohio Volunteer Cavalry was also known as the "River Regiment" since it was recruited from the counties along the Ohio River, including a company from Brown County.

11. The following members of Company B, Fifth Iowa Infantry were transferred to the Fifth Iowa Cavalry: Robert McKee, John Quincy Adams Campbell, Robert Bain, Michael Butler, Daniel Conner, William Fouts, William Graham, Hiram Hall, Godfrey Jerue, William Martins, Ewing McReynolds, Benjamin Stearns, George Watson, and Delano Williams. George Ditto, *Statistical Roster of the 5th Iowa Volunteer Infantry* (Sigourney, Iowa: Smith's Iowa Times Printing, 1897).

12. Confederate general John B. Hood replaced Gen. Joseph E. Johnston as commander of the Army of Tennessee on July 17, 1864. Following the wishes of President Jefferson Davis, he promptly made several attacks on Sherman's armies aimed at driving the Federals away from Atlanta. The attacks caused thousands of Confederate casualties but failed in their purpose. Long, *Civil War Day by Day,* 540–44, 546–47, 550–57, 560–64.

13. Maj. Gen. Joseph Wheeler commanded the cavalry in the Army of Tennessee. Brig. Gen. John Tyler Morgan—not to be confused with the Confederate raider John Hunt Morgan—commanded a brigade in the Cavalry Corps, Army of Tennessee. Warner, *Generals in Gray,* 221–22, 332–33.

14. A veteran of several campaigns with the Union Army of the Cumberland, Maj. Gen. James B. Steedman (not Steadman) commanded the post of Chattanooga during Sherman's Atlanta campaign. His last name was so often misspelled that, when wounded at the Battle of Chickamauga, he instructed a staff officer to make sure it was correctly spelled in his obituary. Boatner, *Civil War Dictionary,* 794.

15. The "negro regiment" was the Fourteenth United States Colored Troops.

Chapter 9. "There Is Hope Yet for America": Final Days in Service, September 15–November 24, 1864

1. Maj. Samuel M. H. Byers was one of dozens of men from the Fifth Iowa who were "gobbled up" at the Battle of Missionary Ridge. See Byers, *With Fire and Sword*, 102–10.

2. Union troops under Maj. Gen. Philip Sheridan soundly defeated a smaller Confederate force under Lt. Gen. Jubal Early on September 19 at the Battle of Third Winchester (also called Opequon Creek). Long, *Civil War Day By Day*, 571.

3. Atlanta fell to Sherman's forces on September 2, 1864. On August 5, 1864, a Union naval squadron under Adm. David G. Farragut successfully entered Mobile Bay, closed the port of Mobile, Alabama, and set the stage for land operations to reduce the two forts at the entrance to the bay. The first of these fell on August 7, the other on August 23. Long, *Civil War Day By Day*, 551–53, 559, 565.

4. Confederate cavalry leader Maj. Gen. Nathan Bedford Forrest led some forty-five hundred horsemen on a sweeping raid into northern Alabama and middle Tennessee in September and October 1864. Long, *Civil War Day by Day*, 569, 572–75, 577, 582.

5. During the Civil War era the United States had no uniform election day (except for president), and states held elections for congressional and state offices on several different dates.

6. After the fall of Atlanta, Hood withdrew his army into northeast Alabama and made several forays against Sherman's exposed railroad supply line in northwest Georgia. Long, *Civil War Day By Day*, 565–67, 577–80, 582–84, 586–87.

7. Sheridan all but wrecked Early's army at the Battle of Cedar Creek on October 19, 1864. Long, *Civil War Day By Day*, 585.

8. "Fall's City" means Louisville, which was established at the Falls of the Ohio River.

9. Mammoth Cave, part of the world's largest system of underground caverns, measures over three hundred miles in extent. It was and remains a highly popular resort and tourist attraction.

10. The vote in the Fifth Iowa Cavalry was similar to the soldier's vote in general. Lincoln received 116,887 votes from Union soldiers, against 33,748 for McClellan. McPherson, *Battle Cry of Freedom*, 804.

11. Lincoln won reelection by a popular vote of 2,213,665 against 1,802,237 for McClellan. The electoral vote was 212 for Lincoln, 21 for McClellan. Philip S. Paludan, *"A People's Contest": The Union and the Civil War, 1861–1865* (New York: Harper and Row, 1988), 257.

12. John Bell Hood hoped to lure Sherman away from Atlanta and Chattanooga, thereby regaining control of those two cities. However, Sherman pursued no

farther than Rome, Georgia. Instead he transferred two corps to Maj. Gen. George H. Thomas at Nashville, where he would be responsible for Tennessee's defense. Thomas then began gathering troops at Nashville which he would use to soundly defeat Hood's Army of Tennessee on December 15–16, 1864. Long, *Civil War Day By Day,* 610–12.

13. On November 15, 1864, Sherman left Atlanta and started for Savannah with sixty-two thousand men. His objective was to obtain a more secure supply base on the Atlantic coast, destroy Southern war resources, and demoralize white Southerners by showing the powerlessness of the Confederate government to protect them. Long, *Civil War Day By Day,* 597.

14. Approved by the U.S. Senate on April 8, 1864, the Thirteenth Amendment abolishing slavery was initially defeated in the U.S. House of Representatives on June 15. The House finally passed it on January 31, 1865. Following its ratification by three-fourths of the states, it went into effect on December 18, 1865. McPherson, *Battle Cry of Freedom,* 823, 838–42.

15. The Spencer was a seven-shot, breech-loading, lever-action carbine.

Appendix: Letters to the *Ripley Bee,* 1861–1864

1. For the Confederate attack on Athens, Missouri, see chapter 1, note 10.

2. Both the governor of Missouri and the state legislature were hostile to the Lincoln administration's policy of maintaining the Union by force. After a riot in St. Louis in which Union troops killed several Missouri citizens, the legislature—already divided between conditional Unionists and outright secessionists—took a pro-Confederate turn. It passed into law several bills intended to place Missouri on a war footing against the Union and left Jefferson City in mid-June rather than submit to Union military occupation of the city. De facto political power in Missouri passed into the hands of a state convention that had adjourned in March after rejecting secession. Members of the convention reassembled in July, constituted themselves the provisional government of Missouri, and ruled the state until January 1865. McPherson, *Battle Cry of Freedom,* 291–93.

3. Fought on June 17, 1861, the Battle of Boonville was a minor action between Union forces under Brig. Gen. Nathaniel Lyon and pro-secession Missourians under Col. John S. Marmaduke. The pro-secession governor, Claiborne Jackson, was present on the field and insisted that Marmaduke stand and fight. Lyon won the ensuing engagement. Jay Monaghan, *Civil War on the Western Border, 1854–1865* (1955; rpt. Lincoln: University of Nebraska Press, 1984), 140–43.

4. For Maj. Gen. John C. Frémont, see chapter 1, note 34.

5. "Puke" was a derogatory term for a poor white Missourian. See Michael Fellman, *Inside War: The Guerrilla Conflict in Missouri During the American Civil War* (New York: Oxford University Press, 1989), 13–14.

6. A U.S. senator from Kansas, James Henry Lane unofficially held rank as a brigadier general and organized the "Kansas Brigade," which operated against secessionist guerrillas in Missouri. In December 1861 he proposed a winter expedition from Kansas into Arkansas and the Indian Territory. Although Lincoln approved the plan, it was derailed by friction between Lane and Maj. Gen. David Hunter, commander of the Department of Kansas. Allen Johnson and Dumas Malone, eds., *Dictionary of American Biography* (New York: Charles Scribners Sons, 1928–58), vol. 10:576–77.

7. Campbell refers to several minor skirmishes in Missouri: Knobnoster (January 22, 1862), Mount Zion Church (December 28, 1861) and Silver Creek (January 8, 1862). *Official Records* 8:2. "The late victory in Kentucky" was the Battle of Mill Springs, fought on January 19, 1862 in the southeastern corner of the state. In this engagement, four thousand Union troops under Brig. Gen. George H. Thomas defeated a like number of Confederates under Brig. Gen. Felix Zollicoffer. The victory broke the eastern anchor of the Confederate defensive line in the western theater. Long, *Civil War Day by Day,* 162.

8. Campbell's remark that "Halleck and Beauregard are playing 'won't and dare not'" comments on the cautious pace of Maj. Gen. Henry W. Halleck's advance on Corinth, Mississippi, and Gen. P. G. T. Beauregard's equally circumspect defense of the strategic rail town.

9. What Campbell terms "Yellow Jack" was yellow fever. Many observers, North and South, did not believe that Union soldiers would be able to stand up to the southern summers.

10. Corduroying a road meant that logs were cut and laid side by side across the roadway. While this made for a bumpy ride, it was necessary on many dirt roads, especially in rainy weather.

11. Beauregard evacuated Corinth on the night of May 29–30 and withdrew to Tupelo, Mississippi, about fifty miles south. Long, *Civil War Day by Day,* 190.

12. Until 1864 it was common for prisoners taken by both sides to be "paroled," that is, released upon a written pledge not to take up arms again until properly exchanged for an equivalent prisoner taken by the other side. Parolees were often interned in parole camps by their own army in order to enforce the exchange cartel arrangement. Boatner, *Civil War Dictionary,* 620.

13. For Brig. Gen. Jacob Ammen, see chapter 3, note 9.

14. Fought on May 31–June 1, 1862, the Battle of Fair Oaks, Virginia, was an unsuccessful Confederate attempt to throw back the Union Army of the Potomac, which was then within ten miles of the Confederate capital of Richmond.

15. For the Battle of Iuka, see chapter 4.

16. While "nixcumerous" does not correspond to any Latin word or phrase, it is possible that Campbell thought he was indicating "nothing doing."

17. For Lieutenant Mateer, see chapter 4, note 3.

18. "From a part we may divine the whole." See chapter 8, note 7.

19. While Grant moved overland toward Vicksburg, an expedition under Maj. Gen.

William T. Sherman steamed down the Mississippi River and disembarked a few miles north of the city. This was the diversionary movement to which Campbell refers. Sherman's force unsuccessfully assaulted the Confederate defenses at Chickasaw Bluffs on December 29, 1862. Long, *Civil War Day by Day,* 301. Brig. Gen. Frederick Steele served as one of Sherman's division commanders during this operation.

20. John Van Buren, son of former president Martin Van Buren, was a New York lawyer and politician. Although a Free Soil Democrat, he supported a convention of the state to arrange guarantees for slavery and denounced Lincoln for calling out troops so precipitously after the firing on Fort Sumter. *Dictionary of American Biography* 19:151. Fernando Wood was the Democratic mayor of New York who, in January 1861, opined that the metropolis should "disrupt the bands" that tied it to upstate New York and become a free city. Although he initially supported the Union war effort, after being defeated for reelection he changed stances and helped to organize the Peace Democrats. *Dictionary of American Biography* 20:456–57. Chilton A. White was the Democratic congressman from Campbell's former home district in Ohio. Critical of Lincoln's war policies and opposed to both emancipation and the draft, he supported a cessation of hostilities and a negotiated settlement with the disaffected South. Twice elected to Congress, he was denied a third term when voters turned him out of office in 1864. John T. Hubbell and James W. Geary, eds., *Biographical Dictionary of the Union: Northern Leaders of the Civil War* (Westport, Conn.: Greenwood Press, 1995), 584–85. The "first day of next January" refers to Lincoln's much anticipated issuance of the final Emancipation Proclamation.

21. For the term "contraband," see chapter 2, note 3.

22. The allusion is to a minstrel song of the day called "Dandy Jim."

23. For background on the Holly Springs debacle and the failure of Grant's campaign, see chapter 4.

24. In classical mythology Tantalus, king of Sipylus, fell into disfavor with the gods and was condemned to eternal torture in Hades. He was staked in a pool of water which rose up to his chin but dried up whenever he attempted to drink; a bough of fruit was placed just beyond his reach; and a stone placed above him perpetually threatened to fall and crush him. Edward Tripp, *Crowell's Handbook of Classical Mythology* (New York: Thomas W. Crowell, 1970), 542–43.

25. For the operations in which Campbell participated during this period, see chapter 5.

26. Vice president during James Buchanan's administration, John C. Breckinridge ran for president in 1860 as a Southern Democrat, then served as a U.S. senator from Kentucky until September 1861. Then, under threat of arrest for disloyalty, he cast his fortunes with the Confederacy, becoming a major general and eventually secretary of war. A resident of Kentucky and (briefly) Iowa, he does not appear to have had property holdings in Louisiana. William C. Davis,

Breckinridge: Statesman, Soldier, Symbol (Baton Rouge: Louisiana State University, 1974).

27. For the operations in which Campbell participated during the main phase of the Vicksburg campaign, see chapter 5.

28. For the Battle of Champion Hill, see chapter 5, note 13.

29. For the Unionist meeting in Huntsville, Alabama, in early 1864, see chapter 7, note 9.

30. For D. C. Humphries and Jeremiah Clemens, see chapter 7, notes 9 and 11.

31. James Buchanan, fifteenth president of the United States, was a so-called "doughface" Democrat who favored placating the slaveholding South at virtually any cost. His response to the secession of the Deep South in the winter of 1860–61 was typical of the man: he simultaneously denied the legality of secession and the federal government's constitutional right to prevent it. See *Dictionary of American Biography* 3:207–14.

32. Campbell here refers to Jefferson Davis, then senator from Mississippi and later president of the Confederate States of America; Christopher Memminger, a South Carolina politician who became Davis's first secretary of the treasury; and Alabamian Leroy P. Walker, who served briefly as Davis's first secretary of war. "Mr. Gilchrist" corresponds to no Southern congressman or prominent Confederate official and is possibly a mistranscription of another name. Biographical sketches of Davis, Memminger, and Walker are in *Dictionary of American Biography* 5:123–31, 12:527, and 19:351, respectively.

33. For Chilton A. White, see appendix, note 20.

Index

Johnston, Albert Sidney, 23
Johnston, Joseph E., 95, 105, 110, 114,
    115, 160, 161, 244n, 246n, 247n, 253n
Jolly, John, 184
Jones, George L., 102
Jones, Isaac G., 4
Jones, Will, 173
Jonesburgh, Mo., 26

Keisler, Thomas, 4, 22, 27, 105, 245n
Kennedy, Simeon, 98
Kennesaw Mountain, Ga., 169, 253n
Kentucky, Confederate invasion of, 39, 56
Keokuk, Iowa, 5–6, 198
Kephardt, William (uncle), 15, 79, 109,
    113, 116, 184, 194, 220
Ketterman, William, 194
King, James, 187
King, John, 75
Kingston, Ga., 167, 168, 170, 171, 173,
    174, 176, 177, 182, 184, 186
Kirk, John, 188
Kirkwood, Samuel J., xiv, 46, 53
Knapp, Mary, 159, 187
Knobnoster (Knob Knoster), Mo.,
    engagement at, 200, 256n
Knoxville, Tenn., 139, 249n
Kokomo, Ind., 158
Kramer, Fred, 201

La Grange, Tenn., 66, 67, 73, 74, 124, 242n
Lafayette, Ind., 153
Lafayette, Tenn., 73
Lake Providence, La., 79, 86, 87,121, 219
Lake Providence canal, 87
Lane, James H., 21, 22, 200, 236n, 256n
Larkinsville, Ala., 144, 145, 146, 167, 180
Lavergne, Tenn., 178
Leavenworth, Kans., 200
Lee, Daniel, 152
Lee, Robert E., 39, 111, 150, 159, 160,
    252n
Lee, Stephen D., 248n
Lexington, Mo., 8; capture of, 12
Limbocker, Jerry, 181
Limestone, Ala., 162
Lincoln, Abraham, 113, 117, 141, 160,
    165, 166, 191, 192, 216, 236n, 247n,
    252n, 254n
Linderman, Gerald F., xvi
Little Rock, Ark., 121; capture of, 248n
Lockland, Ohio, 158

Logan, John A., 140, 244n
"Logan's Car," 105, 245n
Long Pond, Ga., 181, 182
Longstreet, James, 140, 249n
Lookout Mountain, Tenn., 177, 221, 223;
    battle of, 249n
Loudenback, David, 60, 138
Loudenback, Isaac, 48, 138
Loudon, DeWitt, 72
Loughridge, Poultney, 232n
Louisville, Ky., 153, 158, 159, 188, 189,
    190, 192, 194, 254
Lovell, Mansfield, 61
Lowe, George, 60
Lumpkin's Mill, Miss., 68, 72, 212
Lyon, Nathaniel, 12, 199, 234n, 235n, 255n

Madison Station, Ala., 163, 166; engage-
    ment at, 162
Madisonville, Tenn., 177
Mahony, Dennis A., 53, 242n
Mammoth Cave, Ky., 191, 254n
Manassas, Va.: first battle of, 229; second
    battle of, 39, 54
Marietta, Ga., 173, 175, 184
Marmaduke, John S., 255n
Marshall, William, 89
Martins, William, 253n
Maslowski, Pete, xvii
Mateer, Alex L., 2, 14, 16, 18, 51, 60, 61,
    64, 210, 211
Matison, Wesley, 82
Matthews, John, 74
Matthies, Charles L., 10, 19, 48, 53, 60,
    66, 105, 114, 123, 137, 149, 151, 161,
    162, 209, 225, 234n, 240n
Maysville, Ky., 51, 146
McCayne, Tom, 173
McClanahan, Will, 72, 74, 87, 103, 116
McClellan, George B., Jr., 23, 38, 48, 160,
    165, 166, 183, 191, 252n, 254n
McClernand, John C., 81, 98, 243n, 245n
McClure, Samuel, 28
McCook, Ed, Gen., 176
McCord, Dave, 17
McCord, Jim, 17
McCroskey, James W., 4, 60
McCully, William., 98
McElrea, William, 52, 181, 190, 194
McKee, Robert A., 19, 51, 61, 73, 74, 75,
    95, 108, 109, 111, 116, 151, 154, 181,
    183, 253n

The Union Must Stand was designed and typeset on a Macintosh computer system using PageMaker software. The text is set in New Caledonia, the chapter numerals and title page are set in Crinoline, and the ornaments in Wood Type Ornaments. This book was designed by Todd Duren, composed by Kim Scarbrough, and manufactured by Thomson-Shore, Inc. The recycled paper used in this book is designed for an effective life of at least three hundred years.